Good Management

Business Ethics in Action

FREDERICK BIRD
Concordia University

JEFFREY GANDZ
The University of Western Ontario

Prentice-Hall Canada Inc., Scarborough, Ontario

Names and other information have been disguised in certain cases including Cases 1,7,12,13,16, and 20.

Canadian Cataloguing in Publication Data
Bird, Frederick B. (Frederick Bruce), 1938-
 Good Management

ISBN 0-13-359076-3

1. Business ethics. 2. Business ethics—Case
studies. I. Gandz, Jeffrey, 1944-   . II. Title.

HF5387.B57 1991   174'.4   C90-095607-0

Prentice Hall, Inc., Englewood Cliffs, New Jersey
Prentice-Hall International, Inc., London
Prentice-Hall of Austrialia, Pty., Ltd., Sydney
Prentice-Hall of India Pvt., Ltd., New Delhi
Prentice-Hall of Japan, Inc., Tokyo
Prentice-Hall of Southeast Asia (Pte.) Ltd., Singapore
Editora Prentice-Hall do Brasil Ltda., Rio de Janeiro
Prentice-Hall Hispanoamericana, S.A., Mexico

ISBN 0-13-359076-3

Production Editor: Jocelyn Smyth
Coordinating Editor: Elizabeth Long
Production Coordinator: Anna Orodi
Cover Design: Monica Kompter
Page Layout: Sue Boehler, Olena Serbyn

1 2 3 4 5   RRD   95 94 93 92 91

Printed and bound in the United States of America by R. R. Donnelly and Sons

CONTENTS

Video: Alcan Aluminium Ltd.

— $1B Kemano Completion project

— divert water for Nechako River to Kemano River to general electrics

1987 agreement between Fed./prov. & Alcan.

ignore scientific evidence

4 day meeting to review environmental issues

half constructed in June 1991   (environmental review)
 ↳ 2000 people out of work

Native group — aboriginal claims

environmental group → project will populate nature

destroy fish, wildlife hurt the region's tourism potential make crop irrigation impossible

FOREWORD

In an era where change seems to be the only constant, it is helpful for people to know and understand the values and practices intrinsic to their business life. Indeed, a lifetime in business has reaffirmed my belief in a tried-and-true maxim: virtue brings its own reward. But more and more, as business becomes a community affair where numerous and diverse groups have a legitimate and influential voice in the operation of the enterprise, we all need to test constantly our actions against an ethical yardstick. This is why understanding acceptable standards of honesty, integrity, fairness and good faith will never be out of fashion.

I see a growing awareness of the need for more ethical conduct, not only in business but in all walks of life. Apart from good intentions and wanting to do what is right, there is also a compelling pragmatic reason for paying close attention to ethics in business. It really is the only way to run a successful enterprise. Keep in mind that every corporation exists at the pleasure of the public, and if it wants to stay in business it had better keep itself attuned to sharpening public perceptions of social responsibility.

For those readers just starting a career, you should know that a life in business means being accountable to many publics, whose expectations are high to begin with and are constantly changing. For this reason, good ethics are never bad business. They are the grounding for individuals to make sensible decisions in complex, challenging and ever-changing business environments. Never lose sight of the fact that a company's reputation — in other words, one's own reputation — for ethical practices is its most valued asset.

This is why I particularly welcome the work undertaken by Frederick Bird and Jeffrey Gandz. *Good Management: Business Ethics in Action* provides an essential learning tool, not only for business students, but for anyone who is committed to implementing ethical decision-making in the workplace.

When all is said and done, people are led by personal example. It is in this context that every one of us should encourage and participate in widespread debate on ethics and integrity. *Good Management: Business Ethics in Action* is an excellent starting point.

Arden R. Haynes
Chairman and Chief Executive Officer
Imperial Oil Limited

INTRODUCTION

(This is a book about management and ethics.)We make the assumption that those who read it or use it in courses of study want to be both good managers and good people. In writing this book and developing the cases, we have worked to a certain set of beliefs that we have about the value of studying business ethics:

- the conventional business management decision-making model is quite consistent with making decisions involving moral considerations, provided that decision-makers acknowledge and interact with the many stakeholders in business decisions, including stockholders, employees, customers, suppliers, others who are affected by business decisions which, of course, includes society as a whole;
- business decision-making will be improved if managers are more aware of their own values and the social norms and moral standards in their environment and take these into account in their decision-making;
- there will be an ensuing benefit to managers themselves, the business, and society if decision-making incorporates such social analysis and ethical choice;
- various tools of ethical analysis can help managers make better decisions and articulate and justify their actions to relevant stakeholder groups;
- business students and practising managers are perfectly capable of developing ethical decision-making skills;
- it does not make a great deal of sense to study business ethics in the abstract — they should be studied and understood in the context of the real-life situations which managers and executives have to face;
- ethical decision-making is an activity and not just a thought process so that the ethical decision-maker must understand how to act effectively with respect to moral choices;
- senior managers who want to establish and reinforce an ethical corporate culture can use the tools of organizational design — structure and systems — to help them create this moral management milieu;
- senior managers have both the ability and responsibility to give ethical leadership to their organizations, both by exercising their authority responsibly and by articulating and enacting a positive ethical vision for the corporation.

The book combines ten chapters of textual material with 21 substantive, real-life cases which address many of the ethical issues in business and the moral choices which managers make on an everyday or occasional basis. Some of these cases deal with issues at the societal level, some at the corporate level, while others address interpersonal issues. All are based on real situations and most of them call for decisions to be made in the absence of complete information — the essence of managerial decision-making. The textual material does not provide neat templates for analyzing the cases. Rather, the analysis of the cases will be assisted with the concepts developed by reading the text coupled with the reader's existing knowledge and accumulated experience of handling business situations.

[This book attempts to integrate, within a decision-making model, material from several disciplines, all of which, we believe, are relevant to the active management of moral issues in business.]The model is skeletal and we assume that those who use it will want to give it greater body and substance by adding resources. To start this process, we have suggested some additional readings drawn from the fields of sociology, philosophy, political theory, strategic management, and organizational behavior.

OUR MORAL POINT OF VIEW

Any reader of a text on business ethics should ask a simple question — do the authors themselves have some particular moral point of view? We do. And, while it will become more obvious as the chapters are read, we think that there is some value to stating it up front.

We assume that managers hold moral convictions of their own which may represent the cumulative impact of experience, reflections, education, religion and other influences. Although managers frequently hold similar convictions with respect to a number of broad moral principles, they typically hold these beliefs privately, while at the same time differing with respect to the convictions that others hold. Influenced by contrasting political philosophies, by different religious and secular beliefs, by variations in personal values and temperament, there may be significant variance in individual and cultural moral convictions. Some managers are highly sensitive while others are much less so; particular managers are extremely principled while others are more pragmatic; some principled managers hold to different principles than other principled managers; in some cultures certain principles are adhered to, in others they are not. The world of ethical convictions related to business is characterized by pluralism and diversity. This is the human condition and does not warrant despair or cynicism.

We do believe, however, that people with differing beliefs and varying convictions can enter into collaborative arrangements in hopes of addressing problems that concern them all[1] and in this book we have proposed a model to allow people with different moral convictions to address moral issues; it allows people to frame issues, discuss, and act responsibly and collaboratively even though they may vary in many of their beliefs and convictions.

We also assume that the business environment is not amoral. Whether by virtue of social customs, professional codes, laws, or social values the settings within which business operates are structured and influenced by varied moral expectations which shape the ways in which people work, interact, make agreements, contract, communicate and carry out other activities. These moral expectations vary by culture and vary in their strength and compellingness. A business person cannot be morally responsible simply by following these guidelines because, in many instances, they are simply too broad. They must be reinterpreted and assigned priorities before they can serve as useful and valid guidelines for action. In some instances morally responsible business people may well conclude that these expectations are themselves part of the problem either because they are too traditional or too vague, because they are not demanding enough or excessively idealistic, or because they conflict with other standards which are judged, in the circumstances, to be more weighty. The point is that business takes place against a variegated background of normative expectations that must be taken into account as business people attempt to deal with on going moral issues in a responsible manner.

We argue that business organizations exist by virtue of social contractual relations with their stakeholders. It is inappropriate to view firms as autonomous realities existing within well-defined boundaries. Rather, firms are social realities that exist as a result of ongoing, reciprocal yet asymetrical interactions with relevant stakeholders. In keeping with this assumption we argue that it is possible to identify the moral purpose of corporations in relation to these stakeholders. We attempt to address the problems of moral relativity not only by this argument but also by arguing why certain forms of social reasoning possess greater ethical authority than others. In particular, acknowledging the fact of pluralism without surrendering to it, we propose that moral reasoning is most compelling when principled arguments are combined with consequential and purposive arguments. Further, we suggest some ethical principles for determining whether certain tactics are morally acceptable in the pursuit of moral objectives and propose a number of actions that corporate leaders can take to establish morally purposive organizations and demonstrate the marks of ethically good leadership. Finally, we argue that to exercise corporate leadership requires that the leader should take on this responsibility.

F. Bird
J. Gandz
1991

NOTES

1 Barbara Gray, Collaborating: Finding Common Ground for Multiparty Problems (San Francisco: Jossey-Bass, 1989).

DEDICATION

We dedicate this book to the memory of James A. Waters, who, before his untimely death in January, 1989, was our friend and collaborator. The title of this book was proposed by Jim, who was long dedicated to good management as an executive, a teacher helping to train students to become managers, a university administrator, and a scholar. If it were not for Jim, much of the research and discussions which gave rise to this book would not have taken place.

F.B. Bird
J. Gandz
March, 1991

objectives:

- to be a proactive person in the process of business decision making to influence decisions from a broad based background of knowledge on what society's norms & values are.

- to recognize the multi-sided nature about issues & that decision making is complicated & difficult.

PART 1

CHAPTERS

1 Ethics in Management

This is a book about good management, about being an effective and morally responsible manager. The first chapter will outline why ethics are important in management and what is meant by ethical management. It will also give a preview of the material to come in subsequent chapters.

THE RELEVANCE OF ETHICS FOR MANAGERS

Managers make decisions in which some people benefit and others do not. Managers are, therefore, involved in making moral judgements. Whether to bid for a tobacco advertising account, whether to close a factory or run it at an unsatisfactory profit, whether to fire an employee or allow leave to attend an alcohol-abuse program, and whether to charge for a personal expense only indirectly related to business, are all ethical decisions.

Business ethics are about making and implementing decisions involving moral judgements. They may involve major strategic decisions, such as investing in certain industries or countries, or lesser ones such as what kind of performance appraisal to give a particular employee. The rationale for studying and thinking about these issues is to make better decisions which integrate moral factors with other considerations involved in business decisions. When managers judge in a morally conscious, reasoned, and systematic way, they will likely make better decisions.

Better decisions have a number of practical benefits. First, societies benefit. Societies have expectations about how firms should behave and about the consequences of corporate behavior. For example, societies rightfully expect unpolluted air and water, safe workplaces, competitive markets free of price-fixing, safe products and truthful advertising — matters of business ethics which managers should take into account in their decision-making. When business people do transgress societal expectations, a program of business

1

ethics enables others — either within or outside the organization — to call public attention to obvious as well as hidden abusive practices.

Businesses are also beneficiaries of more ethical behavior. In the long term, corporations will prosper only to the extent that they reflect and enhance society's values. Managers are an important link between organizations and society, and part of the managerial challenge is to understand and respond to societal expectations. The failure to think critically and act thoughtfully with respect to ethical issues leads inevitably to increased external control of organizations. Businesses can become entangled in a web of well-intentioned but impossibly complex government regulations, which in turn may result in higher costs. Moreover, the effectiveness and efficiency of working relationships with shareholders, customers, suppliers, unions, employees, and other stakeholders in the firm depend, in large measure, on integrity and trust. These relationships are burdened with extra costs when more energy is devoted to self-protection than to the job itself. Ethical behavior promotes reliable, co-operative working relationships and reduces the risk of costly lawsuits, whistle-blowing, bad publicity, and other damaging consequences of unethical behavior.

At a personal level, long-term career development may well hinge on a reputation for personal integrity. Perhaps nothing will limit a manager's career prospects more than a reputation for being a sharp operator who cannot be relied upon to act fairly, reasonably, and honestly. When unethical behavior becomes illegal behavior the consequences may involve indictments, legal battles, and professional and personal tragedies. Ethical behavior is personally sensible behavior. If management is a career worthy of significant personal investment, it must enhance feelings of self-worth in its practitioners. When people act ethically, especially when it is difficult and costly to do so, their actions enhance feelings of self-esteem and they derive satisfaction from their work.[1] Pride and a sense of accomplishment are important aspects of personal identity; these may be threatened by deliberately unethical behavior or actions which are subsequently shown to be unethical. They are reinforced, however, by ethically-conscious managerial behavior.

WHY THE CURRENT INTEREST?

The term "business ethics" was once considered an oxymoron. Questions of ethics seemed to have little relevance for the "hard-nosed" world of business except, perhaps, for some critics of business practices. However, it is a naive attitude today to overlook the importance of ethics in business. Ethics are being invoked continuously. Alarmed at instances of insider trading, environmental neglect, bribery and collusion, responsible business executives are calling for an ethical business community. This call is being echoed by the many corporations which have drafted their own ethical codes to ensure that those who work with and for them comply with accepted business standards. Ethics are an everyday reality for the business person today. They comprise the standards we set to determine decision-making, including both the minimal obligations which we must satisfy as well as ideals worth pursuing.

A FOCUS ON ACTION

Managers and non-managerial employees, individually and in groups, make choices and implement decisions daily. They face numerous issues, some pressing and others not, some of critical importance and others which are quite insignificant.[2] Whether they openly acknowledge it or not, business people regularly make decisions that reflect moral concerns and produce consequences which either help to realize or frustrate moral objectives. The closure of a factory could result in unemployment and economic and social hardship for employees, but may be deemed necessary for longer-term corporate health, a satisfactory return to stockholders, and job security for the remaining employees. A banker may be asked to finance the hostile takeover of one client by another and feel obligated towards both. An advertising executive might be concerned that highly selective product comparisons are misleading to the consumer, but market research may indicate that the comparison could increase sales. An individual may be offered a hot stock tip from someone with access to confidential information about a potential merger and may deliberate about acting on it.

Human resource management, accounting, financial management, marketing, operations, and other business disciplines involve ethical decisions. Sometimes these affect individuals and focus on personal and interpersonal behavior; sometimes they focus on relationships between groups, departments, divisions, or distinct corporate entities, be they suppliers, customers, or competitors. At other times, ethical issues concern major strategic decisions involving investment or disinvestment, product market entries, or competition.

When coupled with realistic assessments of the managerial role, and when discussed in the context of real management problems and issues, studying business ethics provides an opportunity for current and would-be managers to develop managerial skills necessary to make good, thoughtful and articulate managerial decisions.

MAKING BETTER DECISIONS

While these concepts are presented in later chapters, an example of what we mean by a better decision may be useful. Let us examine the case of an advertising agency executive who is offered the opportunity to make a presentation for a tobacco company account. The "hard-nosed" business decision might look at the costs and benefits associated with taking the account. The revenue, the staff to be hired to service the account, and so on would be considered. Management may also realize that some employees might leave the agency, upset at the prospect of promoting cigarette smoking, and consider this factor in the decision-making process.

An ethically sound decision-maker would consider the rights and obligations of various groups and individuals who have an interest in the decision, namely the stakeholders. Stakeholder analysis — which will be described more fully in a subsequent chapter — will identify, among other groups,

- stockholders, who expect the executive to act in their interests to maximize return on assets. Some stockholders, however, may have invested in the business because it had no tobacco accounts and may be prepared to forego profits from advertising tobacco products;
- employees, some of whom may find advertising tobacco products morally offensive, some of whom may feel there is nothing wrong with it and all of whom may be affected by way of bonuses and profits;
- society, including those whose smoking habit may be initiated or reinforced by the advertising, consumers of "second-hand smoke", and the dependents of smokers who are affected by their health problems.

The decision may involve taking the business, refusing it, or taking it subject to certain conditions, such as refusing to do "lifestyle" advertising or refusing to target certain age groups. The executive will then have to evaluate each of these options. This process might involve reflecting on personal values, discussing the dilemma with others in the advertising agency, their business acquaintances, their families, other board members, key shareholders, etc. In this evaluation executives may use a number of analytical techniques and decision-making rules. They may be influenced by various considerations such as that advertising tobacco products is legal, therefore it must be all right; that if they don't take this account, someone else will, so no good will come to society if the business is turned down; that if they don't take this business, they may have to lay off people; their bonuses would increase significantly if they took this business; or that if they declined this business it might put them in a very good position to bid for a large conservation group's advertising account. These various factors may all be considered in making an ethically conscious choice. Just how they may be considered will depend to some extent on the analytical framework those involved use.

Regardless of what option is chosen, there are likely to be dissatisfied employees, shareholders, and consumer groups. These may include close business acquaintances, squash partners, friends, and even family members. Decision-makers will need to justify their decision and monitor the impact of the decision over time. Did the decision to accept or reject the account attract new customers or lose the agency old ones, did key employees stay or leave because of this decision, what was the impact of the decision on the "bottom line", and how would they handle a similar situation in the future?

ETHICS, MORALITY AND GOOD MANAGEMENT

What do we mean by the words "ethics" and "morality"? They are derived from Greek (*ethos*) and Latin (*mores*) and refer to customary and prescribed communal living standards, broadly considered to be good. These words will be used interchangeably to identify patterns of behavior judged to be right because they adhere to a communally accepted standard. In keeping with philosophical conventions, "ethics" will refer to any communication about right or wrong conduct and "moral" will refer to actual or recommended conduct.

THE NATURE OF ETHICAL DECISION-MAKING

Moral philosophers such as Plato, Kant, Mill and Rawls developed various approaches to ethically responsible decision-making, and their conclusions suggest six major components of the decision-making process. Morally good decisions

- are realistic yet responsive to the issues at hand;
- are fully informed of the views and interests of relevant stakeholders;
- are aware of laws, principles and rules that might have bearing;
- are consciously and reflectively deliberated;
- are intelligently and coherently justified;
- are effectively implemented.

This focus of ethics on good decision-making parallels the concern of management with making and implementing responsible decisions. Good managers should know how to analyze difficult problems, generate and evaluate alternatives and make decisive judgements.

On the surface, at least, there appear to be differences between how ethicists and managers gauge decision-making. The common stereotype is that ethicists seek to apply universalizable standards to decisions whereas managers seek only to realize the economic interests of their operations. But this is really a caricature of both groups. Over the past two decades a number of books and articles on business ethics have attempted to demonstrate how philosophical models of ethical decision-making might be applied in useful ways to many of the tough choices facing business people. Managers are counselled to think about business problems from different perspectives involving, for example, the importance of long-term benefits, the rights of various stakeholders, relevant principles of justice, and relative cultural traditions.[3]

In classrooms and training seminars, managers have discussed real and hypothetical cases involving moral issues using this approach. They have often discovered new options, weaknesses in their initial assumptions, and stronger arguments for their eventual decisions. In the process, managers have discovered the relevance of philosophical ethics and philosophers have started to undestand the decision-making context of business.

By using philosophical models, ethical decision-making consists of rational consideration of the issues, an objective weighing of viable options, thoughtful deliberations and a justification of the decision reached. Managers use this ethical framework to make decisions in which moral considerations stand alongside economic and organizational considerations. This philosophical decision-making approach assumes that moral standards influence affected businesses. Morally responsible decisions are judgements made by invoking moral principles.

THE MANAGERIAL MODEL OF ETHICAL DECISION-MAKING

In the following chapters we set out a managerial model of ethical decision-making. We suggest that ethical decision-making involves identification of relevant stakeholders, consultation with stakeholders, the identification and interpretation of existing cultural norms, reflective reasoning, and the communication of these justifications to others. We also discuss ethical reasoning. Different ways of reasoning are distinguished in order to identify various patterns of deliberating about moral issues. We set out these types of reasoning so that managers can examine how they already think about moral issues and how alternative ways of reasoning may enhance their current practice.

The managerial model assumes but expands upon the simple philosophical model. It identifies decision-making as a social activity rather than a personal one, involving consultation with many people; it recognizes that there are social norms and expectations and codes of ethics and business practices; and it focuses on the real need to develop cogent and compelling justifications for actions.

For analytical purposes we divide the overall process of decision-making into three sets of activities which closely parallel the model of decision-making with which managers and business students are familiar. The first set involves identifying the issues; the second involves choosing between various courses of action, and the third involves undertaking a course of action.

Identifying the issues includes: describing and analyzing relevant information; considering the rights, interests, and expectations of stakeholders; and identifying normative standards that have bearing on the decision. Selecting an option involves: establishing objectives; weighing and interpreting information, stakeholders' views, and normative standards; considering alternative courses of action; and deciding how to act. Action may involve: the choice of tactics; the development of policies and processes at the organizational level; or the steps taken which may be required to achieve the desired outcome. (See Figure 1.1)

1. **Sizing-Up**
   Identifying difficulties, concerns, dilemmas, paradoxes. (Chapter 2)

   Consulting with relevant stakeholders to obtain their views, to listen to their claims and statements of interest, to discuss alternatives. (Chapter 3)

   Critically reviewing relevant social norms and standards and ethical principles in order to define and assign priority to issues. (Chapter 4)

2. **Deliberating and Deciding**
   Setting objectives, identifying and evaluating alternatives, weighing evidence, choosing the best alternative. (Chapter 5)

   Articulating intelligent and persuasive justifications for chosen courses of action. (Chapter 6)

   Defining minimal obligations and standards of excellence. (Chapter 7)

3. **Enacting**
   Developing tactics to realize objectives. (Chapter 8)

   Monitoring results. (Chapters 5 and 7)

   Developing organizational structures, systems and processes to facilitate ethically responsible actions. (Chapters 8 and 9)

   Exerting moral leadership. (Chapter 10)

FIGURE 1.1 **The Ethical Decision–Making Model**

(One of the problems facing managers is to decide whether a particular issue has ethical dimensions.) After all, how many times has a manager suggested to someone that an issue has an ethical dimension only to hear the other person respond that "no really, it's basically a legal issue." And even when an issue is identified as ethical, managers must decide whether to try to address the issue within their organizations. Should a recent business school graduate devote time and effort in attempting to change a company's policy on investment in South Africa? Chapter two addresses these problems and provides a framework for identifying ethical issues and the extent to which people may commit themselves to action.

Chapters three and four consider what is involved in determining the moral dimensions of issues. Chapter three examines these issues from the perspective of relevant stakeholders and chapter four examines them from the perspective of relevant moral standards. Managers often assume rather than fully consider these perspectives. Considering stakeholders' views and relevant norms does not necessarily lead clearly and automatically to ideal solutions. Stakeholders may hold opposing views. Normative standards may conflict and prevailing conventions may seem untenable on closer examination. This information must be interpreted and evaluated in keeping with intended objectives. Analysis leads to and involves deliberation.

Chapters five and six examine the processes of ethical deliberation. Chapter five considers the process of moral deliberation, identifying it as an action-oriented, pragmatic process. Chapter six identifies and discusses the strengths and weaknesses of seven typical patterns of reasoning about moral issues. Various "schools" of ethical reasoning and moral deliberation such as utilitarianism and relativism are also discussed.

These chapters outline a model of ethical decision-making which functions both as an analytical device and a normative ideal. This model can be used to analyze the ways business people make and avoid decisions about moral issues. It can be used to gauge the degree to which stakeholders are actively consulted, relevant cultural norms are considered, and coherent arguments are offered, as well as to evaluate the extent to which moral issues are discussed. The model is also normative since ethically responsible decisions are made as managers identify issues, deliberate, choose and act.

(From the perspective of our model, the fundamental prerequisites of ethical decision-making include a willingness to consult with stakeholders, a determination to consider the moral aspects of decisions, a commitment to think through issues reflectively and critically, a willingness to talk over these matters with colleagues, and a determination to offer clear, coherent and full justifications of decisions made.) This model does not outline a rigid decision-making process comprising a series of well-defined stages. Rather, the model is designed to foster reflection and imagination. Managers may well make responsible decisions in the very midst of their consultations; they may be led to their considered judgements by intuition as much as by logical discussion; and they may articulate their arguments only after they have already made their choices. The model is designed to help managers appreciate the various ways in which they actually reason about moral issues and the strengths and weaknesses of these approaches. It may encourage them to consider alternative, more satisfying ways of thinking about moral dilemmas.

(The model is also designed to help managers improve their capacity for logical reasoning.) Using this model, managers can examine the assumptions and coherence of other arguments and provide a framework for more imaginative and responsible considerations of moral issues. By using this model, managers will gain new perspectives on moral issues.

(We hope, finally, that this model will promote open, forthright debates on the moral aspects of business.) Candid discussions of moral issues will make managers increasingly conscious of moral standards in business; standards which, as individuals, they may hold in common with other managers or organization members.[4] (see Figure 1.2)

To evaluate one's own intuitions and conclusions.

To assess the arguments and decisions of others.

To stimulate new ideas, new perspectives, and moral imagination.

To help in the articulation of more intelligent, articulate justifications for decisions.

To cultivate more open debates with respect to moral issues.

To provide a shared, cognitive framework for dialogue and problem-solving discussions.

FIGURE 1.2 **The Uses of an Ethical Decision-Making Model**

ETHICS IN ACTION

This book emphasizes the process of decision-making. Whether a senior executive or a junior manager, the individual who wants to act on an ethical issue can draw on a number of techniques. The appropriate choice of tactics will often determine the results of the action and certain consequences for the individual. Whether to seek action by persuasion, by building coalitions of like-minded people, by organizing demonstrations, boycotts, or other demonstrations of power, or by "blowing the whistle" to the media or some regulatory agency, are all tactics for the individual who wants to affect organizational or individual decision-making. Chapter Eight discusses various approaches of initiating action.

ETHICS AND ORGANIZATIONS

As well as dealing with ethical dilemmas, managers make choices about organizing for ethical business practice. There are two aspects to this activity. The first, the subject of chapter seven, is the establishment of objectives for the ethically responsible organization. This chapter suggests that there are certain minimal moral standards an organization should comply with and higher standards of excellence to which an organization should aspire. The second activity involves structuring an organization to reinforce an ethical culture. Performance appraisals, internal audits, communications systems, staff training and development, and other structural and systems components of organizational design, impact ethical management practice. A policy which emphasizes cost-reduction at any price, which may condone cutting corners on safety precautions or dumping pollutants into the environment may be as unethical as the individual who turns the valve or favors a particular contractor for personal gain.

ETHICS AND LEADERSHIP

Ethical leadership in organizations, the subject of chapter ten, ensures that problems, issues, and potential solutions are explored so that viewpoints may be considered and decisions may be explained to all who will be affected. Ethical leadership accepts that cogent moral arguments may be raised to support decisions and that the decision-making process is as important as the decision itself. As one chief executive officer wrote:

"Through a legal fiction, a corporation is regarded as a person in relation to the law; but in reality it is more than this abstract concept; it has a human dimension and morality brought to it by its owners, management and employees. A corporation has an ethical reputation; it is judged by those it deals with — employees, shareholders, customers, sales associates, suppliers, and the community — against the same ethical standards as individuals. Our courts ascribe intent, motive, purpose and negligence to corporations. A transfer of thinking from individual values to corporate decisions happens — unconsciously because individuals bring morality with them, and consciously through leadership and a well-established commitment to high standards of ethics in all relationships".[5]

SUMMARY

Ethical management involves action rather than endless, abstract, deliberation. It requires the acceptance of multiple stakeholders and the obligation of making an ethically conscious decision based on reflection, dialogue, and a responsibility towards stakeholders. It requires analysis, decision-making, and implementation.

SUGGESTED READINGS

Barry, Vincent. *Moral Issues in Business.* (Belmont, California: Wadsworth Publishing Co., 1979).

Pastin, M. *The Hard Problems of Management: Gaining the Ethics Edge.* (San Francisco: Jossey-Bass, 1986).

Solomon, R.L. and K. Hanson. *It's Good Business.* (New York: Athenium, 1985).

Velasquez, M.G. *Business Ethics.* (Englewood Cliffs, N.J.: Prentice Hall, 1982).

NOTES FOR CHAPTER 1

1 Scott J. Vitell and D.L. Davis, "The Relationship Between Ethics and Job Satisfaction: An Empirical Investigation," *Journal of Business Ethics*, Vol. 9, No. 6 (1990): 489-494.

2 J. Dutton and E. Ottensmeyer, "Strategic Issues Management Systems: Form, Function and Contexts," *Academy of Management Review*, Vol. 12, No. 2 (1987): 355-365.

3 Karl E. Weick, "Organizational Culture As a Source of High Reliability," *California Management Review*, Vol. 29, No. 2 (1987).

4 J. Waters and F. Bird. "The Moral Dimensions of Organization Culture," *Journal of Business Ethics*, Vol. 6, No. 1 (1987): 15-22.

5 Personal communication from Arden Haynes, Chairman and Chief Executive Officer, Imperial Oil Limited.

2 Ethical Issues

Business people continuously face issues — situations in which alternatives exist and they must choose and defend a particular course of action. Often they simply choose to do what they have done before and, although there may actually be alternatives, choices are made without much thought. Issues emerge only as business people consciously recognize alternatives — whether because of changed circumstances or amended objectives, or because others have called attention to their concerns. Industrial plants, for example, had for a long time been exhausting toxic materials up their smokestacks before public attention made them aware of pollution as a problem. It simply was not a salient issue for most managers. In this chapter we look at what constitutes an ethical issue and how these issues may be identified.

THE SALIENCE OF ISSUES

This almost automatic reaction of simply acting as one has acted in similar circumstances on previous occasions has its virtues, for if every situation in which alternatives existed were viewed as giving rise to weighty issues, it would become impossible to act decisively and effectively. We would divert attention and energy away from current projects in order to deliberate about alternatives, most of which are not worth considering. It is clearly useful to view many possibilities as not constituting genuine alternatives. It is beneficial to establish guidelines for action so that it is not necessary to divert time and energy sizing up every situation as if it were new and unexpected. Most of the time most of us respond to exigencies in keeping with established conventions: and that, precisely, are what our norms, customs, conventional wisdom, principles, and habits are for.

However, business people often err by not recognizing alternatives especially when following them might well be better for their firms and communities.

Responsive managers learn how to distinguish genuine issues from facsimiles and how to pose questions to identify promising possibilities. Responsible managers learn to differentiate fundamental issues from peripheral concerns.[1] Ethically responsible managers learn how to identify the moral aspects of the issues they face.

Ethical issues confronting business people come in different shapes and sizes. Some are obvious: the abuse of expense accounts, the bribing of purchasing agents, the reduction of product quality, and the release of pollutants into the environment. Some are less obvious: the closure of factories, especially in areas of high unemployment; the use of sub-contractors who pay workers at lower rates; the conduct of performance appraisal sessions; and the hiring of minority groups. The latter examples may even be considered by some to have no ethical or moral basis at all.

Even when an issue is defined as "ethical", managers must decide about their own moral standpoint, and whether to ignore the problem, make a decision or encourage someone else to decide. In this chapter we provide a guide to help managers identify the kinds of ethical issues which they may face and to help them realize their personal attitude towards the issue. As we address these two concerns, namely the identification of ethical issues in business and the relationship of managers to them, we also consider why many managers fail to see and respond to these issues.

IDENTIFYING ETHICAL ISSUES

It is not unusual for two managers to confront an issue differently; one as a moral concern, and the other as a practical one. Some financial executives consider the matter of insider trading as an ethical problem while others see it as a matter of securities legislation and regulation. Our understanding of ethical issues is influenced both by what we assume makes an issue ethical in the first place and by corresponding assumptions about different kinds of ethical issues. People hold varying assumptions about what constitutes an ethical issue. These assumptions may be labelled "high" or "low", "broad" or "narrow". These assumptions are summarized in Figure 2.1.

Some people define ethics in terms of high and demanding moral standards with which they seek to comply out of a sense of duty independent of any potential benefits. They may characterize these standards, as the philosopher Kant did, with rationally defensible, universal principles, or with specific forms of behavior which are, for example, altruistic, self-sacrificing, or in keeping with particular religions.[2] Those who adopt an especially high standard of business ethics may either strive to transform business into a more principled activity or cynically conclude that business practices, by their very nature, cannot be judged by ethical standards.

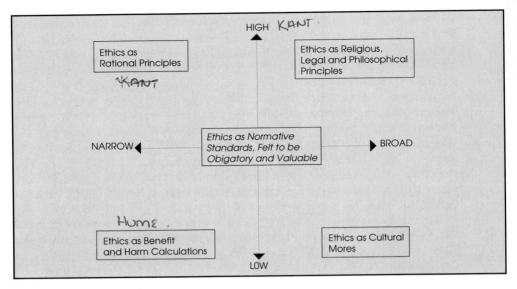

FIGURE 2.1 **Assumptions About "Ethical Issues "**

This "high" view of ethics historically arose in reaction to a "low" view which defined ethics as standards of behavior people adopt because they believe that acting in keeping with them will promote well-being, and acting contrary to them will promote harm. The "low" view was initially defended by the philosopher Hume, who observed that people tend to adopt and defend moral standards because they believe those standards are beneficial. The "low" view holds that any common standards introduced to reduce harm or increase mutual benefits are ethical. In business, then, "ethical" practices are those which increase well-being and "unethical" practices are those which lead to injury and harm. This view of ethics extends the scope of activities regarded as ethically relevant to business and allows and encourages diverse views of what this benefit and injury actually means. When applied to business activities, "low" ethics foster occasional condemnations of potentially damaging activities, as well as activities which produce noteworthy benefits. An exceedingly "low" view of ethics provides no common standards for evaluating business activities aside from calculations of benefits and harms, which are open to varying interpretations.

The "narrow" view of ethics assumes that ethics comprise a distinct reality quite separate from other related disciplines, such as religion, politics, law, social conventions, and etiquette. Legal issues are clearly distinguished from moral or political issues. Unlike law involving compulsory jurisdiction and politics involving power, ethics are associated with voluntarily adopted principles that gain influence without force *or* political persuasion. Unlike religions, which primarily regulate human relations with sacred realities, or customs and social mores which tend to be accepted without reflection, ethics attempt to guide human interaction through standards that are consciously adopted. "Narrow" ethics isolate the role of law, politics, and customs from each other.[4] For business, this means that only a restricted range of issues are considered to be of ethical concern. "Narrow" ethics, in practice, focus attention on obvious abuses, such as violations of conflict-of-interest guidelines, and moral dilemmas that lack clear precedents. Many issues which some managers may find morally problematic are dismissed by other managers as problems for lawyers, accountants, financial advisors, and industrial relations experts.

The "broad" view of ethics, in contrast, does not separate ethics from law, politics, social customs, professional codes, and etiquette. Ethics are social mores, that is, standards of conduct which guide human behavior. Ethics are the action guides or codes which influence how people ought to act. Ethical issues emerge whenever people violate or ignore social mores or whenever individuals or groups seek to change them. When business practices are considered from this "broad" perspective, the scope of potential moral issues both expands and contracts. Moral issues are broadly determined by accepted practices and relative cultural mores which influence how businesses ordinarily make decisions. These standards may be set by professional codes, economic theories, local customs, organizational policies, laws, and religious beliefs.[5] However, while this "broad" view of ethics calls attention to the normative, and hence moral aspects of many economic assumptions and business practices, it provides no basis for questioning these standards or for resolving dilemmas when issues conflict.

Each of these ethical viewpoints is appealing both because of what each values — the emphasis on principles or actual benefits and harms, the recognition of the distinctiveness of ethics or of the pervasive influence of morality on everyday social conventions — and how each complements the other. Recognizing that people hold differing perspectives on the relative value of "high", "low", "broad" and "narrow" ethics, we maintain that aspects of each are all relevant to a balanced ethical perspective. This "middle" position suggests that ethics refer to normative standards for interpersonal behavior, which are regarded as compelling and authoritative (the "broad" view) because acting in keeping with these standards is considered an obligation (the "high" view) and beneficial (the "low" view). Behavior, which corresponds to these standards, is not ethical if it is coerced, or undertaken for private advantage. It becomes moral only to the degree that it is enacted out of conscious voluntary respect for behavioral standards (the "narrow" view). These standards may be based on social conventions, ideologies, laws, philosophies or religions (the "broad" view).

The scope for dealing with ethical issues in business is broad. It includes any act or decision affecting the welfare of businesses and their stakeholders, which may be evaluated and judged by relevant moral standards, as these are recognized by business people and their stakeholders, including the larger society. As we argue in this and the next two chapters the range of these standards is indeed extensive. Moreover as we maintain generally in this book, in order to make business more morally responsible, ordinarily it is often not necessary to introduce new moral standards into business; rather, it is necessary to find ways of encouraging, compelling, rewarding, and — where indicated — punishing business people so that they follow more closely standards they already at least tacitly acknowledge.

(This somewhat theoretical discussion has been introduced because the assumptions people make about the nature of ethics directly affect their practical judgements.) Aside from those few committed moral crusaders and saints, exceedingly high and narrow views of ethics lead most business people to conclude despairingly or defiantly that ethics can have little to say about day to day business operations. In contrast, while excessively "low" and "broad" views acknowledge the moral dimension of business, they often provide little leverage for seeing these issues clearly and critically. Ethics, correspondingly, become blurred with pragmatic, utilitarian calculations and considerations of the deference to be paid to local customs, laws, professional standards, and company conventions instead of reflecting principled, thoughtful, and cogent managerial action.

ETHICAL ISSUES AND BUSINESS DISCIPLINES

(What matters most is not whether we judge particular issues to be ethical, but our judgements about the kinds of ethical issues which confront us.) The term ethics, itself, is too broad a referent. Ethical issues range from pilfering supplies to methods of toxic waste disposal. They range from debates about marketing practices in the Third World to procedures for promotions. Therefore, it is useful to group ethical issues facing managers in relation to the major areas of business activity. Issues may affect functional areas, such as marketing, finance, industrial relations, operations, personnel, accounting, purchasing, and sales, or they may affect relationships with major stakeholders, such as employees, suppliers, investors, creditors, consumers, and community groups.[6] Figure 2.2 presents a listing of some of the ethical issues which managers confront in functional areas. This list alerts managers to the kinds of moral concerns likely to arise in the course of their daily work and encourages managers to examine the relationship between their specific responsibilities and the more general topic of ethics.

It is sometimes difficult for managers to understand the importance of ethics while the discussion of moral issues centres on business organizations as a whole. And, so long as the study of business ethics remains a peripheral subject area, considered only for elective courses or occasional seminars, it is not likely to be integrated into practical debates on business and finance. To the contrary, identifying the ethical issues involved in these functional areas and stakeholder relationships should encourage the consideration of ethics in all business decisions.

General Management:
Choice of business markets
Mergers and acquisitions
Leveraged buy outs
Ecology and environment
Whistle-blowing
Codes of conduct
Ethical appeal mechanisms
Greenmail
Golden parachutes

Human Resource Management:
Employment equity
Psychological testing
Anti-Union activities
Work design
Employment security
Employee discipline
Confidentiality and privacy
Technology induced displacement
Negotiating practices
Performance appraisal
Succession planning
Pay equity

Marketing:
Predatory pricing
Price fixing
Deceptive advertising
Product misrepresentation
Sex/race exploitation
Stereotyping
Consumer privacy
Incentives and promotions
Market research in promotion
Boiler-room telemarketing

Sales:
Deception/misinformation
Gifts/entertainment
Local business practices

Finance:
Loans to foreign countries
Lending criteria

Debt rescheduling
Foreclosures
Disclosure
Insider trading
Insider leveraged buy outs
Management buy outs
Cash management policies
Program (computer) trading
'Pushing' of new securities

Accounting:
Disclosure
Inflation accounting
Provisions for losses
Tax shelters
Conflict of interest
Independence
Self-regulation
Overfamiliarity

Operations:
Plant location
Automation and redundancy
Environmental protection
Safety standards
Technological innovation

Purchasing:
Competitive bidding procedure
Gifts
Reciprocity for friends

Information Systems:
Privacy of information
Copyright infringement
Moonlighting
Intelligence gathering
Liability for errors

Management Science/Operations Research:
Bias in analytical results
Intervention in modelling
Modelling ethical issues/decisions
Confidentiality of models

FIGURE 2.2 **A Non-Exhaustive List of Ethical Issues in Business**

ETHICAL ISSUES AND MANAGEMENT BEHAVIOR

One traditional focus of business ethics is concerned with how people behave and ought to behave according to a set of accepted moral standards. It is, however, a misconception and oversimplification to focus just on conduct that fails to comply with accepted standards. In the first place, non-compliance may assume different forms which ought to be distinguished from each other. In the second place, moral issues may also arise because managers may be interested in pursuing ideals, in raising new and higher standards of behavior, and in encouraging people to aspire to realize them. In the third place, existing moral standards conflict in ways that provide no clear behavioral guidelines. Business people are likely to become more sensitive to moral concerns and more likely to respond effectively if they recognize differences in the ethical character of moral issues and comprehend how these variations call for quite different responses.

Many ethical issues in business arise because business people fail to comply with accepted moral standards, by acting outside of expected roles, by distorting their roles, or by failing to live up to their roles. "Non-role" behaviors include conduct in which business people cheat on expense accounts, embezzle funds, steal supplies, use suppliers in which they have financial interests, engage in insider trading, make false claims for sick leave, and direct company maintenance departments to paint their private residences. Managers, in all these instances, blatantly disregard recognized standards and harm their firms. In all of these cases the costs of such actions are borne by the employees' firms and the payoffs favor the individuals themselves. Managers are tempted to engage in these acts when they feel they will not be caught. Many firms attempt to prevent this behavior by establishing codes of behavior forbidding it, introducing sanctions and maintaining close supervision.

"Role-distortion" acts are also easily recognized. They differ from "non-role" acts in that they are likely to benefit the firms for which managers work. "Role distortion" is used to indicate that managers in these cases do act in keeping with expected standards as managers but they bend, twist, or modify these standards to engage in activities from which their firms gain advantages. "Role-distorted" acts are those in which actors pursue their role mandates, such as increasing sales or reducing costs, but distort that mandate by disregarding widely accepted moral standards. "Role-distortion" acts include bribery, padding insurance claims, price-fixing, unjustified differential pricing, falsifying product safety test results and manipulating suppliers. Other examples of role-distortion acts include reducing the quality of products without informing customers, over-selling products without informing customers, fudging safety or environmental standards, pirating computer software, and discriminating against women or minorities in hiring and promotions. Though these acts would, if widely known, be disapproved of in most organizations, they increase profits at the expense of outside parties, such as customers, suppliers, employees, and competitors.

Because these acts benefit the firms involved, they are often <u>difficult to police and control</u>. Senior management will often officially condemn this behavior while implicitly encouraging subordinates to act in ways that directly advantage their firms. Because their own careers depend in large measure on how well they can contribute to their firms' financial well-being, subordinate managers are sometimes tempted to commit "role-distortion" acts. Over time, some of these "role-distortion" acts have been the subject of legislation which both prohibits specific abuses and establishes regulatory agencies to police them. However, the problem of curtailing these acts continues, not only because many "role-distortion" acts are not precisely illegal and are difficult to detect but also because the surveillance, adjudication and legislation involved in policing these acts are expensive. Nonetheless, regulatory agencies have helped to improve safety standards, to reduce outright discrimination, to minimize collusion in pricing, to set limits on manipulation of suppliers, and to help control pollution.

The term "<u>role-failure</u>" identifies a third group of morally non-compliant acts by business people. These acts include instances in which individuals fail to perform in their roles of managers, executives, and sales personnel as expected. They do not involve explicit cheating either against their firms, as in "non-role" acts or for their firms, as in "role-distortion" acts. Rather, they involve inadequate performance or mismanagement. Some examples will help to clarify the term. Managers may fail to conduct candid performance appraisals, or fail to confront subordinates who have cheated on their expense reports. They may deny promotions or training opportunities to high performers or they may deceitfully "palm off" poor performers to other departments. They may undermine their bosses' authority or slant proposals and withhold information. Though managers do not engage in "role-failure" acts for financial gain, they act selfishly and to the detriment of fellow employees and the firm as a whole.

"Role-failure" acts harm others and often damage business organizations. Although they are not illegal, they do constitute violations of generally accepted normative standards. Again, it is useful to cite examples to demonstrate how pervasive these acts are, and their costs to businesses. For example, senior

---

⓪ **Non-Role**: Acts which are not consistent with the expectations of the role. Not approved by the organization. Often illegal in nature. Benefit the actors and their conspirators.

② **Role-Distortion**: Behaviors associated with carrying out the expected role but which are inconsistent with moral standards. Benefit the organization, not the actors. May or may not be approved by the organization.

③ **Role Failure**: Failure to perform the acts as required by the organization. The organization loses as a result of these failures.

FIGURE 2.3 **Types of Moral Failings**

executives can become so preoccupied by their office power struggles that they fail to keep up-to-date with market developments or technological innovations. Executives may sell off profitable units of their organization to provide short run gains that make them look successful, or, they may dispose of valuable by-products that cannot be used immediately to reduce inventory costs and show higher short-run margins for their units.[8] Sales managers may push their staff beyond their reasonable capacities and may provoke stress and encourage deceitful sales practices. Drug companies may not adequately inform consumers of potentially adverse side-effects to prescription medicine. To expand their own portfolios, credit institutions may provide loans to people and groups who are not good credit risks on the assumption that the value of their present possessions, used as collateral, will remain steady or grow. This last example is a major public concern in both Canada and the United States. Miscalculations, faulty judgements, poor management and competition led a number of savings and loan associations and banks to over-extend themselves. The results have seriously injured investors and disrupted borrowers, including many farmers, who had been encouraged to take out loans for which they were not well-positioned to repay. Eventually tax-payers have been charged with the cost of the debt. Often these acts of mismanagement have few consequences. Sometimes, however, "role-failure" may produce disastrous results. For example, the oil spill in Alaska might have been avoided if the "senior executive" of the Exxon Valdez had assumed more direct supervision for sailing the ship instead of leaving it to a less experienced subordinate. Whether they cause minor or major harm, "role-failure" acts are morally questionable because they are failures of responsible management.

Compared to "non-role" and "role-distortion" acts, "role-failure" acts are more difficult to limit and control. After all, to some extent acts of mismanagement are inevitable. It is difficult to prevent or prohibit all instances of poor judgement and haphazard management. Inexperienced managers are more likely to falter here. But even senior managers err, sometimes out of self-interest and sometimes out of neglect. Especially when the resulting damage from "role-failure" is insignificant or not immediately apparent, it is difficult to exert energy to isolate and punish perpetrators. Attention does need to be drawn to "role-failure", especially by those adversely affected and those who tacitly tolerate it. However, rarely will punishment provide a solution as it does with both "non-role" and "role-distortion" acts. A more fitting response to "role-failure" should include a combination of counselling and training that encourage people to learn from mistakes and poorly considered judgements.

MORAL IDEALS

Moral issues arise, not only when people act in ways that are reprehensible, but when people seek to realize objectives they consider worthwhile. Instead of asking how we can prevent people from acting in proscribed ways we should ask how we can encourage people to act ethically. The distinction we are making here corresponds to the distinction philosophers often make between moral standards which identify basic obligations and moral standards which identify aspired standards of excellence.[9] When people fail to realize basic obligations, we refer to their behavior as being non-compliant but using these words is inappropriate in describing behavior that aims for, but falls short of standards of excellence. Striving to achieve higher standards should not be condemned but praised. The prohibition against intentional lying represents a widely acknowledged moral obligation, the violation of which is, with some exceptions, universally condemned. In contrast, acting altruistically is a moral ideal, which people may honor in varying degrees without moral criticism.

The opinion that businesses ought to pursue certain moral ideals is not a recent one. In the early stages of industrialization, businesses which received public charters were expected to further national interests by representing national governments in colonial areas, by augmenting national wealth, and by developing transportation links within countries. From time to time businesses have been called upon to support charity drives and to help national efforts in wartime and national emergencies. Many businesses have assumed responsibility for developing social and recreational facilities for their employees and other community members. Businesses have patronized the arts and public sport. Although this question has been heatedly debated, many business people believe that corporations have a social responsibility to provide technical, charitable and voluntary assistance to the communities in which their businesses are located. Business people have joined associations, such as the Kiwanis, Elks and Rotary, which promote not only business contacts but useful civic activities.

Businesses have pursued moral ideals not only for their communities but for the way they conduct their business. For example, different ideals have affected corporate treatment of employees. The development of scientific management, human relations, and more recently, human resource management represent different ideals about the ways of treating employees.[10] More generally, it has been argued that the most successful businesses are characterized by a commitment to being service-oriented to customers, people-oriented to personnel, and responsive to the public.[11]

Managers, through their businesses, may pursue specific moral ideals. It is possible to cite examples of businesses which have committed themselves to ideal objectives. For example, firms may make special efforts to foster the career development of their employees; they may establish corporate foundations to help community groups, educational institutions, and the arts; they may institute programs to help employees with drinking, immigration problems or other personal difficulties. Like Chemical Bank, they may use their special competence, as accountants, for example, to help non-profit organizations with their bookkeeping, or like General Electric they may "adopt" inner city schools. To conserve natural resources, they may choose to use only recycled paper and biodegradable packaging. They may also voluntarily reduce toxic contamination of their water and smoke disposal in advance of legal requirements. They may foster a sense of community among employees by sponsoring everything from sports teams to cultural groups.

These ideals create a number of issues for business people. Although businesses may not be faulted for failing to live up to all these ideals, they may leave themselves open to criticism if they remain insensitive to all these issues. Because pursuing moral ideals may be a drain on resources, time, and money, businesses may only be able to commit themselves to certain ideals. This rationale provides no excuse for ignoring these pursuits. Hence, managers need to prioritize moral objectives.[12]

Moral commitment is often ignored or misconstrued in the discussion of business ethics. Frequently, critics ignore the extent to which business people have committed themselves to particular moral ideals. It is too simple to construe policy as totally self-serving. IBM, for example, is a company which has unswervingly committed itself to an employment security policy, incurring costs to relocate employees when operations have discontinued or when plants have been rationalized. Sometimes, businesses are criticized because of shortfalls towards the environment, without considering their commitment to personnel relations and customer services. While it is useful to recall instances where managers pursue ideals for the community with respect to education, we should recognize that this idealism can easily wane. Today, the trend is towards the environment since many people fear that a failure to address concerns now may lead to disastrous long-term consequences.

MORAL DILEMMAS

Ethical issues arise also in response to moral dilemmas. A dilemma exists when there is a need to choose between two or more equally favorable or unfavorable alternatives. For example, after having pursued an aggressive policy of non-discriminatory employment in South Africa, a firm may well debate whether to protest against apartheid, whether to withdraw investment, or whether to turn its plants over to local interests likely to pursue less liberal policies. Sound arguments have been made both for divestment, as a means of registering criticism with policies of apartheid, and for policies of continued investment, together with programs of non-discrimination and integration. In the end, those making decisions must find ways to weigh arguments, to put them in perspective, and to choose decisively, justifying their choices in clear, persuasive terms.

Many moral issues arise in business in the form of dilemmas, some easier to resolve than others. For example, in order to achieve a balanced labor force, should firms adopt a policy of affirmative action, favoring members of minority groups? Or, to reduce pilfering and malingering by employees, should managers use informants? To maintain employment security for all regular employees, should a firm hire casual workers or sub-contract to cheaper foreign workers to meet shifting market demands? Should a firm always use a sealed-bid system with suppliers or establish long-term relationships with particular suppliers, who may be more expensive? Is a leveraged buyout in the best interests of a particular firm, its workers, and consumers? Should workers receive compensation payments for work-related stress? Given limited financial leeway, how fast should firms move on reducing pollution in advance of actual court orders? Should a company close down an unprofitable plant in an area of high unemployment? These are but a few examples of the moral dilemmas which may arise in business practices.

In practice, many ethical issues do not start out as dilemmas. They first catch our attention either because of the failure of individuals and organizations to comply with accepted ethical standards, or because particular moral ideals capture our imagination and we seek to achieve them. Nonetheless, both these aspects may provoke ethical dilemmas as we consider steps to resolve them. Thus, to curtail moral failings, we need to consider how to encourage voluntary compliance as well as strategies for policing unacceptable behavior. As we review alternative decisions, we need to weigh the strengths and weaknesses of each and the extent to which they correspond to our moral convictions. Similarly, as we think about strategies to realize ideals, we need to consider the cost of these policies and the impact of costs on other aspects of the business. As we consider strategies to limit moral failings and encourage moral ideals, we often deliberate about assigning priorities to various objectives and ways of achieving those objectives. As ethical issues are addressed, we must recognize the need to reflect on the moral strengths and weaknesses of the possible alternatives.

THE SCOPE AND DIVERSITY OF ETHICAL ISSUES

Many moral issues in business are overlooked because managers fail to recognize the diverse forms in which these issues arise. Many adopt the tendency to limit "ethics" to blatant "non-role" acts, outrageous and illegal "role-distortion" acts, and the most controversial and publicly-debated ethical dilemmas. This view overlooks almost all "role-failure" acts, "role distortion" acts which are not illegal, everyday dilemmas which are not a focus for heated debate, as well as issues relating to priorities and strategies which realize chosen ideals. As managers recognize the diversity of moral issues, they are more likely to acknowledge their relevance to responsible and effective business practices. They are also more likely to understand the need for varying responses depending on the issues at hand.

INDIVIDUAL MANAGERS AND ETHICAL ISSUES

To respond effectively to ethical issues, managers need to identify not only the kind of issues at hand, but their own personal relationship to them. This relationship is affected by two factors: the structural setting and the importance which individuals assign to specific issues.

Ethical issues facing business people appear at different levels of the business hierarchy. Questions about expense account excesses and the relationship of purchasing agents to suppliers arise at different levels of an organization than do questions about whether to divert a small portion of an investment portfolio into non-profit businesses. Discussions about proper supervision of subordinates occur in different settings than do deliberations about policing environmental guidelines. To clarify this problem, we propose a four-level model that distinguishes issues that arise on a societal, organizational, positional and individual level. (see Figure 2.4) A given issue may impact all four levels or only one. Correspondingly, individual managers may be responsible for specific issues on several levels at the same time. This four-tiered model allows managers to understand their relationships with particular issues.

A number of issues facing businesses call for action at the societal level. This concerns the relationship between businesses and governments, businesses and regulatory agencies, and businesses and community groups. At this level, governments have legislated to establish worker health and safety standards, to reduce discrimination against minorities, to foster private pension programs in small companies, to establish noxious emissions standards, and to guarantee the purity and safety of goods produced. It is often difficult to persuade particular businesses to adopt socially beneficial programs if the costs of

Societal Issues: Relationship between businesses and outside groups such as government, consumer associations, regulatory agencies.

Corporate Issues: Issues within and between organizations, such as supplier and vendor relationships, and corporate policies and practices.

Role Issues: Issues relating to the ongoing discharge of the responsibilities of a designated role including non-role acts, role-distortion acts, and role failure. Poor and biased performance appraisals, excessive business gift-giving to stimulate sales, or misleading advertising campaigns are examples.

Individual Issues: Issues relating to a clash between individuals' value systems and actions of the corporation or other employees. Going along with questionable practices out of a sense of loyalty, whistle-blowing, or quitting a company because of its actions are examples of individual issues.

FIGURE 2.4 **Ethical Issues and Level Of Analysis**

these programs are likely to make them less competitive. Hence legislation and regulations have been adopted, for example, to eliminate the use of bribes and gratuities to secure customers in foreign countries. Businesses are not likely to use more expensive recycled materials or to hire and train the chronically unemployed unless these policies are publicly mandated and rewarded by tax benefits or other subsidies.

Many ethical issues are centered at the corporate or organizational level. These involve issues that arise in and between organizations which can be dealt with adequately without the need for legislation, judicial review, or the policing powers of regulatory agencies. For example, businesses may adopt personnel policies that are more or less humane and more or less sensitive to issues regarding the just allocation of tasks and rewards, personal privacy, and the development of skills. It is at the organizational level that decisions are made about staff cuts, how to adjudicate the relative merits of competing stakeholders, and how to use resources to help local communities. Individual organizations establish policies which affect their moral ethos through the implicit or explicit guidelines they adopt for interacting with stakeholders. Decisions about social audits, investment strategies, and product quality are all made at this level.

The moral issues that most concern managers are not those affecting organizations as a whole but those impinging on their managerial responsibilities. These involve professional ethics as opposed to corporate or organizational ethics and are often considered "managerial" because they concern how individual managers ought to carry out the tasks of their positions. At this level we are concerned with how to discourage business people from abusing managerial advantages. These include the range of moral failings which we considered in relation to "non-role", "role-distortion", and "role-failure" acts as well as the professional conduct of business people as accountants, engineers, lawyers, consultants, sales agents, information systems experts, and human resource directors.

Moral issues also arise at a personal level. As individuals, managers bear personal responsibilities. Managers may need to appease their own conscience even when this means acting against their official roles or organizational loyalties. At an individual level, managers may conclude that there are businesses for which they cannot work because of a particular product or policy. They may feel the need to dissent from organizational policies or role expectations which they cannot, in good conscience, support. Independent of their official roles, managers may be asked to befriend others within their organization, or to "blow the whistle" on any abuses they observe. As individuals they may freely counsel others and help them overcome personal difficulties.

Depending on the relevant issue, managers may be expected to respond on one or more of these levels at the same time. Managers are also limited in their capacity to address issues by their level in the company's hierarchy. Managers in subordinate positions as individuals cannot be expected to respond to many moral issues at the societal or organizational levels. Here they must pursue their objectives at a more personal level, informing superiors of problems, participating in informal coalitions to lobby for specific changes, supporting political groups and community associations to affect legal changes and corporate responses, and possibly, "blowing the whistle" on abuses. Senior executives, on the other hand, can be expected to act on all four levels, at once guiding the policies of their organizations, using their organizational connections to lobby for societal changes, fulfilling their leadership responsibilities, in addition to whatever personal guidelines they may adopt.

ACTING ON ETHICAL ISSUES

How we choose to respond to ethical issues is affected both by our structural relationship to particular concerns and by the extent to which we are personally motivated to take action. The junior manager of a marketing or sales department may simply not be involved, from a structural perspective, with an organization's purchasing practices, its policy on investment in South Africa, or its approach to affirmative action. A junior manager has no formal responsibility for these decisions, may know very little about them, and may have no forum for expressing attitudes towards them.

Some issues are weighty while others are trivial. For example, if someone feels that the company is deliberately ignoring the safety conditions in a mine in order to increase production figures, and that person understands the impact of safety violations on the workforce, then the matter is weighty. It might be even weightier if there are personal consequences, such as the involvement of friends or family, but even without personal considerations, it is clearly an important issue. On the other hand, knowing that someone is claiming for a taxi when they took a bus to the airport may be recognized as a violation of both company rules and the responsibility to be honest, but it may not impel action. Decisions to close down plants clearly affect more people than poor performance appraisals; failure to upgrade equipment and re-train personnel may have more far reaching consequences than failure to contribute generously to local charity campaigns. All these judgements are subject to debate.[13] Weightiness is measured by the scope and urgency of the situation as well as by the importance attributed to particular concerns which reflect value-laden judgements.

The motivation to respond to ethical issues is determined by two factors: the extent to which people are personally affected by the issue and their estimation of the probability that their actions will influence the outcomes. Businesses, as organizations, and managers, as individuals, can attempt to rank moral issues in order of importance and immediacy. Many today consider environmental issues as particularly important. Failure to act responsibly is likely to cause long-term injury to many people and to the natural environment unless steps are taken to reduce the depletion of non-renewable resources, to reduce the contamination of the atmosphere, and to find ways of reducing and securing dangerous wastes. The collective good of a number of firms may be undermined by executives pursuing policies that provide short-run advantages in the form of enhanced personal reputations or fiscal returns that leave organizations demoralized, without clear direction and financially drained. While many mergers are financially beneficial to investors and the executives who arrange them, they do not necessarily use organizational resources more effectively. On the other hand, organizational efforts to increase workers' autonomy to upgrade their skills may be considered morally important because these efforts increase both organizational efficiency and workers' dignity and organizational commitment. Other weighty issues include the role of businesses in Third World economies, the servicing of customers, competing with smaller firms, and discriminating against certain groups.

The relative importance of moral issues varies in relation to our calculations of their objective importance as well as to their impact on our lives. This impact is determined by the immediacy of particular issues and our capacity to respond effectively to them. We are more likely to devote time and energy to issues which directly affect our work, our organizations, and our neighborhoods. One of the most successful ways to arouse moral concern is to demonstrate how events are likely to have an immediate personal impact on people's lives. Environmental groups have been successful in demonstrating the connection between industrial policies, unwelcome environmental changes, such as increased smog and acid rain, and general health.

Our propensity to act on moral issues is also greatly affected by our ability to make a difference. Sometimes, people do become vocal about issues over which they can have little direct impact. They may debate the relative justice of industrial capitalism, the vices of trans-national corporations, and the moral bankruptcy of high finance, without being able to do anything about them. Our capacity to act effectively is conditioned, positively, by opportunities for exerting influence, and negatively, by other constraints on our lives. Morally concerned business people often fail to recognize the variety of options available to them. In most cases, our capacity to act effectively is connected with our ability to form and work with coalitions of other like-minded people and our ability to communicate persuasively. Often, our ability to respond is limited by other factors impinging on our lives, including our interest in other moral issues, our prior organizational commitments, our job limitations, and our lack of experience in successfully raising issues. All these factors do change over time and an individual's capacity to act effectively may improve.

How we relate to moral issues depends on a number of factors. These include our structural relation to concerns, our judgements regarding their objective importance, their likely impact on our lives, and our capacity to forge effective plans of action. There is no way to weigh these factors to determine the relative importance of the issues. Rather, we need, through consultation, to determine our <u>own priorities</u>. We may well acknowledge the importance of certain issues, such as hunger in Africa, for which we can do little in our managerial or organizational roles, even though we may as individuals attempt to do our part. At the same time, we can improve personnel relations and product quality, because these are objectives we can realistically fulfill. (see Figure 2.5)

SUMMARY

If we can ask again why business people fail to acknowledge the moral aspects of so many issues they face, we can see that their reluctance often springs from the assumption that their contribution will not matter. Why discuss issues with no easy solutions? In many instances this question reflects an unthinking reaction. Too often business people do not really think seriously. They fail to imagine alternatives. They too often think they are alone in their dilemmas and are unable to consider options for raising and responding to moral issues that matter to them. Business people can respond as good managers, though, by putting ethics into action.

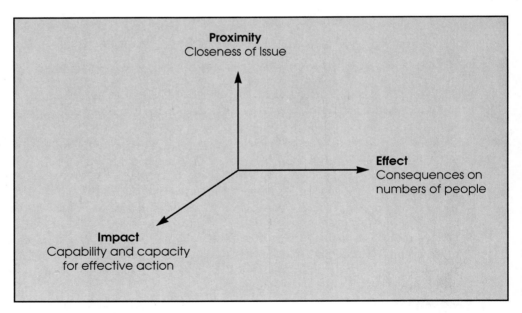

FIGURE 2.5 **Factors Influencing Action**

SUGGESTED READINGS

Beauchamp, T.L. and N.E. Bowie eds. *Ethical Theory and Business* (Cambridge: Harvard University Press, 1979).

Garrett, T.M. and R.J. Klonowski. *Business Ethics*, 2nd ed. (Englewood Cliffs, N.J.: Prentice Hall, 1986, 1966).

Olive, D. *Just Rewards: The Case For Ethical Reform in Business* (Toronto: Key Porter, 1987).

Toffler, B.L. *Tough Choices: Managers Talk Ethics* (New York: Wiley, 1986).

NOTES FOR CHAPTER 2

1 J. Dutton and R.B. Duncan, "The Creation of Momentum for Change Through the Process of Strategic Issues Diagnosis", *Strategic Management Journal* Vol. 8, No. 3 (1987): 279-295.

2 Immanuel Kant, *Fundamental Principles of the Metaphysics of Morals*, translated by Thomas K. Abbott, (New York: The Liberal Arts Press, 1949).

3 D.A. Hume, "An Enquiry Concerning the Principles of Morals" in L.A. Selby-Biggs, *Enquiries Concerning Human Understanding and Concerning the Principles of Morals*, 3d ed., (Oxford: Clarendon Press, 1975).

4 D. Little and S. Twiss, *Comparative Religious Ethics: A New Method* (New York: Harper and Row, 1978).

5 W.G. Sumner, *Folkways* (Boston: Ginn and Company, 1906, 1940).

6 James A. Waters, Frederick B. Bird and Peter Chant, "Everyday Moral Issues Experienced by Managers", *Journal of Business Ethics*, Vol.5, No.5 (1986): 373-384.

7 J.A. Waters and F.B. Bird, "Attending to Ethics in Management" *Journal of Business Ethics*, Vol.8, No.6 (1989): 493-497. Much of the following argument first appeared in this article.

8 Robert Jackall, *Moral Mazes: The World of Corporate Managers* (New York: Oxford University Press, 1988).

9 For a clear discussion of this distinction, see Lon Fuller, *The Morality of Law* (New Haven: Yale University Press, 1964).

10 Reinhard Bendix, *Work and Authority in Industry: Ideologies of Management in the Course of Industrialization*. (Berkely: University of California Press, 1974).

11 Thomas J. Peters and Robert H. Waterman Jr., *In Search of Excellence* (New York: Harper and Row, 1982).

12 James A. Waters, "Of Saints, Sinners, and Socially Responsible Executives," *Business and Society* (1980): 67-73.

3 Stakeholders

We have suggested that ethical decisions require a consideration of the various claims of stakeholders. In this chapter we consider the role of stakeholders in greater depth and develop the position that regular consultation with stakeholders is one way management can identify ethical issues and make informed ethical decisions.

THE STAKEHOLDER CONCEPT

Managers seldom work in businesses which are isolated, autonomous units. Businesses are open systems, inter-related with, and dependent for their well-being on, the activities of different groups which form a part of their economic, social, political, and technological task environment.[1] How successful business organizations realize their objectives depends, in large measure, on how well they manage their relationships with various constituencies of consumers, creditors, investors, suppliers, employees, competitors, local communities and society.) Managers may interact with constituencies in markedly different ways, on a regular or episodic basis. Stakeholders have been defined as "individuals or groups which depend on the company for realization of their personal goals and on which the company is dependent" or, "any group or individual who can affect, or is affected by the achievement of corporation purpose".[2] Accordingly, any groups or individuals who exercise power over an organization or are affected by the exercise of power by an organization are considered to be stakeholders.

This is a very broad view of stakeholders. The problem with this definition is that any business decision can be shown to affect, either positively or negatively, many different people. Indeed, it is a tortuous exercise to identify everyone who might be affected by the closure of a plant, for example. It would affect employees, relatives of employees, residents of the neighboring town whose property values may rise if displaced employees move there, etc.

A more specific approach defines stakeholders as groups and individuals whose legitimate interests must be formally considered. Stakeholders are not just those constituencies with which an organization interacts; stakeholders possess valid and legitimate claims which the organization must honor. As independent corporations were formed on the basis of ownership of capital goods, investors claimed that they were the pre-eminent if not exclusive stakeholders of these organizations. Subsequently, other groups, including employees, local communities, national governments and consumers have also claimed legitimate stakes in the behavior of corporate organizations.

We define stakeholders in relatin to the legitimacy of their claims (a measure of authority) rather than in relation to their influence (a measure of power). Influence by power and influence by legitimate authority are two separate entities. Power is an amoral reality. It identifies the capacity to make things happen even in the face of potential resistance.[3] People may exercise power overtly or covertly, through economic, political or coercive means. The person who has access to a company's packaging line and interferes with it, is exercising power. Legitimate authority, in contrast, is a moral responsibility. Someone is recognized as possessing authority if others voluntarily defer to them in determining how they should behave. The chief executive officer of a company is generally considered to have a legitimate authority to run a business; stockholders are usually considered to have some legitimate authority to influence managerial decisions; consultants or other experts have an authority based on their expertise or status; employees and employee groups, customers and their associations, and even competitors have authority as stakeholders. The definition of stakeholder is complex since it requires a consideration of property entitlements, the law, changing social conventions, and pragmatic considerations of business relationships.

STAKEHOLDER IDENTIFICATION

One of the key issues in ethical decision-making is the identification and validation of the legitimacy of stakeholder claims. We have grouped various stakeholders into six distinct categories: stockholders, managers, non-managerial employees, customers, contractors, and the public.

Stockholders

Traditionally stockholders have been identified as the primary if not exclusive stakeholders of corporate organizations. Investors provide the capital that enables a corporate organization to purchase resources and labor in order to produce and market goods and services. Since they provide the necessary capital for organizational activity, they possess a legitimate claim to direct how the resources, purchased with their investments, will be used. Their claim is justified by the argument that ownership of capital entitles them to use their property as they see fit provided they do not break the law. As a corollary, firms are obligated to realize a profitable return on the stockholders' investments.

(The view that investors are the primary if not exclusive stakeholders has been extremely influential) It has been used since the eighteenth century as an argument for corporate autonomy and minimal state intervention. It was originally used to protest against the mercantilist practices by which firms were publicly incorporated by government decrees. Firms were publicly incorporated because they were expected to promote national policies. During the nineteenth century this view was invoked to oppose and rescind the master-servant labor contract; servants were not free to leave masters at will and masters assumed responsibility for the living conditions of workers. Labor contracts were redefined to give workers the freedom to seek and leave employment and employers the right to pay only for work performed. Capitalists were given the prerogative to make and break labor contracts.[4]

The idea that capital owners were the primary stakeholders arose to free corporate organizations from traditional mercantilist and feudal patterns of incorporation and labor relations. Already, by the nineteenth century, this view was being modified as other stakeholders gained legitimate recognition. But today, this view is still widely held. Today's firms, however, rarely, if at all, seek profit maximization — in the short term — as their primary objective. Rather they seek the achievement of sufficient profit to cover risks of economic activity and to minimize loss. The rhetoric of profit maximization and the corresponding view of stockholders as paramount stakeholders serves other functions, being used now as it was traditionally to argue against governmental intervention and regulations considered intrusive, arbitrary and uneconomical. Increasingly the rhetoric of profit maximization is used to argue that firms have objectives which transcend the specific interests of community groups, employees, consumers, and governmental agencies. That is, the supposed interest of investors, insofar as they do not directly manage firms, are rhetorically invoked to assert the freedom of management to pursue independent corporate ventures provided they are economically sound.

(Profit maximization is largely invoked by business people involved in some mergers and acquisitions, particularly those who specialize in buying companies whose stock prices do not reflect the value of their underlying assets.) These companies — often purchased by taking on high debt — are then broken up and sold in their constituent parts to pay off the debt, to realize a profit for the principals in the reorganization effort, and to pay fees to bankers, lawyers, advisors and other beneficiaries. The fact that viable businesses may be dismembered, plants may be closed despite their potential for profitable production, and reinvestment stopped to pay off debt related to the acquisition, is placed secondary to the goal of realizing a maximum return for stockholders. Such consequences are, of course, quite different to those which result from mergers and acquisitions which are designed to build more effective, competitive organizations which might operate on a global scale, might prosper through synergies between the merged organizations, or have other, more beneficial consequences for employees, society as a whole, as well as stockholders.

Management

Another view claims that management is the major — or, at the extreme, the only — legitimate stakeholder. Managers rather than owners exercise <u>effective control</u> over corporations; the owners of capital in many cases are rarely involved in the on-going operations of firms. Investors are perceived as exercising a more passive role. They seek to obtain reasonable returns on their investments and will sell their shares if profit ratios fall too low for too long. Investors exercise influence, but in a smaller and less active way than in the past, and they exercise little authoritative direction.[5] In the name of their own organizational autonomy, management may remain formally closed, like neutral nations bound by no treaties or international agreements that might modify or limit their sovereign prerogatives. As we have already observed, this view is often supported in practice through the rhetoric of profit maximization, which defends managerial discretion over the claims of other stakeholders.

Non-Managerial Employees

Slowly, and sometimes with much resistance, modern corporations have recognized employees as legitimate stakeholders. With industrialization, wage contracts were deliberately designed to free workers and managers from the rigidity of the feudal master-servant relationship. As wage earners, workers who did not possess a needed skill or craft were formally free but had no influence. This situation changed with the formation of trade unions and social welfare legislation. Where they gained recognition, <u>trade unions</u> were able to bargain with firms for better working conditions. Collective bargaining agreements created rights and privileges for workers. Social welfare legislation was passed because of the pressure exerted by employee groups to modify and enhance the status of workers.

Beginning with laws passed by the German government in the 1880s, industrialized nations have recognized the rights of workers to collective bargaining, to unemployment insurance, to compensation for work related accidents, to public pensions, to health insurance and to safe working conditions. In countries such as Germany and Yugoslavia these rights also include representation on corporate management boards and workers' councils. Trade unions and social welfare legislation have markedly improved the status of workers. Workers are no longer simply factors of production: rather, they have attained the status of membership within organizational polities with corresponding rights and responsibilities. In some areas union membership has made the termination of unsatisfactory, long-term employees very difficult; in others, it has enabled the right to jobs based on seniority, rather than on demonstrably superior skills.[6] Clearly these stakeholder rights have offset those of management and stockholders.

Customers

Already in the eighteenth century the classical view of owners as the primary stakeholders was modified by a consideration of customers as legitimate stakeholders. For example, Adam Smith argued that consumer choice dictated what kinds of goods and services businesses produced. If businesses hoped to survive they would have to respond to customer demand.[7]

The view that consumers are legitimate stakeholders has had an ambiguous history. In market economies consumers exercise considerable influence but little or no acknowledged authority. Consumer choice has been periodically and rhetorically invoked, as in anti-trust actions, to defend smaller enterprises from larger firms. On the other hand, larger firms, such as General Motors, have invoked the ideals of consumer choice to defend their own hegemony in relation to smaller suppliers. In practice, consumers have little authoritative influence. Governments have protected their interests against unsafe and unhealthy products. Only as they have, in recent years, represented their interests through organized associations, have consumers gained any discretionary influence. Organized consumer groups have campaigned with some success for safer automobiles, for safer children's toys, for banning sealing or products made from animal fur, and for products and services suited to particular interest groups such as the aged and handicapped.

Organized consumer groups have probably gained the greatest degree of legitimate influence in local markets where they have campaigned for changes to opening hours and particular services. Many businesses have established consumer advisory boards to research customer attitudes.

The role of consumers as stakeholders, whose choices shape business activity beyond market demand, remains a theoretical argument rather than a practical reality. Although consumers do exercise influence through their choices, it is impossible to represent individual consumers in a broader context since there is no organized way of doing this. Organized interest groups only represent their own focused viewpoints. Thus, only in a marginal way, in relation to selective interests, is it feasible to recognize consumers as stakeholders. Still responsive managers must be sensitive to the interests, needs, and choices of their customers because of the power they exercise as purchasers, as well as the legitimate authority that some organizations accord them.

Contractors

A fifth perspective overlaps but modifies each of these views and holds that stakeholders should be defined by formal contractual relationships. Stakeholders are individuals and groups with which a business interacts in keeping with formal contractual agreements. Formal contractual agreements outline specific rights and responsibilities; they create and identify relations of reciprocity; they are compelling. They have a public character. If one party violates the agreement, then the other party has recourse through courts and regulatory agencies to punish the offender or obtain compensation. Certain laws define conditions for creating, modifying and dissolving different kinds of contractual relations. Contracts may create ongoing relationships, such as joint ventures or partnerships, or remain situational, such as a sealed bid contract with suppliers. It is a mark of industrial capitalism that economic enterprises operate in keeping with privately negotiated contracts.

Depending on the scope of activities they cover, their duration, and their capability for enforcement, contractual agreements impact stakeholders with different degrees of authoritative influence. Whenever interactions are stipulated by a contract, suppliers and consumers gain specific rights and may make corresponding claims. Retail consumers, not covered by formal contracts, cannot make equivalent claims on business organizations. From a contractual perspective, investors, employees, suppliers, franchisers, and consumer groups are all stakeholders, but the weight and significance of their status differs significantly in relation to specific contractual terms. As individuals these constituencies possess little discretionary authority unless appropriately represented by bodies such as trade associations, which can lobby for their individual interests.

Of the groups with which business organizations enter into contractual relations, financial institutions often play a particularly influential role. They are, for example, represented more frequently and in a larger proportion on boards of directors than other constituencies. Their authority and power derives from their capacity to extend credit and establish terms for lending and re-payment. In order that their programs not be blocked by unfavorable credit decisions, businesses often deliberately solicit the favor of financial institutions.

The Public

According to a sixth view, the public, along with other interest groups, ought to be considered legitimate stakeholders. Traditional mercantilist beliefs assumed that businesses ought to be incorporated by special governmental decree and serve the interests of their investors as well as national interests. The British East India Company was chartered both to advance imperialism as well as to pursue business objectives. Incorporation granted firms the authority to negotiate contracts, to hold property and to borrow, but it also made them answerable to governments; this changed, however, as incorporation became a private matter. It was then assumed, in Adam Smith's words, that the public interest would be served indirectly as individual firms pursued their private objectives.

(Starting in the late nineteenth century, governments began to encourage businesses to take <u>public interest</u> into account.) In the public interest, governments passed laws and created regulatory agencies to enforce food and drug safety standards, to minimize predatory competition, and to standardize products. They further promoted the public interest by instituting taxes on corporate profits and for employee social insurance programs. In recent years corporations have been called on to take into account the public interest in other ways. For example, as a result of the efforts of environment protection laws and campaigns by environmentalists, businesses are expected to consider the safe and effective removal of dangerous waste. In addition, local communities often seek to establish formal and informal agreements with businesses so that businesses, employers and investors in local economies, will recognize their importance to local communities, and local communities will in turn provide roads, sewage and garbage services, construction permits, and even temporary tax abatements. Finally, corporations, at times, attempt to respond to the public interest by assuming philanthropic roles through corporate foundations, and involvement in social programs, and by encouraging employees to participate in civic activities.

As these examples indicate, business considerations of the public's interests have varied. Businesses interact with many public groups. Over time, corporations have been persuaded and, at times, forced to be more socially responsible. However, their accountability to the public has been diverse. The public's interest is variously represented by regulatory agencies, some of which are in turn nominated by businesses to protect their own interests, by local and regional governments, by tax laws, and by isolated community representatives on boards of directors.

Stockholders: Owners of common and preferred stock in the corporation.

Management: The management of the organization, who may or may not be significant stockholders.

Non-Managerial Employees: Employees of the organization, as individuals or in association.

Customers: The purchasers of the products and services of organizations, viewed individually or as collective groups.

Contractors: Those who have contractual arrangements with the organization, including vendors, distributors, bankers, and others.

The Public: Everyone who is impacted by the activities of the enterprise.

FIGURE 3.1 **Stakeholders in the Business Organization**

As summarized in Figure 3.1, explicitly and implicitly, corporate organizations have recognized a number of constituencies as legitimate stakeholders. These views have evolved over time. Businesses have often espoused attitudes yet acted contrary to them. For example, while publicly endorsing the view of stockholders as exclusive stakeholders, many businesses accord a stakeholder status to other groups through observing formal contractual relations, government regulations, and taxes which protect the public. On the other hand, these same firms may endorse classical economic arguments which relegate consumers as marginal stakeholders. Most businesses generally treat a number of constituencies as stakeholders, with legitimate rights and claims they must take into account.

STRATEGIES FOR MANAGING STAKEHOLDERS

Businesses interact with diverse constituencies who affect, and are affected by, their well-being. In varying degrees they may openly acknowledge different stakeholders and formally establish the conventions that define mutual expectations. We suggest that there are <u>four</u> dominant stakeholder consultation strategies: avoidance, tokenism, absorption and interaction, as summarized in Figure 3.2.

Avoidance: Ignore them! But this may not be possible over an extended period of time.

Absorbtion: Merge, acquire, co-opt. May be difficult to do and reduces the independent voice of disagreement.

Tokenism: Co-opt dissenting stakeholders but without encouraging and attending to their dissent. Limited and partial communications result and expectations of stakeholder groups may be raised.

Interaction: Interact frequently or continuously and in-depth. Excellent communications and long-standing relationships. A realistic view of the business through others' eyes.

FIGURE 3.2 **Strategies for Managing Stakeholders**

Avoidance

This strategy simply avoids acknowledging most if not all constituencies as stakeholders. Corporate strategists may, to be sure, attempt to take these groups into account. Researchers may be dispatched to poll the attitudes of consumers, investors, and employees. However, formal discussion with these groups will be avoided to prevent obstacles which may limit managerial autonomy. Businesses try to preserve their independence by defining their relationship to all external constituencies as temporary and transitory; on-going and therefore binding agreements are avoided; managers ignore organized worker representatives and establish short term contracts with suppliers and customers; managers treat investors as temporary purchasers of securities rather than as owners with property entitlements.

Avoidance strategy is difficult, if not impossible, to implement. For example, employees have become aggravated and antagonistic in their demands when confronted by an indifferent or hostile employer. Strike activity is higher where employers refuse to recognize the bargaining status of employee groups or when they seek to break the power of these groups. Similarly, consumers may purchase alternative products when their demands are repeatedly ignored and disgruntled investors may mount stockholder challenges in criticism of management policies.

In practice, businesses rarely pursue the avoidance strategy consistently. They often establish on-going relationships with competitors, suppliers and corporate customers through trade associations, contractual understandings, and bidding conventions. In fact, organizations which often seek to protect their autonomy have entered into co-operative arrangements. Where governments are concerned, this strategy calls for organizations to remain as independent of regulatory agencies and tax restraints as possible. However, in practice, firms which publicly espouse free enterprise and oppose government intervention, occasionally use their good influence to seek favorable interpretations of legal rulings. While defending free trade and open competition, one manager cited the example of how his organization persuaded government officials to impose a tariff on a competing product from a neighboring country.[8]

Absorption

Business people often voice the rhetoric of free enterprise to describe corporate organizations as independent economic units bound to constituents by no ongoing stakeholder agreements. However, unless organizations possess considerable power, the absence of on-going agreements may leave them vulnerable to unexpected changes in difficult times. To reduce uncertainty, especially with stakeholders upon whom they feel especially dependent, business organizations sometimes attempt to absorb prized constituents. The strategy of absorption contrasts sharply with the strategy of avoidance. Nonetheless neither strategy regards constituents as legitimate fully-fledged stakeholders.

Depending on which constituents business organizations are concerned with, the strategy of absorption assumes different forms. For example, businesses have sought to regulate employees by denying them the right to form or join independent trade unions by creating company unions. Workers' associations and councils then become part of the internal structure of the larger organization. Workers are allowed to associate and express their feelings in groups which are ultimately subservient to the larger organization.[9] Also, businesses sometimes seek to reduce uncertainty and insecurity with competitors, suppliers and organized consumers by mergers and acquisitions. Instead of being constantly dependent on suppliers who may sell to others or change prices, businesses can guarantee a regular and reliable supply of needed resources by making relevant suppliers into sub-divisions of the larger enterprise.[10] Organizations often <u>merge</u> with competitors when competitive uncertainty is highest.

Absorption is appealing as a strategy for regulating relations with constituents on whom an organization is dependent, but with whom those relations are changeable and uncertain. At one level this strategy is appealing not only because it appears, at least initially, to reduce irregular contingencies, but also because it reduces transactional costs with relevant constituents. When relevant constituents are made part of a larger organization either by vertical or horizontal integration or by creating a company workers' association, the amount of time and energy needed to re-negotiate and re-establish temporary contractual relations is greatly reduced. Much less time needs to be spent allowing negotiators to familiarize themselves and find fitting discourse for negotiations.[11] The strategy of absorption is appealing because it yields quick organizational growth; it produces measurable accomplishments in the form of mergers, acquisition, increased capital and a more cooperative work force to which the executives responsible can point with pride.

Absorbing constituents to reduce uncertainty and irregularity <u>has costs.</u> Constituents who lack independence are not wholly beneficial to the business. Absorption may not overcome difficulties with suppliers or competitors, whose organizational cultures may differ significantly, and whose style of decision-making, rewards, and inter-personal relations are not easily changed. Mergers may lead to demands for organizational change which may <u>reduce the effectiveness</u> of the organizations being merged. When external constituents are absorbed, they may react with hostility that festers, but is not openly confrontational. Employees or competitors may feel that they have been bought off with superficial privileges while losing their autonomy. As divisionalized sectors within a larger organization, constituents who have been absorbed may experience little discretionary authority for social, personnel and consumer programs, and experience increased pressure to produce measurable results. They may comply with the new order and its rules but with low morale and may therefore work at reduced levels of productivity.

Once they have been absorbed, constituents become less vocal about issues which concern them. Loyalty is expected, and sometimes expected to be demonstrated. Constituents who voice criticism make an organization more sensitive to its shortcomings, but this voice may be squashed and prevent on-going give and take relations with regular constituents.[12]

Tokenism

In practice businesses rarely succeed in ignoring or absorbing all their influential constituents. Frequently, they adopt a strategy of cultivating a <u>loose rela-</u>

tionship with a few constituents. This is referred to as tokenism. Organizations respond to constituents as token stakeholders when they formally accord these groups some acknowledged status which allows for at least limited formal communication. The relationship remains a token one so long as their status is marginal and communication remains minimal and one-sided.

A widely used tactic of tokenism is to invite a representative from constituent groups to membership on an organization's board of directors or advisory group. The constituents' group is formally recognized as a relevant stakeholder and both the organization and the stakeholder group gain advantages from this act of formal cooperation. The organization adds legitimacy by gaining support from community groups, employees, creditors, and/or important suppliers who are represented on the board. The organization may also neutralize potential opposition from constituents and use formal representation to make these constituent groups more fully aware of the organization's aims and limitations. Constituents, at the same time, do gain formal recognition and occasional assistance. They are allowed to formally articulate criticisms.[13]

Usually organizations that appoint stakeholder representatives to their boards attempt to meet at least some stakeholder demands. Another way of allowing constituent groups to articulate claims and complaints is by establishing formal offices for that purpose. Depending on the constituents involved, these offices may be referred to as community liaison officers, ombudsmen, or consumer affairs departments. Officers are formally chartered to hear the views of individual stakeholders, to transmit their views to relevant parts of the larger organization, and to seek the cooperation of the organization in attempting to respond to specific complaints. At one level these offices are considered impartial, and capable, because of their neutrality, of speaking out within the organization on behalf of aggrieved stakeholders. At another level these offices, precisely because of their apparent neutrality, function as a buffer to hear and defuse complaints as well as to seek out negative feedback and initiate responses before criticism becomes too intense. Again, both organizations and their stakeholders gain by these arrangements. Constituents feel that their criticism is not simply rebuffed. Often complaints lead to resolution or compensatory actions. Organizations, for their part, learn more effectively of problem areas and dysfunctional operations otherwise overlooked.

Nonetheless, these tactics only grant constituents a nominal status as stakeholders. Communications are limited and incomplete. Conversations are often like mutual monologues: each side states its views and solutions are postponed. As board members, stakeholder representatives are particularly exposed minorities. They often face expectations, as stakeholder delegates, to represent their constituent's interests and to demonstrate that stakeholders can play responsible roles within an organization. They become exposed public figures, vulnerable to criticism while lacking the support from other constituent members. As individuals they have little power except in so far as their constituent groups choose to veto or be uncooperative.[14] Constituent groups gain little authoritative influence by interacting with ombudsmen, liaison officers and consumer representatives. The latter are designed to help individual constituents, not constituent groups. When communications between constituent groups and organizations pass through either constituent representatives on boards or through formal complaint offices, they remain indirect, impersonal, and hence largely ineffective.

Interaction

As a fourth strategy, corporate organizations may interact with constituents as legitimate, full-fledged stakeholders. This kind of interaction differs from token relations in three ways. First, as stakeholders, constituents are accorded formal organizational recognition. This recognition includes, the right to representation on specific decision-making bodies, the right to appeal particular decisions to higher authorities and decision-making councils within the organization, the right to appeal particular decisions to trade associations or public regulatory agencies, and the right to articulate individual claims and complaints to officials such as ombudsmen. Full-fledged stakeholders differ from token stakeholders to the extent that their recognition is usually wider and more likely to be reinforced by impartial, external observers.[15]

Second, organizations develop active, long-lasting, relations with full-fledged stakeholders. These relationships are considered as enduring ones worth cultivating. Business relationships with full-fledged stakeholders are characterized by on-going, active and reciprocal communication. Organizations regularly seek to determine stakeholders' views and keep them informed of organizational developments. This process has been referred to as a "scanning" of constituents and is sometimes improved by a informal "auditing" of the relationship. Whenever on-going relationships between organizations and stakeholders develop, corresponding social conventions develop around consultations, to characterize and personalize the interaction. These conventions communicate deference, as well as a recognition of differences and similarities in status. To the degree that businesses regularly interact with stakeholders, they are less likely to be taken by surprise by changes affecting these constituents.

Third, business organizations interact with full-fledged stakeholders in depth. We use the phrase "in depth" to indicate that consultations do not simply take place between heads of organizations and their designated representatives but that consultations take place at various levels of both organizations. From a structural, organizational perspective, interacting in depth means that appropriate sub-units, whether they be divisions, line supervisors, or staff personnel, are permitted limited discretion to consult and negotiate with relevant stakeholders.[16] In particular, relating in depth with stakeholders requires that middle managers, who regularly interact with particular stakeholders such as suppliers, customers, local community officials, or employees, be viewed as integral members of an organizational strategy. This requires that middle managers perform the following tasks: they assume a primary responsibility as information gatherers to keep track of any alterations in stakeholders and their concerns; they keep stakeholders informed of organizational policies; they judge how stakeholders are likely to respond to proposed new policies; and they use their discretion in consultation with superiors to make adjustments to on-going relations.[17]

(Interacting in depth with stakeholders means communications between constituent groups is sustained by a web of social relationships) At the various contact points where organizations interact with stakeholders, individual managers cultivate contacts and acquaintances with corresponding individuals from stakeholder groups. Conversations between these individuals may be casual as well as formal, may exchange official as well as unofficial information, may deal with personal as well as organizational matters. These conversations are ideally suited to general inquiries, uncensored feedback, precautionary warnings as well as expressions of genuine sympathy. They may encourage the give and take that is part of preliminary negotiations and follow up adjustments and facilitate the transmission of a much wider and more up-to-date range of information. Through these ties, organizations can establish strong cooperative links with stakeholders. Formal relations with stakeholders are more effective because they are embedded in social networks formed through social contacts.[18]

(When constituent groups are treated as full-fledged stakeholders relationships with them become more political.) Various stakeholders continuously seek to defend their interests and advance their objectives, but this does not necessarily lead to chaos.[19] The social networks that accompany relations with stakeholders moderate conflicts and reduce antagonism.

The Case for Stakeholder Consultation

As we have shown, businesses attempt to relate to the many constituencies with which they interact. They may attempt to deny them status, to absorb them, or to establish a formal, stakeholder status, on either a token or fully interactive basis. Given that these methods are so prevalent, is there a preferred way of relating to stakeholders?

(Organizations ought to acknowledge and interact with their major external constituents as full-fledged stakeholders.) Clearly, when considering ethical issues where other groups might be involved, consulting with them is essential:

- Without consultation, organizations lack information about constituent groups, and their positions on issues which are important to organizations.
- If organizations only consult with stakeholders when facing tough choices, then the framework for discussion and conflict resolution will not be in place. Relationships are best developed in the absence of crisis.
- If consultation only occurs periodically, in relation to specific issues, then

constituents are treated as token stakeholders and ethical decision-making is likely to be less responsive and less well-informed. Full and frequent consultation, other than on an as-needed basis, is recommended.

- Acknowledging constituents as stakeholders is a means of recognizing an organization's interdependence with other groups. Interdependence is not dependence. Any business linked to one or two constituents, such as franchised retailers to parent companies or small auto-part suppliers to General Motors, experience dependence. However, as the number of influential constituents increases, organizations gain greater autonomy.

- By regularly consulting stakeholders in depth, organizations maintain up-to-date information about constituencies, whose actions directly affect their well-being. Interacting in depth with constituents provides organizations with relevant data on the changing conditions of constituents.

- Regularly probing stakeholders also provides a reliable evaluation of likely responses to proposed organizational initiatives. These probings protect organizations from and prepare them for adverse constituent reactions. As organizations actively consult stakeholders, they obtain useful feedback on proposed programs and initiatives. This kind of information is of critical importance for ongoing organizational strategies.

- When constituents are regularly treated as stakeholders, they are more likely to develop on-going cooperative relations with an organization. New initiatives are likely to receive greater acceptance and be implemented quicker.

- Organizations enhance their own image by recognizing constituent groups as stakeholders. Stakeholders respect and defer to organizations that respect their claims.

- As organizations recognize constituent groups as full-fledged stakeholders, they enhance innovation. Innovation is likely to occur where people are less committed to preserving traditional organizational practices. When consultations with stakeholders occur regularly at both formal and informal levels, managers are more likely to hear about projects or ideas that might eventually benefit the organization. When top managers see themselves not as innovators themselves, but as sponsors of innovation, it is more likely that innovations will be accepted and implemented.

SUMMARY

No one person or group which can exercise power over an organization is necessarily a legitimate stakeholder. Stakeholders have claims by virtue of property entitlements, contractual arrangements, the law, and social conventions. There is a growing list of groups who claim, and are often accorded, stakeholder status including stockholders, customers, employees, managers, suppliers, sub-contractors and the general public or society. Business organizations deal with stakeholder groups in different ways, by avoiding them, absorbing them into the organizational net, according them token status, or by interacting with them in-depth on a regular basis. We argue that identification of, and interaction with stakeholder groups pays off for businesses by making them more informed and understanding of different perspectives, and in establishing relationships which enhance conflict identification and resolution. In the long term, organizations can only act ethically if they accommodate stakeholder concerns and expectations, and this can only be achieved through on-going, in-depth consultations.

SUGGESTED READINGS:

Freeman, R.E. *Strategic Management: A Stakeholder Approach* (Boston: Pitman, 1984).

Gray, Barbara. *Collaborating: Finding Common Ground For Multi-Party Problems* (San Francisco: Jossey-Bass, 1989).

Mintzberg, Henry. *Power In and Around Organizations* (Englewood Cliffs, N.J.: Prentice Hall, 1983).

Pfeffer, J., and Salancik, G. *The External Control of Organizations: A Resource Dependence Perspective* (New York: Harper and Row, 1978).

NOTES FOR CHAPTER 3

1   James D. Thompson, *Organizations in Action: Social Science Bases of Administrative Theory* (New York: McGraw-Hill, 1967).

2   R. Edward Freeman, *Strategic Management: A Stakeholder Approach* (Boston: Pitman, 1984).

3   Max Weber, *Economics and A Society*, edited by Guenther Roh and Claus Wittich. (Berkeley: University of California Press, 1978) 53.

4.   Philip Selznick, *Law, Society and Industrial Justice* (New York: Russell Sage, 1969).

5   Adolf A. Berle Jr. and Gardiner C. Means, *The Modern Corporation and Private Property* (New York: Commerce Clearing House, 1932).

6   Selznick, op. cit.

7   Adam Smith. *The Wealth of Nations, Books 1-3*, edited by Andrew Skinner (Middlesex, England: Penguin Books, 1970, 1974); John Kenneth Galbraith. *Economics and the Public Purpose* (Scarborough: Signet, 1973) chp. 4.

8   Frederick Bird, Frances Westley, and James A. Waters, "The Uses of Moral Talk." *Journal of Business Ethics*, Vol. 8 (1989): 82.

9   It is this fear which sometimes causes unions to oppose such "progressive" concepts as semi-autonomous teams, quality circles, and so on. See the *CAW Statement on the Reorganization of Work*, 1989.

10   As Pfeffer and Salancik observe, firms typically vertically integrate with suppliers or consumers that create the most problems for them. Jeffrey Pfeffer and Gerald R.

Salancik, *The External Control of Organizations: A Resource Dependence Perspective* (New York: Harper and Row, 1978), chp. 6.

11 Oliver E. Williamson, "Transactional Cost Economics: The Governance of Contractual Relations," *Journal of Law and Economics*, (1980): 233-261.

12 Albert O. Hirschman, *Exit, Voice and Loyalty: Responses to Decline in Firms and States* (Cambridge: Harvard University Press, 1970).

13 Philip Selznick, *TVA and the Grass Roots* (New York: Harper and Row, 1966).

14 Rosabeth Moss Kanter, *Men and Women of the Corporation* (New York: Basic Books, 1977) chp 8.

15 Pfeffer and Salancik, op. cit., chps. 7,8.

16 Ibid., p. 273.

17 Frances Westley, "Middle Managers and Strategy: The Microdynamics of Inclusion," *Strategic Management Journal* (1990).

18 Mark S. Granovetter, "Economic Action and Social Structure: The Problem of Imbeddedness," *American Journal of Sociology* Vol. 91, No. 3 (1985): 481-510.

19 Henry Mintzberg, *Power In and Around Organizations* (Englewood Cliffs, N.J.: Prentice Hall, 1983) chp. 23.

4 Social Norms and Moral Standards

Many issues which managers recognize as ethical recur over time in similar form. Therefore, it is useful for managers to determine what behavioral guidelines already exist and whether those standards are relevant to current decisions.

MANAGEMENT AND MORALITY

(Businesses operate in complex environments where decisions may be construed as immoral or amoral.) Of course, immoral and deviant behavior does occur. Business people may cheat on their income taxes, exploit executive privileges, ignore government safety and pollution regulations, collude on pricing agreements, inadequately appraise subordinates, run deceptive advertisements, offer extravagant kickbacks, and make fortunes in the stock market based on inside information. Illegal and immoral conduct is widespread and should concern us. However, although these examples prove that some people are willing to violate moral standards, they do not mean that moral standards do not exist.

(Similarly, just because business decisions are frequently made on the basis of economic and practical considerations does not mean that moral expectations play little or no part.) Clearly, many decisions concerning organizational practices, marketing, finance, employee relations, and other spheres of business activity are made on the basis of considerations that are morally indifferent. In many settings moral considerations may over-simplify the issues at hand and lead to a preoccupation with image-making rather than the substance of hard-headed problem-solving. Nonetheless, moral standards are relevant to business practices, and many business people themselves recognize this.

(Managers have identified a range of issues where they felt moral expectations establish normative standards for business practices.) Business organizations expect that people will not steal, will not lie, and will manage to preserve minimal degrees of personal self-control. They expect that buyers will not accept extravagant gifts from suppliers, that employees will defer to organizational authority and that managers will work industriously and consistently without supervision. Most businesses establish guidelines to protect confidentiality, to discourage conflicts of interest, and to insure equity regarding salaries and promotions. These standards are both honored and ignored. Some moral standards, such as refusing bribes or being honest with expense accounts, are clearly in the interests of the businesses which promote them. But others, such as supporting charitable organizations or indigenous businesses, are less self-serving.

MORAL MUTENESS

The role of moral standards in management is complicated by the fact that many managers adopt moral standards but fail to publicly support them, a condition which we label "moral muteness". If hypocrisy involves people claiming a moral commitment they fail to honor, then moral muteness involves a compliance with moral standards which is not supported verbally. The failure of morally committed managers to attest verbally to their convictions makes management seem less moral than it really is. It reduces morality to a private concern and limits the capacity for other managers or non-managerial employees to call on them as a resource in decision-making.[1]

MORAL REALISM

Before managers make decisions, they need to examine standards that already influence business practices and critically evaluate their bearing on relevant issues. In business, as in families, local communities, religious movements, and societies, there are guidelines for behavior people regard as so compelling that they seek to comply with them. They do this because they feel compliance is both obligatory and desirable and yet there is seldom uniform compliance with these guidelines, even if the standards are highly regarded. People must often choose between conflicting standards, they may have weak wills, and new and complex situations may arise which they have difficulty analyzing.

MORAL EXPECTATIONS

The moral expectations which influence business practices have been authoritatively communicated as professional codes of practice or standards, laws, organizational codes, managerial and economic ideologies, and societal values. We will examine and analyze moral standards as well as their social relevance and cultural roles.

Professional Codes

Many managers belong to occupational groups which have established profes-sional codes. These codes propose standards of excellence to which managers are encouraged to aspire as well as rules which are to be obeyed. Professional codes have been developed for accountants, engineers, lawyers, advertisers, financial analysts, personnel managers, and computer professionals. These are not just recent responses to highly publicized unethical activities. For example, in the 1920s the American Institute of Accountants published a document titled "Approved Methods of the Preparation of Balance Sheet Statements." These standards were reinforced by security laws in the 1930s, and by 1945, associa-tions of accountants solidified their code of ethics to develop stricter, more uni-form standards.

Lawyers have also attempted to define moral standards for their profession. The American Bar Association has promulgated a code of professional responsi-bilities, which argues that lawyers owe allegiance to corporations as entities rather than to individuals. Associations of advertisers have established guidelines to distinguish between what they characterize as legitimate enhancement and inexcusable falsification of a product. The recently formed profession of computer analysts has endeavored to outline standards appropri-ate for managers working with information systems. They have stressed their commitment to protecting confidential information, to providing quality ser-vices, and to handling responsibly favors solicited by vendors. Codes for finan-cial analysts, management consultants, and almost every group which seeks recognition as a profession have also been devised.

These standards have shaped and determined the conduct of occupational groups: membership to these professions has become valued, in part, because of regulation by the affiliated professional association. Medical doctors must be licensed by their professional body and have attempted to exclude and censure what they have deemed to be the irresponsible practice of medicine. They have attempted to reduce negligence, to increase diligence, and to promote the informed consent of patients. Engineers have succeeded in establishing a com-parable degree of professional identity. They also share membership to an exclusive fraternity with the onus on providing expert service. They share with physicians commitments to practical science and to serving their clients' inter-ests. Both professional associations provide a way to discipline errant members. The professions have also influenced business practices in several ways. Accountants have insisted on independent audits and required standardized methods of accounting to help expose fraud, to identify improper practices with-in firms, and to provide a measure for external investors to assess the economic vitality of firms.

Professional codes of ethics exercise compelling authority because they cre-dential members who excel and control the behavior of members whose conduct violates these standards. Between January 1970 and June 1977, the American

Institute of Certified Public Accountants, for example, cited and censured 121 members for violating professional standards. While many felt that this was far fewer than the number who should have been tried and disciplined, nonetheless these acts of censure help reinforce the strength of the professional code.[2] Clearly, professional associations of advertisers, consultants, personnel managers, and computer analysts are not in as strong a position to discipline members.

B)

Managerial Codes

Although managers may work in specialized areas such as sales, merchandizing, operations, personnel, finance, and customer services, they do not belong to any professional, self-governing association comparable to those to which lawyers and doctors belong. Indeed, the merits of management as a profession are debatable. Associations of managers do not credential and discipline and they have not identified ethical standards, the violation of which would lead to expulsion. Nonetheless efforts are being made to recognize management as a profession. Business schools have championed this project by raising entrance requirements, up-grading the curriculum, and stressing not only the importance of gaining expertise in particular areas of knowledge but also of exercising competently the skills of problem-solving, group facilitation, and communication. Increasingly, a consensus has emerged regarding normative standards that comprise professional business ethics.

This emergent ethic has been demonstrated by various spokespeople on management and by managers themselves. A number of management analysts have argued that managers ought to consider themselves professionals with associated commitments to certain moral standards. Selznick has argued that managers should exert leadership by attempting to realize values through their work. Walton has insisted on the importance of managerial integrity. More recently, Peters and Waterman have asserted that successful managers are distinguished by their moral commitments. The importance of professional moral standards for managers is emphasized in a recent book, *What They Don't Teach You at Harvard Business School*. Ostensibly dedicated to encouraging amoral street smarts, it advocates common courtesy.[3]

Managers themselves often consider a commitment to moral standards as a mark of good management. A survey of managerial attitudes conducted in the early 1950s found that managers highly valued what was referred to as an "austere emphasis on moral responsibility."[4] In the early 1980s, in response to a survey conducted by the American Manufacturing Association, middle managers ranked commitment to ethical standards second only to the right to use and develop their best skills as organizational attributes they valued most.[5]

We can discern three themes in an emergent professional ethic of management. These are: an ethic of courtesy with respect to co-workers, an ethic of responsible workmanship with respect to assigned tasks, and an ethic of service with respect to clients and customers.)

(1) (The ethic of courtesy is spelled out in a variety of precepts regarding subordinates, peers and superiors.) Managers are counselled: to be prompt and efficient; to respect local customs and keep confidences; to help subordinates succeed, assist them in learning from their mistakes, applaud and champion their contributions, and involve them in decisions which affect them; to recognize the limits of subordinates, be explicit in their assignments, welcome their feedback and criticism, and listen to what they say. Managers are expected to establish an objective relationship with co-workers and are counselled to be professional yet candid with superiors.

(2) (An ethic of responsible workmanship means that managers are expected to be attentive to their environments, to learn quickly, and to be flexible to changing circumstances.) Advice such as: "Be flexible and strive for consistency"; "The craft of management involves the ability to think objectively, and to communicate clearly" is dispensed by some writers.[6] Most importantly, good managers are expected to act decisively, especially in settings that are unclear. Decisive action itself is a cipher to describe outcomes produced by abilities to set priorities, deliberate clearly, and offer persuasive justifications. While procrastination is universally criticized, impulsive decision-making is equally censured.

(3) The third theme of an emergent professional ethic highlights the service orientation of managers.(The purpose of management is to provide utilities to customers.[7]) Managers increasingly identify themselves as people, prepared by training and experience, to provide skilled services in administering private as well as public organizations. The recent spate of books urging an improvement to customer service merely reinforces an ethic which has long been associated with successful business enterprise.

There are other emergent ethics which, while not as widespread as those cited above, appear to be gaining recognition. For example, an environmental ethic which stresses the co-existence of business with a safe and self-sustaining environment appears to be gaining widespread acceptance and is influencing decisions ranging from plant location and reforestation, to product design involving bio-degradable materials.[8]

(c) These principles of good management represent an emerging professional ethic which, although coherent, is somewhat formless. They are standards which do not specify professional obligation. However, they are not without influence. These principles are respected, they provide a rule of thumb for applauding exemplary managers and censuring others, and they are often implicitly or explicitly invoked when managers are evaluated for promotion.

Company Codes and Corporate Mores

(Many businesses have established written codes of ethics for their companies.) This has been especially true for large corporations in the 1980s. Ninety-seven percent of corporations with annual revenues above $4 billion have instituted codes compared with only 40 percent of those with annual revenues under $60 million.[9] Many corporations have recently revised, up-dated, or promulgated ethical codes as part of official attempts to institutionalize ethics in their organizations. In the process, copies of ethical codes have been widely distributed to organizational members who have often been invited to discuss these codes with co-workers and supervisors.

Through these activities, managers and employees have become more aware of moral issues in their work. A recently instituted program in ethics at General Dynamics resulted, for example, in increased attention to a variety of ethical issues, especially in the area of human relations. Canadian companies, such as Imperial Oil, have had codes with annual sign-offs by managers for years. Some organizations, such as Imperial Oil, Syncrude, and the Royal Bank incorporate ethics modules in their internal training and management development programs to reinforce the required standards of behavior.

Organizationally mandated ethical codes have articulated moral standards with respect to many issues from the uses of agents in foreign countries, to contributions to political campaigns, from affirmative action to the proper ways to make competitive bids. When these codes are examined comparatively, it is possible to see that certain concerns are much more likely to be included. The standards which were most prevalent are those in which firms seek to protect themselves from illegal or questionable behavior, which would expose them to risk of legal suits, hostile public criticism, or the exploitation of organizational resources for personal advantage. According to one survey, the following standards were found in at least three of every five organizational codes surveyed: conflicts of interest are to be avoided, organizational confidence is to be protected, local and national laws are to be obeyed, questionable payments are to be avoided, and bribes, kickbacks and collusion are censured. Most other standards were found in no more than one in four organizational codes. Thus, concerns regarding honest communication, decent working conditions, environmental protection, and high quality goods and services were listed in less than one fourth of the codes surveyed. Standards with respect to equity in pay, fair treatment regarding promotions, cooperation among co-workers, and the dignity of work were found less frequently.[10]

An analysis of this survey suggests that organizational ethics codes are established by large companies to protect themselves from conduct that is likely to be injurious. Smaller firms are less likely to establish formal codes because the same sets of concerns are likely to be transmitted directly through oral communication and supervisory relations which more closely unite an organization. We have argued in chapter two that the acts which these codes prohibit are ones in which managers or employees are acting against the firm's interest to distort or violate their role expectations. This out-of-role behavior, is more easily observed in small firms.

(Even though these codes have been established to protect organizational interests, they may still communicate significant moral expectations not only with respect to censuring of obviously deviant behavior but also with respect to other matters, such as consumers' rights to privacy and fair treatment of employees.)Written codes do provide a means for reinforcing and defining moral expectations which heretofore have been conveyed orally. Rarely does the promulgation of a written code, by itself, promote an obligation towards compelling moral behavior. Publishing written codes serves either to strengthen and clarify existing moral expectations, to provide new, revised and/or authorized interpretations of conventional expectations, or to censure behavior that is out of hand. For example, organizational codes have recently set forth a stricter attitude towards the use of agents and gifts to facilitate trade relations in foreign countries.

(In addition to explicit policy statements, businesses frequently communicate implicit moral expectations which often embody the moral commitments of the founders of organizations or top executives through the recounting of legends and stories.)Although more elusive and less capable of being documented, these organizational mores may communicate organizationally-specific moral expectations more powerfully than ethics codes.

Law

(Many of the moral expectations that influence business practices have been established by law.)We use the term law to identify statutes enacted by governments, regulations set forth by public agencies, judgements reached by courts of law, as well as legal opinion. Together these establish what we popularly define as what the law says. What matters to most business people is not what statute books actually stipulate but rather what are the probabilities that specific acts will be judged in court to be legally permissible. Since most practical cases are settled out of court, not only the history of court rulings matter but also the history of legal opinion.

The distinction between law and morality may easily be drawn too sharply. Legal systems do establish and communicate moral standards, although in somewhat different ways than religions, social conventions, ideologies and ethics.

It is possible to identify four different ways in which legal and moral standards overlap in business practices. (First, there are moral standards which influence the forms and procedures of modern law.)Referring to these standards as the "Morality of Law," Fuller has argued that laws ought to be stated in general terms, be publicly promulgated, be clear, require what is feasible, be constant over time, and be enforced.[11] Accordingly we expect legal proceedings to honor our shared expectations of due process and we feel exploited when these assumptions are violated. (Second, many statutes regarding business practices directly embody moral assumptions.) The Sherman Anti-Trust Law of 1890 attacked trade cartels in order to protect fair competition. The US Congress passed the Foreign Corrupt Practices Act in 1978 to eliminate bribery in foreign commerce. Over the years, courts and legislators have defined what constitutes reasonable contracts, identifying various morally dubious actions which provide the justification for one party or another to cancel otherwise binding, contractual arrangements. Third, courts frequently draw moral principles to support their judgements. A large number of these principles have gained legal weight, such as, that no one shall be permitted to profit by his own fraud...or acquire property by his own crime. Consider as well the principle of "good faith" in collective bargaining, and the principle that no one is bound by "unconscionable contracts." Finally, in some areas the courts recognize as legally binding conventional practices which have gained normative authority, such as sealed bidding practices.

Public laws communicate a wide range of moral expectations regarding business practices. It is useful to survey the various ways laws influenced by moral assumptions, establish authoritative guidelines within businesses and between businesses and their several constituents. Criminal laws have been passed forbidding embezzlement, larceny, bribery, and insider trading. Civil laws outline liabilities for negligence and violations of copyright, reputations, and patenting. Legal standards have been set to wage levels and working conditions, rights to economic security for regular employees through social insurance programs, and the right to organize collectively to bargain with employers. Laws define the rights and privileges of consumers, stipulate contracting procedures, and establish guidelines for sales practices. Laws have been enacted to regulate utilities as enterprises responsible to the public and the environment. Bodies of law have grown around banking, insurance, security exchanges, partnerships, and property transfers. All these laws bear moral assumptions, as they define and seek to implement notions of responsibility, equality, due compensation, employee rights, honest communication, and environmental protection.

Legal guidelines have been established for a large range of business practices. Like all moral norms, by themselves, these guidelines cannot effectively produce morally responsible conduct. Companies may, and do hire lawyers not only to invoke laws in defense of their interests and to make claims against others, but also to discover ways to reduce the bearing of laws on their own actions.

Economic and Managerial Ideologies

The moral dimensions of business may also be analyzed in relation to ideologies which influence business practices. Economic ideologies are used by North Americans and Europeans in defense of free enterprise capitalism, welfare state capitalism, social democratic capitalism, worker-controlled socialism, and state socialism. These ideologies, in large measure, focus on the relation of business activities to the state, as well as employment practices and pricing mechanisms. They have greatly influenced the overall character of business practices in particular countries. In Canada and the United States economic ideologies have determined different forms of relations between government and business. For example, Canadians have established crown corporations and developed medicare programs while Americans have not. These economic ideologies, however, do not provide much guidance for the day to day management of business. They identify and justify the normative standards which define state regulated market economies.

Management ideologies have played a more immediate role in the relationship of top management to employees and junior managers. Since the industrial revolution, business people have constructed a number of managerial ideologies. These ideologies spell out how managers ought to interact with their subordinates. Some of these ideologies have been identified, such as the "scientific management" and "the human relations" approach to management.[12] Other managerial ideologies have been defined in relation to ideas about "management by objectives", "participative management", "empowered work teams", and "the quality of worklife." These ideologies all establish norms for how managers ought to work effectively to gain the greatest cooperation from subordinates and peers and to manage successful enterprises.

These ideologies also establish standards for the social arrangement of power and privilege. Ideologies function to identify and legitimate patterns of domination or structures of authoritative decision-making.[13] They establish normative standards for the social organization of business enterprises and the relation of these enterprises to other enterprises and government agencies. Economic and managerial ideologies, like all ideologies, are rhetorical. Rhetoric mobilizes passionate commitments to objectives and standards. Unlike laws, ideologies are not set out to warn and to instruct; rather, they are used to engender popular support and to defend, as just and fitting, existing or proposed arrangements of power and privilege.[14] Precisely because of their rhetorical nature, the relationship between the normative standards of ideologies and actual conduct is prone to discrepancies. For example, business executives have articulated entrepreneurial ideologies in defense of corporate structures and monopolistic practices, and trade unions have defended closed shops in the name of industrial democracy.

Organizational Conventions

Moral expectations of business practices are also communicated by the ways businesses are organized. There are, broadly speaking, three sets of organizational conventions which are commonly reflected in the ways managers operate within businesses: bureaucratic, paternalistic, and entrepreneurial.

The bureaucratic model assumes that managers and employees ought to be able to exercise independent discretion within bound jurisdictions without the need for constant supervision. People who continually seek out the advice of superiors or who seek creative, unexpected solutions deviate from the model. According to bureaucratic conventions, conflicts in organizations ought to be resolved rationally through open and full consultations in keeping with recognized procedures. This convention upholds notions of procedural justice. Arbitrary discrimination, favoritism, and nepotism represent violations of the model. In principle conflicts should be resolved by referring to standards and through intelligible discourse. The bureaucratic model has a number of virtues. Office-holders are expected to be able to discipline themselves, work industriously without constant surveillance, act civilly to co-workers, exercise discretion, and be able to balance the relative values of means, immediate ends, and long-range benefits. They are expected to be able to plan ahead and to exercise practical wisdom. They are counted on to be rational, ready to offer intelligent justifications for their actions, to provide coherent instructions to subordinates, and to make sensible and responsible choices.

We use the term paternalistic as a second model for business organization. Organizations which function with this model emphasize personal relationships between leaders, their lieutenants and agents, the identification by group members with leaders, the sense of community reinforced by this identification, the centralization of authority, and the justification of decisions on the basis of honored conventions. Actions are legitimated by precedent rather than by rational principles. Superiors are expected to look after subordinates, to champion their ideas, to sponsor their promotions, to support them in conflicts and to reward them personally for their accomplishments. Subordinates, correspondingly, are expected to defer to superiors, to flatter them on their achievements, and to seek their counsel. They are to consider themselves members of a team and regard their personal deeds by how they affect their team's efforts. Attention is focused on the leaders, who are set apart by special privileges, including opportunities to advance those whose loyalty they can count on. Administrators exercise authority, not primarily by virtue of the office they hold, but because they have been formally and personally authorized by their superiors. Conflicts are resolved by appealing to the wisdom and judgements of superiors. This model emphasizes the importance of personal leadership and the sense of community in business organizations.

The paternalistic model calls for allegiance and deference from subordinates and caring leadership from superiors. Subordinates are not viewed as independent office-holders but as agents of superiors. The value placed on community is expressed by loyalty to co-workers, rewarding those who demonstrate allegiance, appointing senior officials from within the organization, and promoting collective communal activities. Paternalistic patterns of organization assume and esteem especially the virtues of company loyalty, deference and fealty from subordinates, and solicitous, personal, yet statesmanlike leadership from management. The effectiveness of organizations is to be measured, not by gauges of efficiency, but by unswerving commitments to aims, methods, and roles in the community. While efficiency may be important at the base of the organization, leadership is needed at the top to transform office-holding organizations into self-maintaining institutions with distinctive identities, values and purposes.[15]

The paternalistic model, like the bureaucratic one, represents a compelling yet rarely realized ideal. Attempts to replicate parts of the model while ignoring others has resulted in distorted caricatures. Often subordinates fawn over superiors who may be more concerned with status than responsibility. Often managers promote colleagues on the basis of deference and loyalty rather than on objective achievements. Still, this model continues to inspire those who seek to make their organizations more personal and communal, and encourages executive direction based on influenced leadership.

According to a third set of social conventions, businesses ought to function as entrepreneurial enterprises. These assumptions are usually applied to smaller companies, the leadership apex of large companies, and units within larger organizations which are expected to be creative and innovative. The entrepreneurial organizational ethic especially values the ability to adapt, to compete aggressively, and to form new alliances. These assumptions are frequently conveyed in discussions of organizational innovation, adhocracy, networking, and competitive advantages.

The entrepreneurial model insists that organizational structures be subordinated and responsive to goals and objectives. The ideal organization is one able to respond quickly and effectively to environmental changes and opportunities. An entrepreneurial business is not tied down by traditions and rules. Conventions and principles are treated as guides for behavior but may be altered and amended when needed. The relationships within these organizations are expected to be personal. It is assumed that people can work together most effectively if they regard each other as friends and colleagues, not as impersonal co-workers. Personal relationships are fostered because they facilitate immediate and wide-ranging communication. Within entrepreurial organizations workers are assigned, not so much to specific offices with bound jurisdictions, but to sets of tasks. Managers gain legitimacy as authorities by virtue of their performances. Similarly, conflicts are resolved, not by appeals to higher authorities or some established judiciary system, but by encouraging competition, by rewarding those who make identifiable contributions, by allowing those who lose to try again, and by allowing contestants to form whatever kinds of alliances will advantage their campaigns.

These assumptions again presuppose several explictly moral expectations. It is assumed that workers and managers ought to be evaluated on the basis of their unique contributions. What is especially valued is innovation. While the entrepreneurial ethic places little worth on organizational community as such, it does value alliances and friendship among workers, colleagues, and outsiders. The entrepreneurial ethic emphasizes a cluster of virtues. Managers are expected to be creative, to exercise initiative, to be able to respond quickly to change, to be able to form friendships, and to communicate directly, and persuasively. Entrepreneurs, like bureaucrats, are expected to be self-disciplined and able to manage independently. However, self-management is accomplished not so much by rules but by developing a strong sense of one's potential and capabilities. Entrepreneurs are expected to be gamesmen.[16]

These bureaucratic, paternalistic, and entrepreneurial models represent powerful currents of opinion about how business enterprises ought to be organized and how business people ought to act. To the extent that individuals value membership to organizations based on these models, they will tend to abide by these conventions. Following orders without question is normal behavior in a paternalistic organization; asking for them in writing, perhaps with the right to question them before a review board, would be normal in a bureaucratic organization; ignoring them if they don't seem sensible or relevant to the bottom line might be consistent within an entrepreneurial organization. To foster standards of morality, the bureaucratic organization would require strong, official, documented, statements of desirable ethical and moral practices. The paternalistic organization would require a leader or leaders with high moral standards. The entrepreneurial organization would require most people in positions of power to have well-developed moral characters.

Societal Values

Businesses are influenced by moral expectations communicated as societal values. We use the words societal values to identify compelling and authoritative moral standards of particular societies. Equal opportunity, for example, is a basic ethos of our society. Societal values are not just theoretical ideas. Rather, these standards influence how people talk and act. Societal values often influence business practices even though these standards do not directly relate to business.

Societal values have often been considered integral to religious, political and national traditions. Several examples will demonstrate the role of societal values, and their impact on business. By tradition, Muslims forbid interest payments on loaned money. This is derived from ancient prohibitions against usurious lending to the poor. Muslim banks have developed ways of encouraging creditors and investors to extend loans and make investments without making explicit interest payments. Catholics also traditionally opposed usury but eventually found a means, by distinguishing carefully between usury and interest, to prohibit the former and allow the latter.[17] Christians have traditionally opposed work on Sundays just as Jews opposed work on Saturdays. Businesses operating in areas influenced by these religious traditions have had to modify their working hours accordingly. A more recently established societal value is the public commitment to health and medical insurance. A number of countries have instituted public health services or Medicare plans financed by payroll taxes and contributions by employers. Finally, even before industrialization, a number of European societies began to place increasing value on an attitude towards work, wealth, and time that emphasized self-discipline, the reduction of waste, and future planning.[18]

In recent years societal values have come to the attention of businesses in two ways. On the one hand, transnational businesses have become aware that conventions in countries abroad differ from those at home. Business people have especially noticed differences in the expected ways contractual arrangements are formulated. Negotiating agreements in some foreign countries are of a more personal nature. Favors are expected to be granted and repaid in keeping with particular assumptions regarding reciprocity. Often what has seemed to critics like corruption has been a conflict between older patterns of commerce that reinforced traditional kinship and village bonds, and more recent, bureaucratic models of administration and business.[19] However, traditional patterns of personal and reciprocal contracting do not amount to paying off local officials or agents. A careful study of the role of American corporations in the Middle East indicates that payoffs to government officials increased recently as a result of the expansion of these countries' government offices, even though the governments themselves officially opposed such bribes.[20] Those involved in transnational business have also become conscious of other differences in societal values related to working hours, the degree to which employers are expected to assume responsibility for the living conditions of workers, and the more active role of government officials.

On the other hand, in Europe and North America reform movements have from time to time challenged businesses to honor fundamental societal values. For example, since the 1880s, reformers attacked monopolies in support of fair and open competition. At various times reformers have demanded that businesses stop discriminating against particular groups, including trade unionists, immigrants, Blacks, and women.

Several clusters of societal values have played important roles in North America. The first cluster is the liberal democratic commitment to equal opportunity. This social creed has been expressed by reference to civil liberties, civil rights, and equality before the law. The fundamental assumption is that people have the right to develop and exercise their talents, to compete openly for opportunities, and to be rewarded fairly on the basis of efforts and achievements.

This creed does not require rewards to be distributed equally, however. It does expect fair competition for positions and rewards by avoiding favoritism to any groups or individuals. The commitment to publicly-supported education demonstrates the liberal democratic belief in schooling as a means of establishing equal opportunity. Fair competition has been protected by rulings against monopolies, by insisting on equality before the law, by championing civil liberties that encourage individuals to develop and express themselves, and by outlawing laws and conventions that discriminate against groups and individuals, especially minorities. Over time, commitment to equal opportunity, articulated first by enlightenment philosophers such as Locke, and by the founders of the American republic, has broadened and deepened its scope and meaning. Only gradually did liberal democratic men recognize equality of the sexes. Some liberal democrats have been much more consistent in their defense of equality than others. Andrew Carnegie, the rich steel magnate, true to his belief in individualism, advocated a very heavy inheritance tax that both encouraged the rich to support private charities and reduced the special advantages enjoyed by children of the wealthy.

North Americans and Europeans also support a second value cluster that emphasizes the rights of citizens to certain minimal social benefits. Depending on the country, these social rights may be broad or narrow. In most countries social benefits include the right to education, compensation for workers suffering from employment-related accidents, unemployment insurance, and public pensions for retired workers. Some countries support job retraining for the unemployed, medical insurance for all, the guarantee of minimum wage levels, and generous maternity leave. The social rights of citizenship are a manifestation of the emergence of the welfare state, with its programs for workers' compensation, unemployment insurance, medical insurance, and old age pensions.

According to a third cluster of societal values, citizens are expected to protect natural resources and the environment. The environmental creed was initially voiced as part of a conservation movement during the late nineteenth century and early twentieth century. The original commitment was to protect land and resources from commercial exploitation. This commitment has not always been honored. In recent years environmentalists have asked government and business to reduce pollution, to control and limit toxic waste, to replenish natural resources, to limit the use of non-renewable natural resources and, where possible, to compensate for damage to the environment.

The commitment to justice represents a further societal value. Arguments about reasonable competition, fair treatment, and equitable pay are often considered issues of justice.

It is possible to identify common assumptions among the various theories of justice. Justice is associated with equity, with just allocation, with fair treatment, with the acceptable distribution of social goods, and with due entitlements. All theories assume that each person or group ought to receive its due, and that the overall division of social goods and burdens ought to be reasonable, fair, and well-ordered.

Finally, while societies may assign relative importance to the value of ethnic and linguistic traditions, most societies assign prominence to a series of moral standards which are universally regarded as authoritative. These standards include the commitment to confidentiality, to not harming others, to helping each other out where possible, to respect for individuals and their property.[21] Because these standards are self-evident, they are often assumed rather than stated, except when they are blatantly violated.

THE MYTH OF AMORALITY IN BUSINESS

We have attempted to demonstrate that business people often refer to and attempt to comply with a wide range of moral standards. In various settings they invoke professional, legal and company codes as well as economic and

---

Professional Codes
For particular professions, like Law, Engineering, Accounting; an emergent professional ethic for management.

Company Codes and Corporate Mores
Ethical policy statements; corporate mores.

Law
Statutes, court decisions, decrees of regulatory agencies; legal opinion.

Economic Ideologies and Managerial Ideologies
Economic ideologies (free enterprise, etc.).
Managerial ideologies (scientific management, human relations, etc.).

Organizational Conventions
Assumptions about how organizations ought to be structured: bureaucratic, patrimonial, entrepreneurial.

Societal Values
Values of less developed societies.
Religiously influenced societal values.
Societal values honored in industrially developed societies: liberal democratic defense of equal opportunity; defense of social rights; defense of the environment; defense of justice.

FIGURE 4.1 **Forms by Which Moral Expectations for Business Are Communicated**

managerial ideologies, organizational philosophies and societal values. By citing these standards and corresponding examples of business practices, we counter the conventional attitude that business is amoral. While some businesses do ignore or violate moral standards, many business people and organizations do attempt to comply with these expectations. As Etzioni has recently argued, there is a moral dimension to business. It makes good business sense to keep promises, to treat personnel and stakeholders fairly, to conserve resources, to abide by legal structures, to provide quality services to consumers even when these actions entail at least short-term economic costs.[22]

Many businesses do not readily acknowledge the moral dimension of their activities. Instead, many people hold that business decisions and practices are pursued without moral considerations. This attitude has been supported for a number of reasons.

Much media attention has been focused on the illegal, deviant, and irresponsible activities of business people. Often, the phrase "business ethics" brings to mind examples of the opposite: references to hostile take-overs, damaging oil-spills, laundered money made from criminal activities, unsafe merchandise, abuse of executive privileges, the dumping of toxic waste, and international bribery. Certainly a long list of morally questionable business activities could be produced. We cannot deny that business people engage in misconduct. However, we maintain that these activities are not common and not generally tolerated. In the meantime, media attention to these practices gives the impression that, for the most part, business is unconcerned with moral standards. As they expose these wrong-doings, however, the media and public often forget that the standards they use to judge these actions are standards often endorsed by businesses as well.

Managers do find it convenient on occasion to ignore or violate particular standards. Many managers are selective in their adherence to moral standards. One transportation company took care to avoid discrimination and to use surveillance techniques that were not invasive. At the same time this company defended pricing policies that favored customers who were larger and could therefore bargain harder. These policies protected particular activities the company did not want openly examined. Business people who cite the myth of moral neutrality often do so because they don't want others to look too closely at activities they themselves may acknowledge to be questionable.

This myth is not only invoked by those who seek to reduce public scrutiny or internal debate. It is also invoked by those who use moral crusades as excuses for intrusive and arbitrary interventions in business activities. Many managers associate the concern over business ethics with attempts to extend and reinforce government regulations. Business ethics seem to them to be the rally cry for more regulatory agencies, more inspections, more rules, more citations, and more litigation. On the other hand, the call for business ethics often comes from various interest groups who seek to advance their own causes rather than the overall good of business organizations. Cornered by moral crusaders, many managers defend themselves from what they perceive to be unnecessary intervention that renders responsible management more difficult.

It is simplistic and wrong to assume, either that moral standards are ignored by managers and their businesses, or that they are all-pervasive. Reality is more complex. In all walks of life, people do not fully and consistently comply with the moral standards they respect and hold. This is because people often adopt standards without intending to comply with them. It also occurs when morally committed people cannot reconcile conflicts. Conflicts may arise between personal and company standards, and between professional norms and organizational conventions. Discrepancies also occur because people become morally weak. They may be confused or tired, lack social support, be distracted by opinions or impulses, and may momentarily err.

THE ACCEPTANCE OF MORAL STANDARDS

The relationship between moral standards and business practice is unique. We have identified moral standards that businesses recognize and seek to honor. Nonetheless, these standards are less compelling and authoritative than they might be. Their limited authority results from such factors as debates over the meaning of particular standards, and the lack of institutional grounding for many standards. We have already observed that many of the standards that affect business practices cannot be strictly enforced. The consequences are that business people individually endorse moral standards but do not hold them in common with others. They uphold private standards inspired by their professional, ideological, and societal commitments. Yet when they discuss moral issues they have faced in their work, managers similarly invoke a core of moral principles. These principles respect standards for business practices and beliefs concerning the moral purpose of business.

For example, when questioned about their ethical judgements, managers again and again cite several common standards. As they talk about ethical issues they invoke similar standards to criticize, to praise, to analyze, or to defend their own actions.[23] The accompanying table lists a series of standards to which individual managers refer when they were asked to discuss examples of moral issues they have faced in their work. Managers invoked these standards as they discussed cases in which they, and others, both complied with, and violated, moral expectations. Many managers respect moral standards and usually attempt to comply with them, even though they sometimes find excuses to ignore them. They refer to these standards as they make personal judgements of others' behavior.

THE FUNDAMENTAL PURPOSE OF BUSINESS

When we discuss the fundamental purpose of business, we cannot simply define the goals of particular firms or the social functions of business activity. Goals are objectives that are generally realized. These objectives may be defined in relation to profit margins, consumer satisfaction, personnel relations, or financial gain. Goals are set in relation to hoped-for outcomes. Goals may be influenced by economic, political, and social considerations. In contrast, the fundamental purpose of business is determined by how business directs on-going activities. For example, one of the fundamental purposes of business is to produce and market goods and services of good quality at reasonable costs in response to consumer choices.[24] Firms may seek to realize this aim by setting

Honest communications

Promise-keeping/keeping of confidences

Fair treatement

Special considerations

Safe and useful, high quality service/goods

Fair competition

Organizational responsibility

Law-abiding

Corporate social responsibility

Avoidance of conflicts of interest

FIGURE 4.2 **Moral Standards Referred to by Managers**

goals to gauge their accomplishments. This purpose, however, is a fundamental end of business whereas goals, such as increased consumer satisfaction, higher sales to particular groups, improved quality-control, greater consumer recognition of trade names, all identify specific objectives.

The fundamental purpose of business is <u>not limited</u> to the social functions of business. Firms perform a variety of social functions. They market goods, provide jobs, make investments, pay taxes, provide environments for people to meet others, exercise power, and use natural resources. In market economies, businesses are central to the social organizations of society. They establish networks of power and privilege, provide means of exchanging goods and information, and function to allocate status and material benefits. Many of the social functions of business are side-effects of business authority. Nonetheless, the social functions of business and its fundamental purpose may overlap to the extent that it represents the basic aim of the organization.

What distinguishes the fundamental purpose of business from specific organizational objectives and social functions is that the former possesses a <u>moral character.</u> When managers talk about this purpose, they acknowledge that aims lead to worthwhile ends. Nonetheless, although fundamental moral purposes can be identified and have been acknowledged by many business people, these purposes are often lost to sight as business and stakeholders shunt them aside for specific objectives. The <u>fundamental purpose of business</u> may be stated as follows:

- to produce quality goods and services at reasonable costs in response to consumer choices;
- to use natural and human resources efficiently;
- to allow all employees to use and develop their own skills individually

and in cooperation with others;
- to offer investors and lenders a fair return on their investments;
- to benefit the communities in which they operate.

These purposes are widely acknowledged by business people. Both classical and neo-classical economists assumed that business ought to produce in response to consumer choices. Business, correspondingly, ought not to ignore or manipulate choice. Executives often invoke the second purpose by arguing that firms ought to do what they know best, and not venture into areas where they possess less natural competence.[25]

The third purpose, regarding efficiency, has been recognized as a virtue since condemnation of wasted time and resources by Protestant reformers. Efficiency is so often invoked that its wider, moral applications are frequently overlooked. Too often efficiency is gauged in relation to a short-term reduction in operating costs, however this may be achieved. Efficiency should be measured in relation to which human and natural resources are used effectively over time without injury or waste. The fourth purpose, regarding the recognition and cultivation of worker competence, has long been emphasized by human resource experts. Humans are not machines. Businesses are likely to gain the greatest efforts from workers who feel their skills are valued. Businesses, according to the fifth purpose, are expected to benefit those who invest in them. This is one of the six aims of business. It is neither the sole not the most compelling purpose of business. Business must meet expectations of many people, including those who contribute to a business's well-being by consuming goods and services, by supplying them with goods and services, by working for them, and by investing in them. Finally, businesses exist because societies grant them charters of incorporation, provide infrastructures of utilities, roads and by-ways, potential consumers and investors, and protect them from thieves and embezzlers. Correspondingly, by an implicit social contract, businesses should seek to benefit the societies in which they operate.[26]

These purposes are not empty ideals. Businesses feel obliged to respect these purposes, often demonstrating this respect through public relation efforts. Business people rarely discuss these purposes openly, however. Rather, they focus their attention on specific objectives, or restricted versions of these purposes. We believe, however, that business people do recognize the authority of these purposes and that these are a reference managers can use to identify moral issues, set their objectives and deliberate about how to act.

SUMMARY

Our survey reveals that businesses are influenced by a wide range of moral standards. Moreover, moral expectations have increased over time. Nevertheless, these expectations are not clear, consistent and compelling. Many standards conflict with each other. Professional standards clash with bureaucratic principles which in turn compete with an emphasis on community and personal leadership. Managers may, at the same time, strive to fulfill the ethics of their profession and promote good relations with colleagues and subordinates in ways that may seem personally taxing and confusing. In addition, legal codes may conflict with societal values. Many feel, for example, that current laws allow for pollution in ways that violate the commitment to preserve the natural environment.

The business environment is also ambiguous because so many of the moral expectations of business are privately held. Few of the expectations we have surveyed are publicly acknowledged practices. To a great extent, these standards have a private status. As we have observed, managers, when interviewed, frequently identified common sets of moral expectations which guide their actual decision-making, but they rarely discuss how these standards might be interpreted, and what discretion might be taken in applying them. Alternately, the moral dimensions of business law are often obscured. Frequently, lawyers are used as technical specialists to determine what is legally allowable and to defend business interest against governments and other businesses. Managers simply allow legal counsel to handle matters as professional concerns without personally considering the moral issues involved. Finally, while many managers do identify with codes of professional ethics, these standards are considered private guides rather than corporate principles. The social dimensions of standards, laws, and codes are therefore frequently lost to sight.

SUGGESTED READINGS

Bird, Frederick B. and James A. Waters. "The Nature of Managerial Moral Standards," *Journal of Business Ethics* Vol. 6 (1987): 1-13.

Etzioni, A. *The Moral Dimension: Towards a New Economics* (New York: The Free Press, 1988).

Moss Kanter, Rosabeth. *Men and Women of the Corporation* (New York: Basic Books, 1977).

Sutton, Francis X., et al. *The American Business Creed* (Cambridge: Harvard University Press, 1956).

Peters, Thomas J., and Robert H. Waterman, Jr. *In Search of Excellence* (New York: Harper and Row, 1988).

Waters, James A. and Frederick B. Bird. "The Moral Dimension of Organizational Culture," *Journal of Business Ethics* Vol. 6 (1987): 15-22.

NOTES

1   Frederick B. Bird and James A. Waters, "The Moral Muteness of Managers," *California Management Review*, Vol. 32, No. 1, 73-88.

2   Briloff, Abraham J., "Codes of Conduct: Their Sound and Their Fury," *Ethics, Free Enterprise, and Public Policy*, edited by Richard T. DeGeorge and Joseph A. Pichler (New York: Oxford University Press, 1978).

3   Philip Selznick, *Leadership in Administration: A Sociological Interpretation (Evanston*, Illinois: Row, Peterson, 1957) chp. 4; Thomas J. Peters and Robert H. Waterman, Jr., *In Search of Excellence* (New York: Harper and Row, 1983); Mark H. McCormack, *What They Don't Teach You at Harvard Business School* (Toronto, New York: Bantam, 1984); Clarence C. Walton, *The Moral Manager* (Cambridge: Ballinger Publishing Company, 1988).

4   Francis X. Sutton, et al., *The American Business Creed* (Cambridge:Harvard University Press, 1956).

5   George E. Green, "Middle Management Morale in the 80s," *The AMA Survey Report* (New York: The American Management Association, 1983).

6   Mark H. McCormack, *What They Don't Teach You at Harvard Business School* (Toronto, New York: Bantam, 1984) chp. 1.

7   Peter F. Drucker, *Management: Tasks, Responsibilities Practices* (New York: Harper and Row, 1973); Thomas J. Peters and Robert H. Waterman, *In Search of Excellence* (New York: Harper and Row, 1982).

8   Walter E. Block, *Economics and The Environment: A Reconciliation* (Vancouver, B.C.: The Fraser Institute, 1990); World Commission on the Environment and Development: *Our Common Future* (New York: Oxford University Press, 1987).

9   Charles McCoy, *Management of Values: The Ethical Difference in Corporate Policy and Performance* (Boston: Pitman, 1985) chp. 2.

10 Mark L. Taylor, *A Study of Corporate Ethical Policy Statements* (Dallas: The Foundation of the Southeastern Graduate School of Banking, 1980).

11 Lon Fuller, *The Morality of Law* (New Haven: Yale University Press, 1964).

12 Reinhard Bendix, *Work and Authority in Industry: Ideologies of Management in the Course of Industrialization* (Berkeley: University of California Press, 1974).

13 Max Weber, "Types of Legitimate Domination" and "Domination and Legitimation," *Economy and Society: An Outline of Interpretive Sociology,* edited by Guenther Roth and Claus Wittich (Berkeley: University of California Press, 1968, 1978) Part One, chp. 3 and Part Two, chp. 10.

14 Clifford Geertz, "Ideology As a Cultural System," *The Interpretation of Culture* (New York: Basic Books 1973) chp. 9; Alvin Gouldner. *Dialectic of Ideology and Technology* (London: MacMillan, 1976) chps. 1-4.

15 Philip Selznick, *Leadership in Administration: A Sociological Interpretation Evanston*, Illinois: Row, Peterson, 1957) chp. 4.

16 Michael Maccoby, *The Gamesman* (New York: Simon and Schuster, 1976).

17 Benjamin Nelson, *The Idea of Usury* (New York: The Free Press, 1949).

18 We make reference here to the so-called Capitalist Work Ethic; see Max Weber. *The Protestant Ethic and the Spirit of Capitalism*, translated by Talcott Parsons (New York: Scribner's, 1930).

19 W.F. Wertheim, "Sociological Aspects of Corruption in Southeast Asia," *East-West Parallels: Sociological Approaches to Modern Asia* (The Hague: J. van Heneve Ltd., 1964) chp. 5.

20 Kate Gillespie, "The Middle East Response to the U.S. Foreign Corrupt Practices Act," *California Management Review*, Vol.29, No. 4 (1987) 9-30.

21 May Edel and Abraham Edel, *Anthropology and Ethics; The Quest for Moral Understanding* (Cleveland: Press of Case Western Reserve University, 1968).

22 Amitai Etzioni, *The Moral Dimension: Toward a New Economics* (New York: Free Press; London: Collier Macmillan, 1988).

23 Frederick Bird and James A. Waters, "The Nature of Managerial Moral Standards," *Journal of Business Ethics*, Vol 6. (1987) 1-13.

24 Thomas M. Garrett and Richard J. Klonoski, *Business Ethics*, 2nd ed. (Englewood Cliffs, N.J.: Prentice Hall, 1986) chp. 2.

25 Peters and Waterman, op. cit.; Selznick, op. cit.

26 John Kenneth Galbraith, *Economics and the Public Purpose* (Boston: Houghton Mifflin, 1973) Parts III, IV and V.

5 Moral Deliberation

Whether managers make ethically defensible choices for the moral issues they face depends on how they think about the issues and communicate these thoughts to others. Ethical decision-making involves consulting with stakeholders, identifying the issues involved, and determining relevant moral expectations. There are often conflicts between the rights of stakeholders and moral expectations. This chapter and the next consider how these conflicts may be analyzed and resolved.

MORAL DELIBERATION AS ACTION

Moral deliberation is the process by which people make judgements and articulate the grounds for their choices. There are two very different approaches to moral reasoning. To some people, reasoning involves the application of a set of moral principles, such as utilitarianism, the categorical imperative, or principles of justice which are rationally defined. Choices are presumed to result from logic and reason; moral deliberation is therefore viewed as the process by which people argue for the merits of particular sets of reasons in relation to the practical issues under consideration. Often these reasons are associated with particular philosophical models. As a result, moral deliberation becomes a debate over the relative merits of reasons championed by utilitarians, Kantians, Rawlsians, Aristotelians, Marxists, or defenders of natural law. Moral argument often leads, not to agreement, but to greater disagreement.[1]

This understanding of moral reasoning fails to appreciate the degree to which reflective ethical deliberation involves several activities, including interpreting data, weighing claims, and articulating justifications capable of persuading others. Aristotle demonstrated this point as his lectures on ethics were complemented by lectures on politics and rhetoric. To identify moral reasoning as the process of identifying and stating reasons, overlooks attempts to understand the issues, identify objectives, and persuade others to condone decisions reached.) We do not want to belittle the importance of reason in the making moral decisions; however, we do want to emphasize that moral deliberation is more than the application of reason. It is a social activity.[2]

THE PRACTICALITY OF MORAL DELIBERATION

We also view moral deliberation as a practical activity which can be useful in helping people make better decisions in business organizations. (Its aims are to foster collaboration and workable answers among people by critically examining moral assumptions, by encouraging people to be clear about their priorities, and by identifying objectives that are morally worthy and standards for acting that are morally compelling.[3]) Deliberation is open-ended, self-critical and seeks agreement among people for specific judgements. Moral deliberation also seeks both to foster critical reflection regarding accepted conventions and assumptions and to persuade people to act in morally fitting ways. Moral deliberation proceeds by those making judgements outlining their justifications so that others may understand and question them.

THE DIMENSIONS OF MORAL DELIBERATION

Moral deliberating involves five basic steps, summarized in Figure 5.1, namely: interpreting evidence; evaluating the claims of stakeholders; setting realistic objectives; considering and ranking alternative courses of action; and articulating justifications for decisions reached.)

1. **Interpreting evidence:** Analyzing the facts of a particular situation, objectively and subjectively.
2. **Evaluating information:** Weighing and ranking information, claims and expectations.
3. **Setting objectives:** Establishing long and short-term objectives; prioritizing among worthwhile objectives.
4. **Identifying and evaluating alternatives:** Developing possible alternatives to meet objectives and evaluating the alternatives by weighing and assigning priorities to relevant factors.
5. **Articulating justifications:** providing reasons for choice.

FIGURE 5.1 **The Multi-Dimensional Nature of Moral Reasoning**

① Interpreting

Moral deliberation involves interpreting issues. (Moral issues are defined by how we view problems, by how various stakeholders view problems, and by the moral standards which people invoke in the process.) The same problem is likely to look very different from different viewpoints. So-called facts do not speak for themselves. Making sense of them involves interpretation.

What is relevant to the following case? A large corporation which extracts natural resources is about to close a local mill. They claim the mill, which has not been updated, is unprofitable, given changes in market demand. They claim that current tax laws discourage modernizing plants because present depreciation allowances are too low. They argue that the work force, which is unionized, has become less productive and is unwilling to consider wage rollbacks that could make the plant more profitable. The trade union, in turn, argues that management has been authoritarian, unapproachable, and unimaginative. The union argues that management has stuck to a traditional management structure that has been unresponsive to change.

(A fact-finding team sent to this mill could collect extensive information on its capital value, the condition of its machinery, the impact of the plant on the local economy, the tenure of the work force, alternative uses for the plant, and relevant policies of the parent corporation.) Still, all this information has to be interpreted considering likely effects on all the stakeholders involved. The eventual statements of fact are likely to reflect various stakeholder interests, as well as the objectives they seek. It is easy to see that this data would be interpreted quite differently by those who argue that the plant should be kept in operation and those who argue that the plant should be closed.

Facts are not just a matter of subjective interpretation. Through public discussion, it is often possible to achieve consensus regarding the information deemed most relevant. Nonetheless, data must be interpreted and interpretations are shaped by objectives which people pursue and the moral arguments they use to justify their decisions.

② Evaluating

(Moral deliberation involves evaluating information, stakeholder claims, and moral expectations.) We have already discussed how stakeholders make various claims and how management is often influenced by professional, organizational, economic and societal standards which may be heterogeneous and conflicting. To be sure, often these claims and expectations are muffled and obscured because they are referred to in morally neutral terms. As a result, evaluating information, stakeholder claims, and moral expectations is done tacitly, and is justified in political and economic terms. Nonetheless, all decisions involve the deliberate or tacit act of assigning importance to data, significance to the claims and interests of stakeholders, and weight to moral expectations that are relevant to the issues.

Often this evaluative ranking is done tacitly as the following example illustrates. A transportation company justified its decision to charge different customers different rates for the same service by arguing that some customers ought to be rewarded for hard bargaining. This argument makes a number of evaluative assumptions. It assumes either that customers share equal information or that providing different information is not a moral problem. It assigns greater prominence to the moral value of contract negotiation than to the moral value of equal treatment. Any evaluation of moral claims, expectations, and information involves assigning priorities to social obligations. The latter may arise from explicit contracts, from legal stipulations, from tacit promises, or from personal commitments.

Setting Objectives

Moral deliberation involves setting valued objectives. Objectives are what people hope to accomplish from actions. As people consider important decisions, they think about objectives — personal and organizational, divisional and corporate, short and long-term. Setting an objective involves allocating priorities to various goals, all of which may be legitimate and worthy.

The manager of a family-run clothing manufacturing business pondered what to do about several long-term employees who were in their mid sixties, were becoming less effective workers, but had no pension provisions apart from public insurance and minimal savings. The company had never instituted a company pension plan for its employees, who were non-unionized. There was high morale among workers and managers. A plan to develop a company pension plan would not benefit these employees. As the manager considered his options he reviewed a number of possible objectives all of which seemed worthwhile. The company cultivated morale by encouraging managers to offer personal services to employees in need. Still, the clothing business was competitive and the company had survived by working people hard, by cutting corners when necessary, and by keeping the union out. It was easier to let go of old employees who were not likely to complain and who had families that would take care of them.

Whether consciously or unconsciously, managers identify and rank objectives in the short and long term to their own personal moral purposes, as well as to the larger organizations of which they are a part. Ethicists have urged business people to adopt a long-range view, not in terms of the present year's budget. A long-term view would tolerate temporary losses incurred by a morally sound decision because the decision may protect communal support and employee morale.[4] A few ethicists have argued that short-term consequences must still be considered, that current financial responsibilities cannot be ignored, and that ethics can help managers run economically successful businesses by helping them make hard choices.[5]

We advocate a balanced view of the relevant objectives. We feel that objectives ought to be considered in terms of the institutional identity of the organization and the moral identities of decision-makers. It is also important to ask what kind of moral character the organization has had and would like to strive to attain, and the values the organization wants to institutionalize.[6]

How we set and identify our objectives is influenced by other aspects of moral deliberation. Our interpretation of data, our evaluation of information and moral claims, and the rationales we articulate, all influence how we rank and identify our objectives. Nonetheless, long-range objectives decisively influence how we establish identities, set priorities, and delineate the parameters in relation to which other matters are considered.[7] Whether they are tacitly assumed, or publicly defended, these long-term objectives mark out the boundaries for the staging of subsequent discussions.[8] Therefore, we think it is useful early on in any process of moral deliberation to consider critically and to assign priorities to relevant objectives. It is necessary to consider the meaning and influence of the long-term moral objectives of organizations, because these are likely to influence subsequent debate.

As individuals and organizations establish their objectives, they make assumptions about what will promote well-being and the likelihood of their present activities achieving that end. Objectives are valued as a means for attaining this state of well-being. However, people define "well-being" in many different ways. Does the well-being of a business organization consist in its survival over time, its expansion, its profitability, the on-going contributions it makes to its several stakeholders? Alternatively, does well-being consist of skilled performance or in the cooperation of workers? Is the organization's well-being maximized by seeking to further the well-being of its members? We do not intend to answer these questions here. Rather, we wish to argue that organizations seek to realize what those with effective influence understand as well-being. They may seek a bigger market share, happy employees, or higher productivity levels depending on the alternatives they might judge to be more worthwhile. Alternatively, they may refuse to accept trade-offs and pursue multiple objectives such as the realization of greater economic return and the growth and development of employees, where the second of these is valued as an objective in and of itself and is not merely instrumental to the attainment of profit.

We raise this point because it is easier to arouse and sustain people to act morally if they feel that their well-being and the well-being of their associations are likely to be enhanced by certain activities. The issue here is not simply to define well-being in one way or the other. It is rather a practical matter. People are more likely to make decisions that will enhance their own lives.

Identifying and Evaluating Alternatives

Moral deliberation involves identifying, ranking, and choosing alternative courses of action. Facts are interpreted, claims evaluated, and objectives set in order to help determine a decision. A plan of action is often adopted because it is <u>a preferred alternative</u>. The consideration of alternatives provides a means of weighing and assigning priorities to the diverse factors which affect an issue. Decision-makers attempt to balance costs and benefits, existing obligations and ideal objectives, the claims of diverse stakeholders, short- and long- term advantages, normative expectations and realistic responsibilities. The very act of constructing alternatives makes people much more aware that possibilities for different decisions exist and that each alternative assigns greater or less moral and practical weight. (Reviewing alternatives raises consciousness and makes people more aware of their assumptions and priorities.) The process encourages them to <u>articulate sound reasons</u> for accepting and dismissing alternatives.

For example, a sub-contractor in the construction business debated whether to take a contractor to court for late payment for work already completed. He was short of funds to pay his employees. He recognized that litigation would be costly, would delay the payment, would result in a compromise decision that awarded him only a portion of the amount due, and would alienate him from the contractor, a very large firm, from whom he still hoped for future work. The alternative, however, was to meet current costs out of his own pocket while awaiting eventual payment, but because of the delay the payment would be smaller, in real terms, than the contracted amount. The sub-contractor faced this dilemma several times. Sometimes he sued contractors when payments were delayed and sometimes he waited and made payments out of his personal funds.

(It is crucial to identify the alternatives in moral deliberation.) Frequently people feel little room to maneuver simply because there are not enough viable alternatives. In the example just mentioned, the sub-contractor felt he had only two alternatives. Perhaps other alternatives might have been considered. The sub-contractor might have attempted to join with other sub-contractors to lobby for quicker payments. He might have threatened to delay completion of the work until partial payments were made. He might have worked with the contractor to secure advance, partial payments from customers. He might have leaked a story to the local press exposing the problem. Or, he might have sought to join other sub-contractors in a series of lawsuits against the contractor. Several of these alternatives might have been pursued at the same time. <u>Moral dilemmas</u> seem intractable when the range of alternatives is restricted. The range often seems narrow because alternatives have not even been entertained much less thoughtfully considered.

(Considering alternatives <u>calls for imagination</u>; looking at issues from new perspectives, stepping outside conventional wisdom, and examining examples of how others creatively respond to similar situations) Often by considering seemingly unlikely alternatives, people learn to imagine new ways of satisfactorily balancing claims and interests. The capacity to think imaginatively is a valuable skill for moral reasoning.

It is, of course, easier to acknowledge the value of imagination than it is to institutionalize ways of encouraging imaginative thinking about moral issues. Imaginative thinking is sometimes discouraged because it is iconoclastic. Because they do not want to be too closely associated with ideas that are later judged to be unacceptable, managers are often inclined to propose only ideas that are likely to be adopted.

There are several ways to encourage imaginative responses to moral issues. We have already argued that on-going in-depth consultations with relevant stakeholders draws attention to new ideas and possibilities. These consultations encourage imaginative responses. Imaginative consideration of alternatives is also strengthened by organizational tolerance for dissent. Managers are likely to propose more creative and innovative responses to moral dilemmas if they are not likely to be penalized for advocating positions not later adopted. Finally, imaginative thinking is always triggered by considering examples of how other businesses have responded to similar problems. Managers can often generate a wider range of alternatives by looking over reports by other organizations.

Once a list of alternatives is generated, options must be weighed and ranked. Often this evaluation of alternatives focuses on narrow objectives. Alternatives are judged in terms of probable benefits and costs. Although, this framework is useful, it should not be used exclusively. This narrow, or utilitarian framework, too easily devolves into an economic analysis of costs and benefits, ignoring non-utilitarian moral values which ought to be considered.[9]

Articulating Justifications

Finally, moral deliberation involves the articulation of appropriate and persuasive justifications for action. Justifications are the reasons people cite to defend judgements and actions. They involve more than the citing of particular standards, such as fair treatment or conflict of interest guidelines. Justifications spell out the reasons for judgements and actions as well as the reasons for invoking specific standards on normative grounds. For example, a manager justifies a decision to institute an affirmative action program, not only by invoking principles of justice, but by arguing the importance of these standards at this moment in time.

Justifications invoke other dimensions of moral deliberation; namely, the way relevant information is to be interpreted, the way claims and obligations are to be evaluated, the kinds of objectives which are to be pursued, and the ranking of viable alternatives. Openly or tacitly, justifications make sense of data, claims, ideals, and alternatives so that choices can be understood and defended.

Justifications are persuasive. Justifications are used to seek cooperation from those whose compliance and consent are needed, and acceptance and deference from those who may otherwise criticize. As people voice justifications, they explain their decision, reinforce their own commitments, and motivate others to agree with them. Justifications often appeal to the heart and imagination as much as to the mind. Justifications are as much influenced by rhetoric as by logic. Justifications are used, after all, to gain the voluntary consent of others.

As managers state justifications for their decision, they are involved in communication. They seek the passive assent of some and the active agreement of others. They seek to make their chosen course of action so appealing that those whose cooperation is desired will voluntarily consent. Workers who willingly consent to wage freezes, for example, are much more likely to continue to work industriously and effectively than workers who have been forced to accept them, or are unconvinced by managerial arguments. Justifications are also offered in defense of decisions made, so that criticism is neutralized, and potential attacks are disarmed.

Decisions may precede or follow from agreements about justifications for action. Sometimes, a course of action is chosen because a justifying argument provides a way of clearly ranking alternatives. Moral choice follows from moral deliberation. On the basis of on-going consultations with stakeholders as well as intuitive reflections, a decision may seem morally correct, even though those involved have not yet hit on a convincing justification. Before finalizing their decision, individuals involved must search for persuasive rationales that will not only gain the consent of others but clarify their own commitments. Typically, when the deliberating process moves from reaching a decision to arriving at justifications, the activity of articulating reasons produces a clearer and more compelling understanding of the decisions themselves.

Justifications explain how decisions have been reached and set out the steps that led to the decision. They answer the question "why" a decision was made by indicating the considerations, claims, and facts that eventually resulted in a decision. Justifications provide histories about the factors that preceded, and prepared the way for the decision. Justifications also look to the future by directing people how they ought to act in order to realize valued objectives.

Managers face several problems as they seek to articulate justifications for business decisions. These problems influence how moral arguments are confronted or avoided by business people. Thus, managers often seek the cooperation of various stakeholders to support a particular course of action. Different rationales are likely to be persuasive with different constituent groups. However, if different justifications are used for different groups, managers are likely to be accused of talking out of both sides of their mouths. Hence, they must seek rationales they can use consistently while still adapting them to different interest groups. Managers should avoid using moral justifications like propaganda, simply to persuade others. Moral discourse, like propaganda is persuasive. However, unlike propaganda, moral discourse offers authentic reasons for acting and an assurance that recommended actions are morally correct.[10]

THE MARKS OF GOOD MORAL DELIBERATIONS

(Moral deliberations in practice may successfully facilitate the kinds of sound judgements and viable agreements that allow for responsible action.) Several factors influence the extent to which actual deliberations foster this facilitating role. These factors, which affect the character of these deliberations, together constitute a set of moral guidelines for good moral deliberations. (Good moral deliberations are vocal, honest, issue-oriented, thoughtful, rational and imaginative.)

Good moral deliberations are vocal. People speak up with respect to their concerns and commitments, and they allow and encourage others to speak up as well. They are not silent or silenced. The vocal character of good moral deliberations has several consequences. To some degree organizations that allow these kinds of voicing are likely to be noisier and also more lively and engaged. The relationship between superiors and subordinates is likely to change so that both in some measure feel free to set agendas and tones for their interactions. If superintendents only set direction and subordinates primarily provide feedback, these exchanges will remain stilted, corresponding more to mutual monologues than interactive dialogues.[11]

Good moral deliberations are honest. People involved in these deliberations neither directly lie or dissimulate. Honest deliberations do not require that they expose all that they know. Often it is necessary to protect valued secrets. Moreover, often in negotiations it is important to delay the disclosure of information so that it is balanced with the unfolding disclosures of others, as negotiating parties become clearer about final agreements with which they can live. Honest deliberations are not, however, deliberately misleading. Nor do those deliberating honestly cloak their convictions in borrowed language. It is better to speak using one's own expressions, even if these do not seem to be terms formally used in ethics, so that one can directly communicate one's own judgements.

Good moral deliberations are issue-oriented. They retain a problem-solving, realistic, here and now focus. People often allow themselves to become distracted when they deliberate. They may slide off topic by invoking ideal states or by talking in vague generalities. Moral talk itself sometimes distracts when problem-solving discussions get side-tracked into considerations of blame and praise. Because of the tendency to personalize moral issues, people often distract themselves as they allow discussions regarding viable alternatives to devolve into considerations regarding the guilt, irresponsibility, excellence or exemplary character of those most directly involved. Frequently what might have been problem-solving deliberations about ethical issues turn into settings where people use moral talk to complain about others, to rationalize their own actions, or to recite their ideological beliefs. This kind of carping, excusing, and posturing facilitates neither sound judgements nor viable agreements.[12]

Good moral deliberation is _rational_. We make this observation recognizing that there are many different ways of being rational. Good moral deliberations are rational in several senses. They are, for example, intelligible. They are articulated so others can comprehend their meaning. They are reasonable. They set forth articulate arguments. They are considered and thoughtful. Often when moral issues arise, people respond by stating their feelings and views. They preface every observation or proposition with qualifying phrases such as "I feel" or "It is my opinion that...". As a result their observations remain undebatable. One cannot debate another's feelings. Arguments, as contrasted with opinions, are thoughtful and debatable. They represent considered judgements. They connect conclusions together with premises in ways that allow others to discuss assumptions, recommendations, and the ways these are inter-related.

Finally, good moral deliberations are _imaginative_. One of the major differences between good and restrictive moral deliberations is that the former open up people's minds and imaginations so they see possibilities where none before seemed to exist. When the aim of ethics is to facilitate sound judgements and viable agreements, then it is helpful when moral discourse works to overcome resistances while still deepening convictions, to explore alternatives while still retaining commitments. When moral discourse becomes too straight-laced it frustrates the facilitative role, which calls for a continuous negotiating between basic convictions, particular exigencies and the morally defensible claims of others. Moral deliberation best plays this role when by re-telling stories, citing examples, and brainstorming, people are able to see their way through to new judgements and agreements.

SUMMARY

By consciously engaging in data interpretation, evaluation, the setting of objectives, identifying and evaluating alternatives, and justifying choices, managers must inevitably end up consulting with stakeholders to ascertain how they see situations and how they feel about them. This process of moral deliberation is independent of the types of reasoning about moral issues which we describe in the next chapter. But, when consciously engaged in, it takes ethics from the realm of the intellectual and abstract to the action environment of managerial decision-making.

SUGGESTED READINGS

Dutton, Jane, and R.B. Duncan. "The Creation of Momentum for Change Through the Process of Issues Diagnosis," _Strategic Management Journal_ Vol. 8, No. 3 (1987): 279-295.

Freeman, R.E., and David R. Gilbert, Jr. *Corporate Strategy and the Search for Ethics* (Englewood Cliff, N.J.: Prentice Hall, 1988).

Stout, J. *Ethics After Babel: The Languages of Morals and Their Discontents* (Boston: Beacon Press, 1988).

NOTES FOR CHAPTER 5

1   Alasdaire C. MacIntyre, *After Virtue: A Study In Moral Theory* (Notre Dame, Ind.: University of Notre Dame Press, 1981) chps. 1-6.

2   We are thereby following the lead of philosophers like Ludwig Wittgenstein, *Philosophical Investigations*, translated by G.E.M. Anscombe (Oxford: Basil Blackwell, 1972); Hannah Arendt, *The Life of the Mind*, Vol. I "Thinking" and Vol. II "Willing" (New York: Harcourt Brace Janovich, 1978); John Searle, *Speech Acts* (Cambridge: Cambridge University Press, 1969); and John Austin, *How To Do Things With Words* (Cambridge: Harvard University Press, 1958). Other philosophers who view moral reasoning primarily as a social activity include Richard Rorty, *The Consequences of Pragmatism* (Minneapolis: University of Minnesota Press, 1982) chp. 9; Albert R. Jonsen and Stephen Toulmin, *The Abuses of Casuistry: A History of Moral Reasoning* (Berkeley: The University of California Press, 1988); Sabina Lovibond, *Realism and Imagination in Ethics* (Oxford: Basil Blackwood, 1983); Amitai Etzioni, *The Moral Dimension: Toward a New Economics* (New York: The Free Press, 1988) chps. 8-11.

3   Barbara Gray, *Collaborating: Finding Common Ground for Multi-Party Problems* (San Francisco: Jossey-Bass, 1989); see also Dutton, op. cit.

4   Roberet C. Solomon and Kristin R. Hanso, *It's Good Business* (New York: Atheneum, 1985); Charles McCoy, *Management of Values: The Ethical Difference in Corporate Policy and Performance* (Boston, Mass.: Pitman, 1985); R. Edward Freeman and David R. Gilbert, Jr., *Corporate Strategy and the Search for Ethics* (Englewood Cliffs, N.J.: Prentice Hall, 1988).

5   Mark Pastin, *The Hard Problems of Management: Getting the Ethics Edge* (San Francisco, Calif.: Jossey-Bass, 1986) chp. 1,2,8.

6   Philip Selznick, *Leadership in Administration* (Evanston: Row, Peterson, 1957).

7   Talcott Parsons and Edward A. Shils, "Values, Motives, and Systems of Action," in Talcott Parsons and Edward Shils, eds., *Toward A General Theory of Action* (New York: Harper and Row, 1951) Part Two, chps. 1 and 3; Clyde Kluckholm, "Values and Value Orientations in the Theory of Action: An Exploration in Definition and Clarification," in *Toward A General Theory of Action*, op. cit., Part Four, chp. 2; Charles Morris, *Varieties of Human Values* (Chicago: The University of Chicago Press, 1956).

8   Erving Goffman, *The Presentation of Self in Everyday Life* (Garden City, N.Y.: Doubleday, 1959).

9   Amitai Etzioni, *The Moral Dimension: Toward A New Economics* (New York: The Free Press, 1988).

10   Jurgen Habermas, *The Theory of Communicative Action*, trans. by Thomas

McCarthy (Boston: Beacon Press, 1984) Vol. I, chp. 3.

11 Frances Westley, "Middle Managers and Strategy: The Microdynamics of Inclusion," *Strategic Management Journal*, (1990).

12 Frederick Bird, Frances Westley, and James A. Waters, "The Uses of Moral Talk: Why Do Managers Talk Ethics," *Journal of Business Ethics*, Vol. 8 (1989) 75-89.

 6 Moral Reasoning

The previous chapter analyzed moral deliberation as a practical, social activity. We observed how this activity involved interpreting information, evaluating claims of those involved, identifying objectives and alternative ways to realize these, as well as articulating persuasive justifications for the choices reached. We concluded the chapter by spelling out several marks that characterized good, as opposed to not so good, moral deliberations. This chapter focuses on just one element in the deliberating process, namely, the way people justify their moral judgements. It analyzes the alternative ways by which people reason or argue as they attempt to render moral judgements, the strengths and weaknesses of these alternatives and ways they may be combined.

FOCUS ON MODES OF REASONING

This chapter focuses on the forms of reasoning which people use to justify moral judgements and not on ethical theories or specific beliefs they may invoke as part of their arguments. The typology found in this chapter provides a model which may be used both to analyze how people already form their arguments as well as to identify alternative ways of reasoning that may be utilized to strengthen one's own position. People use quite varied patterns of arguing to justify their moral decisions, often without knowing much about existing ethical theories. Their modes of reasoning may in fact correspond to theories of which they are as yet not fully aware.

Our model is designed as an analytical typology to distinguish the different ways people actually put together their moral arguments.[1] Responsible adults have almost certainly utilized each of these forms of reasoning on occasion and they need not be mutually exclusive. In fact, people often utilize several forms of reasoning at the same time without necessarily being inconsistent. A too-exclusive use of any form of arguing may lead people to overlook important information and considerations. Utilizing several forms of reasoning at once, in contrast, provides an opportunity to compensate for this one-sidedness.

APPLYING THEORIES OR DEVELOPING ARGUMENTS?

Moral reasoning primarily consists in the development of cogent, persuasive, defensible arguments rather than in the artful application of particular theories. Business people may well be able to gain insight regarding moral issues, strengthen their own arguments and become more critical of the arguments of others by gaining knowledge of various ethical theories. A serious reading in moral philosophy can be recommended not only for these utilitarian reasons but also because of the cultural and personal significance of these works.

Formal ethical theories articulate both specific moral principles — such as justice, honesty, employee rights — and the arguments used to defend these principles. It is often assumed that the appropriate way to integrate ethics into business decision-making is to find ways of applying given ethical theories to particular business problems and decisions.

There are three basic problems to the theory-application approach. First, it fails to distinguish between moral standards for behavior and the reasoning used to justify these standards. The same standards, such as honesty or privacy, may be justified by different kinds of arguments.[2] For example, lying, under certain circumstances, might be justified by the end justifying the means, the lesser of two evils, or the desire to be compassionate at the expense of the truth. However, when ethical deliberation involves applying ethical theories, the distinction between standards for action, and justifications of these standards, is often obscured.

Second, this theory-application model also suggests a knowledge-based approach to moral deliberation. Morally sensitive managers are expected to use a working knowledge of ethical literature which they are to apply, like engineers apply scientific knowledge to construction or production. In contrast, we think that the point of moral deliberation is to think imaginatively, to argue persuasively, and to judge critically. Developing competence in this process results more from cultivating skills than from gaining more knowledge. These skills are less likely to develop by concentrating on the theory-application model.

The theory-application model of moral reasoning also tends to ignore the extent to which managers already use moral arguments in their justifications. Most people make moral arguments in spite of being unfamiliar with ethical theories. A manager's reasoning may not be refined and may be inconsistent, but it may very well correspond to classical patterns of ethical argument. For such managers, ethical knowledge is likely to be less useful than becoming more aware and more critical of their own arguments and assumptions. So equipped, managers will be better able to recognize and criticize implicit moral arguments, understand their moral convictions, and be more articulate in their justifications.

TYPES OF MORAL REASONING

(We have identified seven distinct types of moral reasoning: traditional, principled, consequential, purposive, consensual, subjective and charismatic.)The main characteristics of each of these is summarized in Figure 6.1.

TRADITIONAL

Citing relevant precedents: deferring to traditions, recognized conventions, and oft-cited cases.

PRINCIPLED

Identifying rational, coherent, universal principles: arguing on the basis of principles, standards of natural law, the nature of human action, and self-evident assumptions.

CONSEQUENTIAL

Maximizing beneficial consequences: means, ends and secondary consequences are compared and balanced in hope of maximizing morally good benefits at least cost.

PURPOSIVE

Identifying intrinsic purposes and ends: intrinsic purposes are identified in relation to historical processes, institutional roles; means are derived from chosen ends.

CONSENSUAL

Seeking informed, intelligent consensus: defended by both social contract and democratic theories; reasoning proceeds by attempting to cultivate informed, intelligent consensus among those involved.

SUBJECTIVE

Identifying personally acceptable rationales: deliberations proceed to identify rationales that are subjectively satisfying, that allow individuals to act with a sense of integrity and authenticity.

CHARISMATIC

Deferring to inspired authorities: authorities defend their arguments as inspired, fitting to the situation, facilitating relevant action; others defer to them because of their charisma.

FIGURE 6.1 **Typology of Moral Reasoning**

Traditional

We use the word "traditional" to describe moral reasoning which attempts to make decisions by identifying and following relevant precedents. The key to this approach is the identification and interpretation of relevant precedents. Not all past experiences are likely to be relevant. Precedents may be chosen from the recent or distant past; from one's own experience or the experience of others. If we follow the example of case law, precedents are chosen because they are both instructive and authoritative. In case law, however, it is not always clear which precedents are most relevant. When precedents are used in moral deliberations, they are invoked as sources of wisdom, not simply as examples of behavior to be slavishly followed.

When traditional patterns of moral reasoning are used among a group of people, and precedents are continually cited, deliberating tends to reinforce a sense of community. At IBM, for example, managers often cite the wisdom and example of their founder, Watson, to justify current practices. In the process of re-telling stories, managers strengthen the sense of community they share not only with previous managers at IBM, but also with current associates.

Traditional patterns of moral reasoning possess a number of advantages. This pattern of deliberating recognizes that much can be gained by reviewing relevant past experiences. By examining past experiences and former debates, we learn ways of dealing with contemporary problems. Our own deliberations are more rigorous for examining the deliberations of others who have already considered similar issues. Moreover, since people defer to precedents, they are more likely to consent to contemporary judgements which use them to justify and defend decisions.

Using relevant precedents for moral reasoning has a number of limitations. Precedents may be arbitrary and amoral. People may cite precedents that legitimate privilege and power. Following precedents may render people inflexible to contemporary change. One of the limitations of traditional moral reasoning is that people too often view traditions as behavioral norms rather than as sources of wisdom. It is as a source of wisdom that past experiences have relevance for moral deliberating. Citing relevant precedents, as a form of moral reasoning, is also likely to be more useful in settings with rich traditions of moral debate, such as case law, talmudic debate, and philosophical ethics. In many organizations a tradition of moral reasoning is scant, and relevant precedents are only found outside the organization and its history.

Principled

We use the word "principled" to describe moral reasoning based on universally valid ethical principles. The focus is on means not ends, on good or morally acceptable behavior rather than on possible benefits. These principles establish general guidelines for acceptable conduct. Decisions are made based on what is permissible and recommended according to these fundamental principles.

Several examples of these basic principles are well known. According to the Golden Rule, people ought to act towards others, as they expect others to act towards them. Kant's categorical imperative states that people ought to act in such a way that they treat other people as ends and not means and that standards used to justify actions ought to appeal to all morally aware people. Other philosophers have identified other basic principles, such as the obligation to keep confidences, and to be honest, to avoid inflicting injury and to act fairly. A number of basic moral principles are defended as rights, such as equality of gender, age, or race, and freedom of speech and action.

In practice, principled moral reasoning involves the application of these principles to decisions. For example, the question about whether to institute secret surveillance of workers in the stockroom to reduce theft, would involve a discussion about whether this could be justified by the Golden Rule or by Kant's categorical imperative. Clearly, stealing company supplies is wrong. The question becomes one of determining how this wrong can be limited in ways that do not involve equally reprehensible behavior. Is subversive, yet unobtrusive

---

Principled Reasoning — Kant:

There is therefore but one categorical imperative, namely this: Act only on that maxim whereby thou canst at the same time will that it should become a universal law. . . . Act as if the maxim of thy action were to become by thy will a universal law of nature. . . . A man . . . finds himself forced by necessity to borrow money. He knows that he will not be able to repay it, but sees also that nothing will be lent to him unless he promises stoutly to repay it in a definite time. He desires to make this promise, but he has still so much conscience as to ask himself: Is it not unlawful and inconsistent with duty to get out of a difficulty in this way? . . . How would it be if my maxim were a universal law? Then I see at once that it could never hold as a universal law of nature, but would necessarily contradict itself. . . . Accordingly, the practical imperative will be as follows: so act to treat humanity, whether in thine own person or that of any other, in every case as an end withal, never as means only . . . . He who is thinking of making a lying promise to others will see at once that he would be using another man merely as a means, without the latter containing at the same time the end in himself.

Immanuel Kant, *Fundamental Principles of the Metaphysics Morals*, translated by Thomas K. Abbott (New York: The Liberal Arts Press, 1949) pages 38, 39, 40, 46, 47.

Principled Reasoning — Gert

A moral rule is unchanging or unchangeable; discovered rather than invented. A moral rule is not dependent on the will of any one man or group of men . . . moral rules have a status similar to the laws of logic or of mathematics.

We now have ten rules:

1. Don't kill
2. Don't cause pain
3. Don't disable
4. Don't deprive of freedom or opportunity
5. Don't deprive of pleasure
6. Don't deceive
7. Keep your promise
8. Don't cheat
9. Obey the law
10. Do your duty

Everyone is always to obey the rule except when he could publically advocate violating it. Anyone who violates the rule when he could not publically advocate such a violation may be punished.

Bernard Gert, *The Moral Rules: A New Rational Foundation for Morality* (New York: Harper and Row, 1966, 1967, 1970), pages 67, 68, 125.

surveillance an unjustifiable invasion of privacy? Can we compel people to act the same way towards us? Principled moral reasoning would raise these kinds of questions and arrive at conclusions without asking pragmatic questions about whether certain actions would yield desired results, such as less pilfering of supplies. Ordinarily, people use principled forms of moral reasoning to demonstrate why specific judgements ought to be made based on specific principles. While one manager justifies the closed-bid process because it seems fair, another may justify developing closer relations with suppliers who provide good service on the basis of reciprocity or loyalty.

Principled forms of moral reasoning are ethically attractive for a number of reasons. In so far as the principles cited are widely recognized as authoritative, this form of reasoning is compelling to broad groups of people. These principles are morally pre-eminent even to those who are sceptical about the role of ethics in management. They are not only universally appealing: they are certain and fixed.

Principled forms of moral reasoning are especially attractive because they provide a telling, unambiguous guard against self-serving rationales. People often cloak actions undertaken to further their own interests in moralizing language that excuses particular actions in terms of larger social benefits.

Principled forms of moral reasoning function both to expose such abuse of moral language and to guard one against doing the same thing. This happens because principled reasoning always requires that particular decisions be defended in relation to principles that have equal moral weight for all.

However, principled forms of moral reasoning possess several notable limitations. In the first place, these principles are abstract. While at a theoretical level they are compelling, it is often not clear how to interpret them and which should have priority. For example, should justice be applied to the fair distribution of goods or to fair procedures for their distribution? Many of these principles are better at indicating what kinds of action should be avoided than at providing guidelines when several alternatives are morally permissable. It is easier, for instance, to determine and censure outright, intentional deceit than to establish guidelines for professional and organizational secrecy, acceptable disclosure of information and permissible exaggeration in negotiations and advertising. The general nature of principled moral reasoning conflicts with specific issues associated with group membership, roles, or organizations.

Consequential

Consequential patterns of moral reasoning focus on the attempt to find the fit between desired ends and means which will yield benefits for the greatest number of people. As individuals deliberate, they use this pattern of reasoning to inquire about probable benefits and losses measured in the short- and long-terms. To be moral, these results must be judged to be good or worthy because

---

Consequential Reasoning — James

The pragmatic method in such cases is to try to interpret each notion by tracing its respective practical consequences . . . . No particular results then, so far, but only an attitude of orientation, is what the pragmatic method means. The attitude of looking away from first things, principles, "categories," supposed necessities; and of looking towards last things, fruits, consequences, facts . . . . Pragmatism, on the other hand, asks its usual question. "Grant an idea or belief to be true," it says, "what concrete difference will its being true make in any one's actual life? How will the truth be realized? What experiences will be different from those which would obtain if the belief were false? What, in short, is the truth's cash-value in experiential terms?"

William James, "What Pragmatism Means" and "Pragmatism's Conception of Truth," *Essays in Pragmatism*. (New York: Hafner Publishing Company, 1948), pages 142, 146, 160.

of their benefits or the excellence they achieve. (Next, the focus shifts to the means available to attain these objectives) Means are justifiable insofar as they help to realize morally good ends. Means not likely to achieve desired benefits are morally questionable: they may involve costs without any corresponding benefits. Morally good objectives, which cannot realistically be attained by available means, are also morally questionable. Unrealistic objectives may occasion either the adoption of questionable means, or expressions of malingering resentment. (Hence, consequential moral reasoning is characterized by the attempt to balance means, ends, and secondary consequences to maximize benefits at minimal costs.)

Consequential Reasoning — Mill

. . . the Greatest Happiness Principle, holds that actions are right in proportion as they tend to promote happiness, wrong as they tend to produce the reverse of happiness. By happiness is intended pleasure and the absence of pain; by unhappiness, pain and the privation of pleasure . . . the happiness which forms the utilitarian standard of what is right in conduct is not the agent's own happiness, but that of all concerned.

John Stuart Mill, "Utilitarianism" in the *Essential Works of John Stuart Mill*, edited by Max Lerner (New York: Bantam Books, 1963) pages 194, 204.

This mode of reasoning has wide appeal. It views moral actions in relation to the good they generate. Those using this form of reasoning assert that there is little moral virtue in abiding by moral rules that do not improve well-being. (Consequential reasoning calls people to consider action that is morally appropriate in considering the benefits and costs that are likely to result.) In the second place, consequential forms of moral reasoning are easy to understand and use. One can attempt to identify, evaluate and balance moral benefits and liabilities without special education or knowledge. In the third place, this form of moral reasoning allows ends to be defined contextually. Which particular moral good people seek to realize is seen as a matter of choice and circumstance. One business might define good in terms of improved services to consumers while another sees its good in relation to satisfying and cooperating with its workforce. In the fourth place, consequential reasoning allows for a critical investigation of the relation between means and ends. Are the benefits desired being achieved? Do the means facilitate or thwart the realization of these ends? Can the ends or means be adjusted to realize a better fit? All these questions can be empirically analyzed in ways that allow for informed discussions.

Consequential forms of moral reasoning are also subject to a <u>number of lim-itations</u>. This form of reasoning provides no basis for excluding morally unac-ceptable means, provided beneficial consequences result. There may be no compelling argument for providing a decent standard wage unless it can be argued that low wages produce disgruntled employees who work less efficiently. This form of reasoning makes the moral status of questionable actions, such as bribery or misleading advertising, uncertain, subject to long-range calculations of overall cost and benefits for intangible and uncertain consequences.

Consequential reasoning is open to tolerating morally questionable actions as well as to losing sight of worthwhile objectives. As managers reflect on the moral benefits they would like to realize, their thinking may well be predeter-mined by their assumptions about available means. They may well lose sight of desired benefits because they are preoccupied by costs. How can a mill elimi-nate toxic matter from its smoke stacks and sewage pipes in a short time with-out burdening themselves with excessive costs they cannot hope to recoup through greater sales or reduced wages? How can a steel mill modernize its equipment at enormous costs especially when the international market has driven down the selling price for steel products? Again some ethicists, using consequential patterns of reasoning, invoke the long-term to provide a way around dilemmas where the judgements based on available means rule out any attempts to pursue a desired moral good. By using a longer time frame, they seek a fit between ends and means that focuses on maximizing moral benefits. Nonetheless, this strategy is often not convincing, especially in turbulent times when long-term projections are difficult to make and the organization is in dan-ger of not surviving the short-term.

Consequential moral reasoning is also <u>morally limited</u> because of its ten-dency to devolve into simple, practical, amoral calculations of costs and bene-fits. Because of its empirical nature, this form of reasoning often seeks to gauge benefits solely in measurable terms. Finally, consequential reasoning is limited because the good it seeks to realize is often imprecise, intangible, or vacuous.[3]

Purposive

Purposive moral reasoning approaches decisions by examining how the <u>intrin-sic purpose</u> of organizations, groups or individuals illuminates present action. Some leaders argue that the intrinsic business of business is to maximize profit and it is wrong to focus on corporate social responsibility unless that can be shown to directly influence stockholder returns. Other business leaders might argue that the purpose of business is to offer moral leadership, even at the cost of return on investment.[4]

In this purposive pattern of reasoning, the objectives of any action cannot be selected either by votes or by considering the balance between objectives and available means. Rather, ends are predetermined by <u>human nature</u>, or commu-nities, or social roles. Moreover, the choice of means is not a matter for discre-

Purposive Reasoning — Aristotle

It is thought that every activity, artistic or scientific, in fact every deliberate action or pursuit, has for its object the attainment of some good. We may therefore assent to the view which has been expressed that 'the good' is 'that at which all things aim' . . . . By human goodness is meant not fineness of physique but a right condition of the soul . . . .

Aristotle, *The Nicomachean Ethics*, translated by J.A.K. Thomson, (Middlesex, England: Penguin Books Ltd., 1953), pages 25, 51.

tion. Rather, <u>fitting means</u> are those actions best suited to realize intrinsic ends. Purposive reasoning assumes a dynamic developmental perspective that identifies the essential character of persons, or organizations, or groups in terms of the purposes they are, by nature, compelled to realize. Moral reasoning is not calculative. People do not seek ways of balancing means, ends and secondary consequences. Instead, reasoning attempts to identify links between predetermined ends and corresponding means. The aim of moral action is not to maximize benefits nor to honor obligations but to excel at realizing and furthering <u>intrinsic purposes.</u>

Purposive Reasoning — Aquinas

First, there is present in man the inclination toward the good on the level of the nature which he shares with all substances, inasmuch as each substance desires the preservation of its own existence according to its own nature . . . . Second, there is present in man an inclination toward some more special things, on the level of the nature which he shares with other animals. And on this level, those things are said to belong to natural law "which nature teaches to all animals" . . . . Third, there is present in man an inclination toward the good that is in accord with the nature of reason, and this is proper to him. Thus, man has a natural inclination toward knowing the truth about God, and toward living in society. On this level, those things within the scope of this inclination pertain to the natural law; for instance, that man should avoid ignorance, that he should not offend those with whom he must associate . . . .

St. Thomas Aquinas, *Summa of Theology I-II*, Q, 94, 2, c. found in *The Pocket Aquinas*, edited by Vernon J. Bourke (New York: Washington Square Press/Pocket Books Publication, 1960), page 198.

This form of reasoning has often been defended by <u>religious ethicists</u>. St. Thomas Aquinas employed purposive reasoning, as did Aristotle, to identify the intrinsic objective of human life, namely unity with God, and the corresponding virtues, the cultivation of which would help realize this end. He identified the purpose of the state and guidelines for political life. Calvin argued that the chief purpose of life was to glorify God. This was pursued by transforming institutions to reflect God's purposes.

Purposive reasoning may be used to examine business activities. In a recent book, Pastin called for greater attention to organizational purpose as a means of gaining perspective on moral issues and promoting organizational success.[5] Freeman and Gilbert argued that the most promising ethical organizational strategies are those which make the identification and implementation of organizational purpose a pre-eminent objective, and Bowie organized his introductory business ethics text by discussing the purpose of business organizations and managerial positions.[6] He argued these included the efficient use of human and natural resources to produce quality goods and services for consumers, and which allowed employees and managers to use and develop skills, and provided investors with fair returns on investment.

It is characteristic of purposive moral reasoning that questions regarding how we should act are addressed by asking, instead, what kind of persons, organizations or managers <u>we wish to be.</u> Questions of action are turned into questions of fundamental moral identity. Actions which correspond, reinforce, and further moral identity are to be encouraged. Actions which compromise moral identity are to be discouraged.

Purposive moral reasoning may be applied both to business organizations and to individual human behavior. In relation to moral issues in advertising, this form of deliberating would ask about the purpose of advertising to inform and solicit consumers by fairly representing advertised products. It might be argued that the essential purpose of sales representatives is to provide high quality services to customers. Human resource managers may use purposive moral reasoning to promote actions which cultivate the trust of employees because they see their function as promoting personal development and the dignity of individuals; controllers may institute audit procedures because they see their essential purpose as the protection of corporate assets and property against a minority of dishonest and irresponsible employees.

Purposive moral reasoning has <u>many strengths</u>. This form of deliberating directs attention to those aims which are intrinsic to particular activities and institutions. Because it is so easy to get distracted by objectives which are not integral to institutions, such as high sales, generous perks, lucrative payoffs, enhanced status, leisure time and increased power, purposive moral reasoning re-asserts the pre-eminence of goods which are essential to the organization. Profit-making, for example, is not an intrinsic purpose of business: it is rather, a sign of economic health and for many a motive for extra effort. The intrinsic aim of business is the production and marketing of useful goods.[7] This form of deliberating allows those making a decision to see the relation between particular judgements and the overall, ongoing purposes of their organization.

Purposive moral reasoning is subject to several limitations. Often it is difficult to achieve consensus on organizational or positional purposes. One stakeholder's purpose may not harmonize with another's. It is often easier to identify specific objectives or particular obligatory standards than to determine institutional character or identity. Precisely because purposes are generally defined, it is often difficult to find direction from considering purposes. Finally, purposive moral reasoning can become dogmatic. Sure of their own understanding of sound management, some people, especially those who hold executive positions, may tolerate little open discussion with regarding an organization's mission or fundamental purpose.

Consensual

The basic premise of consensual moral reasoning is that the best decisions are made by consent. In contrast, bad decisions are those in which compliance is demanded from those who do not consent. To be sure, various factors including a consideration of traditions, general principles, and intrinsic purposes as well as calculations of costs and benefits, may well influence how people are disposed to decide. However, in the end these factors are all relative. The decisive factor involves the informed judgements of those directly involved.

Consensual reasoning is best demonstrated by examining the assumptions regarding informed consent, the virtues of give-and-take argument, reasoned judgements, and collective representation. Consensual reasoning assumes that

---

Consensual Reasoning — Locke

The only way whereby any one divests himself of his natural liberty and puts on the bonds of civil society is by agreeing with other men to join and unite into a community for their comfortable, safe, and peaceable living one amongst another, in a secure enjoyment of their properties and a greater security against any that are not of it . . . . For when any number of men have, by the consent of every individual, made a community, they have thereby made that community one body, with a power to act as one body, which is only by the will and determination of the majority . . . . And thus every man, by consenting with others to make one body politic under one government, puts himself under an obligation to everyone of that society to submit to the determination of the majority . . . .

John Locke, *The Second Treatise of Government*, edited by Thomas P. Reardon (New York: The Liberal Arts Press, 1952), pages 54, 55.

---

decisions, even morally good ones, ought not be forced on people. Insofar as cooperation is solicited, people ought to be fully and objectively informed under circumstances that allow them to choose freely and intelligently. The first requirement of consensual reasoning is that those involved be adequately informed. The second feature of consensual reasoning is the assumption that morally good decisions are reached after an interactive process of discussion and argument. During this process various arguments are likely to be put forward, criticized, and reformulated, as people develop their opinions and attempt to take account of the opinions of others. Give-and-take allows good arguments to become better and more convincing, considers alternatives, and discards poor arguments.

Consensual reasoning presupposes that argument will proceed as people reason rather than simply state unreflective opinions. If discussions of moral issues are to be open and full, then it must be possible to raise questions about the arguments of others and to defend one's own position against criticism.

Finally, consensual reasoning assumes that the best decisions represent collective judgement. Usually the advocates of consensual reasoning assume that the best collective decisions are made by representative councils who act for the larger community. The virtue of these councils is that they allow public deliberation, which is why Europeans often refer to them as parliaments — places for talking.

Consensual reasoning occurs in business whenever smaller or larger groups actively and openly debate issues. This give-and-take may occur among sub-groups of selected managers, employees, and work units. The establishment of quality circles, for example, provides occasions for free-wheeling discussion between employees and managers about how work is to be done. When mining companies meet regularly with environmental groups to exchange views about issues such as acid rain, this type of reasoning takes place.

As a mode of deliberating, consensual reasoning shifts the focus from types of reasons and beliefs to the process of arguing as an interactive and self-correcting action. Consensual reasoning focuses on process because it makes two assumptions about human reasoning and ethics. This pattern of deliberating recognizes more fully than other perspectives discussed so far, the limits of human reason and the historical particularity of most moral judgements. The capacity of human reason to resolve moral dilemmas is limited by human ignorance, by the diversity of moral beliefs and types of reasoning, and by the unpredictability of human developments. Acknowledging the plurality of perspectives and points of view, consensual reasoning seeks to generate consensus through informed public debate. Consensual reasoning seeks to minimize ignorance by active consultation. Finally those using consensual reasoning acknowledge the historical significance of their judgements. They argue and make decisions, not to establish universally valid principles, but to deal with particular problems in specific settings.

Consensual Reasoning — Rousseau

. . . . social order is a right — a sacred right, which serves as the basis for all other rights; it does not, that is to say, flow from force. Yet it does not flow from nature either. It therefore rests upon agreements . . . . The oldest of societies, and the only society that is in any sense natural, is the family. Yet we must not overlook the role of agreements even here; the children do not remain tied to the father beyond the period during which they have need of him in order to preserve themselves . . . If they continue together, they no longer do so out of natural necessity but rather out of choice, so that thenceforth even the family keeps itself alive only by agreement . . . . No man, as we have seen, has any natural authority over his fellow-man, and might, as we have seen also, makes no right. We have nothing left save agreements, then, to serve as a basis for all legitimate authority among men . . . .

Jean-Jacques Rousseau, *The Social Contract*, translated and edited by Willmoors Kendall (Chicago: Henry Regnery Company, 1954), pages 2, 3, 6 (From Book I, chps. 1, 4).

Consensual reasoning is susceptible to a number of limitations. Outvoted minorities often feel that their rights, their interests, and their moral arguments are ignored. Sometimes majorities feel the same way when particular elites dominate the process of deliberation and control the councils where decisions are made. The process of consensual deliberation may be undermined if those making decisions fail to represent the concerns and arguments of those affected by their judgements. The major weakness of consensual reasoning is its susceptibility to becoming excessively politicized. Even when the problems of minority and majority rule and opinion-mongering are contained, consensual reasoning remains vulnerable to manipulation by powerful political interests. Consensual reasoning goes astray when public debate is controlled and limited, and moved along more by reference to the power of those speaking than by reference to the cogency of their arguments. Because people are likely to influence discussions and are inclined to exert the force of their positions, it is difficult to prune consensual reasoning of its political character. This political character can, at times, threaten to undermine consensual reasoning as a process of rational deliberation.

Subjective

We use the word "subjective" to identify those forms of moral reasoning which argue that individuals should make choices and provide reasons which authen-

Subjective Reasoning — Smith

When I endeavour to examine my own conduct, when I endeavour to pass sentence upon it, and either to approve or condemn it, it is evident that, in all such cases, I divide myself, as it were, into two persons; and that I, the examiner and judge, represent a different character from that other I, the person whose conduct is examined into and judged of... and it is only by consulting this judge within that we can ever see what relates to ourselves in its proper shape and dimensions; or that we can ever make any proper comparison between our own interests and those of other people.

Adam Smith, *The Theory of Moral Sentiments* (Indianapolis: Liberty Classics, 1969, 1976), pages 206, 232 (Part II, chps. 1, 3).

tically reflect their own personal commitments.) Subjective reasoning means acting on conscience. When making decisions, individuals reflect on their own convictions, capacities, limitations, and contingencies, and then make decisions based on their own views and capabilities. Moral deliberation is a personal, reflective activity. The ideal is to act with integrity, not being set off course by tempting choices which do not harmonize with personal commitments.

(A variety of philosophical and therapeutic movements have argued for subjective moral reasoning.) Many Epicureans and Stoics viewed moral reasoning in these terms, insisting that individuals ought to reflect seriously on their own goals and commitments and act in keeping with them.[8] Psychoanalytically influenced ethicists like Fromm make a similar argument. Fromm maintains that individuals ought not allow themselves to be misled by the ethics of others: they should devise their own ethics, grounded on affirming their own being.[9] Existentialists assume a parallel position. Every person is thrown into a world not of their own construction; they should resolutely acknowledge the limits placed on their lives and act with care.[10] Subjective reasoning is defended as well by Intuitionists. This form of deliberating is, however, most commonly encountered not as it is articulated by various philosophers but as it is used by consultants, teachers and counsellors in value clarification exercises. These exercises are used to encourage people to think about the convictions they already hold but have not clearly analyzed. People are encouraged, not only to become more self-aware, but also to assign priorities to their convictions and become more confident defending their commitments.

(The most obvious characteristic of subjective reasoning is the activity of personal reflection.) With subjective reasoning distinctions between knowing, feeling, and willing are discarded. Thinking is a passionate and cognitive activi-

Subjective Reasoning — Sartre

Man is nothing else but that which he makes of himself. That is the first principle of existentialism. And this is what people call its "subjectivity"... man is responsible for what he is... man is condemned to be free. ...the destiny of man is placed within himself... the one thing which permits him to have life is the deed. Upon this level therefore, what we are considering is an ethic of action and self-commitment... Man makes himself; he is not found ready-made; he makes himself by the choice of his morality, and he cannot but choose a morality, such is the pressure of circumstances upon him...

Jean-Paul Sartre, "Existentialism is a Humanism" in *Existentialism From Dostoevsky to Sartre*, edited and translated by Walter Kaufmann (New York: Meridian Books, Inc., 1956) pages 291, 295, 302, 306.

ty. Full self-knowledge cannot be attained without consulting one's feelings, including one's aspirations, affirmations, and doubts.[11] Reasoning itself is viewed as a reflective activity, that finds truth from deeper meanings and authentic insights.[12] One aim of reasoning is the attainment of personal insights that clarify the issues at hand.[13]

Subjective reasoning can be applied to moral issues in business in several ways. Managers may opt for subjective reasoning especially when they face conflicts between company policies and their own personal convictions. Having made a commitment to give up smoking because of its dangers to health, can an advertising executive, in good conscience, take on a tobacco company as a client? How can a sales manager at once interact in his own organization with one set of standards and interact with foreign sales people with another? Managers resort to personal reflections on their own commitments, both when they are considering blowing the whistle or quitting, and when they are attempting to act with integrity in different cultural environments. As the ideal of executive integrity itself gains prominence, subjective reasoning will become more widely and frequently employed. Individuals will consider how they ought to act so they remain true to their own consciences.[14]

Subjective reasoning has two special strengths. First, as we reason subjectively, we must recognize that the choices we make or consent to are really our own. We must assume responsibility no matter what logic we use. We may have invoked honored traditions, universal principles, sacred purposes, greater benefits, and the willing support of those affected. Nonetheless, if things turn out differently than we expect, we must take full responsibility for the consequences. The same is true, of course, if things turn out as we expect or better. Second, this mode of reasoning, more than others, directly appeals to our sense of conscience. As a result, reasoning subjectively often arouses and sustains our motivation to act more than other forms of reasoning. Individuals are much more likely to act when their reasons for acting are closely connected with a personal sense of who they are and what they believe in.

Subjective reasoning is vulnerable to several limitations. This form of reasoning provides no basis for determining how groups of people or organizations ought to behave. It remains personal and individual. At best it can only complement other forms of reasoning which address questions about corporate and social action more directly. This form of reasoning provides no rational basis for resolving disagreements between people. Although it helps people determine their own roles in organizations, it does not provide organizational direction. Depending on which particular expression of subjective reasoning — whether Existentialist, Stoic, Intuitionist, Psychotherapeutic — and depending on personal interpretations of these views, individuals may state reasons for acting that are only more or less comprehensible to others.

Charismatic

We use the word "charismatic" to identify a seventh type of moral reasoning, which involves deference to a person or work of literature with an invested authority to resolve moral issues. The basic idea is that some people or documents are more able to find compromises, to articulate moral visions, and to inspire others. Charismatic figures inspire confidence and commitment because of their capacity to invoke powerful visions and elicit personal commitment from those who defer to them. Their messages are considered wise and valid, not by virtue of tradition or logic, but by virtue of their source and popular appeal.

The most obvious charismatic examples are religious prophets, political visionaries, and sacred texts. Many people seek to resolve their own moral dilemmas by consulting the wisdom of others. Many people have determined how they should behave by asking whether particular acts are allowed or required by the Bible, the Koran, Rabbinic Responsa, the works of Karl Marx or the Book of Mormon. Others in turn regularly consult their Hassidic Rebbe, their Imam or Papal Encyclicals. It is worth noting that the compelling aura of charismatic figures or writing arises from the fact that so many people trust them and identify with them. Charisma for the most part is in the eye of the devoted follower, not in the characteristics of these figures.[15]

Charismatic reasoning cannot be dismissed as wholly irrational. Rather, as a form of reasoning, it is especially characterized by imagination and by balancing and integrating opposing factors. Charismatic reasoning does not usually consist of blind deference to authority. Rather, charismatic reasoning consists in the imaginative capacity to connect basic truths to particular settings in ways that seem particularly fitting. The ancient Israelite King Solomon exemplified charismatic reasoning by being able to determine which of two women who claimed to be the mother of a child was in fact the real mother by knowing what kinds of questions to ask.

Charismatic reasoning has influenced business practices in two different ways. On the one hand, as devoted Christians, Jews, and Muslims, managers have at times deferred to the rulings of sacred authorities with issues regarding interest payments.[16] On the other hand, many business people defer to particular executives as charismatic authorities themselves. A number of executives have exercised charismatic authority over their organizations, such as Ford of the automobile company, Watson of IBM, Iaccoca of Chrysler, Welch of General Electric, and de Gaspe Beaubien of Telemedia. In recent years advocates of charismatic leadership have argued that executives are particularly able to provide the kind of vision and energy to transform otherwise stagnant organizations. Because these leaders are able to elicit the support of co-workers and articulate compelling visions, they are able to inspire greater industry and increased commitment. Most importantly, they are able to spell out reasons for acting that seem credible and immediate. They transform work into a worthwhile mission.[17]

The appeal of charismatic reasoning is twofold. In the first place, this kind of reasoning, more than others we have examined, embodies contemporary wisdom. Charismatic reasoning often seems multi-dimensional, as it connects various considerations into larger, more encompassing holistic visions. Many people who defer to biblical rulings, for example, do so not out of narrow-minded conviction that these particular rulings are especially inspired, but out of respect for biblical teachings as a whole. Unlike traditional reasoning, charismatic reasoning is believed to be intrinsically contemporary. The charismatic prophet gains a following from those who believe their situation is being addressed. Those who adhere to sacred texts do so because they believe them to be of timeless relevance. In the second place, charismatic reasoning, like traditional reasoning, gains appeal because it provides a basis for, and reinforces, communal loyalties. Charismatic figures often serve as symbolic representatives for communities of people. A sense of loyalty is strengthened by identification with the charismatic figure.

There are several limitations to charismatic moral reasoning. This type of reasoning may be prophetic and inspiring, but it does not allow for discursive criticism and debate. The messages are unique. One may dissent or distance oneself from such a vision. It is difficult, however, to enter into a mutual discussion in the hope of proposing alternatives. As a result, while those citing charismatic messages sometimes succeed in identifying encompassing visions, they are not very amenable to negotiating resolutions with those who use principled, consequential or consensual arguments. Compromises rob visionary messages of their charisma.

RELATIVITY AND RESPONSIBLE DECISION-MAKING

When we recognize that there are several different ways of deliberating about moral issues, we are confronted with the problem of attempting to choose which

Forms of Reasoning	Strengths, Advantages, Special Appeals	Weaknesses, Limitations, Disadvantages
Traditional	Reliance on past experience and wisdom. Precedents are often emblematic of community.	Precedents may be arbitrary and may preclude innovations and adaptations.
Principled	Helps to avoid self-serving arguments. Universal arguments are morally persuasive. Heightens sense of certitude regarding rights and obligations.	Principles may be overly abstract and unresponsive to contextual setting. Principles tend to ignore communal loyalties. Principles may serve as check to immoral acts but not as guides to constructive action.
Consequential	Focuses on maximizing benefits. Reduces questions of means to calculable gauges. Easily understandable way of reasoning. Recognizes importance of contextual setting.	Practicality becomes a substitute for moral issues. May deteriorate into pure cost/benefit analysis which ignores issues of justice. Tendency to treat means as morally indifferent, focusing only on ends.
Purposive	Raises fundamental questions regarding goods which are integral and intrinsic to our institutions and activities. Considers activities by raising question of identity and character.	Not always easy to reach agreement regarding essential purposes or ends. May become unyielding and dogmatic with respect to particular views.
Consensual	Appeals to active consent of those involved. Invites open-ended conversation about moral issues.	Consensus-forming process may be manipulated by minorities. Process may neglect out voted minorities. Process may lead to politicization of moral issues and opinion-polling.
Subjective	Appeals to sense of personal responsibility, integrity and conscience.	Reasoning tends to be private and personal. Provides no rational basis for discussing and resolving disagreements.
Charismatic	Allows for deference to those who have exhibited clear moral wisdom and leadership. Reinforces communal feelings.	Reasoning process tends to be arbitrary and undebatable.

FIGURE 6.2 **Strengths and Weaknesses of Schools of Ethical Reasoning**

is most appropriate. As the previous discussion shows, and as Figure 6.2 summarizes, there are strengths and weaknesses to each school of moral reasoning. It is clear that people think about moral issues differently, they use varied moral languages, and reach contrasting and at times opposing conclusions. This diversity does not result simply from variations in personal points of view, as a naive relativist might argue.[18] These differences matter. The fact of diversity causes misunderstandings and disagreements, but this problem need not be intractable. The forthright recognition of diversity renders the problem more manageable, and morally responsible decision-making can provide a workable means for dealing with this diversity.

The first step in addressing this problem responsibly is to recognize that it cannot be solved by identifying or creating a universal moral Esperanto, a pattern of moral discourse that will be universally accepted. Certain philosophers have attempted to disagree however. For example, natural law theorists argued that the principles they identified by their reasoning were principles which all humans could assent to on the basis of consistent reasoning. Believing that the principles of natural law were limited and arbitrary, Hume assumed that he had identified an even more universally valid ethic when he observed that people everywhere established moral standards to enhance human well-being. Kant criticized Hume's theory which, he argued, did not distinguish between amoral hypothetical imperatives designed simply to achieve particular ends, and genuinely moral imperatives which were universal. This debate continues, articulated by contemporary philosophers who hope to find a universally valid foundation for all moral judgements.[19] However, the arguments of these proponents have resulted, not in substantial agreement, but in ongoing debates and increasingly refined disagreements.[20]

Our approach is less ambitious. We believe that the best way to cope with moral diversity is to recognize four factors:

- that there are significant agreements about moral standards which cut across cultures;
- that a process of in-depth discussion is beneficial and essential;
- that different situations call for different types of moral reasoning;
- that it may be necessary and useful to combine different patterns of reasoning to deal with different issues.

Common Moral Standards

It is useful to acknowledge agreements about a number of common moral judgements. For example, anthropologists have discovered cross-cultural consensus prohibiting stealing, lying, causing of needless injury, and incest as well as parental standards and communal responsibilities. Universally, cultures expect people to keep promises, to reward acts of courage and charity, and to forbid slavery. Increasingly, people believe that humans possess certain inalienable rights as individuals, even though there are varied track records with respect to the protection of those rights.[21]

We have identified a broad number of standards with respect to fitting conduct as well as standards of intrinsic excellence which businesses ought to pursue. Thus, in spite of the fact that we may use quite different reasoning patterns, we often agree, at a general level, to a number of significant moral standards.

In-depth, Recursive Discussions

This moral diversity can be managed by engaging in reasoned in-depth debate with those who hold different perspectives about the moral issues at hand. To be sure, several forms of deliberating rely more heavily on uncontrollable factors, such as majority views, charismatic prophesy, and personal integrity, than do others. However, by arguing with others we can learn about different points of view. Through give-and-take we can modify our own views and attempt to take the views of others into account.

Situation-Based Moral Reasoning

The problem of moral diversity becomes more manageable when we recognize that particular forms of reasoning are used more appropriately in different settings and with different audiences. Decisions are made differently by individuals and organizations. Different arguments are used as people work towards a judgement and communicate that judgement convincingly to others. It is a mistake to ignore variations in setting and audience. Variations in settings directly affect the roles people play: as chief executives, they have different decision-making responsibilities than as line supervisors or as non-managerial employees. Different normative expectations accompany each of these roles. These expectations do influence how we deliberate about moral issues. Similarly, variations in audiences influence how we can attempt to persuade others to agree with us or consent to our recomendations. When we vary how we communicate moral reason we often explain this diversity by referring to cultural differences. Cultural variations may be associated with professional, organizational, social, ethnic, national and religious differences. Clearly, to be understood it is necessary to translate one's arguments into prevailing cultural idioms.

Variations in setting and audience help to explain why people in different circumstances are likely to use different patterns of moral reasoning. We can illustrate this kind of diversity by examining briefly the relevance of specific forms of reasoning for particular settings or audiences. For example, whenever a group of people, whether directors or supervisors, have to work closely with each other on an ongoing basis, consensual reasoning is especially appropriate. Other forms of reasoning may be used while final decisions are reached through argumentation and group decision-making. However, decisions about whether to dissent from, or comply with, morally troubling policies may best be made by subjective reasoning. Sometimes, charismatic reasoning is effectively used when there is a need to mobilize popular support for policies. At the same time traditional reasoning is often used with equal effectiveness for the same objective, since the citing of familiar precedents gives credibility. While purposive reasoning may be utilized to gain perspective on very difficult matters, eventual decisions may be communicated in consequential and principled arguments that are more readily understood. As we have already observed, each of these modes of reasoning possess specific virtues and limitations, which render them more or less suitable for moral deliberation in different circumstances.

(Variations in the uses of moral reasoning are influenced by the diversity of settings and audiences of moral deliberations.) In making this point we are not endorsing role and social group relativism.[22] Role and social group relativists make arguments which appear to be similar but differ in that relativists simply invoke prevailing practices, and do not make any moral claims. Practices and customs have no moral status by themselves. Relativists may attempt to justify their own positions by invoking either the existing normative expectations or by the prevailing moral conventions of their groups. Relativists excuse their own judgements by arguing that alternatives are not possible because of the weighty influence of norms and conventions, and can be criticized for substituting abbreviated excuses for genuine moral arguments.

COMBINING MORAL REASONING PATTERNS

No one form of reasoning is entirely adequate in dealing with moral issues that arise in business, and in fact, the exclusive use of any one form may render people blind to considerations of moral weight. Principled, purposive, and consequential reasoning provide the basic frameworks for intelligent, fruitful public debates on business practices. Purposive reasoning emphasizes the good we seek to realize; principled reasoning emphasizes the right and wrong forms of conduct we allow, encourage or censure; consequential reasoning calls for us to balance considerations in relation to realistic appraisals of actual conditions. These three forms of reasoning check and balance each other. No matter how worthy the good is which we seek to realize, principled reasoning reminds us that there are ways of acting that remain morally intolerable. Lest we become too focused on specific rules, or the absence of rules, purposive reasoning reminds us about our moral identities as guides for action. So we do not become too idealistic or too principled, consequential reasoning reminds us that the ultimate objective of moral action is to maintain or enhance the actual well-being of those likely to be affected by our decisions.

It is impossible to establish any permanent ranking among the purposive, consequential, and principled forms of moral reasoning. We do believe that purposive reasoning ought to be used early on in moral deliberation so that those involved think about the essential moral purposes of their institutions, offices, and activities. For the same reason that we argued that the setting of clear objectives ought to occur early on in moral deliberation, we maintain that purposive reasoning ought to be used to explore the relationship between policy objectives and the overall mission of organizations. This reasoning puts issues into a perspective, grounded not on changing goals but on the essential purpose of institutional existence. Principled and consequential reasoning operate, much like a tag team, pushing and pulling, to keep in focus the relationship of means and ends to actual consequences and decisions which are acceptable and unacceptable according to principles. One of the particular roles of principled reasoning is to identify generally applicable ethical standards.

(Subjective and charismatic patterns of reasoning are especially inapplicable for reaching decisions regarding corporate policy.) Neither allow for give-and-take debate. Traditional moral reasoning is a useful guide rather than a fundamental basis for judgements. The traditions of any single business or industry are likely to be too narrow, too sparse, and too diverse to serve as an ultimate guide for decision-making.

We have not yet discussed our ranking of consensual reasoning. When this form of reasoning is viewed in relation to its final product, namely consent by some form of vote or statement of willingness to comply, this form of reasoning functions as a secondary guide to communicate to those making decisions what people are likely to comply with or tolerate. Consensual reasoning fosters a process of debate and argumentation. We may illustrate the uses of consensual reasoning by the following example. A manufacturing company with high risk technology polls its workers to determine whether they would agree to a mandatory drug testing program of all employees. This poll provides the company with workers' opinions. It also provides senior management with guidance on what is likely to be acceptable. Senior managers then discuss the issue among themselves. Consensual reasoning is now carried on in its public form as managers argue with each other, stating their reasons and criticizing the arguments of others, responding to criticisms, adjusting positions to take the views of others into account, and seeking a reasonable resolution.

SUMMARY

We make moral judgements as human beings in different contexts and assume responsibility for those decisions. These decisions are made by individuals who use reasoning to guide their reflections. In the process we may use, or at least consider, arguments posed in relation to all seven models of moral reasoning.

Insofar as we use principled, purposive and consequential reasoning, and seek to translate their meanings across cultural lines, our arguments will be comprehensible to people of different backgrounds. We believe this is morally desirable. Nonetheless, in the end, the responsible moral judgement, no matter how rationally articulated, involves risk. Guided by diverse considerations, we make the best judgements we can.

SUGGESTED READINGS

Aristotle, *The Nicomachean Ethics*. Translated by J.A.K. Thomson. Middlesex: Penguin Books, 1953.

Derry, R. "Moral Reasoning in Work-Related Conflicts." *Research in Corporate Social Performance and Policy*, Vol. 9, JAI Press, Inc. (1987) 25-49.

Derry, Robbin and Ronald M. Green. "Ethical Theory in Business Ethics: A Critical Assessment." *Journal of Business Ethics*, 1989.

Frankena, William K. *Ethics*. Englewood Cliffs, N.J.: Prentice-Hall, 1963.

Kant, Immanuel. *Fundamental Principles of the Metaphysics of Morals*. Translated by Thomas K. Abbott, New York: The Liberal Arts Press, 1949.

Mill, John Stuart. *Utilitarianism*. (New York: Bantam Books, 1961).

NOTES FOR CHAPTER SIX

1   Our model is similar to that developed by Kohlberg, although it is not developmental. Kohlberg identified six sequentially ordered stages of moral reasoning, which he sub-divided into pre-conventional, conventional, and post-conventional groupings. On the basis of empirical tests conducted in varied settings and in different countries, he argued that most North American children justified their moral decisions on the basis of pre-conventional moral arguments which defined the first two stages of his model. He concluded as well, that by late adolescence or adulthood, most North Americans defended their moral choices using the conventional modes of arguing typical of the third and fourth stages of his model. Only rarely or occasionally did some adults exhibit the post-conventional forms of reasoning which corresponded to the fifth, sixth and subsequently added seventh stages of his model. As a moralist, Kohlberg defended the forms of reasoning characteristic of the sixth and seventh stages because they were principled and altruistic. Lawrence Kohlberg, *The Philosophy of Moral Development* (San Francisco: Harper and Row, 1981); Lawrence Kohlberg, *The Psychology of Moral Development* (San Francisco: Harper and Row, 1984).

2   Sissela Bok, *Lying* (New York: Pantheon Books, 1978); Stanley I. Benn, "Privacy, Freedom and Respect for Persons," *Privacy*, Nomos, Vol. 13, edited by J. Roland Pennock and John W. Chapman (New York: Atherton Press, 1971): 1-26; Charles Fried, "Privacy: A Rational Context," *An Anatomy of Values* (Cambridge: Harvard University Press, 1970), chp. IX.

3   Amitai Etzioni, *The Moral Dimension: Towards A New Economics* (New York: The Free Press, 1988; London: Collier Macmillan, 1988).

4   Milton Friedman, "The Social Responsibility of Business is to Increase its Profits," *New York Times Magazine* (September 13, 1970).

5   Mark Pastin, *The Hard Problems of Management* (San Francisco: Jossey-Bass, 1986), chp. 8.

6   R. Edward Freeman and Daniel R. Gilbert, Jr., *Corporate Strategy and Search for Ethics* (Englewood Cliffs, N.J.: Prentice-Hall, 1988), chp. 4; Norman Bowie, *Business*

Ethics (Englewood Cliffs, N.J.: Prentice-Hall, 1982), chps. 2,3; see also Etzioni, op.cit., Part I; Thomas M. Garrett and Richard J. Klonuski, *Business Ethics*, Second Edition (Englewood Cliffs, N.J.: Prentice-Hall, 1986, 1966), Chps. 1, 2.

7   Peter Drucker, *Management: Tasks, Responsibilities, Practices* (New York: Harper and Row, 1973).

8   Marcus Aurelius, *Meditations* (Baltimore: Penguin Books, 1966); Epictectus. Enchiridion (Chicago: Henry Regnery Company, 1956).

9   Eric Fromm, *Man For Himself; An Inquiry into the Psychology of Ethics* (New York, Rinehart, 1947).

10   Martin Heidegger, *Being and Time*, translated by John Macquarrie and Edward Robinson (London: SCM Press, 1962; Oxford: Blackwell, 1961).

11   Michael Polanyi, *Personal Knowledge; Towards a Post-Critical Philosophy* (Chicago: University of Chicago Press, 1958), chps. 6, 8, 9, 10.

12   Friedrich W. Neitzsche, "Beyond Good and Evil" in *The Philosophy of Nietzsche*, translated by Marianne Cowan (New York: Modern Library, 1927, 1957).

13   Herbert Fingarette, *The Self in Transformation* (New York: Basic Books, 1963), chps. 1, 2; Walter E. Conn, *Conscience* (Birmingham, Ala.: Religious Education Press, 1981), Part Three.

14   Suresh Srivastva and Associates, *Executive Integrity: The Search for High Human Values in Organizational Life* (San Francisco: Jossey-Bass, 1988).

15   Max Weber, "Types of Legitimate Domination" and "Charisma and Its Transformation" in *Economy and Society*, edited by Guenther Roth and Claus Wittich (Berkeley: University of California Press, 1968, 1978), Part One, chp. 3 and Part Two, chp. 14; Chester Barnard, *The Functions of the Executive* (Cambridge: Harvard University Press, 1938).

16   Benjamin Nelson, *Usury: The History of an Idea* (New York: The Free Press, 1949); Aaron Levine, *Free Enterprise and Jewish Law* (New York: KTAV Publishing House, Inc., Yeshiva University, 1980).

17   Jay A. Conger and Rabindra N. Kanungo and Associates, *Charismatic Leadership: The Elusive Factor in Organizational Effectiveness* (San Francisco: Jossey-Bass, 1988).

18   Freeman and Gilbert, op. cit., chp. 2.

19   Alan Donagan, *The Theory of Morality* (Chicago: The University of Chicago Press, 1977); Alan Gewirth, *Reason and Morality* (Chicago: The University of Chicago Press, 1978).

20   MacIntyre, op. cit.; Jeffrey Stout, *Ethics After Babel: The Languages of Morals and Their Discontents* (Boston: Beacon Press, 1988).

21   May Edel and Abraham Edel, *Anthropology and Ethics: The Quest for Moral Understanding* (Cleveland: The Press of Case Western Reserve University, 1968).

22   Freeman and Gilbert, op. cit., chp. 2

- stakeholder model
- moral standard
  ↳ obligation to stakeholder.
- moral standard rating scale
- purity of motives

7 Ethically Responsible Organizations

Morally good management is characterized not only by the capacity to identify and respond to relevant moral issues, and by competently making ethical decisions, but also by the pursuit of moral objectives. But before we can consider what managers can and should do to create and sustain ethically responsible organizations, we have to tackle a more immediate question: what does an ethically responsible organization mean? How would one decide if an organization was morally responsible? Organizational leaders and critics must use some kind of yardstick to measure their current status and future development.

MORAL REALITIES

We suggest that the morally responsible business organization strives to achieve moral objectives, including being socially responsible to the communities in which it does business, producing products and services which provide good value for customers, compliance with relevant social conventions and laws, using and conserving all its resources effectively, and others. While it is difficult, if not practically impossible, for organizations to excel at a wide range of moral objectives all at the same time, organizations may and ought to meet minimal standards with respect to many of them. Attempts to excel in any of these dimensions of a good organization entail costs in terms of extra efforts and sacrifices, and may well limit its ability to achieve in other areas.

People and organizations inevitably make moral mistakes. Sometimes, faced with hard choices, they opt for an expedient decision. Frequently, in retrospect, they recognize errors of judgement or judgements that were less than scrupulous. Often, the pursuit of moral objectives is shunted aside, delayed, or assigned a lesser importance as organizations and executives are distracted by opportunities to advance their own power, by challenges to their current positions, or by risks to their corporate survival.

THE STAKEHOLDER MODEL FOR MORALLY RESPONSIBLE ORGANIZATIONS

Corporate organizations can be evaluated by their moral commitment to major stakeholder groups: stockholders, employees and annuitants, customers, suppliers, competitors, and society (see Figure 7.1). Organizational conduct can be evaluated using scales which measure the extent to which organizations meet minimal obligations toward stakeholders, fail to meet them, or exceed them. But to be useful to the organization, this evaluation must be candid and forthright.

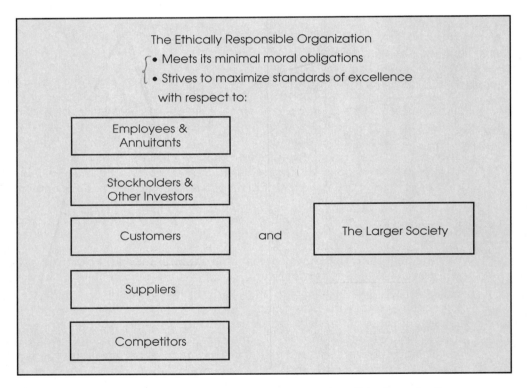

FIGURE 7.1 **The Stakeholder Model of Ethically Responsible Organizations**

The stakeholder model for judging the moral performance of businesses has a number of advantages over alternative ways of gauging corporate morality. This model recognizes that the morality of organizations is multi-dimensional.

Often corporations are praised or castigated because of their relations with certain stakeholders. A pharmaceutical company recalled medicine that the public feared might be dangerous because of several incidents that resulted in death. The recalls cost millions of dollars but the ongoing repute of the company for reliable products was safeguarded. While such an action ought to be applauded, it is still fitting to inquire how characteristic it is of relations with other stakeholders. A petroleum company with otherwise good records for safety, community action, and employee relations, was responsible for a sizable oil spill. While the damage caused must be considered serious, it remains to be seen whether this accident should be considered typical and symptomatic of the moral responsibility of the company.

Other indicators may be used to determine a company's moral commitment. We may consider whether organizations match employee contributions to charities, whether they have been indicted for violations of anti-trust statutes, whether they have used inside information to make successful bids for government contracts, and so forth. Some researchers even suggest that indicators such as whether an organization is unionized, or whether it has laid people off in the last few years are related to the ethical performance.[1] These and other questions are useful indicators for gauging the social performance of organizations although they fall short of being reliable or valid measures of ethical performance. However, we do believe that these questions ought to be raised in relation to more general principles used to evaluate the conduct of business organizations in relation to their stakeholders.

This model of the ethically responsible organization reinforces the conviction that businesses exist and thrive only by virtue of their ongoing interactions with relevant stakeholders. This model is relational and dynamic. It draws our attention not to long lists of rules but to the character of ongoing interactions between business organizations and constituents. Many businesses have developed handbooks or codes stating organizational standards with respect to varied activities. Most of these policy statements amount to lists of ideals and prohibitions. Johnson and Johnson's, creed, "Our Credo," first formulated in 1945 (see Figure 7.2), differs slightly but significantly. As an organizational code of ethics, it is distinctive because it is brief and simple and because it expresses, reflects, and helps to reinforce an organizational ethos that seems real and important to the people who work there. What is interesting is the way it assumes and underlines a stakeholder view of organizational ethics. The beliefs listed are grouped in order to communicate that this organization will responsibly interact with its stakeholders where issues will affect the company-stakeholder relationship.

When we morally evaluate organizations, we do so to gauge their strengths and weaknesses, and to establish benchmarks for ethical reform. Correspondingly, the standards we use should allow us to judge the relative moral stature of these organizations. Organizations can honestly appraise their developments, recognize the costs involved in instituting genuine reforms (as well as potential benefits), and acknowledge areas where their performance is morally better or worse than others.

Johnson and Johnson's <u>Credo</u> [2]

Customers

We believe our first responsibility is to the doctors, nurses and patients, to mothers and all others who use our products and services.
In meeting their needs everything we do must be of high quality.
We must constantly strive to reduce our costs in order to maintain reasonable prices.
Customers' orders must be serviced promptly and accurately.

Suppliers and Distributors

Our suppliers and distributors must have an opportunity to make a fair profit.

Employees

We are responsible to our employees, the men and women who work with us throughout the world.
Everyone must be considered as an individual.
We must respect their dignity and recognize their merit.
They must have a sense of security in their jobs.
Compensation must be fair and adequate, and working conditions clean, orderly and safe.
Employees must feel free to make suggestions and complaints.
There must be equal opportunity for employment, development and advancement for those qualified.

We must provide competent management, and their actions must be just and ethical.

The Larger Society

We are responsible to the communities in which we live and work and to the world community as well.
We must be good citizens — support good works and charities and bear our fair share of taxes.
We must encourage civic improvements and better health and education.
We must maintain in good order the property we are privileged to use, protecting the environment and natural resources.

Resources

Our final responsibility is to our stockholders.
Business must make a sound profit.
We must experiment with new ideas.
Research must be carried on, innovative programs developed and mistakes paid for.
New equipment must be purchased, new facilities provided and new products launched.
Reserves must be created to provide for adverse times.
When we operate according to these principles the stockholders should realize a fair return.

MORAL STANDARDS

(Basic to the assessment of the relative moral stature of organizations is the distinction between standards which constitute minimal obligations and those which comprise standards of excellence) <u>Minimal obligations</u> must be met. The failure to do so is morally wrong. No matter what else, organizations must reduce and attempt to eliminate wrongs, but because humans are often motivated by self-interest and seek their own power and advantage, eliminating wrongs is not always easy.

There are other moral standards which organizations and individuals often strive to attain — standards of excellence. These ideals may be difficult to attain, despite the fact that they may be both intrinsically and extrinsically rewarding. Failure to attain these standards of excellence does not usually bring external criticism or reprisals which might well be the consequence of failure to meet the minimal obligations.

There may be many different ways of stating both minimal obligations and ideals for organizational performance with respect to stakeholders. Clearly, a person's sense of what constitutes the obligations of a business enterprise is shaped by political ideology and may well be couched in self-interest. The following set of minimal and ideal expectations is culled from the vast number of corporate codes of conduct, ethics guides, and statements of purpose that corporations produce and distribute. They reflect a North American corporate consensus. There are references to issues (such as the environment) which might not have been included in a similar list twenty-five years ago. We also expect that this list will change over time.

Obligations to Investors

People who invest in the common and preferred stocks of companies have a right to expect the management of the enterprise to look after their investment and to try to improve the value of this investment by taking prudent risks commensurate with the stated risk profile of the company. This may vary with the type of company and the type of stock. For example, stock in junior exploration companies carries with it a certain expectation of risk that the informed investor understands and this expectation would be different for preferred shareholders of a major chartered bank.

At a minimum, managers should act with prudence and should not make investments and undertake business ventures which are incompatible with stockholders' expectations. They should not, for example, make a leveraged buy-out bid which so burdens the company with debt that the value of the company's regular bonds or preferred shares is severely affected. At a minimum, stockholders should be kept informed of developments which might have a material impact on their investment and they should receive clear and honest reporting of financial information.[3]

Some stockholder responsibilities go beyond minimal obligations. Management may state performance objectives in shareholder reports and explain their performance in relation to these objectives. They may structure their companies to ensure that all shareholders, whether large or small, receive the same price for their shares in a takeover situation. Some companies report extensively and openly on their performance, make executives and managers available to shareholders for questions and enquiries, and encourage questions and discussions at annual meetings. Such companies often tie executive compensation to shareholder value, seeking to make the interests of shareholders and senior management more convergent. They may use cumulative voting for directors, so that minority shareholders are represented in major policy decisions and they may also specify a significant number of external directors who represent shareholders as well as the management team.

(While managers clearly have responsibilities to investors, they also have responsibility for managing their firm's internal resources efficiently over time.) This responsibility may be viewed both substantively, as their organizational responsibility, and formally as their responsibility to keep account of the firm's activities, assets and liabilities. Substantively, managers are expected to do what is good for their organizations as a whole, in the process seeking to reduce needless waste, to resolve dysfunctional conflicts, to facilitate cooperation, and to increase efficient uses of capital, fiscal, natural and human resources. Formally, management is expected to keep strict accounts to ensure that these resources are used as intended. Ideally, internal auditing procedures ought to enable firms to keep track of their activities as a whole, the processes as well as the result, the parts as well as the whole, thereby expanding the role of the internal audit function to focus on business practices, broadly defined, rather than just the integrity of the financial reporting system.

> "The company endeavors to provide an appropriate return to shareholders through its dividend policies and through growth in the value of its assets . . . . Shareholders are encouraged to identify with the company, to take an interest in its affairs and to develop informed positions on vital issues . . . . The company communicates with shareholders candidly and promptly, providing the information necessary to evaluate the management and investment worth of the company. In providing this information, the company meets and, in most cases, exceeds the mandatory requirements."
>
> Imperial Oil

Obligations to Employees and Annuitants

(Employees should be treated fairly with dignity and respect.) The minimum organizational obligation is that they should abide by human rights codes, equal opportunity employment, labor statutes, and occupational health acts.

The <u>Moral Obligations</u> of Business Organizations

STAKEHOLDERS	EXAMPLES OF MINIMAL OBLIGATIONS	EXAMPLES OF STANDARDS OF EXCELLENCE
Stockholders and other investors	Increase shareholder value while acting with prudent risk commensurate with investor's expectations. Clear and honest reporting of relevant information.	Explicit performance objectives. Equal treatment to all classes of shareholders. Extensive and open reporting. Consultations with shareholders. Executive compensation tied to shareholder value. Cumulative voting for directors. Outside directors on the board.
Employees	Treat employees and annuitants with respect and dignity. Abide by relevant statutes and regulations. Provide safe and healthy workplace. Avoid discrimination. Protect privacy. Train employees properly. Provide feedback on performance and corrective steps prior to disciplinary action.	Employment security. Careful human resource planning. Opportunities to develop skills and abilities. Cross-training, retraining and relocation assistance. Job posting. Employees exercise discretion over their work. Feedback and objective performance appraisals. Competitive salaries and benefits. Employee assistance programs.
Customers	Accurately labelled, safe goods and services of good value. Adequate customer information. Respect promises on delivery and performance.	Active dialog with customers. High value products and services. Prompt response to customer complaints, questions, and requests. Sensitive and informative advertising and promotion. Fair allocation of goods and services in short supply.
Suppliers	Contracts and commitments are honored. Closed bid purchasing processes are respected. Ideas and proposals from suppliers should not be utilized without compensation or advance notification.	Opportunities for fair profit. Fair bidding process. Respect for supplier inputs. Keep advised of developments which may impact them. Provide assistance to maintain relationship. Build the customer-supplier partnership.
Competitors	Avoid untrue comparative advertising and promotion, and predatory pricing. No interference with competitive activities.	Avoidance of comparative advertising. Share potentially damaging information without collusion.
The larger society	Compliance with relevant laws, statutes, rules, conventions, societal values and codes. Avoidance of harm to environment. Compensation for damages done to community and environment.	A "balance of trade" with the society. Conservation of physical, financial and human resources. Improvement of community infrastructures and environments. Contribute to charities and community institutions.

(Organizations should avoid discriminatory treatment, and provide working conditions that are safe and healthy.) They should protect the privacy of their members and allow freedom of expression. Employees should be properly trained for their job responsibilities. When performance is below standard, employees should be advised of the problem, assisted to correct it, and warned before disciplinary action is taken. Annuitants should have their pensions safeguarded. These are minimal standards.

(But many corporations strive for much more than this, believing that it is both morally right and good business to pursue standards of excellence with respect to employment.) Such standards often include lifetime employment security. When IBM trims its workforce, for example, it has usually attempted to do so through attrition or voluntary retirement, with substantial severance payments. They, and many other organizations, are able to do this because they carefully plan human resources, because they provide employees with opportunities to develop their skills and to advance within the organization on the basis of accomplishments, and because they consistently train and cross-train employees so that their skills and abilities evolve with changing technologies and business requirements. Some organizations, such as General Motors, are actively involved with adult literacy programs, sometimes in cooperation with trade unions. When it comes to layoffs, companies with high standards of excellence in treating employees provide opportunities for relocation and/or retraining. They post job vacancies so that employees can see what is going on and apply for positions that they want.

There are other standards of excellence that some companies pursue and which should form part of organizational objectives. Employees should be able to exercise discretion in the performance of their work and be encouraged to demonstrate innovation and creativity. They should be listened to and objectively appraised. They should be given feedback on their performance and be rewarded for their contributions to the organization. Compensation and benefits should be competitive with leading organizations in their industry. Organizations should have appeal boards for employees who disagree with management actions. Responsible whistle-blowing should be encouraged. Employees ought to be able to perform tasks with a sense of independence and responsibility. The system for allocating tasks, burdens, privileges, and rewards ought to be just and compassionate. Some organizations assist employees in resolving personal, family, and work-related problems through employee assistance programs, clearly demonstrating concern for the whole person and not just the part of the person "bought" for wages. Annuitants — many of whom have spent all their working lives with the organization — should be kept informed about what is happening in the organization, invited to visit, and have their pensions adjusted to reflect inflation.

"Champion wants to be known for its fair and thoughtful treatment of employees. We are committed to providing equality of opportunity for all people, regardless of race, national origin, sex, age, or religion. We actively seek a talented, diverse, enthusiastic workforce. We believe in the individual worth of each employee and seek to foster opportunities for personal development."

The Champion Way

"All employees have the right, if in their opinion they feel such steps are necessary, to discuss their concerns with the level of management they feel is appropriate to handle the situation. Any effort to prevent an employee from going to higher-level managers, through intimidation or any other means, is absolutely contrary to company policy and will be dealt with accordingly. Using the open door policy will not in any way impact any evaluations of employees or subject them to any other adverse consequences."

Hewlett Packard Open Door Policy

"To fulfill our corporate and social responsibilities, which include affirmative action for women and minorities, General Mills will strive, through aggressive recruitment and individual development programs, to achieve full utilization of minorities and women available in our labor forces."

General Mills

Obligations to Customers

Organizations ought to provide goods and service of good value to their customers. Goods and services should not be overpriced relative to their quantity or quality and they should match purchaser expectations. Minimally, organizations should produce products that are accurately labelled, safe, and easy to use. They should strive to meet promises of performance and delivery, and avoid misleading advertising or promotions.

Again, many organizations act beyond minimal standards. Organizations embracing standards of excellence for consumers engage in dialogue with them to produce products that are of good value, and developed for customer needs. All questions, complaints, and suggestions from customers are promptly addressed. When goods or services are in short supply, allocations are made fairly. Advertising and promotion is informative, misleading comparisons are not made, and care is taken to ensure that hyperbole in advertising is not misleading and sensitivity is shown in representing sexual and racial groups.

"We believe that the consumer has the right to quality products, consistent with cost; therefore it is the policy of General Mills to market products that are not only safe, but of uniformly high quality and priced to represent good value to the consumer. To meet this responsibility, standards have been established for all raw materials, ingredients and finished products and for their storage, processing, and distribution. In order to ensure that these standards are met, skilled personnel continuously test and monitor all those elements involved in a total quality control program . . . . We believe that the consumer has the right to products which are honestly packaged and which provide adequate product information to facilitate wise choice and use of products by the consumer. General Mills' packaging is designed to meet consumer needs and to protect the product. Package labels are designed to inform the consumer and to enhance comparative shopping."

General Mills

"Staff members and their families may not solicit or accept any gifts of significant value, lavish entertainment or other valuable benefits intended to influence Chase's business. Staff members may not solicit or accept personal fees, commissions or other forms of remuneration because of any transactions or business involving Chase."

Chase Manhattan Corp.

In relation to customers and suppliers, firms ought to negotiate contracts without employing bribes or kickbacks. As consumers of goods and services, most firms officially denounce these practices, although some allow for occasional gratuities. In contrast, as sellers, many firms complain that such practices are necessary in particular markets, especially in foreign countries, and in 1978 the US passed the Foreign Corrupt Practices Act forbidding US firms to exercise these practices in other countries.[4]

Obligations to Suppliers

Suppliers have a right to be treated fairly. At a minimum this means that contracts and commitments should be honored, closed bid purchasing competitions should be conducted fairly, and organizations should not use designs and ideas provided by suppliers to give to other suppliers unless this is clearly permitted.

Again, motivated by both moral considerations and good business practices, many organizations go well beyond minimal obligations to embrace standards of excellence with supplier relationships. They require that suppliers be given an opportunity to make a fair profit and to bid for business on a fair basis. Suppliers are advised of developments within the organization which might

"It is the policy of Citicorp to purchase all equipment, supplies and services needed by it on the basis of quality, utility, and the price offered by the vendor. Under no circumstances will customers of Citicorp be given preferential treatment in vendor negotiations or transactions involving Citicorp purchases . . . . It must be kept in mind that not only will customers of Citicorp be given no preferential treatment on purchases, but care must be taken so that no vendor is left with the impression, however erroneous, that it is necessary or helpful to him or her as a vendor, to purchase products or services which are offered by Citicorp."

Citicorp

"It is the policy of The Equitable to promote the economic development of firms controlled by minorities, women, and handicapped individuals. To accomplish this objective, we have established a purchasing program designed to increase the volume of purchases from firms in which such people have majority ownership. It continues to be basic policy that we make purchases at the lowest price consistent with specified quality and service standards, solicited through competitive bids. We expect to increase our business with the firms above, while continuing to adhere to this procedure."

Equitable Life Assurance

impact their own economic future in time to make the necessary adjustments. Organizations may give help to long-term and good suppliers to make necessary technical modifications, to increase their quality, and sometimes even to refinance their operations or to weather periods of depressed economic activity. Some organizations, such as Imperial Oil, have clearly stated preferential treatment for smaller suppliers within their community, seeing such policies as ways in which the company can contribute to the benefit of both suppliers and the community in which they and the suppliers operate. In many cases the distinction between a company and its suppliers is becoming blurred as many organizations pursue single-company sourcing to cement a partnership relationship.

Obligations to Competitors

In developed capitalist economies where business organizations compete there has always been an assumption that competition will be fair. At a minimum, organizations ought to abide by relevant competition laws and avoid untrue comparative advertising, predatory pricing, and monopolization of trade outlets. Sales people should not tell lies about competitive products and services or

"Fair competition is fundamental to continuation of the free enterprise system. We support laws prohibiting restraints of trade, unfair practices, or abuse of economic power. And we avoid such practices everywhere — including areas of the world where laws do not prohibit them. In relationships with competitors . . . . Caterpillar employees are directed to avoid arrangements restricting our ability to compete with others — or the ability of any other business organization to compete freely and fairly with us, and with others. There must be no arrangements or understandings with competitors, affecting practice, terms upon which products are sold, or the number and type of products manufactured or sold — or which might be construed as dividing customers or sales territories with a competitor. Suppliers aren't required to forego trade with our competitors in order to merit Caterpillar purchases."

Caterpillar Tractor Co.

"It always has been IBM's policy to provide the best possible products and services to customers, and to sell on the merits of our own products and services — not by disparaging competitors, or their products and services. In short, sell IBM. Disparaging remarks include not only false statements but also information which is misleading or simply unfair. Even factually correct material can be disparaging if it's derogatory and irrelevant to the particular sales situation. This includes casting doubt on a competitor's capabilities or making unfair comparisons."

IBM

about the ways the competition conducts its business. They should not deliberately interfere with their competitors' products or their displays.

It is more difficult to identify standards of excellence with respect to competitors although formal codes of ethics or business practices sometimes refer to these. Some organizations are scrupulous in avoiding comparative advertising on the basis that it nearly always involves selectivity. Others make sure that information which might damage competitors severely is made known to them. Needless to say, helping one's competitor must be done with regard for the law which prevents collusive practices and recognizes the value of competition. Firms ought to avoid predatory competition: that is, temporarily lowering prices and assuming losses to force one or more competitors out of the market.

Obligations to the Larger Society

In addition to specific obligations to stakeholder groups, organizations also have obligations to the larger society within which they operate. Members of society have the right to expect business organizations to be "good corporate citizens." At <u>a minimum</u>, this requires that corporations comply with relevant moral expectations as these are expressed in laws, rules, conventions, societal values and codes. Even where specific statutes or regulations do not prohibit action, organizations should not impose harm on the environment through pollution, should respect the customs and mores of communities, and should make restitution to communities which may be disadvantaged by their actions. The organization which stripmines has an obligation to restore the environment to its natural state after it has extracted minerals; organizations exploring for oil should not upset aboriginal hunting rights; when they exit a community to relocate elsewhere companies should attempt to help the community compensate for the loss by attracting other industries.

Many business organizations strive for <u>standards of excellence</u> as corporate citizens. They attempt to return to these communities (in taxes, charity, services, investments) conserved and recycled resources, community services for organization and members and the general public, available resources, accessible markets, and community good will. Such organizations see a responsibility to conserve and use physical, financial and human resources efficiently without needless waste. Organizations seek to improve local communities and enhance natural environments. They support local educational institutions such as

---

" . . . we publicly affirm our belief that corporations and their shareholders have a direct responsibility for the environment. We believe that corporations must conduct their business as responsible stewards of the environment and seek profits only in a manner that leaves the Earth healthy and safe. We believe that corporations must not compromise the ability of future generations to sustain their needs . . . . We will minimize and strive to eliminate the release of any pollutant that may cause environmental damage to the air, water, or earth or its inhabitants. We will safeguard habitats in rivers, lakes, wetlands, coastal zones and oceans and will minimize contributing to the greenhouse effect, depletion of the ozone layer, acid rain, or smog . . . We will make sustainable use of renewable natural resources, such as water, soils and forests. We will conserve nonrenewable natural resources through efficient use and careful planning . . . . We will minimize the creation of waste, especially hazardous waste, and wherever possible recycle materials. We will dispose of all wastes through safe and responsible methods . . . . We will take responsibility for any harm we cause to the environment and to compensate those persons who are adversely affected."

Valdez Principles

Coalition for Environmentally Responsible Economies

---

schools, colleges and universities; they offer public support and appreciation for local services such as police and firefighters. A number of firms have decided to divert a small portion of their total investment portfolio into what are considered ethical investments, that is, community development projects and mutual funds dedicated to humanitarian or environmental projects. They willingly accept smaller rates of return on these investments because the latter further social programs that make the communities in which these firms are located better places to live.

Obligations of Stakeholders to the Organization

Organizational moral obligations to stakeholders should be reciprocated. Employees are obligated to give a fair day's work for a fair day's pay, to safeguard confidential information, to look after organizational equipment, and so on. Stockholders have an obligation to inform themselves regarding their companies, and to read reports. Suppliers have obligations to meet delivery dates, and to safeguard proprietary information.

Businesses cannot dictate that their stakeholders act in certain morally prescribed ways. However, insofar as they acknowledge that their interactions with stakeholder groups are ongoing, and reciprocal, they can influence the character of these relationships in two ways. In the first place, they can insist on acceptable levels of moral conduct with particular stakeholders, such as employees, suppliers, and some customers, by threatening to withdraw from contractual relations if minimal standards are not respected. Firms may use direct pressure in this way especially with respect to illegal and blatantly unethical practices. In the second place, businesses can work at making and keeping their relationships with stakeholders as open to in-depth two-way communication as possible. By this approach businesses do not attempt to pressure stakeholders directly. Rather, they encourage communication between themselves and their stakeholders, including their criticisms and hopes.

MULTI-DIMENSIONAL MORAL EVALUATION

It is possible to evaluate organizations on the extent to which they satisfy minimal and ideal standards by using a simple rating scale such as the one shown in Figure 7.2. Managers who want to guide their organizations towards improved ethical performance should be pursuing some mix of minimal obligations and standards of excellence such that all minimal obligations are met while as many standards of excellence are being pursued as is practicable.

In practice, individual businesses differ considerably in terms of how well they act in relation to their stakeholders, and correspondingly in relation to their overall relative moral stature. In relation to one or more groups of stakeholders, many firms fail to meet the minimal standards we have just reviewed.

1. Unacceptable: In one or more ways, the organization fails to meet minimal standards.
2. Barely acceptable: The organization appears to stay out of trouble, if caught not satisfying minimal obligations then the organization corrects its actions.
3. Acceptable: The organization fully satisfies its minimal obligations.
4. Good: The organization fulfills minimal obligations and strives to achieve standards of excellence.
5. Exemplary: The organization consistently establishes and works toward achieving high ideals and standards of excellence with respect to all stakeholder groups.

FIGURE 7.2 **A Moral Standards Rating Scale**

While some of these firms have been indicted or fined for illegal acts or charged with ethically irresponsible conduct, many firms succeed in staying out of trouble even though they do not strictly abide by minimal standards with respect to all stakeholder groups. Other businesses, in contrast, fulfill all minimal obligations. They do not act in ways that are obviously or surreptitiously unethical but they also do not strive to excel to realize higher ideals. They are responsible organizations. Quite different are those firms that seek, and succeed, in realizing higher ideals in relation to several of their stakeholder groups. All businesses are not alike either in their uses of technology, their innovativeness, their organizational culture, or in their relative moral character and stature.

PURITY OF MOTIVES

Whenever someone points to a company which appears to be doing the right thing morally, a cynic is often quick to point out that it is only acting in its own best interests. For example, the St Joseph's Printing Company has a program called "Partners for Growth" in which the company pays for the planting of one seedling for every tree which is used up in producing customer order forms, and it advises customers of this on its statements. Cynics might argue that the company is exploiting environmental issues by employing a "marketing gimmick" or "public relations ploy." Clearly the company derives some benefit from this program — customers feel good, employees feel good, and that's good for business. But it is also good for the environment and it represents a morally good action which most other companies may not have been creative enough or committed enough to take.

SUMMARY

While many criticize the amorality or immorality of business this is often balanced by business people trying to guide their organizations towards achieving positive benefits for multiple stakeholders. The balance between the interests of various stakeholders is the modern-day version of the social contract. In Alcan's statement of objectives, this balance is a key objective:

> To recognize and seek to balance the interests of our shareholders, employees, customers, suppliers and governments and the public at large, while achieving Alcan's business objectives, taking into account the different economic and environmental aspirations of the communities within which we operate.[5]

It has been argued that business organizations have "a conditional licence to operate" which is granted to it by society and which may be withdrawn or restricted should the organization fail to discharge its moral obligations.[6] This is the ultimate sanction which could befall organizations which are unable to keep their sense of moral equilibrium.

SUGGESTED READINGS

Aupperle, Kenneth E. "An Empirical Measure of Corporate Social Orientation," *Research in Corporate Social Performance and Policy*, Vol. 6, JAI Press, Inc. (1984): 27-54.

The Business Roundtable. *Corporate Ethics: A Prime Business Asset*, 1988.

Clarkson, Max. "Corporate Social Performance in Canada 1976-1986," *Research in Corporate Social Performance and Policy*, Vol. 10, JAI Press, Inc. (1988): 241-265.

Mowday, R., W. Parker, and R.M. Steers. *Employee-Organizational Linkages: The Psychology of Commitment, Absenteeism, and Turnover*. New York: Academic Press, 1982.

Tuleja, Tad. *Beyond the Bottom Line: How Business Leaders Are Turning Principles into Profits*. New York: Facts on File Publications, 1985.

NOTES FOR CHAPTER SEVEN

1   The practice of listing various social indicators and linking them to constructs such as corporate ethical performance should be viewed with some caution since many of these indicators could well be related to ethical behaviors (such as cleaning up the environment) even though they may result in closing down operations and causing unemployment.

2 The headings have been added by the authors to emphasize the various stakeholder groups identified in the J & J Credo.

3 F.P. Schadler and J.E. Kearns, "The Unethical Exploration of Shareholders in Management Buyout Transactions," *Journal of Business Ethics*, Vol. 9, No. 9 (July 1990): 595-602. There is an alternative perspective, which suggests that managers' only obligations to shareholders are those embedded in corporate charters and relevant statutes, represented in W. Irvine, "Corporate Democracy and the Rights of Shareholders," *Journal of Business Ethics*, Vol. 9, 99-108.

4 Kate Gillespie, "The Middle East Response to the U.S. Foreign Corrupt Practices Act," *California Management Review*, Vol. 29, No.4 (1987): 9-30.

5 *Alcan, Its Purpose, Objectives and Policies.* Alcan Aluminum Limited, Montreal, Canada, September 1987.

6 David Grier, an executive with The Royal Bank, in a speech to the Corporate Ethics Forum, Toronto, Canada, September 1989.

Ethics in Action

In the previous chapters we examined how managers can identify relevant stakeholders, address social norms and moral standards, deliberate about moral issues, and use ethical theories and frameworks in the process of reaching decisions. But ethical management goes beyond making decisions — it calls for action. And it is not always easy to realize moral objectives since there may be considerable vested opposition which cannot be ignored. To be ethically responsible we must continuously seek to realize our objectives, adjusting short-term goals in relation to particular circumstances, while still pursuing ultimate goals. This chapter discusses the strategies and tactics that managers can use to turn decisions into effective action.

THE BASIS FOR ACTION

In earlier chapters we suggested that specific guidelines for action have to be developed in keeping with the relevant issues. Therefore, it is inappropriate to spell out simple recipes for effective moral action. Instead, this chapter consists of useful ways for thinking about alternative courses of action.

To act effectively requires persuasion or power, which is the capacity to secure desired outcomes in the face of opposition. People and organizations possess power to the degree that they are able to realize objectives, "to carry out (their) own will (even) in spite of resistance, regardless of the basis on which this possibility exists."[1]

Persuasion

Those who want to make ethical decisions must gain the cooperation of others or minimize their resistance. They may gain cooperation and minimize resis-

122

tance either by persuasion or power or a combination of both. It would be ethically desirable if we could realize most moral objectives primarily by being able to convince others to cooperate through discussion and debate even if coercion may be justifiable under certain circumstances.

It is often possible to convince people to adopt moral objectives simply by providing relevant information and persuasive arguments. In these instances ethical decision-making results in effective action by virtue of well-argued, informative, and well-targeted communication. It is useful to review several examples to see how effective good communication can be in realizing moral objectives. The adoption of the Sullivan principles by firms operating in South Africa exemplifies how much can be accomplished by persuasive arguments. In 1977, the Rev. Leon Sullivan convinced the board of General Motors to adopt principles which called for an end to discrimination in hiring and promotions in their South African firms, and to find housing for employees in spite of their race. General Motors, in turn, persuaded other firms to adopt this policy. These principles were adopted because the arguments used in their defense were persuasive. Or to cite another example, the popular music star Bob Geldoff persuaded a number of musicians, recording companies, and broadcasting corporations to donate their services for a special concert, held simultaneously in England and the United States, to raise funds for hunger relief in Ethiopia. The Live Aid Concert raised nearly $80 million for famine relief. One person was able to persuade many others to cooperate together for this project.

Some other examples may also be useful. Nielsen cited a number of cases where individual managers have succeeded in persuading others in their organization to cease unethical practices. In one instance, a broker persuaded others in his group not to trade on inside information. In another instance, a sales manager for an insurance company succeeded in persuading his boss to hire more women sales representatives by demonstrating that women could be particularly successful at selling insurance to married women, who contributed large portions of their salaries to home mortgages.[2]

Cogent arguments and relevant information can be very persuasive in moving otherwise reluctant individuals and organizations to support ethically mandated changes, especially when these arguments appeal to moral standards and long-term benefits. More humane personnel policies, more service-oriented marketing strategies, more communication with stakeholders may easily be defended in these terms. Ethics may be considered good for business.[3] On the basis of a survey of over 100 member companies, the Business Roundtable recently concluded: "One of the myths about business is that there is a contradiction between ethics and profit. That myth is thoroughly debunked by the attitudes and actions of top managers in the companies that contributed to this report. There is a deep conviction that a good reputation for fair and honest business is a prime corporate asset ..."[4] When business people are thoroughly convinced that it makes good sense to be ethically responsible, it will be easier to persuade them to respond to particular moral concerns.

However, it is probably naive and certainly simplistic to assume that managers and corporations will agree with most ethical proposals for business simply because they find the arguments of moral campaigners to be persuasive and informative. This view overestimates the power of reasoned and objective arguments. It fails to recognize the degree to which other non-rational, but nonetheless broadly moral factors, such as social obligations, concerns to preserve reputations for reliability, probity, and consumer concern, and the desire to limit costs in court fees and lost business from wrong-doing, all play a part. People rarely decide to comply with moral expectations for altrustic reasons alone, even though this often helps convince them. Rather, the motivation to comply springs from a number of interrelated sources, including the desire to keep promises, feelings of social obligation, an interest in achieving and preserving a sense of moral worth, a desire to gain benefits and avoid possible punishments, and a respect for moral teachings (see Figure 8.1).

The Dimension of Social Obligation. Persuasive arguments call into play feelings of social obligation, gratitude and indebtedness to others.

The Dimension of Moral Worth. Persuasive arguments encourage the pursuit of feelings of moral worth, that is, good repute both in one's own eyes and in the eyes of others.

The Dimension of Promise-Keeping. Persuasive arguments invoke the sense of responsibility to honor commitments entailed in previously made explicit promises and tacit agreements.

The Dimension of Rewards and Benefits. Persuasive arguments encourage people to realize selected benefits and avoid harm by acting in keeping with specific moral guidelines.

The Dimension of Altruism. Persuasive arguments appeal at once to people's idealism and altruism, as well as to their pragmatism.

FIGURE 8.1 **Dimensions of Morally Persuasive Arguments**

In making these observations, the power of moral argument is not being understated. However, its power lies as much in rhetoric as in logic. Moral discussion is persuasive to the degree that it identifies issues, provides good reasons for acting, and evokes factors which affect our moral motives. These factors include our indebtedness and gratitude to others from whose efforts we in part benefit, the desire to attain and maintain feelings of moral worth, an interest in preserving reputations of trustworthiness, etc. It is possible to see how these factors influenced firms to adopt the Sullivan principles in the late 1970s and early 1980s, and more recently a number of firms, in the petro-chemical industries to adopt the Valdez principles regarding responsible environmental policies. Although these factors may be vague, in concert they greatly move people to act responsibly.

B) Power

In many settings, however, it is difficult to gain a hearing for moral arguments. Customs and traditions discourage alternative ways of looking at problems. Moral arguments fall on deaf ears or, at least, on ears which are unreceptive. On many occasions, people are deaf to moral persuasion because the costs seem excessive. To secure a hearing, managers who want to pursue moral objectives must gain the attention of their audiences long enough so that these costs can be considered. When moral arguments lack power, it is often necessary to find ways of exerting power more directly by using pressure tactics, invoking authorities, making promises, voicing threats so that these arguments are heard.

In some situations, simply threatening to inform others about a person's misdeeds compels the individuals involved to listen to moral arguments and agree to act in keeping with them. Nielsen cited a number of examples where this threat to inform persuaded others to curtail unethical practices. For example, in one organization a salesman anonymously threatened to inform the local newspaper if a sales manager continued to promote a morally dubious sales technique. The sales manager ceased the practice before any exposure occurred. In another case a female employee asked a male supervisor to cease harassing female subordinates or she would inform his superiors.

These examples are quite typical. For moral arguments to gain credibility, it is necessary to find ways of dealing with existing authorities and generating one's own authority.

Moral action and power are related in two ways. One, any attempt to initiate moral action takes place in a network of relationships already shaped and structured by existing arrangements of power. Large corporations, regulatory agencies, courts, trade unions, consumer associations, mutual funds, and supervisors all exert power. Anyone contemplating moral campaigns must take these powers into account. Ethical decisions can only be actualized by limiting or neutralizing opposing powers and by drawing on and aligning with agreeable powers. The community organizer and social radical Saul Alinsky wrote: "The basic requirement for understanding the politics of change is to recognize the world as it is. We must work with it on its own terms if we are to change it to the kind of world we would like it to be."[5] Two, since we are interested in being as effective as possible, we also need to explore how we can generate as much power as possible in support of our own ethical objectives. We need to examine various tactics we might use to enhance our own positions. Moral crusaders who fail to consider these issues doom themselves to self-righteous posturing.

WORKING WITH THE POWER STRUCTURE

Managers operate in organizations in which power is exercised by various individuals and groups. To accomplish ethical objectives, they must find ways of limiting those in power that might oppose them and gaining assistance from those who might support them.

Morally committed managers may engage existing powers with three different strategies. They may simply acquiesce, deferring to their superior influence or they may seek to limit or neutralize the influence of these powers to pursue their objectives. They may explore ways of exploiting or channelling existing power on behalf of their own aims. These strategies are distinctly different but not mutually exclusive. Moral campaigners may acquiesce on certain fronts, seek to limit the influence of existing powers on other fronts, while funnelling off some of these powers for their own purposes. In the process, moral campaigners may seek to advance quickly on projects which are easily attainable but move slowly and steadily on difficult projects (see Figure 8.2).

To Acquiesce or Defer: To Do Nothing

    (a) By default: in bad conscience or without conscience

    (b) Tactically: with good conscience

To Neutralize or Limit: Policies of Containment

    (a) To identify zones of indifference

    (b) To insulate or protect particular projects by creating moral fiefdoms; by asserting civil rights

    (c) To create countervailing power

To Exploit or Rechannel: Policies of Counteraction

    (a) To attack or threaten possible reputation

    (b) To sue or threaten to sue

    (c) To boycott

FIGURE 8.2 **Strategies for Engaging Existing Powers**

Acquiescence

One obvious response to the opposition of moral objectives is to do nothing at all about it. Many managers adopt this position either because they never consider the ethical aspects of their work or because they see no alternatives. Nielsen cited the example of a manager with the United Fruit Company who only considered, after the event, whether his company ought to have been involved in a coup against the Guatemalan government. In another case, a manager tacitly went along with offering sizeable kickbacks to suppliers.[6] Many managers acquiesce to morally ambiguous practices but don't feel good about it. Toffler cited the example of an executive who was asked to spy on his co-workers. He was especially annoyed because the superiors who requested him to do this, later attacked him on the matter.[7] Because many managers simply go along with the directives of authorities, they often feel that their own moral sentiments are largely ignored.

(Acquiescing is not always an unwise policy. Deference may be momentary or tactical. It may be used to stall for time or put people off guard.) One of the best examples of deference as a tactical political strategy is the way Gandhi encouraged Indians to cooperate with the British with military support in World Wars I and II, while continually seeking independence. Civil disobedience employs deference selectively, by agreeing to act respectfully and accept punishment, while at the same time defying particular laws judged to be unjust. Managers may use deference as a tactic in less dramatic ways. A manager feeling threatened at losing his job if he publicly informs others of a bid-rigging scheme in the electronic industry might well wait, as one manager did, until he had left the firm before exposing the scandal. In another case, a manager who felt that his company ought to honor pollution guidelines struck a compromise with superiors who argued that strict compliance was too expensive and would force them to close down a local plant. The manager agreed to go along with current practices while stricter controls would be gradually introduced.[8]

Neutralization and Limitation

(A second response to the opposition of moral projects is to limit or neutralize the influence of such opposition.) This aim is largely defensive. The objective is to enhance one's own capacity to act morally by finding ways to check, defuse, or divert the power of those who might interfere. This goal may be pursued by using any of the following strategies: by identifying areas of business activity which existing powers are not directly concerned about, by insulating and protecting particular moral projects, and by countering negative influences.

Existing powers are not equally concerned about all the issues that confront them. As moral reformers seek to develop priorities for moral projects, it is useful to identify matters about which existing powers are likely to feel indifferent.[9] Often, but not always, these zones of indifference correspond with activities that have no major associated costs. For example, without directly confronting the issues surrounding the social role of corporations, a number of businesses have undertaken investing small portfolios into low profit community projects. Some firms have been coaxed into matching employee contributions to specific charities. These projects have been adopted because goodwill occasioned by this exercise has compensated for the financial cost involved. Identifying moral projects likely to fall within zones of indifference is an especially useful tactic, not only because it is often easy to sell these programs, but because these projects make those ordinarily resistant to such projects aware of their advantages.

A second means of limiting or neutralizing existing powers focuses on developing a way to protect or insulate moral programs from hostile intervention. This aim is realized by creating fiefdoms, in which moral purposes may be protected organizationally from the intrusion of otherwise stronger, opposing powers. Creating a company foundation is a means of developing such a moral fiefdom. Corporate foundations are then in a position to pursue various objectives in keeping with overall guidelines without organizational obstruction. Particular units within a business may succeed in achieving a degree of autonomy, extended to them in the belief that well managed units, characterized by sound commitment by participants, will be more productive in the long run. Often similar insulation from intrusion is achieved when a particular project, such as, for example, one which includes greater decision-making by all workers, is treated as experimental and short-term. These projects need not be subject to the same kind of surveillance, financial accounting, and organizational control as regular, ongoing activities.

A way of protecting moral objectives from hostile intrusions is to demonstrate how these activities are guaranteed in relation to legally-defined civil rights. By their nature, civil rights identify prerogatives which individuals and groups of individuals may exercise free from the intervention of others, especially of governments. Governments are mandated to protect these rights, so that people may freely express themselves, form associations, enjoy their privacy, and be protected against discrimination of gender, age, race or religion. Correspondingly, we may view attempts to assert rights as a means of limiting or neutralizing possibly hostile intervention of existing powers. This strategy need not involve direct appeal to courts and regulatory agencies. Because most businesses tacitly acknowledge that their members possess various rights, this general belief may be invoked successfully to specific objectives which aim to reduce discrimination against women, indoor pollution in the work place, or similar events.

The capacity of existing powers to obstruct moral projects may be limited or neutralized by a third set of tactics which generate countervailing powers against opposition. Accordingly, the discretion of existing powers to obstruct moral purposes is reduced and contained by exerting or threatening to exert influence that opposes them. This strategy overlaps both with tactics to exploit existing powers and tactics that help to expand one's own power and influence, because it is by directly demonstrating power that one is able to limit the otherwise unimpeded exercise of opposing influences and forces. Since we will examine ways of developing and expanding power later, we will only consider the negative aspects of this demonstration of power for the moment.

(3)

Exploiting and Rechanneling

A third approach to powers that oppose moral projects is to discover ways of diverting or limiting their influence. It is sometimes possible to draw on the energy of an assault and turn it back on the assaulter, as in the martial art of tai chi. Recognizing that power is derived from many sources, it is sometimes possible to defend particular moral projects by tapping one or more of these sources in opposition to other sources. It is at times possible to draw on the power of an organization's bill of legal health, their repute and legitimacy, and the personal loyalties they inspire, to oppose or limit the power of their economic strength and organizational authority. Companies that have gained public reputations for civic responsibility, integrity, fairness, and/or responsiveness to consumer interests, do not like to see this reputation endangered. Such organizations, and their executives, are much more likely to respond to threatened exposures which would reveal practices that countervene this image. Even secretly communicated threats to inform the media of practices that violate accepted standards are likely to provoke a response, because these organizations do not want to lose the influence gained by virtue of their public reputation. Similarly, a moral crusader may draw on the legal recognition of some businesses by threatening to sue when legal violations are discovered.

One of the most widely used tactics for counteracting existing powers is the boycott by powerful groups within an organization. These groups may face economic recriminations and organizational penalties. However, to the degree that the power of the organization for working well depends on their expertise, their special knowledge, and/or their particular resources, they may eventually force the resisting organization to listen more attentively to their concerns. Striking nurses, police officers, and technicians are just a few examples. However, boycotts are sometimes most effective when they are threats. Even the prospect of a boycott by consumers of food products in which dangerous pesticides were used has persuaded many growers to adjust their practices. Work-to-rule campaigns, which might be considered partial boycotts, have been used effectively to campaign for better working conditions. Probably, over time the most effective boycotts have been exercised by creditors (although rarely for moral objectives). In all these examples, the powers-that-be are likely to become more responsive when they feel that their overall power is likely to be diminished by a group able to withdraw or threatening to withdraw their services.

PROMOTING POWER FOR EFFECTIVE ACTION

We have briefly reviewed tactics which moral campaigners might use to further their objectives in the face of opposition. We will now examine tactics they may use to enhance their positions. We will review how moral actors may enhance their projects by developing coalitions, augmenting their legitimacy, using their control over scarce or valuable resources, and exploiting legal opportunities (see Figure 8.3).

PEOPLE POWER

To solicit individual commitment and to organize networks and coalitions, lobbies, caucuses, and formal associations.

MORAL POWER

To cultivate credibility and legitimacy for activities and organizations, through ideologies, moral arguments and media attention.

TACTICAL POWER

To threaten to withdraw valued services, to trade use of expertise for desired moral objective.

LEGAL POWER

To exploit legal remedies in defense of moral projects.

COERCIVE POWER

In the absence of other sources of power, moral actors may seek directly to realize moral objectives, compelling others — without persuasion — to comply.

FIGURE 8.3 **Tactics for Promoting Power for Effective Action**

People Power

The basic tactic for strengthening a position is to solicit and organize support from groups of people. The more people involved, the greater the influence. To make a difference, this support must incorporate a readiness to act rather than just verbal acquiescence. Characteristically, individuals vary in their degree of commitment to particular causes, from a central core of enthusiasts ready to assume considerable risks to fringe supporters willing only on occasion to act publicly when the costs are not too high. The basic tactic, then, is to recruit fringe supporters and then to coax as many of them as possible to become more committed. Core members often display their commitment such as Gandhi's followers in India who wore homespun clothes rather than cotton clothes manufactured in Britain, or draft resistors during the Vietnam war who turned in their draft cards. It is also necessary to solicit at least marginal commitment from many others willing to write letters, attend public meetings, and adopt symbolic gestures, to express their support. Moral crusades may falter from either a lack of committed core supporters or less involved sympathizers.

People power may be expressed through different types of social groups, from spontaneous crowds to tightly disciplined sects, from loose networks to intentionally organized causes. The basic step is to form a viable coalition among people willing, in varying degrees, to support a particular project. Coalition building assumes several typical forms. One approach is to start afresh confronting people as individuals, putting the case to them, and inviting them to join with like-minded people. For example, a manager concerned about internal air pollution might discuss this concern with co-workers, determining their willingness to join him or her in a petition to demand that larger spaces within the business environment be designated for non-smoking. Much can be accomplished in this manner, if issues are raised and discussed. Personal support for moral principles is often much greater than most individual managers recognize, simply because these concerns are so seldom voiced even in informal ways. Coalitions may be formed by inviting potential supporters to public gatherings, which in turn serve as demonstrations of support. People are especially likely to attend gatherings when the issues are easy to identify with. Public meetings and demonstrations have been held to defend and criticize government trade and tax policies, to oppose plant closures, and to champion less discriminatory hiring practices.

It is often convenient and useful to form coalitions by appealing to existing groups as alliances. Rather than forming new organizations, it is possible to seek support from individuals already associated in existing groups, whether by occupation, work stations, divisions, professional associations, or informal caucuses. Coalitions formed by federations of existing groups have the advantage that little energy needs to be vested in group maintenance. Existing channels of communication can be used without having to forge new ones. Community organizers often use this coalition building strategy among unorganized low-income groups by linking up with existing religious groups, trade unions, nursery schools, neighborhood associations, athletic teams, youth gangs and play groups. In businesses this approach to coalition building may be constructed within and between firms by developing alliances for moral projects with working groups, divisions, service organizations, professional groups and trade associations.

Coalitions create power in several ways. They demonstrate how people feel, and they can demonstrate the support which specific policies are likely to generate, as well as the drop in support if proposed objectives are not adopted. Temporarily at least, coalitions can mobilize people to act together to disrupt ordinary business practices long enough to gain attention for their causes. For example, to persuade a large department store to consider hiring more minority group members, the community organizer Saul Alinsky used a coalition to mobilize a massive "shop in" by group members, who crowded the aisles of the store and obstructed business. This demonstration convinced the store to change its policies, as they recognized the support they might gain, and acknowledged the power of these people to disrupt ordinary business.[10]

Moral Power

(Moral advocates can enhance the power of their causes by incorporating popular beliefs about what is legitimate and what matters) It is much easier to organize people on behalf of projects they deem worthwhile. It becomes increasingly difficult to perpetuate policies that have become morally questionable, even if they are legal. We can observe the impact of changed beliefs by examining business responses to environmental issues over the past two decades. Initial resistance in almost all quarters has given way to partial support and in some cases active initiative. Some retailers have decided that they may gain sales by eliminating some non-biodegradable packaging from their merchandise and using recycled materials. Environmental activists have gained power as greater numbers of people have become even more convinced that these policies are important. In the 1960s, ecological arguments were supported by intellectuals, conservationists, students, and the political left. The apocalyptic disasters they predicted, if policy changes were not instituted, seemed unbelievable to most businesses.[11] Little by little as evidence accumulated regarding air and water pollution, as the case for conserving and renewing resources was made over and over, as stories circulated about the harm done to people exposed to dangerous waste, ecological arguments gained more believers. In many areas, ecological proposals seemed so valid that no arguments needed to be mounted in their defense. In the process, businesses and governments began to view environmental issues as urgent and important.

We could also examine the way changed attitudes influenced occupational health and safety standards, the rights of women in the work place, the status of trade unions, the prerogatives of public utilities, adolescent wages, and mandatory retirement ages. Occasionally changes in attitude occur rapidly, as happened with the Three Mile Island nuclear accident. Ordinarily changes in beliefs occur gradually as large groups of people consider and become convinced by relevant arguments, as appears to be happening with issues such as employment equity and the environment.

Changing beliefs about the legitimacy of business practices may greatly alter the balance of power between those who advocate and resist moral reforms. Beliefs considered conventional reinforce existing power arrangements. Like ideologies, they define what is and what ought to be, and thereby legitimate current distributions of authority and influence. Changes allow for new arrangements of power.

However changes are not easily achieved. Those who campaign to reform need to commit themselves to the long-term. They must be willing to undertake crusades aimed at distributing information, instructing people again and again why issues are important, and finding ways to break through resistance by people to consider issues from new perspectives. Currently, a number of company executives have committed themselves to educating their work forces to moral concerns by developing ethical codes, distributing copies of these to their employees, and holding seminars to discuss them. In the process, these executives are attempting to set ethical standards for business. In keeping with existing beliefs, these codes still direct business people to comply with the directives of their organizations, avoiding unethical acts which disadvantage their firms. At the same time, by promulgating these codes, corporate executives are recognizing that ethics have a business application.

Tactical Power

Individuals and groups may enhance and strengthen their positions through the exercise of what we call tactical power. The idea here is simple. To the extent that they control the access and allocation of particular valued resources, whether they be economic goods, technical know-how, sales contacts, credit ratings, or organizational promotions, individuals and groups bargain in strength with those who need their resources. For example, because bankers judge who gets credit and on what terms, they may powerfully influence the policies of organizations that either seek loans or seek to re-finance existing debts. To advance their own projects, moral campaigners need to determine which resources can be used for bargaining for moral demands.

It is useful to examine several examples of tactical power to illustrate the ways moral crusaders might use this approach. For example, as investors, people may threaten to withdraw their funds unless an organization decides to change its policies. Investors have organized to persuade companies to divest their holdings in South Africa and to increase minority group recruitment. Consumer groups have sometimes successfully asserted their power by boycotting particular products or services, such as non-union harvested grapes. Working-to-rule is another tactical exercise of power by which particular groups of workers, such as nurses or engineers, refuse to undertake any work not directly stipulated by their job descriptions and organizational rules. Occasionally, units within companies temporarily refuse to cooperate until a particular problem is resolved. Often these temporary refusals to cooperate are used to expedite promised improvements to working conditions.

The tactical exercise of power works most effectively where there exists a strong moral argument and where the resource or skill being withheld is highly valued and not easily replaced. Nonetheless, the tactical exercise of power may backfire. When air traffic controllers went on strike in the US in the early 1980s, they found their power taken away from them. Although their services were highly valued, it was possible to find others to fill in for them and the public was prepared to cope with reduced service levels.

Legal Power

Moral advocates may enhance their power by making use of legal remedies. Legal tactics attempt to draw on the power already institutionalized in courts, regulatory agencies, and legislatures. Legal tactics are not used to create new bases of power nor to persuade people to alter their commitments. Rather, they aim to channel existing sources of public power on behalf of particular objectives.

We will cite a number of examples where moral reformers have used legal tactics. In Canada, anti-smoking crusaders have successfully lobbied legislatures to restrict or ban smoking in public places, government offices and government agencies. In the US and Canada, reformers have used legislatures to raise standards of car and industrial plant emissions. In the past, reformers have effectively lobbied for workers' rights, including minimum wage laws, adequate unemployment insurance, and workers' compensation laws. Other reformers have kept up pressure on regulatory agencies, sometimes providing them with information on violations and sometimes simply goading them to improve standards. These agencies have played an active role, attempting to maintain safe and healthy working conditions, to reduce trading on inside information, to indict influence peddlers, and to reduce racial and sexual discrimination. Typically, these agencies perform their functions best where public interest groups function as watchdogs to push them to act.[12] Moral reformers may also appeal directly to the courts, launching lawsuits when they believe harm has been done, or when laws and contracts have been violated. In Canada, moral reformers successfully petitioned the courts in the mid 1970s to stop the construction of an oil pipeline down the Mackenzie River Valley, because they argued that such a project ought not to proceed until the land claims of the native people affected by the pipeline were settled. A manager with a public utilities company in the US anonymously informed the justice department of long time bid-rigging among a number of large electrical contractors. These companies have subsequently paid millions of dollars in fines for their abuses.[13]

Coercive Power

Coercive power is another way of strengthening a moral position. When we use coercion, we seek to force our positions onto others. It is a means of last resort. Often, people resort to coercive tactics when they feel otherwise powerless to prevent actions they consider objectionable. Ordinarily, these tactics would be considered unjustifiable means of realizing moral objectives. Moral reformers should realize their objectives by exerting power in non-coercive ways that allow those who oppose them room to consent voluntarily to moral objectives. Insofar as coercive tactics involve direct assaults on individuals or property, they should be avoided. However, coercion may also involve outright non-compliance with commands or rules without harming others. An individual may, contrary to directives from superiors, proceed to hire minority group applicants or divert what seems excessive funds for public relations into a community development project. However, whenever one sabotages the policies of a company, whether openly or secretly, one must be prepared to accept full responsibility for the consequences of being caught. Occasionally sabotage provides time during which moral crusaders may succeed in persuading superiors to change policies. For example, a program manager for a social welfare agency refused to obey a superior's orders to drop clients. The manager instigated a paper work chain in cahoots with other agencies so that the mandated dropping of clients was delayed. In the end, this strategy delayed the decision long enough for the superior to change his mind.[14]

ETHICS, POLITICS AND RESPONSIBLE ACTION

We have reviewed a number of ways managers can use existing powers and promote their own powers in support of moral objectives. We recognize, at the same time, that these same tactics may be used to advance unethical interests. By themselves these tactics for limiting opposing powers and enhancing the power of moral reformers are neither moral nor immoral. Nonetheless, they may be employed in ways that are more or less ethically acceptable. Hence, as we complete this discussion of tactics, we need to consider guidelines for assessing their moral character.

Broadly understood, the use of tactics is a political activity. Politics, neutrally defined, refers to the various activities people utilize as they seek to strengthen their power and influence decision-making within specific organizations. Politics may occur within clubs or clans, within corporations or jurisdictions. It is pervasive in organizations.[15] Sometimes, we are inclined to use the term politics perjoratively to refer to the pursuit of power and self-serving abuse of power. However, if we restrict politics only to these abuses, then we have no term to refer to legitimate uses of power. Hence, we shall use the term politics to describe all efforts to enhance power or affect decision-making in organized associations.

Understood in these terms, politics is closely connected with ethics as classical ethicists have demonstrated. Aristotle's *Ethics* and *Politics* are best viewed as a single set of lectures, the latter providing a sociological setting for the former. It is almost impossible to distinguish between the ethical and the political in the writings of Plato, Hobbes, Montesquieu, Rousseau, Locke, Hegel, and Rawls. This connection exists because ethical deliberations become politics whenever people consider ways of implementing moral judgements. It is also through political manoeuvering and judgements that many ethical decisions are made.

In his essay "Politics as Vocation" Weber argued that one could assume either a pragmatic or idealistic approach to politics. One could adopt either an "ethic of responsibility" based on realism and pragmatic possibilities or an "ethic of ultimate ends," which endorsed non-violence, justice, and individual rights as non-negotiable points of reference.[16] For the most part, Weber argued in defense of the ethic of responsibility.[17] Nonetheless he concluded that those persons who truly had a calling for politics were able to integrate both ethics: they were pragmatic; they were partisan and yet principled; they combined realism and idealism.

Like Weber, we hold that politics should be guided by a balance of realism and idealism. We believe that it is possible to spell out specific ethical guidelines for politics, assuming, as we do, that the endeavor to act ethically frequently involves politics. We distinguish between obligatory standards that cannot be ignored and ideal guidelines which consist of standards of excellence to which those involved in political action ought to aspire. Failing to honor the first set of guidelines amounts to immoral or deviant behavior. People may fall short of the second set of standards without morally deviating. The visionary, principled, and consensual political styles influenced by ideal moral guidelines enhance the legitimacy and power of those committed to this kind of political action. Idealistic politics has its corresponding political reward (see Figure 8.4).

Obligatory Standards

We have identified four obligatory standards for political action. The first standard is realism. For anyone committed to realizing moral objectives, realism is necessary. Realism highlights limits and obstructions as well as opportunities and alternatives. Realism provides lessons in the art of doing what is possible and in expanding the limits of the possible. As consequentialists argue, it is ethically responsible to be realistic. Realism does not require that people alter either their ultimate objectives or the normative principles that guide their behavior. To be responsible does, however, call for responsiveness to contemporary situational exigencies and a willingness to alter or adapt proximate objectives in relation to these circumstances.

Managers committed to reducing industrial damage to the environment face varied options depending on the existing practices of their companies, the cost involved in instituting improved practices, the positions they hold within their organizations and the support for these improvements from other colleagues. Depending on the circumstances, they may work directly to eliminate pollution, establish a timetable for reduction over a space of years, build a coalition among other managers in support of these activities, protest against current practices, secretly blow the whistle, or publicly expose the conditions. The long range objective of eliminating toxic wastes and pollutants may be pursued by different strategies, which reflect realistic assessments of current limitations and possibilities.

Realism is a virtue for those who wish to enact ethical decisions. It calls for people to consider opposing powers as well as powers that may be mobilized on behalf of particular objectives. The aim of realism ought to be to promote effective action. Sometimes, however, realism is invoked to discourage moral action or moral reform. Realism is evoked to identify difficulties that stand in the way of ethically responsible programs for change. This recognizes limitations and not possibilities, obstructions and not alternatives, difficulties in realizing ultimate objectives and not prospects for pursuing proximate strategies.

Obligatory Standards

Actors should be realistic about what is possible, ignoring neither viable possibilities nor the limitations they impose.

Actors should act in keeping with legal rulings. However, people may protest against laws judged to be immoral by seeking legislative changes, judicial re-interpretations and/or acts of civil disobedience.

As members of organizations, people should seek and use power for the good of the organization rather than for their own personal advantage. Conflict of interest rules in part guard against this abuse.

Coercive tactics ought not to be used unless other means have already been used and proved ineffective. Coercive tactics should largely be used in defense against those using coercive tactics. It is better to seek to persuade than to force or compel compliance.

Standards of Excellence

Politics ought to be visionary. Politics is a means of gaining power in order to fulfill desired objectives. Politics without guiding purposes becomes merely the base pursuit of power. Politics ought to be purposive.

Politics ought to be principled. Not any means are acceptable. Some means are preferable to others. It is vital to act with integrity and inner consistency.

Politics ought to be consensual. Whenever possible, people should seek and use power with the consent of those affected. They should seek power through voluntary cooperation and commitment. Moreover, they should seek consent by persuading others through open discussion and debate rather than by using open or veiled threats.

FIGURE 8.4 **Ethical Guidelines For Political Action**

The next three obligatory ethical standards for political action are widely recognized. The second calls for the observance of legal rulings. However, sometimes specific laws are morally questionable and we are not able to seek changes in them through legislative action. The question then arises, especially when dealing with the laws of other countries, is it permissable to ignore or evade immoral laws? The position we have taken is that developed by defenders of civil disobedience: people may choose not to abide by immoral laws so long as their acts of legal disobedience are public and they are willing to suffer possible punishment for their violations. These public acts call attention to immoral aspects of current laws, seek to arouse opposition to these laws, and hope to transform these laws either through judicial re-interpretation or legislative reform.[18] Thus, civil disobedience seeks to change bad laws not by circumventing them but by altering them and forcing the legal process to confront them directly.

People who are politically involved face the temptation of using their influence and position for private advantage rather than the greater common good. Governments and business organizations develop conflict of interest guidelines to minimize this problem. Because this temptation is so great and so hard to resist for those involved in politics, many people simply use the word "politics" derogatively to identify the self-serving pursuit of power for personal gain. Without reviewing the strategies that have been employed to reduce or limit this problem, we may simply argue that people ought not abuse their positions in organizations for personal advantage.

Insofar as possible we should not resort to coercive tactics. Coercive tactics do not allow for voluntary compliance. They are used to force people to act in prescribed ways whether they wish to or not. Moral tactics seek to persuade people to comply voluntarily. Coercive tactics leave no room for debate or reflection. They are used most appropriately to neutralize or limit the power of others already using coercive means toward immoral ends.

We consider these standards generally acceptable. They identify the parameters for permissable political action by proscribing questionable political conduct. Even by these standards, politics is clearly not a morally indifferent activity.

Standards of Excellence

Political actions ought to be guided, as well, by three additional standards. These standards are not as universally recognized. They are, however, particularly relevant to those who are engaging in politics for moral purposes. We argue that political action, as far as possible, should be purposive, principled, and consensual. We have already identified much of what we mean by these terms when we analyzed purposive, principled, and consensual forms of moral reasoning.

Purposive politics are visionary. Power is not sought for its own sake. It is pursued not simply to exert influence or to gain control but as a means of realizing valued objectives. Visionary politics are antidotes to politics preoccupied by pragmatic considerations. Visionary politics remind people that proximate goals are only proximate: they are relative, historically conditioned objectives that must always be evaluated in terms of their prospects for rendering the realization of the long range objectives more possible.

Principled politics point to standards for action that must be honored. In particular, principled politics call for people to act with integrity and for organizations to act with consistency. They call for managers to publicly honor common standards such as fair treatment, honesty, organizational responsibility, good products, and social responsibility.

(Consensual politics call for us to seek the open, forthright <u>consent</u> of those who are affected by our policies.)Rather than seeking power by using open or veiled threats, or by extending or withdrawing valued resources, consensual politics call for the pursuit of power by seeking fully informed and voluntary commitments from others. Consensual politics assumes that the fundamental base of power rests on the free consent of groups of people whose support has been solicited.

SUMMARY

Effective moral actors understand how to turn thoughts and decisions into behavioral realities. Few moral actors occupy positions of unchallenged authority where their will is automatically converted into action. Hence, moral actors must be both strategists and tacticians, understanding the power arena in which they operate and how to develop the power and influence needed to pursue moral objectives and convert good intentions into effective action. Correspondingly, moral actors can analyze power configurations and use personal, interpersonal, and political skills to develop and sustain coalitions to pursue their aims.

SUGGESTED READINGS

Alinsky, Saul David. *Rules for Radicals: A Practical Primer for Realistic Radicals.* New York: Random House, 1971.

McCoy, Charles. *Management of Values: Ethical Differences in Corporate Policy and Performance.* Boston: Pitman, 1985.

Nielsen, Richard. "What To Do About Unethical Practices." *The Academy of Management Executive* (1989): 124-129.

Weber, Max. "Politics As A Vocation," *Essays in Sociology: From Max Weber.* Translated and edited by H.H. Gerth and C. Wright Mills. New York: Oxford University Press, 1946.

NOTES FOR CHAPTER EIGHT.

1   Max Weber, *Economy and Society*, edited by Guenther Roth and Claus Wittich (Berkeley, Calif.: University of California Press, 1978; New York: Redminster Press, 1968), 53. See also Talcott Parsons, "On the Concept of Political Power" in *Class, Status and Power*, edited by Reinhard Bendix and Seymour Martin Lipset, Second Edition (New York: The Free Press, 1966); Steven Lukes, *Power: A Radical View* (London: Macmillan Press, 1974).

2   Richard Nielsen, "What to Do About Unethical Practices," *Academy of Management Executive* (1989): 124, 125, 127. A number of the examples in this chapter come from Nielsen's studies.

3   Charles S. McCoy, *Management of Values: The Ethical Difference in Corporate Policy and Performance* (Boston, Mass.: Pitman, 1985); Mark Pastin, *The Hard Problems of Management: Gaining the Ethics Edge* (San Francisco: Jossey-Bass, 1986).

4   The Business Roundtable, *Corporate Ethics: A Prime Business Asset* (February 1988).

5   Saul David Alinsky, *Rules for Radicals: A Practical Primer for Realistic Radicals* (New York: Random House, 1971).

6   Richard P. Nielsen, "What Can Managers Do About Unethical Management?" *Journal of Business Ethics*, Vol. 6. (1987): 309-320.

7   Barbara Ley Toffler. *Tough Choices: Managers Talk Ethics* (New York: Wiley, 1986), 86-88.

8   Nielsen, 1987, op. cit., 311.

9   Stanley Milgram, *Obedience to Authority: An Experimental View* (New York: Harper and Row, 1974), 202; Herbert Simon, *Administrative Behavior: A Study of Decision-Making Processes in Administrative Organizations* (New York: Macmillan, 1967).

10 Alinsky, op. cit.

11 Robert L. Heilbroner, *An Enquiry into the Human Prospect* (New York: W.W. Norton and Co. Inc., 1975); Donella Meadows, Dennis L. Meadows, Jorgen Randers, William W. Behrens, III. *The Limits to Growth* (New York: Signet, 1972).

12 Philippe Nonet, *Administrative Justice: Advocacy and Change in a Government Agency* (Berkeley: University of California Press, 1969).

13 Nielsen, 1989, op. cit., 125.

14 Nielsen, 1987, op.cit., 311.

15 J. Gandz and V.V. Murray, "The Experience of Workplace Politics," *Academy of Management Journal*, Vol. 23, No. 2 (June 1980).

16 Max Weber, "Politics As A Vocation" in *Essays in Sociology: From Max Weber*, translated and edited by H.H. Gerth and C. Wright Mills (New York: Oxford University Press, 1946).

17 Wolfgang Schluchter, "Value Neutrality and the Ethic of Responsibility" in *Max Weber's Vision of History: Ethics and Methods*, edited by Guenther Roth and Wolfgang Schluchter (Berkeley: University of California Press, 1979).

18 John Rawls, *A Theory of Justice* (Cambridge: Belknap Press of Harvard University Press, 1971), chp. 6.

- communicating ethical expectation
- policy & practice (2)
- developing moral character (4)
- controlling behaviour

- modeling behaviour
= the important of the whole

- comprehensive approach

Designing Ethically Responsible Organizations

Many senior executives who want managers and their employees to behave ethically ask the question: "What do I have to do to ensure ethical behavior throughout my organization?" They recognize that business organizations become morally responsible not only by committing themselves to honoring sets of principles but also by _acting_ consistently with those principles. If ensuring ethical behavior means guaranteeing it then that is probably impossible and the question must go unanswered. But there are many things that executives can do to ensure that people do not act unethically because they are ignorant, because they are pressured, or because they do not know that the organization values ethical behavior. This chapter outlines the ways in which the tools of organizational design — structure and systems — can create and maintain the ethically responsible organization.

COMMUNICATING ETHICAL EXPECTATIONS

Thomas Watson Jr, of IBM, noted that the great organization "...owes its resiliency not to its form of organization or administrative skills, but to the power of what we call beliefs and the appeal these beliefs have for its people"[1] and Isadore Sharp, the chairman of Four Seasons Hotels, has referred to values as the company's "psychic core."[2] These are organizations which disseminate ethical expectations and moral values throughout the organization.

Following one particularly distressing event in which a manager of a company was found to have lavishly entertained a client, including arranging for various sexual favors, to secure an opportunity to bid on a contract, the CEO of the company said in exasperation: "Surely to goodness, Fred knows we don't condone that kind of thing around here." Well, as it turned out, Fred didn't_ know_ that at all. And the CEO could never remember when he had last discussed the issue with Fred or anyone else. Somehow staff were just supposed to know!

With constant pressures to act in the interests of efficiency, employees who are good, honest people may well take short cuts and "do the wrong thing" because it is expedient to do so, because they fear punishment if they don't, or because they believe they may be rewarded if they do. Or they may simply not realize that what they are doing — taking the hockey tickets, paying the agent a secret commission, promising a supplier that they'll get the next job if they charge a little less on this one — is wrong and is not desired by the organization. When a chemical company manager released toxic effluent into the river he wasn't deliberately committing an evil act; he was reacting to severe cost-cutting pressures that the corporation had imposed. He didn't react in a sensible way and it ended up costing the company millions of dollars in fines and clean-up costs. But he was reacting rationally to a series of intense pressures. When Fred hired an "escort" for the oil company buyer he was trying to make his sales quota, the importance of which had been emphasized to him at the national sales conference three weeks previously and in a telephone call from his regional sales manager the day before.

One way to avoid this problem is to publicize senior management's values and the behavior which is valued by the organization. Statements about ethics and the corporate ethical stance should be published and distributed to employees; when unethical events occur they should be publicized together with the actions taken as a result of their discovery; when codes are developed and revised they should be circulated and discussed at employee meetings.

When managers are exhorting employees to cut costs, sharpen pencils, offer better deals and outdo market competition, they can spend time emphasizing the principles which will guide such efforts. To stress that cost cutting will not come at the expense of safety or environmental integrity, that competition will take place on the basis of product quality and price rather than on personal favors to the purchasing agent, is to balance the messages that people receive and will allow them to make better decisions.

Many firms have attempted to represent their shared moral values by drawing up organizational codes and credos. We have already referred to the credo of Johnson and Johnson. Ninety percent of *Fortune Magazine's* 500 largest firms in the US have codes or credos. As the Business Roundtable asserts: "Codes are important for communicating clear expectations."[3] Codes express the ethos of organizations. Johnson and Johnson's credo expresses shared understandings that have been important for 40 years. Its credo is vital because it is an everyday reality, and it expresses the commitment of the organization to maintaining reciprocally beneficial interactions with major stakeholders. If company codes are to be more than sets of platitudinous ideals and lists of forbidden misconduct, then they must reflect the beliefs and commitments which already guide the morally responsible conduct of organizational members. In this way, codes may be viewed not so much as agendas for changing behavior but as ways of highlighting existing morally responsible conduct.

POLICY AND PRACTICE REVIEW

An organization's policies and practices must be consistent with its espoused values and beliefs if those values and beliefs are to be respected. Yet frequently there is a gap between stated values and various business practices. For example, if an organization espouses values of "empowerment," "trust" and "equality" for employees yet maintains executive dining rooms, separate classes of travel for different levels of executives, and various other perks, executives and managers will be received with cynicism.

In particular, human resource management policies and practices seem to be critical indicators of how employers perceive the values of an organization. How a company closes down or reduces an operation is interpreted as the real statement about individual dignity. Is adequate notice given? Are timely explanations provided? Is assistance given to retraining or relocation? Are severance payments made?[4] When an organization claims that "people are our most valued asset" but then does little to ensure that people get good career planning and performance appraisals, then the pious statements are undermined by corporate practices. It is inevitable, then, that statements about corporate social responsibility or ethical behavior become viewed within the corporation as glib public relations.

There are two kinds of policies and practices which must be regularly reviewed. First, there are those which deal directly with ethical issues such as purchasing policies, gifts and donations to political parties, payments to foreign agents, reporting of financial transactions, investment policies, and many others. Then there are those which do not apparently deal with ethical issues but which might be the source of unethical behavior. So, for example, a corporation's recruitment policy might favor graduates of specific schools and this might result in unintentionally screening out minority group applicants, or another company might rate summer employment in physical labor, such as construction work, very highly in selecting people for permanent employment and might be systemically discriminating against women when they do this. Many companies have disciplinary policies, or at least ways of dealing with "problem employees" and these should be reviewed for their ethical underpinnings.

In recent years, many businesses have augmented auditing activities to take account of the moral performance of organizational members and units. Ethical auditing has assumed several forms. A number of organizations have established social audits. Using various time frames, annually or more frequently, they measure how well units within the organization, as well as the organization as a whole, have performed in relation to affirmative action policies, hours lost for safety or ill health, and investments in local industries. Most social audits focus on indices of social responsibility and the fair treatment of personnel. Usually units within firms and top managers make these assessments about those aspects of the organization for which they are formally responsible. The social audit serves as a reminder of ethical goals.[5]

Organizations may also ethically audit themselves by using survey forms to gain anonymous, confidential information on attitudes and activities of organizational members. Organizations which have instituted such surveys have inquired about the knowledge members have of the organization's ethical guidelines, about grey areas in which members face hard-to-resolve ethical dilemmas, and about members' own satisfaction and organizational commitment. Surveys both inform organizations of troubling areas where they may need to concentrate additional energy and allow members to voice concerns anonymously.

DEVELOPING MORAL CHARACTER

Organizations can foster morally responsible behavior by recruiting, selecting, and promoting people who possess exemplary moral character, training and developing their employees so that they are sensitive to the ethical issues and develop skill in making morally responsible decisions, and reinforcing such behavior through performance appraisals and other control systems.

Recruitment and Selection

Perhaps the most obvious way in which organizations influence their organizational cultures is through the people they hire. The hiring decision is critical to the development of an ethical organizational culture since it is generally considered very difficult to influence deeply held values once people have reached early adulthood.

Organizations may seek to attract people with strong moral character. Candidates may be attracted through advertising, word-of-mouth reputation, recruitment literature, or through managerial and executive search consultants who are briefed to approach people who fit a certain value profile. Organizations such as General Mills, Hees International, and Pepsi-Cola have explicit statements of values, emphasizing good moral character, which they publicize, use in briefing executive recruiters, and in interview questions for prospective candidates. Some organizations, such as General Electric, have widely publicized values which they consider to be important to their organizations.[6]

Sometimes, candidates themselves approach companies because they are attracted to ethical commitment. The popularity of books, such as *The 100 Best Companies to Work For in America* (and its Canadian equivalent) and *Rating America's Corporate Conscience,* indicate that many do consider the moral climate of organizations when they are looking for jobs. In courses which feature teaching cases about ethical organizations, it is not unusual for students to approach their professors and say: "I'd like to work for an organization like that

. . . how do I get in touch!" Indeed, organizations might sponsor the development of such case studies to raise their on-campus profile and attract the kinds of people they want.

An examination of these values indicates variations. Some firms emphasize loyalty, innovativeness, or reliability. Others give prominence to integrity and social commitment. Such variance has made us look at what the "ideal" manager's moral profile might be and we have settled on a short list. We propose that managers should be courageous, temperate, just, prudent, caring, and have a high level of integrity. The importance of these elements of moral character are summarized in Figure 9.1.

Identifying these character traits in people is not simple since direct questions tend to elicit socially desirable responses. For example, asking people in a job interview if they have integrity is highly unlikely to result in a "no" or "I don't think so." It is possible to determine character traits by administering various tests and questionnaires, behaviorally linked questions such as "have you ever been in this situation [specifying some moral dilemma] and how would you act?," assessment exercises, and clinical interviewing by skilled specialists.

Courage allows managers to assume reasonable risks. When they believe something is wrong, they will speak up. They demonstrate initiative but are not foolhardy.

Temperance allows managers to channel their drives and ambitions in creative and useful ways that avoid excesses. When faced with moral issues they will seek organizationally approved ways of dealing with their concerns rather than rush to use force or blow whistles.

Justice is the virtue associated with trying to find fitting balances between competing forces and is essential to considering and balancing stakeholder claims. Just managers respect others' rights and interests and honor principles.

Prudence is the virtue of practical wisdom. Such managers will not get paralyzed by dilemmas, paradoxes, and crises, but will bring their intelligence to bear on the moral issues in practical ways.

Caring managers respect others and keep their well-being in mind in the decisions that they make. They don't have to be reminded of the impact of their decisions on others.

Managers with strong **integrity** are characterized by internal consistency, acting in concert with their values and beliefs.

FIGURE 9.1 **Key Elements of Moral Character**

In practice, the process of recruiting and hiring people with strong moral character may overlap with the process by which businesses may seek to attract and employ people whose beliefs and personalities seem congruent with their organizations. The latter process seeks people who are like-minded and are therefore likely to fit in. Often industrial psychologists and executive search consultants are used to help firms select employees with this kind of congruence. Often this congruence is associated with moral characteristics like "straight-shooting," "integrity," "hard-working" and "assertiveness." However, recruitment, when seeking this kind of fit, is not the same as recruitment which seeks to attract people with moral character. The search for congruence between employees and organizations is likely to be greatly influenced by concerns for compliance rather than independent strength of character. Moral character, in contrast, is associated with the capacity for autonomy, individual discretion, initiative, the capacity for respectful dissent, and strength of convictions — traits which may not seem congruent when too great a focus is placed on conforming.

Reward and Punishment Systems

Through reward and punishment systems, organizations and managers send signals about the extent to which they value various virtues. When someone is disciplined for disloyalty (either directly or by the withholding of organizational rewards such as pay increases and promotion) because they raised concerns about some corporate or senior manager's practices, then the development of moral character is retarded. When they are praised or promoted because they took action to improve safety, stop misleading advertising, expose expense account cheating, or focus on stakeholder concerns, then such moral character is reinforced and reaffirmed as a desired characteristic by the organization.

Firms may use regular performance appraisal procedures to signal their interest in moral character. At this time, managers under review may call attention to services and noteworthy activities they have performed, discuss dilemmas and hard cases where they have had to exercise discretion, and review evidence with respect to their courage, self-discipline, sense of justice, practical wisdom, caring and integrity. It is, of course, exceedingly important that these reviews not be reduced to witch hunts used to gauge and search out instances of non-compliance with company codes. Many companies do ask their managers and subordinates to regularly assess their conduct with respect to company codes. While this exercise helps to arouse a lively interest in these codes, it does not really cultivate and reward strength of character. The latter is most likely gauged by examining how people deal with difficulties where they must exercise discretion and take initiative not dictated by organizational guidelines.

Promotion and Career Development

Even more important than recruiting new, morally sound employees to an organization, is the selection of people who will advance to become the organization's formal leaders. And here, values are tremendously important. In one large multi-national enterprise, two of the six criteria for promoting senior executives are candor and integrity.[7] In a recent speech, the chairman of one of Canada's five top banks proposed that integrity be the first variable considered in promotion matters and that it be a binary, "yes/no" variable — candidates for promotion who did not receive a clear yes would not be considered further, no matter what their other attributes or achievements might be.[8]

The emphasis on values has both emotional and practical dimensions. Among the top ten reasons cited for executive failure in one empirical study was "betrayal of trust — failure to meet commitments," which ranked number three after both "insensitivity to others" and "coldness/aloofness/arrogance."[9]

④ Training and Management Development

One way to emphasize top management's commitment to ethical behavior is to address ethics in staff training and development. Both Exxon and its Canadian affiliate, Imperial Oil, put all managers through internally developed ethics workshops; ethics are also addressed in management development programs in IBM, General Electric, Syncrude, The Royal Bank, and other leading organizations. It is also being found as a topic area on executive and business degree programs at an increasingly large number of North American and European business schools and management development institutes. Professional associations such as the Purchasing Management Association of Canada, and the Canadian Institute of Chartered Accountants also offer courses in ethical issues relating to their professions.

Most often these programs are based on case discussions of situations which managers are likely to experience and focus on specific situations relevant to the functions of the people who are being trained. So purchasing ethics will be taught to purchasing managers, marketers may examine deceptive advertising practices, and so on. Increasingly, though, senior management groups seem interested in exploring the broader, non-functional issues which they may have to deal with as executives, directors, and community leaders.

The inclusion of ethics in management development and training serves three functions. First, it increases awareness of ethics issues among managers; second, it provides tools and techniques to help managers resolve moral dilemmas they face; third, it reinforces the importance of ethics to an organization.

⑤ Formal and Informal Discussions

One other approach to developing the moral character of organizations is to encourage regular discussions between managers about problems that they may face. Whether these are departmental meetings in which senior staff share their experiences and insights with each other or discussions between peers, they help focus organizational attention on moral issues and build awareness and skills among those who participate.

Businesses may indirectly foster moral character by encouraging members to form friendships and affiliative links among themselves. It is within these personal relationships in particular where managers can interact with others who personally praise and criticize their acts in ways that allow them to save face and learn from mistakes.[10] This kind of mutual correction and encouragement, which in turn fosters personal learning and character development, rarely takes place in public or semi-public venues. Organizations are therefore well-advised to foster and allow for these informal networks without attempting to intervene too directly in their management.

Structural Approaches

While most organizations rely on managerial judgements to ensure that policies and practices are ethical, several larger companies are establishing special committees, sometimes of the board of directors, to examine these. For example, Royal Trust has a Business Conduct Review Committee which examines on a routine and ad hoc basis corporate policies and how they might apply to specific situations, and Imperial Oil has appointed a corporate controller to manage employee complaints or concerns about ethical behavior. Many public sector organizations, including universities and colleges, have appointed an ombudsperson to investigate complaints ranging from sexual harassment to favoritism in promotions and transfers. While some private sector corporations have created these roles, others have designated certain individuals as corporate ethical controllers and have publicized their existence and their terms of reference to employees. Increasingly, corporate directors are insisting that such reporting relationships be established, and that they report to outside directors of the board rather than directly to management.

Such actions establish clear channels of communication for employees who suspect unethical behavior within the organization. Often these channels by-pass the traditional hierarchy, designating an individual within the organization who will receive such complaints and investigate them thoroughly while maintaining the confidentiality of the complainant or, at least, shielding them from repercussions. This recognizes several realities. First, that it is difficult for employees to accuse their bosses of unethical behavior, either face-to-face or by going over their heads. Second, if the alternative is whistle-blowing, an anonymous tip-off to the media or government regulators, the damage to the organization may be substantial and could be avoided if prompt action is taken to either confirm the unethical behavior or correct the misunderstanding.

In many cases it is not possible to protect the confidentiality of the informant since he or she may be the only source of the information and may be readily identifiable as soon as an investigation begins. Complainants who approach in confidence must have their privacy respected, even if this makes investigation difficult. By the same token, however, if and when the identity of the complainant becomes known, it may require a great deal of management support for that person, particularly if the complaint turns out to be groundless. Employees may make errors in judgement about the ethical nature of business decisions and practices, and their punishment may deter future vigilance.

One of the great blocks to institutionalizing ethics in business organizations is the fact that so much organizational communication, especially about ethical matters, is one-way. Executives send messages to employees, stating their ideals and identifying restrictions. Employees communicate isolated concerns they become aware of: resentments about discriminatory behavior, complaints about unfulfilled promises, whistle-blowing about inferior products, and concerns regarding difficulty in meeting specific goals.

The child psychologist, Piaget, once described the conversations of juveniles as mutual monologues. Juveniles took turns talking about what mattered to each individually, acknowledged that they had listened to the other, but never really engaged in reciprocating conversations where the course of discussions was affected and shaped by the alternating responses of those involved. At best, many communications in organizations between superiors and subordinates are mutual monologues, even when subordinates feel free to voice their concerns.[11]

If businesses want to be responsive to their members, then internal communications must be open, and ongoing. If not, the concerns of lower managers and employees will be filtered out and the concerns of the organization will not reach those most directly involved. If communications are to be genuinely two-way, then both superiors and subordinates must feel free to set agendas for their interactions and be able to express their feelings. Give-and-take interactions, which allow people to adjust and re-define their objectives and strategies, can only take place under these circumstances.

CONTROLLING BEHAVIOR

It is possible to compensate for the absence of required values, or even to maintain an ethical organization in the presence of contrary values, by directly controlling behavior. At its simplest, a company can control expense account cheating or poor quality through rigid policing of financial records and very tight quality control inspection. This can be done directly through management or supervisory inspection, or institutionally through auditing procedures. If the probability of being caught is high, and the penalties are stiff, the behavior can be deterred but the policing function can be extremely expensive as has been found in the attempt to control drunken driving or drug abuse.

Indeed, the relative cost of establishing values which influence behavior or trying to control behaviors through policing, rewards and punishments may only now be being fully realized. It may be simplistic to suggest that corporations used to hire people without consideration of values and then fire them once they were caught in unacceptable behaviors, but they now find this extremely expensive. They have to catch them, deter them, but in the meantime damage is done. This realization may well be the reason for the current interest in values-based recruitment and selection and the other values-shaping activities described in this chapter. Organizations may simply be recognizing that it is less expensive to work on values than to try to control behaviors.

(Organizations use three basic approaches to control behavior: they can use the reward and punishment system which we described above; they can watch and inspect the way people work through supervisory controls and direct surveillance techniques; and they can audit business and individual practices.) Some companies have quite elaborate audits of business practices which go well beyond the traditional financial audits that internal auditors do. They may audit personnel files to ensure that performance appraisals are being done, they may check purchasing files to ensure that unbiased multi-supplier bidding is carried out, they may require employees to file statements of personal financial transactions and ask them to waive their rights to confidentiality or privacy in personal financial dealings. Many organizations require senior managers and executives to make an annual statement — a declaration that they have personally reviewed the ethics of the business practices within their departments and hold them responsible for any untoward incidents.

(Organizations often seek to curb slack, ineffective, shoddy and deviant behavior by instituting tighter surveillance over workers.) To reduce careless workmanship and to decrease pilfering of company supplies, organizations place supervisors closer to workers and require more detailed reporting on performance. When sales agents use their independence to their own advantage, organizations often restrict their discretion and require fuller accounts of actual negotiations. Organizations typically gear up their surveillance systems when they feel that individual managers and employees have been acting in ways that adversely affect their firms. Businesses have instituted closer supervision to limit the misuse of gratuities, the abuses of executive privileges, business arrangements that represent conflicts of interests and petty pilfering.

Surveillance has limitations and drawbacks. Closer supervision may be used to guarantee that people comply with minimal obligations. (They do not encourage people to aspire to act in keeping with standards of excellence.) They may help to reduce deviance but they do not foster devotion or dedication. More importantly, close supervision is correlated with comparatively lower levels of organizational commitment. Workers exhibit higher levels of identification with, and loyalty to, organizations, and greater commitment to organizational objectives in settings where they feel they are working with more autonomy and less surveillance.[12] Recent experiments with quality circles and past "Quality of Working Life" experiments indicate that employees work best when direct supervision by superiors is reduced and more surveillance is assumed by groups of workers as teams.

In complex organizations, systems of reward and punishment need to be standardized and situationally adjusted if they are to be fair. We do not wish at this moment to consider problems associated with instituting fair reward and punishment systems. We do wish to call attention to this concern and to several of the noticeable ways in which reward/punishment systems may discourage morally responsible behavior. Many organizations believe that it is good to be uncompromising with employees who have been found guilty of violating ethical codes. One organization proudly acknowledged that it had fired employees not only for accepting bribes but also for minor manipulations of records, petty cheating on expense accounts, and failure to disclose information. Such a punitive response to morally reprehensible behavior may well be ethically dysfunctional if it is not administered fairly. Exemplary punishment for individuals whose misdeeds happen to be publicly disclosed, especially when their actions are at cross purposes with their firms, may well breed cynicism and duplicity if misdeeds of others, known privately, go unreported and unpenalized. Severe punishment of notorious misdeeds seems to suggest that all the other actions of firms and their employees are morally good or morally indifferent, as if no other mistakes, poor judgements or indiscretions ever occur. This policy is likely to seem hypocritical to organizational members who know that this is rarely the case. A severe and punitive policy of punishment produces an additional, morally questionable consequence. Fearing exposure or public condemnation for mistakes, bad judgements or careless errors, managers and employees often become more preoccupied with their repute than their actual performance. Because they seek to look good in the eyes of superiors and avoid marks on their records, they shirk difficult decisions, attempting, when they can, to pass them on to others, and camouflage failures and shortfalls, especially morally questionable ones. As managers in one company saw it, the situation called for everyone to cover their rears. Duplicity became an integral leitmotif of organization life, occasioned by a reward and punishment system that was especially punitive with respect to misdeeds and mistakes, and rendered the fear of failure endemic.[13]

OTHER INIATIATIVES

Businesses may also realize particular moral objectives by creating institutions with specific moral mandates. Many corporations have created charitable foundations, charged with distributing funds to worthwhile artistic, athletic and community endeavors. These corporations enjoy certain tax advantages in the process while contributing to special needs and interests of the community. Many corporations help underwrite costs for educational scholarships, endowments for the arts, and economic development projects in poor neighborhoods. The Chemical Bank initiated several programs to help low income groups. They created street banks to extend banking services to impoverished neighborhoods. They established seminars to instruct non-profit organizations on how to manage their finances. A number of businesses have developed specific programs to encourage the hiring and advancement of employees from minority groups. Both the Chemical Bank and Norton have established programs to reward managers who succeed in hiring minority group employees. A number of companies have instituted consumer advisory boards, sometimes comprised of consumers not usually represented, to monitor efforts at meeting consumer needs

and provide them with acceptable services. To insure that the goods they produce are of excellent quality, many organizations have established internal
quality control offices.

(Many businesses have instituted recreational, legal, and health services for
employees.) A number of businesses operating in foreign countries deliberately
encourage local suppliers and invest in local businesses. By creating special committees and offices, organizations can call attention to particular objectives and
assign people the responsibility to realize these goals. Whether such projects
amount to anything depends on how well they are funded and, more decisively,
how much power they are given to realize their mandates. Consumer advisory
boards, quality control offices, ethics committees, and corporate foundations may
be underfunded and given little real authority. A measure of the success of these
special programs is the extent to which they have been able to realize their agen-
da and modify the policies and practices of the larger organization.

MODELING BEHAVIOR

(Needless to say, probably the most critical influence on employees' behavior is
the behavior of immediate supervisors and managers) A senior manager who
makes disparaging comments about someone of a certain gender, race, or ethnic
background is presumed to be reflecting organizational values, not just her or
his personal values. Sometimes junior managers or those who have been recently appointed to management positions may fail to realize the extent to which
their personal behavior is a model for others and the value implications inherent in such behavior.

Corporations may also serve as models in many ways. They may support
organizations such as the United Way, food banks, or other charitable organizations. They may develop policies which encourage personal development such
as educational assistance and retraining. They may also establish facilities to
help employee groups in community work. Here again, when such activities are
inconsistent with day-to-day behaviors, there is the very real risk of cynicism
about the motives and intent of management.

A SENSE OF THE IMPORTANCE OF THE WHOLE

(In the final analysis, the degree to which businesses are able to institutionalize
ethics depends on the extent to which they become morally responsive organizations and embody genuine concern for their members and constituents and seek
to realize worthwhile purposes.[14]) If organizations are to become responsive, fair
institutions, then they must both identify their particular purposes, and establish and maintain procedures so that those who work for, and interact with,
them feel they are treated fairly and decently.

Many managers and employees, many customers and investors, many suppliers and sub-contractors feel they are treated unfairly.[15] Too often, they say,

what seems to count is gaining the favor of particular executives, who are themselves on the make. Enormous deference is paid to particular executives, who in turn enjoy extensive privileges and display great power. To get things done, to obtain the necessary financial or organizational support, to gain promotions, one has to get and keep the attention of these executives. Often this end is best served by obtaining noticeable results over relatively short periods of time. As a result, in spite of an official commitment to long range efforts, individually, managers often seek to produce demonstrable short-term improvements, even though these may deplete stocks and adversely affect long-range developments.

Many businesses are feudal in nature. Executives manage their particular fiefdoms, which they zealously protect. Subordinates pledge their fealty because they know their advancement and power depends on maintaining the favor of these superiors. In the process, many employees, at all levels in organizations, feel that their ongoing efforts are not being fairly assessed. Moreover, if they happen to raise questions about the way these personal interests distort the long-range good of the organization as a whole, they may be excluded from promotion opportunities.[16]

If organizations are to be fair and responsive to members and constituents, they must endeavor to make sure that the ongoing efforts of these groups are not undermined by specific groups or individuals who seek to exploit the organization and its resources for their private purposes. A number of individuals may exploit organizations in this way, from militant, uncompromising trade unionists to executives interested in their own power. Most recently, the threat of extraneous exploitation has been experienced in relation to the chance that particular firms are likely to be bought, merged, or closed, in spite of the hard work and industry and social responsibility exhibited by organizational members. Such moves are often made because they temporarily improve the overall capital assets of an organization or because they allow the organization more versatility in competition with other conglomerates. Such moves are sometimes made because the executives or managers who engineer them, as well as those who finance them, immediately stand to gain wealth, prestige, and power. To be sure, sometimes these transactions can be defended, especially where they allow for greater cooperation between firms or where they are necessitated by changing market conditions. However, these transactions become morally questionable to the extent that unique purposes and strengths of particular organizations are ignored, and the energy and efforts of local firms to improve their productivity and raise their relative moral stature are not taken into account.

A COMPREHENSIVE APPROACH

Organizations which are committed to ethical standards of behavior use an amalgam of value-shaping and behavior-controlling systems and approaches.

While they make every effort to select ethical employees, train and educate them, model desired behaviors, they also routinely audit business practices and require managerial employees to comply with a variety of policing mechanisms.

Clear and concise corporate statement of business principles.

Review of policies and procedures.

Departmental codes and guidelines.

Annual review and sign-off of principles and codes.

Key ethical principles and expected standards of behavior in recruiting materials, interview schedules, candidate profiles, and position (job) descriptions.

Establishment of training and management development programs in business ethics at corporate and departmental levels.

Frequent reference to ethical principles in senior management communications including annual reports, employee newsletters, speeches, and so on.

Internal audit of business practices.

Designated person or organizational unit within management to receive enquiries and complaints about business practices.

Independent business conduct committee of the board.

FIGURE 9.2 **Designing the Ethical Organizational Culture**

This leads to our statement about what it takes to ensure that people in an organization understand the compulsion to act ethically. We suggest the following:

- A clear and concise corporate statement of business principles which includes, but may not be limited to, the moral principles which the company expects to be followed by all employees;
- Review of policies and procedures — specifically those which relate to human resource management — to ensure that they are consistent with the espoused principles and objectives;
- For departments faced with potential ethical dilemmas, to implement departmental codes and guidelines which deal with the most frequently encountered ethical problems and moral dilemmas;
- An annual review and sign-off of principles and codes by managerial personnel and others in positions of trust. When responsible executives or managers do this sign-off they should also commit to reviewing the key elements with their staff in a discussion session;
- A statement of key ethical principles and expected standards of behavior

as a part of recruiting materials, interview schedules, candidate profiles, and job descriptions;

- The establishment of training and management development programs in business ethics at corporate and departmental levels. The key to the effectiveness of these programs is to ensure that senior executives and managers actually attend them. Their conspicuous devotion of time to these emphasizes the importance of the programs to the organization;
- Frequent reference to ethical principles in senior management communications including annual reports, employee newsletters, speeches, and so on;
- An internal audit of business practices to check consistency with ethical principles, extending the role of the auditor from illegal financial transactions to questionable business practices;
- Establishing a designated person or organizational unit within management to receive enquiries and complaints about business practices and to investigate those complaints while maintaining the confidentiality of the complainant;
- Setting up an independent committee of the board, comprised of outside directors, to provide a final avenue of appeal for stakeholders who feel that they cannot go through the management chain of authority or who receive unsatisfactory responses to their problems from senior management.

SUMMARY

In this chapter we have suggested numerous ways that organizational leaders can seek to establish and reinforce an ethical organizational culture. Clear communication of expectations, reviews of practices and policies, and management of the reward and control systems all play their part, as does the recruitment, selection, training, development and advancement of people with moral character. Providing opportunities to discuss moral and ethical issues can help foster an environment which clearly establishes a balance between the achievement of desirable economic goals and good ethical performance.

SUGGESTED READINGS

Jackall, R. *Moral Mazes: The World of Corporate Managers.* New York: Oxford University Press, 1988.

Olive, D. *Just Rewards.* Toronto, Ontario: Key Porter, 1987, chps. 5,6,7,8.

Torbert, W. *Managing the Corporate Dream: Restructuring For Long Term Success.* Homewood, Ill.: Dow Jones-Irwin, 1986.

Waters, J.A. "Catch 20.5: Corporate Morality as an Organizational Phenomenon", *Organizational Dynamics* (Spring 1978): 3-19.

NOTES FOR CHAPTER NINE

1   Thomas J. Watson, Jr., *A Business and Its Beliefs* (New York: McGraw Hill, 1963).

2   Isadore Sharp, Chairman and CEO of Four Seasons Hotels in a speech to the graduates of the University of Guelph's Advanced Management Program for the Hospitality Industry, Spring 1988.

3   Business Roundtable, *Corporate Ethics* (1988), 6.

4   Cynthia Hardy, "Investing in Retrenchment: Avoiding the Hidden Costs," *California Management Review*, Vol. 29, No. 4 (1988): 111-125.

5   John J. Carson and George A. Steiner, *Measuring Businesses' Social Performance: The Corporate Social Audit* (Committee for Economic Development, 1974).

6   Noel Tichy and Ram Charan, "An Interview with Jack Welch," *Harvard Business Review*, Vol. 67, No. 5 (September/October 1989).

7   Ibid.

8   Donald Fullarton, Chairman of the Canadian Imperial Bank of Commerce, in a speech to Institute of Canadian Bankers, November 1989.

9   W. McCall and R. Lombardo, "What Makes a Top Executive," *Psychology Today* (February 1983).

10   Erving Goffman, *Interaction Rituals* (Garden City, NY: Doubleday, 1967); Georg Simmel, *Conflict,* translated by Kurt H. Wolff and *The Web of Group Affiliations,* translated by Reinhard Bendix (Glencoe, Ill.: The Free Press, 1955); Emile Durkheim, *The Division of Labour in Society*, translated by George Simpson (New York: The Free Press, 1933).

11   Jean Piaget, *The Language and the Thought of the Child*, translated by Marjorie Gobain (New York: Meridian Books, 1955).

12   Richard T. Mowday, Lyman W. Porter, and Richard M. Steers, *Employee-Organization Linkages: The Psychology of Commitment, Absenteeism and Turnover* (New York: Academic Press, 1982); Charles Glisson and Mark Durick, "Productivity and Job Satisfaction and Organizational Commitment in Human Service Organizations," *Administrative Science Quarterly*, Vol. 33, No. 11 (1988): 61-68; James P. Curry, Douglas S. Wakefield, James L. Proce, and Charles W. Mueller, "On the Causal Ordering of Job Satisfaction and Organizational Commitment," *Academy of Management Journal*, Vol. 29 (1986): 847-858.

13   R. Jackall, *Moral Mazes: The World of Corporate Managers* (New York: Oxford University Press, 1988), chp. 2.

14   Philip Selznick, *Leadership in Administration* (Evanston, Ill.: Row Peterson, 1957), chp.4.

15   Alex C. Michalos, "The Impact of Trust on Business, International Security and the Quality of Life," *Journal of Business Ethics*, Vol. 9, No. 8 (1990): 619-638.

16   R. Jackall, *Moral Mazes: The World of Corporate Managers* (New York: Oxford University Press, 1988).

- marks of leaders (~)
  def.
- tasks of leaders (5)
- leadership styles (3)
-        : strategies (4)
- good ethical leadership (3)
- importance of lead
- benefits of acting morally
  responsible

10 Ethical Leadership

To translate concepts, ideas, and objectives into actions, people with moral convictions must be able to inspire others. Ideas lead to action because some people assume leadership: they proclaim what needs to be done, initiate action, and mobilize others. Ethical leadership is exerted whenever anyone assumes this responsibility, whatever his or her formal position. Ethical leaders are people who make a difference; who translate moral commitments into effective action by encouraging, guiding, and recruiting others.

LEADERS AND MANAGERS

Leadership is basic to ethical issues. Businesses cannot adequately respond to moral concerns unless they are able to take initiatives and mobilize people with these initiatives. Certainly it is possible, following managerial guidelines, to keep order within organizations and to promote greater compliance with existing moral standards. Many people characterize well administered, law-abiding businesses, able to guarantee high levels of compliance with organizational codes as ethically superior. However, such organizations may remain unmoved by the changing claims of stakeholders, unresponsive to new concerns, unwilling to acknowledge, much less resolve, internal dilemmas and conflicts, and incapable of inspiring moral idealism. Using their managerial positions, leaders initiate, inspire, and mobilize others so that ethical issues become lively concerns.

Whether they assume line or staff responsibilities, executive or supervisory roles, whether they work largely on their own or direct the activities of many, managers are expected to act in keeping with their job description. They are usually expected to establish plans, to supervise budgets, to organize activities and to control the conduct of those answerable to them.[1] They are organization people. They work according to organization rules and expectations within limited jurisdictions; they are answerable to superiors and they make subordinates

157

answerable to them; the positions they fill are identified by specific tasks which they have been trained to perform; they are assigned authority to use their discretion to make fitting decisions in keeping with their positions.[2] Whatever their specialized responsibilities might be, managers are expected to cooperate with others so that the organization as a whole realizes its objectives most effectively.[3]

If we use Kotter's definition of <u>leadership</u> as "the process of moving a group (or groups) in some direction through mostly noncoercive means," then it is clear that not all managers or even all senior managers are leaders.[4] Many senior executives are good administrators; planning, budgeting, coordinating and controlling the conduct of others, without ever moving others in new directions. Managers in various positions may exert leadership, but merely holding a senior position of authority does not, by itself, mark anyone as a leader.

What leaders do, and what managers do when they lead, is to go before others who follow their lead. Leaders <u>show</u> others <u>the way</u> to go, create conditions which motivate them to head in a certain direction, and support them in achieving their desired goals. Leaders cultivate and foster followers. Like team members and their captains, followers and leaders may work closely together like peers. Or, like a Pope and his followers, the relationship may be distant. In either case, people become leaders because they are able to inspire others to follow their direction willingly. Leadership fosters a sense of community both among followers and between leaders and followers.

LEADERS MOBILIZE

Leaders mobilize people: they move them by inspiring them. Although the term leadership is sometimes used to describe institutions and organizations, fundamentally individuals exercise leadership. Leadership is inherently personal because individuals choose to follow the direction of another for who that other person is. The first mark of leaders is that they are able to encourage, arouse and sustain followers who follow their direction out of regard for them as individuals.

Managers as executives, supervisors or colleagues may or may not be able to foster this following. Without exercising real leadership over others, they may still be able to gain the willing cooperation of peers and subordinates. However, others cooperate because of organization rules and contracts and their job descriptions, because they are responding to the system of rewards and punishments in the organization or out of their own commitment to the good of the organization. When a manager exercises leadership, this cooperation may well come easier, as others defer and join in coordinated ventures, not simply out of respect for organizational standards and contractual obligations, but because of their personal regard and respect for the manager.

②

LEADERS INITIATE

Initiative is the second mark of leaders: they take people beyond where they have been before. Leaders may be innovative, ingenious, and creative. However, their leadership does not necessarily have to consist in ground-breaking, revolutionary or startlingly new actions. They may initiate action by showing the way to respond to new contingencies. Whether it be dramatic or prosaic, initiative is required in a number of settings. The world does not stand still. Markets evolve, work-forces age, the economy fluctuates, competitors become more aggressive, conflicts develop, and new technologies are introduced. As managers, individuals respond to these developments in keeping with existing guidelines and past experiences. Often routine managerial responses are sufficient. Leadership is valuable precisely because leaders show new ways to respond to developments. Leaders are not just reactive; they are proactive. Responsive to changing circumstances, they initiate steps to keep ahead of evolving conditions. In order to respond adequately in these settings, managers must be willing to experiment, to try new ways, to explore alternatives. Leaders are people who show the way through new territory.

Many corporations have policies, rules, procedures, and enforcement mechanisms to ensure that employees obey laws. They have codes of ethics; they may have audits; they may train employees to resolve moral dilemmas; they may encourage employees to participate in worthwhile causes such as the United Way or summer camps for children with cancer. They are morally responsible, managing the ethical dimensions of organizational activities. But occasionally someone will lead an organization beyond reactive initiatives. They will move beyond important but prosaic activities and raise the organization to new heights of ethical consciousness. The challenge may be to focus on environmental improvement, or to enhance educational opportunities for the disadvantaged, to improve economic opportunities for native and aboriginal people, or to develop a new consciousness of the role of private sector organizations in community welfare.

THE TASKS OF LEADERS

To inspire and mobilize others and to lead them, leaders perform a series of interlocking tasks. It is useful to distinguish these sub-tasks to examine closely what people do when they function as leaders and to explain how differences in leadership styles reflect variations in the strength with which leaders perform their tasks.

There are five components to the leadership role, as shown in Figure 10.1. First, leaders respond to current circumstances and exigencies which, when they are successfully exploited, become opportunities. Leaders are characterized by an alert responsiveness which enables them to look for and see possibilities in ongoing developments and to do this by listening to what various informed groups have to say. They meet with consumer and special interest groups to recognize concerns about privacy of information, gender bias, copyright infringement, or environmental concerns, well before government regulations force action. They engage in full and active consultation with a variety of stakeholder groups and sub-groups, in ways described in chapter three. In one well-known example, William Norris, the head of Control Data — a large multinational computer company — recognized the social dangers of the decay of the inner cities in the United States and set out to engage community leaders in a discussion of the way his company could help reverse this decay.[5] The result was a commitment to locate plants in the inner cities, drawing on the existing labor pool of unemployed, educationally deprived residents of some of the country's most depressed and crime-ridden areas. His objectives — broadly shared by many stakeholders in the company — were to help develop those communities by providing well-paid employment and a sense of dignity and self-esteem. Norris firmly believed that this was the way for business to demonstrate its commitment to the society in which it was located.

Second, leaders are able to size up situations and determine what really matters. They exercise the capacity for critical judgement. They are able to process information and make sense of it. This talent for judgement is really what in chapters five and six we referred to as the capacity for deliberating. There were many things Control Data could have done with its resources. It took the leader's judgement to recognize that the provision of basic skills and knowledge was the best way out for a generation which was developing a chronic welfare dependency.

Third, and only because they are able to judge situations, leaders are able to articulate appealing visions. Like visionaries, seers, and prophets, leaders are able to articulate images of what really matters in terms that are intelligible and appealing to those who follow them. Like ancient sophists, leaders know how to convey their messages persuasively. Like students of rhetoric and elocution, they know how to speak powerfully in terms that recognize present exigencies for what they are and inspire people to act. Leaders excel at communicating; whether by words or examples, they know how to put their message across with immediacy and cogency. They seem to know what images to use to refer or allude to complexities of the situation yet to make it seem more manageable.[6] Many people spin visions of the world that are too simplistic, complex, utopian, or uninspiring. The visions of leaders differ because they connect them to immediate courses of action. The leader of Control Data used his personal skills to make meaningful to others — employees, shareholders, local community leaders, the media, and other business leaders — his vision of a more educated and productive community.

The fourth task of leaders consists in linking visions to programs of action. Often the link is made by spelling out a course of action. Funds must be raised, resources identified, and people must see that there is a road map to achieve a worthwhile goal. In the Control Data case, the chief executive assigned personnel and operating funds to make it happen, signalling that the initiative was beyond mere rhetoric.

(Finally, leaders are able to arouse and mobilize followers.) What distinguishes leaders is that others look to them for direction and willingly adhere to their guidance. Whatever their formal, organizational relationships, the relationship between leaders and followers is personal. A subordinate may defer to a superior out of respect for the latter's position and obligations to his own position. Insofar as the subordinate looks to the superior as a leader, then a personal sense of loyalty and commitment is added. Leaders gain followers by being able to touch people's lives. Depending on their responses, followers nourish leaders, much like audiences encourage and inspire actors. By their own responses, they may actively help to shape how the central message is to be interpreted and communicated. By their varied enthusiasm, they signal leaders, applauding some of their actions more than others, thereby helping to shape the directions which leaders eventually take.

(Leaders link their visions to courses of action by recruiting collaborators, and forming coalitions of people willing to spread their messages and work zealously to realize their visions.) Like successful politicians, leaders communicate their vision by creating caucuses of dedicated supporters. Leaders need staff, spokespeople, proselytizers, loyal henchmen, and party whips to attract and organize their following. As one person, Norris of Control Data could have done something; by mobilizing others — managers, employees, educators, community leaders, etc. — his efforts were multiplied incalculably. But, sadly, in the face of unsatisfactory financial performance, he lost control of the company and his initiative collapsed.

People who succeed at leading often perform these tasks in a circular fashion. Leaders gain followers because they are responsive. They provide direction because they exercise critical judgement. They collect and marshall collaborators and lieutenants because they articulate persuasive visions. They keep followers because these coalitions keep the ties with followers open and reciprocal. All of these spokes keep the wheels of leadership rolling.

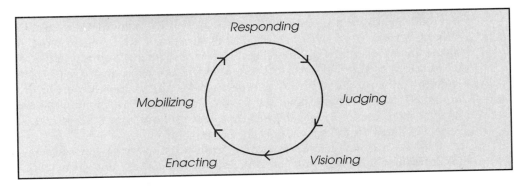

FIGURE 10.1 **The Tasks of Leaders**

Too often, followers are defined as people whose relationship with leaders is remote. The followers of many political and religious leaders often only know their leaders from a great distance. In smaller associations, however, the relationship between leaders and followers may be much closer. Groups may be directed by informal leaders who possess no formal authority but to whom others may look to set the tone, to establish priorities, and to give direction. In some loosely structured organizations that are sometimes referred to as adhocracies,[7] leadership may move around, depending on the tasks being performed. A leader may be a first among peers, a team leader, a player coach, or a committee chairperson, as well as a figure more resembling a priest among parishioners, or politician among constituents.

This observation is made to squelch two popular, romantic views of leadership. According to the first view, leadership is associated almost exclusively with one or two of these tasks, such as articulating visions and arousing followers. While some leaders have clearly excelled at these tasks more than others, it is a mistaken oversimplification to fail to see the degree to which these leaders also perform other tasks or rely on others to perform tasks for them. The other misconception of leadership is to assume that people who lead perform all these tasks with proficiency. In practice, most leaders demonstrate more strength and competence at some tasks than others.

Because of their responsiveness to others and to possibilities, some leaders are more like pastors or forecasters. Because of their skills at sizing up situations and making judgements, some leaders are more like judges. Because of their competency at articulating compelling visions, some leaders are more like seers, oracles, or visionaries. Some leaders fit a more political mold because of their exceptional talent for coalition-building. Finally, because of their capacity to excite and attract groups of followers, some leaders correspond more to what the ancient Greeks called demagogues or what we today refer to as charismatic figures. It is the rare and exceptional leader who excels at all these tasks.

Not all leaders are effective. The effectiveness of leaders is not gauged by how well they perform tasks. A leader may have great appeal, like Hitler, but may not be effective in moving people in ways that benefit them best. The best way of determining the effectiveness of leaders is to measure what has happened to the people who have elected to follow them. We may judge leaders to be effective to the degree that these people have been energized, to the extent that internal conflicts in the groups they lead have been resolved or at least managed, to the extent that they have found ways of responding adequately to new developments, to the degree that groups have found ways of interacting peacefully and cooperatively with others in their environment.[8]

Not all authority figures become leaders. Many who have become leaders for groups of followers are not effective leaders. They may gain followers who are not energized. They may establish initiatives that exacerbate conflicts, and fail to allow for creative and fitting responses to changing developments, and aggravate relations with external groups. We are interested in examining effective leaders who exert their leadership on behalf of ethical issues, wherever these leaders are found in organizations.

ETHICAL LEADERSHIP STYLES

Leaders are expected to be able to mobilize their followers to act cooperatively to realize visions. There are different ways of gaining compliance. In order to call attention to these differences, we will briefly describe three leadership styles, which we will refer to as authoritarian, transactional, and transformational. These leadership styles, summarized in Figure 10.2, correspond to differences in patterns of organizational controls which may be coercive, utilitarian, or normative.[9]

---

① Authoritarian
Exercise legitimate power to mobilize cooperation and gain compliance. May use sanctions but mainly rely on threats of sanctions. Followers comply to the minimal extent necessary to avoid punishment or, unthinkingly, merely accept the dictates of the leader.

② Transactional
Exchange rewards and punishments for compliant behaviors based on the principle of fair exchange. Followers comply or support to the extent that they understand the terms of the contract and the benefits of compliance or support exceed the costs, where the costs also include the benefits of non-compliance or support.

③ Transformational
Encourage beliefs and dispositions which foster identification by the followers with the goals and aspirations of the leader by intellectually stimulating followers with compelling and exciting visions and fostering identification with the distinctive purposes of their organizations.

FIGURE 10.2 **Types of Ethical Leaders**

Authoritarian leaders seek cooperation and gain compliance by exercising their legitimate power. They do not invite but command followers to interact in specified ways. Furthermore, they make it clear that non-compliance will be swiftly and effectively punished by imposing penalties, by public ridicule, by demotions, or by expulsions. They exercise a powerful influence that may at times become coercive. However, ordinarily such leaders only rarely need to impose these kinds of sanctions. Followers comply because they regard leaders and their directives as legitimate on the basis of the positions they hold and because they wish to avoid penalties. Authoritarian leadership is especially effective in well-disciplined, hierarchically structured organizations such as the military, the police, tightly organized religious orders, medical practice, and paternalistic businesses dominated by powerful figures.

Authoritarian leadership can be exercised to produce effectively coordinated, well-ordered organizations where followers seek to pursue goals they share in common and where leaders continue to evoke respect and devotion. This kind of leadership is often accepted in times of crisis. However, in less critical situations or over time, the aura which legitimates these leaders declines. Correspondingly, compliance of followers becomes less eager and more calculating. Often we use the term authoritarian to refer to leaders who have lost most of their legitimacy and who gain compliance largely by threat and coercion. Followers comply to avoid punishment. Exercising ethical leadership on an authoritarian basis is not unusual, particularly when the founder of an organization has strong moral principles.

Transactional leaders seek to mobilize followers by establishing implicit or explicit contracts or agreements with them based on fair exchanges. The leader offers rewards — in terms of wages and salaries, status, opportunities for promotion, economic security, organizational perks, fringe benefits, improved working conditions, longer vacations — in return for willing cooperation and compliance. When followers fail to live up to expectations, inducements are withdrawn proportionately to the degree they miss the mark. Extra rewards are offered for those who excel. The relationship between leaders and followers is viewed like an open market: leaders and followers negotiate until they arrive at agreements that maximize their interests. Leaders are expected to remain attentive to the needs and desires of followers so that they can respond to the latter in ways that also serve their own objectives. The relationship on both sides is voluntary and calculative, and subject to changes as leaders and different groups of followers seek to improve their relative positions or gain greater rewards or compliance from each other. Transactional leadership has been effectively exercised by many corporate executives as the standard model for mobilizing employee cooperation.

Transactional leadership works well so long as the exchanges which underpin it are seen to be fair and reasonable, and so long as followers are able to see the link between rewards and expected behavior. Transactional leadership is subject to various breakdowns. One area of concern is the match between rewards or inducements and desired conduct. Leaders may offer increased benefits in the form of higher wages and more job security, with little noticeable results, switching in disenchantment to closer surveillance in hopes of improving performance. Countless studies have been conducted to determine what combinations of rewards and threatened penalties raise the commitment level of workers.[10] There is, of course, no final answer to this question. Leaders and followers must continuously re-negotiate. Three factors seem to be important in these exchanges: followers are most likely to maintain higher levels of commitment if the overall system of exchanges within organizations is fair and reasonable, if they are allowed some discretion without too close supervision, and if their work obviously makes a difference to others.[11] Transactional leadership works so long as leaders can provide meaningful rewards. There are, however, limits to the rewards that managers are able to offer those who report to them.

There are many ways in which rewards and punishments may be tied to ethical behavior and some of these were discussed in the previous chapter. Performance reviews, the forfeiture of pay or promotion for ethical trangressions, praise given for acting morally are all examples. But it is also clear that there are rewards for engaging in "non-role" and "role-distortion" acts. The huge sums of money to be made from insider trading, the big bonuses for maximizing short-term profit, the opportunity to grasp the brass ring for keeping costs down or fixing prices, receiving kickbacks from suppliers, are all factors in determining the value of ethical behavior in purely transactional terms. Put quite simply, the organization may find it impossible to structure its reward and punishment system to counterbalance these pressures and, even if it does, may be unable to enforce compliance.

Transformational leaders seek to mobilize followers by exercising normative controls, that is, by encouraging loyalty among followers. Authoritarian and transactional leaders often gain, at best, minimal compliance. Transformational leaders seek something more: a disposition among followers to seek to realize the ends of the organization as desirable and obligatory. Transformational leaders attempt to communicate their visions so appealingly that followers will identify with them as if they were their own. Often, transformational leaders seek to encourage this by fostering closeness between themselves and their followers. To the extent that the leader's vision is based on the desire to satisfy the needs of their followers, there will be a long-lasting and deep leader/follower commitment. Such transformational leaders develop followers who are loyal, committed, and involved in achieving their vision.[12]

Transformational leadership has been exercised effectively in organizations whose objectives and operating standards are shaped by moral vision, such as many religious and political organizations, business organizations dominated by charismatic figures, and any organization governed by a recognized sense of mission or purpose. Transformational leadership is also subject to its own limitations and weaknesses. Many executives, for example, lack the gifts for personalized leadership. In addition, transformational leaders become distracted by their own private goals, which they pursue more avidly than the goals of their organizations.[13] Too often, in their effort to personalize their role, transformational leaders are tempted to make a cult of their own leadership.

It is useful to recognize that the identification of followers with a moral vision and their loyalty to the organizations which seek to realize this vision may be fostered without drawing attention to the role of leaders. Transformational leaders may well make themselves servants of the visions which they articulate. They need not possess any charismatic attributes.

Rather, they may lead by identifying and seeking to realize the distinctive purposes that make their organizations worthy institutions.[14] Managers may become transformational leaders because, through their direction, their organizations adopt aims and standards which appeal to the members' sense of loyalty, industry, and commitment. Transformational leaders, in the end, deserve this label only if they do just that: occasion transformations in their organizations so that members are motivated to follow them and to seek organizational objectives not simply because they are ordered to do so, and not merely because they calculate that such compliance is in their interest, but because they voluntarily identify with the organization and willingly seek to fulfill its purposes. When ethical leadership takes place in this transformational mode, then there is a greater chance that followers will become more committed to ethical behaviors within their organizations and that this will endure.

ETHICAL LEADERSHIP STRATEGIES

Managers exert ethical leadership whenever they act as leaders with respect to moral issues. Depending on the kinds of issues which they address, they may lead their organization to limit moral failure, including acts that contravene legal and company codes as well as "role-failure" acts of mismanagement, or they may assume initiative in addressing moral dilemmas, or in inspiring their organization to pursue standards of moral excellence. The leadership of managers is more or less ethical depending on the degree to which they assert their leadership on behalf of these issues.

Ethical leadership is defined in terms of the responsibilities leaders assume, rather than in terms of their character traits. It is possible to evaluate managers in terms of their strength of character. In earlier chapters we argued that recruiting, promoting, and rewarding managers with strong moral character was an essential means for creating ethically responsible organizations. Clearly, leaders who can act with courage, self-discipline, and integrity, using practical wisdom, and acting with compassion and justice are likely to act in morally exemplary ways. Independent of the issues they address, the leadership these people provide is certainly virtuous. We suspect that virtuous leaders are especially likely to exercise leadership on behalf of particular moral issues.

Depending on their positions and the character of the organizations to which they belong, managers may exert moral leadership from four different stances. They may develop ethical leadership strategies characterized, as shown on Figure 10.3, by protest, dissent, insulation, or reformation.

---

1. Protest: Exposing wrong-doing, criticizing moral laxity. May involve personal cost.
2. Dissent: Call attention within the system to particular problems. Form caucuses and groups to promote change. Negotiate to increase influence.
3. Insulation: Focus on own area of authority and responsibility. Set example to influence the larger part.
4. Reformation: Utilize legitimate authority, power and influence to reform or transform organizations.

FIGURE 10.3 **Ethical Leadership Strategies**

Protest

Ethical leaders may lead others to protest moral abuses. When little opportunity exists for constructive reform, it is morally fitting to expose wrong-doing and to criticize moral laxity. Protest is a vital moral role. It highlights unacceptable practices that would otherwise be passively tolerated. Many of the moral issues that especially concern business people today, including fair treatment of minorities and pollution, initially surfaced as moral concerns when some individuals and groups exposed their questionable aspects. Protests encourage people to think twice about customary practices, sometimes more defensively, but sometimes recognizing that changes are both desirable and necessary. Protests publicize issues.

Typically, protests are staged by groups and individuals who are either in subordinate positions within organizations or are marginal to them. People protest when they judge that they are unable to work for changes within organizations, either because organizations themselves resist change or because they lack power to institute reforms. Protesting is often costly. Organizations do not like to be publicly exposed and openly criticized, even if attacks are warranted. They are likely to attack back by criticizing their critics, exposing the moral failings of those who exposed them, and punishing the protesters. Depending on their organization, managers who voice moral protests may be faced with situations in which they are requested to become silent or quit. For this reason, ethical protests against business practices are often led by groups and individuals outside of management, such as trade unionists, consumer advocates, caucuses of investors, and community groups. However, courageous managers, who are unable to continue to acquiesce in the face of immoral practices, such as the unannounced cheapening of products or the disregard for adequate safety precautions, have openly led protests.

Dissent

As ethical leaders, managers may dissent. Typically, as dissenters they call attention to particular problems rather than systematic abuses. They form caucuses to lobby for specific changes and criticize specific abuses. Dissenters often enter into compromises. To secure some progress, they relax certain demands. While protesters seek their own moral autonomy, dissenters often willingly become entangled in negotiations where they end up supporting programs and policies they oppose in principle, in return for organizational support for their own projects. As loyal opposition, dissenters often mute their public criticism in hopes of gaining influence for their views through hard bargaining. Dissenters seek to work for changes within organizations by raising probing questions, by calling attention to overlooked information, by building coalitions willing to support changes and, at every turn, proposing compromises that seem feasible and morally principled.

Dissenters play a vital, but very demanding ethical leadership role in business organizations. When they are able to find a fitting balance between loyalty and dissent, they may become the consciences of their organizations. This is, however, not an easy achievement. They are likely to be attacked and sometimes threatened by those in authority. Unless their organizations tolerate criticism, dissenters are likely to be pushed towards open protest or forced compliance. At the same time, dissenters are also likely to be attacked by their followers for bending their principles in the hope of gaining trivial consolations from top management. Both to their opponents and their supporters, ethical leaders who play the role of dissenters seem vulnerable to compromising too much. Still, when organizations welcome feedback and the airing of moral concerns, dissenters perform an influential role in helping to promote candor and concern about ethical issues, and in helping to cultivate commitment for new ventures reflecting these commitments.

Insulation

Without being able to influence the moral direction of their organization as a whole, managers may at times exert ethical leadership within particular areas or units which are insulated from others. These units may vary in size from whole divisions to work areas. Often large organizations will allow smaller groupings to experiment with different patterns of management, for example, with greater worker participation in administering quality and quantity controls or with more service-oriented marketing strategies, just to see how they work. Divisional structures often allow sub-groups more autonomy in setting goals, in developing their own ethos, in setting their own standards. Managers may seek to exert ethical leadership by attempting to secure positions of authority within units of large business organizations, by exerting leadership with respect to these units, and by insulating them insofar as possible from counter-influences that might undermine or subvert ethically responsible policies that differ from those of the larger organization. Rather than attempt to reform large, complex organizations, managers may exert leadership by seeking to influence small, manageable units where their leadership is more likely to be acknowledged and welcomed. These efforts may, by good example, influence the larger organizations of which they are a part.

Many morally committed managers would like to be in positions where they could demonstrate ethical leadership within smaller, manageable units of their organizations. They would like to be able to identify their units, whether they be plants, regional sales forces, laboratories, or accounting departments, as fiefs over which they can exert independent moral leadership. The problem is that large organizations often resist this independence, particularly when managers exploit autonomy to pursue their own private interests at the expense of the organization. Hence, to create independence for their units, managers must insulate them from ordinary practices and policies that might subvert their moral purposes. Depending on the unit, this is often easier to envision than to accomplish. Organizations sometimes favor autonomy with respect to personnel practices, community relations, and purchasing, but then insist on centralized accounting practices that measure overall activities only in relation to short-term budgets. Nonetheless, although organizations object to independent fiefdoms, it is possible for well-administered units to gain the jurisdiction to experiment with ethical policies currently resisted by the larger organization.

Reformation

Operating within the existing structures of authority, managers may also exert ethical leadership by directly using their influence and discretion to reform their organizations. Using the legitimacy they already possess as executives, supervisors, and directors, managers may exert leadership to attack moral abuses, to confront and resolve dilemmas, to encourage the pursuit of ideals, to cultivate an ethically responsible culture, and to foster and reward those who act with moral integrity. The leadership of these managers reforms or transforms organizations. Unlike managers who lead through protests, dissent, or isolated experiments, reforming managers lead by seeking to remake their overall organizations. The stakes are higher, and the accomplishments likely to be more decisive. However, reforming is only possible by those who are already vested with some measure of organizational authority as senior managers. Managers may provide ethical leadership from any of these four stances: by protest, dissent, experiment, or reform. However, for the most part they must concentrate their energies on a single approach.

The choices between these stances are influenced by the positions of managers within their organizations and by their own moral convictions. Typically, managers with the least influence are more likely to adopt a stance of protest or dissent while those with greater authority are more likely to undertake experimental projects or organizational reformations. Which leadership stance morally committed managers adopt is influenced not only by their organizational power, but by their assessment of the organization's willingness to adopt moral objectives. Ethical leadership adopts a strategy of protest or dissent when organizations seem especially resistant to moral reform. Experimental projects and reformational leadership are more suited to organizations that are open to moral transformation. Finally, leadership grows out of personal convictions. Concerned about particular abuses, some managers are more inclined to leadership by protest; more inclined to diplomatic negotiations; more disposed to dissenting leadership; more eager to experiment on smaller cases and provide leadership in their own units; and more concerned to provide moral leadership through organizational reforms.

These leadership strategies identify the ways morally concerned managers deal with specific issues. It is useful to recognize that several alternatives are possible. These leadership stances describe different orientations for leaders and their organizations. We must now consider something which has been assumed up to this point, namely, the relationship between managers as ethical leaders and those who look to and follow their direction. Whether they are protesters or dissenters, experimenters or reformers, managers adopt styles of ethical leadership which are more or less preferable to those who follow them. Some styles of leadership are more likely than others to promote ethically responsible business practices.

GOOD ETHICAL LEADERSHIP

The term "leader" is morally neutral. A leader is someone capable of moving others to act because the latter look to the former for direction and inspiration. However, in common usage leaders are judged to be good or bad depending on how they lead. Most people understand the difference between good leaders and those who are judged to be false, misleading, or reprehensible. There is common consensus that good leaders promote the well-being of those who follow them while bad leaders make empty promises; good leaders are responsive to the interests of followers while bad leaders are authoritarian. It is helpful to examine good and bad leadership in more detail to see how those who seek to be leaders might avoid the traps associated with misguided leadership and cultivate the characteristics of good leadership.

Our discussion of ethical leadership is not morally neutral. We recommend that those who wish to be leaders, and ethical leaders in particular, seek to develop and limit specific characteristics. We seek to identify the marks of morally good leadership. Rather than characterizing good and bad leadership globally, it is useful to examine the tasks which managers as leaders perform, and analyze various ways of performing these tasks which are ethically justifiable.

Responsive to followers
- Welcoming positive and negative feedback
- Staying in touch
- Incorporating followers' needs and aspirations in their visions
- Recognizing contributions of others
- Sharing power with subordinates

Accountable to followers
- Sharing information
- Owning up to mistakes

Offer visionary leadership
- Exercising good judgement
- Make and keep promises
- Communicate comprehensible messages

FIGURE 10.4 **Good Ethical Leadership**

Whether good or bad, all leaders are expected to be <u>responsive to change</u>, especially with respect to stakeholders, to judge what is at stake, to communicate to others a vision of what needs to be done, to find ways of translating this vision into action, and to mobilize the support of followers to realize this objective. Whether good or bad, all leaders generate followers, articulate visions, elicit trust and confidence, and produce results. However, when we examine the alternative ways of performing tasks, we can distinguish different leadership styles.

Leaders are expected to be responsive to changing contingencies. Some leaders are more sensitive to change and are more likely to identify opportunities. Leaders may be more or less responsive to their followers and stakeholders, more or less open to take account of their interests, and more or less accountable to them for their actions. If leaders are to set agendas that represent the interests of their followers, they must be continuously sensitive to their points of view. They must welcome positive and negative feedback, applause and dissent. Good leaders invite two-way communication, which is often noisier and more disruptive than less open communication. Good leaders do not only encourage followers to identify with them and their <u>visions</u>, but they formulate visions that take into account the needs and hopes of their followers. Their relationship is reciprocal, ever open to new input. As a measure of their responsiveness, good leaders call attention to the accomplishments of subordinates. They make sure that all those involved in worthwhile new ventures receive due credit. They do not take all the praise. Good leaders often <u>allow subordinates</u> and stakeholders to set agendas for their interactions. Surveys of middle managers indicate that senior managers rarely extend this privilege to subordinates.

Senior managers call on those below them to implement their directives and to provide feedback to their questions. Rarely do they take them into their confidence or allow them to suggest what should be considered. However, good leaders do just that: they include subordinates in their counsel so that conversations between them are open and reciprocal.[16]

(The responsiveness of good leaders is measured, not only in terms of their sensitivity to the concerns of their followers, but also by the degree to which they make themselves accountable to them.) Good leaders recognize that they are answerable for their actions. The buck stops with them. They do not attempt to divert blame to subordinates. They own up to their own mistakes. They allow their own accomplishments to be judged openly. Good leaders recognize that their well-being as leaders is bound up with the well-being of those they are leading.

(Many leaders who are quick to <u>seize opportunities</u> are less than fully responsive to the concerns of those they lead.) Many leaders advance so quickly in pursuit of their visions that they leave their followers behind them. They become insensitive to followers' needs and aspirations, and become unaccountable to them. Many business organizations encourage a lack of responsiveness among managers in the process of becoming leaders. They move them from one assignment to the next, promoting them to larger responsibilities, often on the basis of short-term performance. There is no doubt that these fast tracking managers produce benefits for their organizations at least in the short-term. However, aiming at ever higher advancements, they often have little time to spend cultivating open and reciprocal interaction with subordinates. These fast tracking managers often outrun the ordinary mechanisms of accountability. Marshalling personal and material resources to produce demonstrable accomplishments, they may well deplete these resources in ways that only show up some time after they have moved up to more senior posts.[17] Such managers may well demonstrate leadership by their innovation, vision, and capacity to attract allegiance even though they remain comparatively unresponsive to the concerns of subordinates and are unaccountable to them. Such leadership may at times be effective but it is not good. A leader who outruns his or her followers is no longer a leader.

One additional point should be made. It is very difficult for leaders to be genuinely responsive to their followers if the rewards they receive for their efforts — in praise, status, salary, fringe benefits, and privileges <u>far exceed</u> that of their followers.) Leaders are expected to receive greater benefits. However, when their remuneration and rewards reach disproportionate heights, then they are likely to become distracted by these advantages and distance themselves from the concerns of their followers.

(Leaders are expected to be able to judge what is at stake in <u>changing circumstances.</u>) Leaders identify issues, deliberate on alternatives, and determine courses of action. When they are able to see opportunities, to find resolutions for dilemmas, to find direction in the midst of confusion, we often describe leaders as visionary. Some leaders are more skilled at finding resolutions to problems and clear direction than others.

It is possible to distinguish visionary leadership that is morally better or worse. Three traits characterize good visionary leaders: they exercise good judgement, they make promises which they help to realize, and they communicate messages that are comprehensible. Leaders exercise good judgement when they deliberate thoughtfully and fully, avoiding hasty conclusions and arbitrary, one-sided decisions. Good judgements are not gauged by how fast or slow decisions are made but by the degree to which relevant considerations are taken into account, and intelligible justifications are offered for courses of action decided on. The mark of good judgement is thoughtfulness.

Good visionary leaders promise only what they can deliver. When business leaders promise more than can be realized, they mislead. This is a constant temptation for visionary leaders. By their very character, they articulate ideals. If they were practical pragmatists, their visions would fade. Good visionary leaders find ways to strike a balance between their visions and practicality; they are "chastened utopians."[18] They seek "proximate solutions to impossible problems."[19] Nonetheless, many visionary leaders promise more than they can deliver. The visions they articulate are so appealing that they maintain support, in spite of their lack of accomplishments, by excusing their failings as a lack of dedication from their followers or the guile of opponents.

Good leaders articulate visions that are comprehensible. Comprehensible messages are ones that can be readily understood and acted on. Leaders often communicate messages that are contradictory. Consider the following examples, where followers are supposed to make sense of conflicting statements by leaders: "Take initiative" but "don't break the rules;" or "think of the organization as an entity" but "don't trespass into others' areas of responsibility;" or "think in the long-term" but "you will be rewarded and punished in relation to present performances."[20]

Often, contradictory messages are accidental; sometimes they represent the attempt to push onto subordinates contradictions which leaders have not directly confronted themselves. The visions of leaders may not be fully comprehensible by being, for instance, vague and indistinct. Slogans about being service-oriented may convey little significance apart from illustrations or operational guidelines that spell out what these words mean. Some leaders deliberately cultivate an image of themselves as clear-sighted but can only articulate their visions abstrusely. Indirectly, they ask their followers to trust them and their visions which they discuss in vague, general terms. Intentionally or unintentionally, visionary leaders have been tempted to mystify their followers, to hide their lack of clarity, and to reinforce their superior status.

ETHICAL LEADERSHIP: GETTING FROM HERE TO THERE

Without leadership, organizations grind to a halt. They stagnate. They routinize. They lose balance. In fits and starts they may attempt to overcome their stupor. But they are likely to lack direction, purpose, calling, and vitality.

Without ethical leadership, moral issues remain private concerns, personal quandaries, and occasional public outcries against violations of recognized standards. Leadership gets things going.

There are <u>many good reasons</u> for acting in morally responsible ways and for taking the initiative to make ethics an integral part of business. Businesses ought to act morally to comply with existing laws, professional codes, organizational conventions and societal values. Businesses ought to assume ethical responsibility for their actions because acting in these ways occasions both short- and long-term <u>benefits</u>, including more cooperative relations among personnel, higher regard from stakeholders, and less cheating and deception from organizational members. Businesses ought to be moral because acting in keeping with moral convictions preserves a sense of moral worth and self-esteem. Businesses ought to be ethically responsible because there are principles which should not be violated.

Minimally, at least, businesses often comply with moral standards even though they may be quick to argue that this compliance is incidental to <u>good business practic</u>es. Managers possess some moral sensibility but they rarely talk directly about it. As a result, moral amnesia ensues, in which business people fail to recognize the degree to which ethical concerns influence their practice. This moral amnesia calls for ethical leadership. What is required is that concerned managers assume the leadership of identifying the moral aspects of issues facing business, in acknowledging the ethical standards on their practices, and in discussing these matters among themselves and with their stakeholders. Individuals are needed who are willing to assume initiative in transforming their organizations, or parts of their organizations over which they have some influence.

We have argued that individuals may assume this leadership within the <u>limitations</u> of their authority. They may assume leadership from various parts of their organizations, adopting different leadership stances depending on their organization locations and their own capacity for leadership. Some managers may lead through protests and criticisms. Others may lead by raising questions and dissenting. Others may lead by creating their own model units. Some may lead by using existing positions of authority to bring about a renewal, or a moral revitalization of their organizations, as a whole. At the same time, from whatever stance, some may lead like prophets, and others by serving as collaborators, colleagues, and salespeople for moral reforms. What matters is that <u>initiative</u> is taken and supported.

SUMMARY

How business people respond to ethical issues matters a great deal. In some cases immoral acts are also <u>illegal</u>. In many instances failure to act in morally responsible ways results in consequences that are <u>harmful</u> to employees and customers, and costly to organizations and the public.) The unsafe use of toxic materials has resulted in illness and physical harm to employees and customers. The myopic pursuit of their own advancement through ill-planned but attention-getting deals has caused a number of executives to make decisions extremely costly to their businesses. Customers are harmed by deceptive advertising. Workers are mistreated when they are discriminated against. Investors and customers are injured when banks make too many risky loans.

(The major problem may lie in refusing to establish an ethical organization and demonstrate ethical leadership.) Failure to identify and respond adequately to ethical issues is not only harmful, but it also means that businesses lose opportunities to develop closer, more reciprocal relations with workers, customers, and community groups. Ultimately, failure to deal responsibly with the moral aspects leads to a lack of clarity and direction regarding the fundamental purposes of business. Preoccupied by current tasks and crises, driven by their own ambition and fears, buffeted by competitors, critics, and clients, they lose sight of the larger good of their organization, its stakeholders, and society.

Throughout this text we have held the position that business has a fine social purpose and that through socially responsible business activity there is considerable social and personal gain. We have held this position despite realistic assessments of the problems facing people in trying to act in a socially responsible manner and resolving moral dilemmas in ways which can be articulated and justified to stakeholders.

We are acutely aware of the difficulties associated with formulating socially responsible and ethical positions, of the added time involved in considering stakeholders, consulting with them on an in-depth and ongoing basis, identifying the various ethical and moral aspects of their decisions, agonizing over alternative approaches, and laying reputations and careers on the line trying to persuade others who are reluctant to adopt the right approach.

What are the rewards for all this? We suggested that there were three sets of rewards: society benefits through ethical business practices; business itself, and the constituent parts of business — industries and enterprises themselves — also benefit from relative freedom from excessive regulation, reduced transactional costs, and the goodwill of society; and individual managers benefit. To be an ethical manager within an ethical business is to have purpose within a purposive organization. When all is said and done, there must be value to being able to say, at the end of a day that "I did some right things the right way today."

SUGGESTED READINGS

Barnard, C. *The Function of the Executive.* Cambridge: Harvard University Press, 1942.
Kotter, J.P. *The Leadership Factor.* New York: The Free Press, 1988.
Selznick, P. *Leadership in Administration.* Evanston, Ill.: Row, Petersen, 1957.

Conger, J.A., R.N.Kanungo, and Associates, eds. *Charismatic Leadership*. San Francisco: Jossey-Bass, 1988.

NOTES FOR CHAPTER TEN

1   John P. Kotter, *The Leadership Factor* (New York: The Free Press, 1988; London: Collier Macmillan, 1988), chp. 2.

2   Max Weber, "Bureaucracy," *Economy and Society: An Outline of Interpretive Sociology*, edited by Guenther Roth and Claus Wittich (Berkeley: University of California Press, 1978), Part Two, chp. 11.

3   C. Barnard, *The Functions of the Executive* (Cambridge: Harvard University Press, 1942), chp. 5, 6, 7.

4   Kotter, op. cit., p. 16.

5   The William Norris story has been told in many places but a good account of his ethical leadership, together with those of other business executives, is found in *Tad Tuleja. Beyond the Bottom Line* (New York: Facts on File Publications, 1985).

6   J.A. Conger, and R.N. Kanungo, "Towards a behavioral theory of charismatic leadership in organizational settings," *Academy of Management Review*, 1987, 12:637-647; B.J. Avolio and B.M. Bass, "Charisma and beyond," in *Emerging Leadership Vistas,* edited by J.G. Hunt, B.R. Baliga, H.P. Dachler, & C.A. Schriesheim, (Lexington, MA: D.C. Heath, 1988), 29-49; R.J. House, "A 1976 theory of charismatic leadership" in *Leadership: The Cutting Edge*, edited by J.G. Hunt & L.L. Larson (Carbondale, Ill.: Southern Illinois University Press, 1989), 189-204.

7   Henry Mintzberg, *The Structuring of Organizations: A Synthesis of the Research* (Englewood Cliffs, N.J.: Prentice-Hall, 1979), chp. 21.

8   Kotter, op. cit. chp. 1.

9   Amitai Etzioni, *A Comparative Analysis of Complex Organizations: On Power, Involvement and their Correlates* (New York: The Free Press of Glencoe, 1961).

10   Ibid.; B.M. Bass, *Stogdill's Handbook of Leadership* (New York: Free Press, 1981); B.M. Bass, *Leadership and Performance Beyond Expectations* (New York: The Free Press, 1985).

11   Charles Glisson and Mark Durick, "Productivity and Job Statisfaction and Organizational Commitment in Human Service Organizations," *Administrative Science Quarterly*, Vol. 33, No. 11 (1988): 61-68.

12   Burns, 1978, op. cit.; Bass, op. cit.

13   J.M. Howell, "Two Faces of Charisma: Socialized and Personalized Leadership In Organizations," In *Charismatic Leadership*, edited by A.J. Conger & R.N. Kanungo , (San Francisco: Jossey Bass, 1988).

14   Philip Selznick, *Leadership in Administration* (Evanston, Ill.: Row Peterson, 1957), chp. 2.

15   Samuel A. Culbert and John J. McDonough, *The Invisible War: Interests at Work* (New York: John Wiley and Sons, 1980).

16 Frances Westley, "Middle Managers and Strategy: The Microdynamics of Inclusion," *Strategic Management Journal* (1990).

17 R. Jackall, *Moral Mazes: The World of Corporate Managers* (New York: Oxford University Press, 1988).

18 Peter Berger, *Facing Up to Modernity* (New York: Basic Books, 1977).

19 Reinhold Niebuhr, *Children of Light and the Children of Darkness* (New York: Charles Scribner's Sons, 1944).

20 Bjorn Hennestad, "The Symbolic Impact of Double Bind Leadership," Paper presented at 4th International Conference on Organizational Symbolism and Corporate Culture, 1989.

PART 2   CASES

1 Acme Hardware

INTRODUCTION

John Smith, CA, was recently assigned the responsibility for auditing Acme Hardware, a new client. He was wondering what action, if any, he should take about the way certain stores of Acme Hardware were accounting for inventory and advertising costs. As a result of his pre-audit review of the previous auditor's files, he thought it probable that certain store managers, motivated by the company's management and control system, were taking advantage of discretionary accounting alternatives. A complete investigation would be disruptive and expensive and its impact on the company's financial statements might be immaterial.

THE COMPANY

Acme Hardware was a rapidly-expanding chain of hardware stores which operated in southern Ontario. All stores were company-owned.

By the beginning of the 1987/88 fiscal year Acme had 14 stores, four of which had been opened in the previous five years. Total sales in 1986/87 were $30.7 million (up from $21.4 million in 1982/83), resulting in a net income—after corporate expenses and income taxes—of $1.2 million ($650,000 in 1982/83). Total assets as at March 31, 1987, were $17.4 million.

Acme's success was attributed to several factors, but the most important was considered to be the generous bonuses ($15,000) payed to store managers when the budgeted net income for the year was met. Budgets were set by head office, after negotiations with store management. Net income was computed in accordance with accounting policies laid down by head office, and in the event of disagreement, Acme's auditors, who also reviewed each store's records, were to act as arbitrators. The previous audit firm had not been required to arbitrate disagreements about income computations in the preceding five-year period.

PREPARATION FOR THE AUDIT

Acme had recently engaged a new firm of auditors, A B & Co, and John Smith was the person assigned to the job. In planning the work to be performed for the first year—the year ended March 31, 1988—he reviewed the previous audit firm's working files. John found that the bonus arrangement had been identified as a potential "audit risk,"[1] pressuring store managers to achieve budgets.

John reviewed the budget and net income figures for the previous five years, to see how frequently the budgets had been met, and the bonuses paid. He noted that, for 10 stores he examined, because they had been in operation for some time and had an established pattern of operations, bonuses had been paid on 23 occasions (out of a maximum of 50). He also noted that, when a budget was met, the tendency was for it to be met by a narrow margin, but, when missed, by a much wider margin.

ANALYSIS OF INCENTIVE SYSTEM

To examine this issue more closely, John prepared a table setting out the budget and actual net income figures for the 10 stores over the five-year period (see Table 1.1). He separated the 10 stores into two groups:

1. Three stores (North York, Hamilton, and Waterloo) in which:
    (a) budgets were met four times out of a possible 15 (27%);
    (b) the margins by which the budgets were met were $10,000, $3,000, $9,000 and $6,000 (average $7,000); and
    (c) on the 11 occasions when the budgets were not met, the margins ranged from $5,000 to $1,000 (average $2,800).

2. The other seven stores, for which:
    (a) budgets were met 19 times out of a possible 35 (54%);
    (b) the margins by which the budgets were met ranged from $2,000 to $5,000 (average $3,300); and
    (c) on the 16 occasions when the budgets were not met, the margins ranged from $7,000 to $18,000 (average $11,200).

John concluded that there was a strong

---

1 "Audit risk" is the risk that the audit firm would fail to express a reservation in its opinion on Acme's financial statements if they were materially misstated. Such material misstatement would not have been prevented or detected by Acme's internal controls, and would not have been detected by the audit firm.

probability that the managers of seven stores were manipulating net income computations. Based on his experience, John thought that the most likely way of doing so would be by advancing or deferring—from one period to the next—the recognition of income and/or expenses. For example:

1. by deferring the recognition of income or advancing the recognition of expenses, it would be easier to meet the budget in the next period. Managers would be tempted to do this when it was apparent—say by the tenth or eleventh month of the fiscal year—that (a) the current year's budget could not be met, or (b) the budget had already been met; and

2. by advancing the recognition of income or deferring the recognition of expenses, it would be easier to meet the budget in the current period. This would be particularly tempting when, without action of this kind, the budget would probably be missed by a fairly narrow margin.

John reviewed the monthly income statements for the individual stores, all of which followed a standard format (prescribed by head office), based on the income and expense accounts in the general ledger. He concluded that the two most likely areas for manipulation were:

1. Inventories:
   These were valued at the lower of cost (determined on a FIFO—first in first out basis) and net realizable value. The write-down to net realizable value was largely a matter of judgement, particularly in respect of seasonal merchandise, eg garden supplies, and products for which expected new models might make present ones obsolete, eg power mowers.

2. Advertising Expenses:
   Company policy required the cost of local advertising to be expensed in the period the campaign was run. However, store managers had discretion when a

TABLE 1.1: **Budget/Actual Net Income Figures For Ten Stores**
(all figures in $000)

	1982/83 Income		1983/84 Income		1984/85 Income		1985/86 Income		1986/87 Income	
	Budget	Actual	Budget	Actual	Budget	Actual	Budget	Actual	Budget	Actual
Oshawa	$125	$129*	$136	$118	$132	$135*	$140	$132	$145	$147*
Scarborough	180	173	195	198*	212	217*	228	216	236	240*
Markham	76	65	84	88*	102	86	120	125*	138	121
North York	202	198	212	208	220	218	235	245*	250	247
Mississauga	168	171*	175	165	185	189*	197	186	202	205*
Hamilton	136	139*	142	137	148	146	158	167*	168	165
St. Catherines	94	85	98	100*	105	96	110	112*	114	102
Guelph	85	76	88	92*	95	98*	101	92	104	106*
Waterloo	148	146	154	160*	163	160	172	170	185	184
London	189	192*	195	184	198	201*	205	195	209	213*

*Bonus paid to store management.

campaign should be run, and it would be quite possible to advance a campaign scheduled for the first week of April to the last week of March. (Experience had shown that some advertising campaigns result in increased sales over the next few weeks, rather than only in the period in which the advertisements are run.)

CONCLUSION

John was familiar with these incentive schemes because of their use by many of his other clients. He was also aware that senior management recognized that any management control system had flaws. However, these systems motivated operating managers to maintain a focus on net income and to maximize revenues and minimize costs.

John also recognized that, unless several stores manipulated their results in the same direction in any year, the impact on the corporate financial statements would probably not be material. He now had to decide what, if any, action was necessary.

2 Barb and Ed Roberts

In early June 1988, John Hope, a financial planner with the London, Ontario, branch of Versatile Financial Planners, met with Barb Roberts. Barb and her husband Ed were planning to renew their mortgage in a week. Barb presented John with information on their current financial situation and asked for his advice as soon as possible. She was particularly interested in how to better utilize her salary. John was to review their situation and prepare a financial plan.

VERSATILE FINANCIAL PLANNING CORPORATION

Versatile Financial Planning Corporation was an Ontario-based company with 10 offices. The company's head office in Toronto was the administrative centre. Each field office had an office manager who was also a

financial planner. Versatile was formed in 1975 as an independent financial service organization. As an independent dealer in investment funds and life insurance, Versatile advertised itself to be in a unique position to offer objective advice to clients. Versatile's planners were free to deal with any independent mutual fund. Their financial planners assessed a client's present position, identified goals and priorities, and devised strategies specifically tailored to the client's circumstances. The financial planners' salaries consisted mainly of commissions on the products they sold to their clients and, to a lesser extent, on the fees charged for detailed financial planning. Versatile's clients, unlike those of many other companies in the business, "belonged to" the financial planners. In other words, if the financial planner left Versatile, the clients were allowed to remain with the financial planner.

Unlike employees in many related industries, financial planners were not required to hold a licence or pass tests. However, "professional designations" were available through two organizations, the Canadian Association of Financial Planners (CAFP) and the Canadian Institute of Financial Planning. The CAFP awarded the Registered Financial Planner designation to members who met its educational requirements, upheld its Code of Professional Ethics and Guidelines, and had been in financial planning for at least two years. The Canadian Institute of Financial Planning offered a similar designation known as Chartered Financial Planner. The financial planning industry had recently received media attention. Debate centred on whether the financial planning industry should be regulated and a professional designation required of all financial planners. A major argument against regulation was that most financial planners received the majority of their compensation from the sale of such products as mutual funds and life insurance which already required licences.

John Hope

John Hope had been a financial planner at Versatile for the last two years. John's background included a BA in history from York University in 1975 and an LLB from the University of Windsor in 1978. He practiced law for three years and joined Crown Life Financial Services for one year prior to moving to Versatile. John had successfully completed the Chartered Investment Financial Planner course which allowed him to sell mutual funds; he also had a licence to sell life insurance products. John's legal background gave him valuable experience which he used in his financial planning for clients.

After a free initial consultation, John charged $50 per hour for clients requiring detailed financial planning. He felt this fee was fair compensation for his efforts and the advice was of good value to his clients. John's main source of income was from commissions on sales of financial products to his clients who currently numbered 75. He was actively seeking to expand this client base; he gained the majority of his clients through referrals from satisfied customers. Many of John's clients were inexperienced in the field of investment, and for their entry into the financial market, John would recommend mutual funds since he saw this as the best way to achieve diversification with even a small investment. John's view of mutual funds was that no one fund was the very best all the time but it could be consistently above average. Consequently he would look for funds that were consistently among the top 10 performers in a particular category, such as growth funds or income funds. Exhibit 1 contains a description of the major types of mutual funds as well as the funds which John was currently recommending in various fund categories. Exhibit 2 provides performance data on these funds along with average performance data of all funds in various categories, as compiled by the *Financial Post*.

John's view of financial planning included four basic steps: (1) budgeting, (2) eliminating non-tax deductible debt such as a mortgage, (3) maximizing RRSP contributions, and (4) wisely investing any remaining funds. He did not encourage his clients to borrow for investments but he was a firm believer in dollar cost averaging, that is, investing a set sum of money each month.

Barb and Ed Roberts: Background

Barb, age 49, and her husband Ed, age 55, were in good health and had no children. Until 1980, Barb had not been employed outside the home, although she had performed some volunteer work with underprivileged children. In that year, she decided to seek salaried employment, and was hired by a small local corporation. Applying her experience from volunteer work, Barb demonstrated a natural aptitude in personnel and was promoted quickly. In her present position as supervisor, Barb was earning more money than Ed. Barb derived great satisfaction from her job but was always worrying about the future, in particular, about how Ed truly felt about her working and earning more money than him.

Ed Roberts was a foreman for a local manufacturer where he had worked since he was 18. Ed used to believe that he should be the bread-winner, but now had to acknowledge that without Barb's income, they could not enjoy the modest lifestyle they were accustomed to. Still, he insisted on paying for almost everything. He felt proud of Barb's accomplishments but inadequate because of them. Nevertheless, Barb and Ed were very happily married and dedicated to one another.

The Robertses' Current Financial Situation

In order to devise a financial plan, John gathered relevant financial information from Barb. The Robertses' statement of personal net worth is outlined in Exhibit 3 and their income and their expenditures in Exhibit 4. Both Ed and Barb had group term life insurance at their places of employment: Barb was insured

for two times her annual salary and Ed for 3.5 times his annual salary. In addition, Barb had disability coverage which paid 60 percent of her salary in the event of a long-term disability. Both Barb and Ed had defined-benefits company pension plans. Benefits at age 65 were anticipated to be $27,000 for Ed and $20,000 for Barb. Exhibit 5 is a simplified 1988 tax form including selected relevant tax information.

The Robertses' house mortgage was up for renewal in one week. Their initial mortgage was taken out in 1978 for $45,000 at an annual rate of 10.25 percent, and an amortization period of 25 years. The mortgage was renewed for five years in 1983 at a rate of 13 percent on the balance of $42,388. The current balance was $39,139.

Barb was also considering investing a portion of her money in stocks, since she had heard that after the crash in October 1987, stocks were now a good deal. She was unsure what stocks, if any, she should invest in, whether she should consider equity mutual funds, or whether she should consider some other type of mutual fund. She had never previously invested in stocks. Exhibit 6 summarizes recent stock market conditions.

Current Economic Situation

The political climate was uncertain pending a federal election. Mutual fund sales were down from the pre-crash period, although consumer confidence was surprisingly high. The economy was growing at a greater-than-expected pace, causing the Bank of Canada to tighten monetary policy in order to attempt to curtail inflationary pressures. Exhibit 7 contains excerpts from some newspaper articles describing current economic conditions. Exhibit 8 summarizes statistical trends of market conditions. Exhibit 9 details current interest and mortgage rates.

John Hope's Assessment

After gathering the relevant financial information, John's next task was to assess his clients' goals, and then try to determine an appropriate financial plan that would help them achieve these goals. The Robertses had two major financial goals: first, they wanted to pay off their mortgage; second, they wanted to plan for retirement so that they could continue to live their current lifestyle.

An important consideration in recommending investments for clients was their attitude towards risk. John used the form in Exhibit 10 to assess the Robertses' risk preference. He planned to discuss with Barb and Ed the implications of this assessment, and how it demonstrated their attitude towards risk.

John's next step was to examine various mortgage renewal options. He began by determining the monthly payments associated with renewing the mortgage for five more years at an annual rate of 11.25 percent, based on an amortization period of 15 years. He also calculated the weekly payments associated with paying off the mortgage within five years. Exhibit 11 outlines details of the amortization schedules. He realized that there were many other combinations of frequency of payments and terms. For example, one-year rates and variable rates were much lower than five-year rates; however, there was uncertainty as to what future rates would be. John realized that he could not examine the mortgage question in isolation but would also have to examine the Robertses' complete financial situation.

With the information he had gathered, John began to prepare a financial plan for Barb. He knew he would have to meet with both Barb and Ed in the near future, since they would have to make a decision on the mortgage renewal within one week.

EXHIBIT 1

John Hope's Mutual Fund Recommendations

Money Market Funds

Provide a high level of interest income while maintaining stable capital with excellent liquidity. Primarily invest in federal government treasury bills, bank certificates of deposit and short-term corporate debt.

  Recommendations: Bolton Tremblay Money Fund
         Trimark Interest Fund

Bond, Mortgage & Preferred Dividend Funds

Bond and mortgage funds provide high income with the prospect of capital appreciation while maintaining safety of capital.

  Recommendations: Bolton Tremblay Bond & Mortgage
         Bolton Tremblay Income Fund
         Dynamic Dividend Fund
         Dynamic Income Fund
         Noram Canadian Convertible Securities
         Talvest Bond Fund
         Talvest Income Fund

Balanced Funds

Provide potential for capital appreciation by ownership of common corporate shares together with the safety of capital provided by bond, preferred share or treasury-bill investments.

  Recommendations: Bolton Tremblay Canadian Balanced Fund
         Dynamic Managed Portfolio
         Industrial Income Fund
         Mackenzie Mortgage & Income Fund
         Talvest Diversified Fund
         Trimark Income Growth

Exhibit 1 cont'd

Exhibit 1 cont'd

Equity Funds

Provide potential for capital appreciation by ownership of common corporate shares. Fund managers may hold investment funds in cash or treasury bills. These funds can be distinguished geographically but it must be stressed that the role of the fund manager and his or her specific investment strategy is of the utmost importance in this area.

Recommendations:

A) Canadian
- Canadian Cumulative Fund
- Industrial Growth (Horizon & Future) Fund
- Talvest Growth Fund
- Trimark Canadian Fund
- United Accumulative Retirement Fund
- Universal Savings Equity Fund

B) Canadian (Resource)
- Morgan Resource Fund
- Planned Resources Fund Ltd
- Universal Savings Natural Resources Fund

C) American
- Industrial American Fund
- Universal Savings American Fund
- Noram Convertible Securities

D) Far East
- AGF Japan Fund Ltd
- Global Strategy Far East Fund
- Universal Savings Pacific Fund

E) Global
- Bolton Tremblay International
- Cundill Value Fund
- Templeton Growth Fund
- Trimark Fund
- United Accumulative Fund
- Universal Savings Global Fund

EXHIBIT 2

Financial Post Mutual Funds Performance Survey, May 16, 1988
John Hope's Recommended Funds Compared With Average Performance Within Each Category

	TOTAL ASSETS $ MILLIONS	NET ASSET VALUE/SHARE APR. 30	AVERAGE ANNUAL COMPOUND RATE OF RETURN 10 YR	5 YR	1 YR	VARIABILITY 5 YR	REWARD/RISK RATIO 5 YR	EXPENSE RATIO %	MAXIMUM SALES/REDEMPTION CHARGE %
MONEY MARKET FUNDS									
Bolton Tremblay Money Fund	150.4	1.00	n.a.	+9.2	+8.5	avg	+8.28	0.50	2.00
Trimark Interest Fund	24.1	10.00	n.a.	n.a.	n.a.	n.a.	n.a.	0.75	2.00
AVERAGE OF 27 FUNDS	50.1		+11.0	+8.9	+7.6	1.6			
BOND, MORTGAGE & PREFERRED DIVIDEND FUNDS									
Bolton Tremblay Bond & Mortgage Fund	78.3	10.40	+9.6	+6.9	+2.4	avg	+0.38	1.06	5.00
Bolton Tremblay Income Fund	11.6	5.1	n.a.	n.a.	+5.0	avg-	n.a.	1.25	5.00
Dynamic Dividend Fund	91.5	5.33	n.a.	+11.3	+5.6	avg	+/-0.61	1.00	5.00
Dynamic Income Fund	11	10.27	n.a.	n.a.	+2.7	n.a.	n.a.	n.a.	9.00
Noram Canadian Convertible Securities			n.a.	n.a.	n.a.	n.a.	n.a.	n.a.	9.00
Talvest Bond Fund	10.6	10.07	+11.8	+12.2	+7.8	avg	+0.46	1.68	9.00
Talvest Income Fund	6.2	10.56	+10.7	+10.7	+8.4	avg-	+0.94	1.45	4.00
AVERAGE OF 20 FUNDS	93.6		+11.3	+9.1	+1.8	25.8	+0.36		
BALANCED FUNDS									
Bolton Tremblay Canadian Balanced Fund	123.8	14.17	+14.3	+6.4	-9.8	avg	+0.12	2.00	9.00
Dynamic Managed Portfolio	123.0	5.75	n.a.	n.a.	-2.5	n.a.	n.a.	2.00	9.00
Industrial Income Fund	128.9	10.03	+11.5	+15.1	+11.3	avg	+0.65	n.a.	9.00
Mackenzie Mortgage & Income Fund	135.8	1.16	+13.1	+14.6	+10.6	avg	+0.64	n.a.	9.00
Talvest Diversified Fund	19.0	5.65	n.a.	n.a.	+2.7	avg	n.a.	1.77	9.00
Trimark Income Growth	18.3	5.15	n.a.	n.a.	n.a.	n.a.	n.a.	n.a.	9.00
AVERAGE OF 30 FUNDS	53.3		+11.8	+9.1	-4.4	36.41	+0.33		
EQUITY FUNDS									
A) Canadian									
Industrial Growth Fund	1,652.7	15.00	+18.1	+14.8	+3.3	avg	+0.31	n.a.	9.00
Talvest Growth Fund	61.6	8.92	+14.9	+11.4	-5.0	avg	+0.23	2.04	9.00
Trimark Canadian Fund	457.3	10.43	n.a.	+13.8	+.08	avg	+0.26	1.62	9.00
United Accumulative Retirement Fund	162.6	10.87	+18.9	+12.4	-4.0	avg-	+0.32	1.80	9.00
Universal Savings Equity Fund	124.1	11.17	+18.3	+15.8	+6.7	avg	+0.31	2.00	9.00

	Total Net Assets	Net Asset Value per Share		Average Annual Compound Rate of Return		Variability	Reward/Risk Ratio	Expense Ratio	Maximum Sales/Redemption
AVERAGE OF 120 FUNDS	94.1		+13.7	+8.7	-9.8	56.32	+0.17		
B) Canadian Resource									
Morgan Resource Fund	24.9	7.71	n.a.	n.a.	+8.1	n.a.	n.a.	1.95	9.00
Planned Resources Fund Ltd.	45.8	10.98	+14.1	+3.7	-18.5	avg+	+0.05	2.00	9.00
C) American									
Industrial American Fund	424.9	7.41	+19.2	+12.3	-7.3	avg	+0.20	n.a.	9.00
Universal Savings American Fund	48.8	9.46	n.a.	+13.5	-6.4	avg	+0.23	2.00	9.00
AVERAGE OF 30 FUNDS	52.8		+14.5	+7.6	-14.8	63.96	+0.12		
D) Far East									
AGF Japan Fund Ltd.	107.9	6.67	+23.7	+34.5	+15.3	avg+	0.51	1.72	9.00
Global Strategy Far East Fund	22.6	11.02	n.a.	n.a.	+0.3	n.a.	n.a.	1.73	9.00
Universal Savings Pacific Fund	35.0	9.28	n.a.	+29.4	+2.3	avg+	+0.39	2.00	9.00
AVERAGE OF 6 FUNDS	110.2		+22.9	+33.4	+17.0	66.06	+0.50		
E) Global									
Bolton Tremblay International	439.2	6.83	+19.8	+14.7	-10.4	avg+	+0.18	1.84	9.00
Cundill Value Fund	273.8	12.18	+21.5	+13.8	+12.7	avg-	+0.39	1.82	8.75
Templeton Growth Fund	1271.6	17.10	+17.3	+14.1	-11.0	avg	+0.026	0.73	8.50
Trimark Fund	570.1	10.76	n.a.	+14.4	-2.2	avg	+0.022	1.59	9.00
United Accumulative Fund	236.9	9.77	+16.7	+12.6	-13.8	avg	+0.024	1.70	9.00
Universal Savings Global Fund	43.0	5.16	n.a.	n.a.	-7.3	n.a.	n.a.	2.00	9.00
AVERAGE OF 30 FUNDS	164		+17.4	+13.2	-9.1	36.41	+.033		

Total Net Assets - is total assets minus current liabilities; it shows the size of the fund at April 30, 1988.

Net Asset Value per Share - is total assets minus current liabilities divided by number of shares outstanding. Investors buy at this value, plus sales charge if any, and sell at this value, minus redemption charge if any.

Average Annual Compound Rate of Return - measures the average annual change in net asset value per share assuming all dividends and capital gains are reinvested on the date of distribution or realization. no sales or redemption charges are considered in the calculations. Average annual compound returns provide an appropriate measure of comparison with returns on other investments. Investors should examine performance over two or more markets cycles (four or more years). The 10-year average return is calculated from April 30, 1978.

Variability - this is what the statisticians call the standard deviation and it shows the annual variability of the return. It provides a measure of volatility, and therefore of risk. Funds are ranked as average, above average or below average relative to other funds in the group.

Reward/Risk Ratio - is the compound rate of return divided by the variability. A fund with a high ratio has the potential for high reward relative to risk. Comparisons among mutual funds and between the funds and market benchmarks are measures of past performance.

Expense Ratio - is total operating costs (exclusive of any sales or redemption charge) as a percentage of assets.

Maximum Sales/Redemption - is the commission - or load - paid at the time of purchase or redemption

EXHIBIT 3

Statement of Net Worth - June 1, 1988

Assets

Cash Reserve	- Chequing Accounts	Barb	3,600	
		Ed	565	
	Joint Savings Account (Daily Interest)		7,835	
	Credit Union (Daily Interest)	Barb	6,400	
				$ 18,400
Investments	- CSB's (1988 Series)	Barb	8,600	
		Ed	7,200	
	RRSP (1 Year GIC @ 9%)	Barb	15,000	
	(1 Year GIC @ 9%)	Ed	1,500	
				$ 32,300
Real Estate	- Principal Residence			$120,000
Capital Assets	- Automobiles: (LeBaron - 1988)		14,000	
	(Jetta - 1987)		10,000	
	Furnishings		60,000	
	Miscellaneous		20,000	
				$104,000
				$274,700

Liabilities

	- Auto Loans (2 Yrs. @ 11%)	Barb	3,000	
	(5 Yrs. @ 10%)	Ed	7,000	
	- Home Improvement Loan (5 Yrs. @ 9.5%)		15,000	
	- Mortgage		39,139	
				$ 64,139
Net Worth				$210,561

EXHIBIT 4

Monthly Income Statement - June, 1988

Income	- Employment	Barb	$2,916.67	
		Ed	2,333.33	
	- Investment	Interest	200.00	
				$5,450.00

Expenditures				
Necessities:		Food	400.00	
		Clothing	300.00	
		Mortgage[1]	444.73	
		Utilities	180.00	
Protection:		Life Insurance[2]	0.00	
		Automobile Insurance	60.00	
		Home Insurance	20.00	
Taxes:[3]	Income	- Barb	780.00	
		- Ed	694.00	
	Property		83.42	
Investments:[4]	Credit Union (Daily Interest)		100.00	
	CSB's	- Barb	200.00	
		- Ed	100.00	
Loans:[5]	Cars	- Barb (2 Yrs. @ 11%)	146.00	
		- Ed (5 Yrs. @ 10%)	153.88	
	Home Improvement	(5 Yrs. @ 9.5%)	325.55	
				$3,987.58
Net Remaining				$1,462.42

---

1 Based on renewal for 5 years at 11.25% amortized over 15 years.
2 Both have group term insurance through employers; Barb is insured for two times her salary, Ed is insured for 3.5 times his salary.
3 Based on 1987 tax laws.
4 These investments are payroll deductions.
5 Term remaining and rates are in brackets. All loans are open with no prepayment penalties.

EXHIBIT 5

Simplified 1988 Tax Form

1. Employment and Other Income
2. Less: RRSP Contributions
3. Taxable Income (1-2)
4. Federal Tax: % of Line 3 - See Table Below
5. Less Tax Credits:
   Basic $1,020
   Dependent $ 65
6. Basic Federal Tax (4-5)
7. Ontario Provincial Tax (51% of 6)
8. Federal Surtax (3% of 6)
9. Total Tax Payable (6+7+8)

TAXABLE INCOME	FEDERAL MARGINAL TAX RATE
Up to $27,500	17.00%
$27,501 - $55,000	26.00%
$55,001 and Over	29.00%

EXHIBIT 6

Stock Market Information

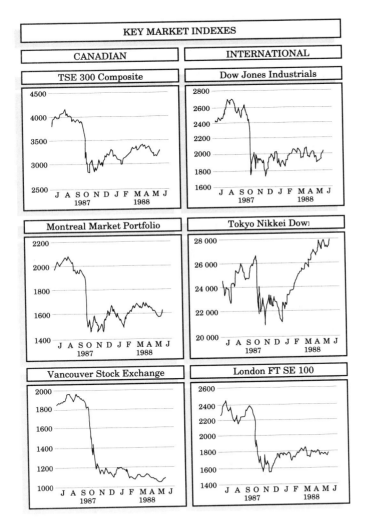

TSE 300 Composite Index:

June 6, 1988 Close	3325.03
1988 High	3405.07
1988 Low	2976.32
1987 High	4118.90
1987 Low	2873.30
P/E Ratio	12.40
Dividend Yield	3.16

Source: *Globe and Mail*, June 6, 1988

EXHIBIT 7

Economic Conditions

Economic forecasts signal PM to call vote this year: Outlook less rosy beyond 1988

Economic forecasters are sending Prime Minister Brian Mulroney a message: if he wants to piggyback on the strength of the economy in his run for re-election, he should call the vote this year. The outlook for the rest of 1988 is good, according to most forecasts. And while no one is predicting that Canada will enter a recession in 1989, the forecasters agree that the medium-term signals are pointing the wrong way. Economic growth, consumer spending and housing starts are heading down, forecasters believe, while inflation, unemployment, and wage growth are all pointing up as the Canadian economy heads towards 1989.

Globe and Mail (May 10, 1988)

Mutual fund sales recover from crash but can't match first quarter of 1987

Sales of mutual funds in the first three months of 1988 surpassed those of the post-crash period last year, but were well below sales chalked up in the booming first quarter of 1987, according to the Investment Funds Institute of Canada. Net sales (sales minus redemptions) were $442 million in the first quarter, only one-fifth of the $2.9 billion recorded a year earlier, but up 23.7 percent from the last three months of 1987, the Institute said. Mutual fund assets stood at $21.8 billion on March 31, up 6.9 percent from the previous year's $20.3 billion. There was a dramatic shift in the type of funds purchased. While half last year's sales were stock funds, today's cautious buyers are choosing only income funds.

Globe and Mail (May 16, 1988)

Service sector propels surge in economy

After two successive months of faltering growth, economic output surged ahead in March, propelled mainly by a pickup in activity in the service industries, Statistics Canada says. Gross domestic product at factor cost — one of the broader measures of the country's economic health — jumped .09 percent in March after a decrease of .02 percent in February and a .01 percent again in January. Economists seemed unwilling to give much significance to the March rebound in gross domestic product. "More important than the March number is the (.5%) quarterly number (for GDP)," said George Vasi, director of economics for Toronto based

<u>Exhibit 7 cont'd</u>

Exhibit 7 cont'd

Data Resources of Canada. "In the quarterly figures, you see the first tentative evidence that the Canadian economy is gearing down from the heady pace of growth last year."

Globe and Mail (June 1, 1988)

Confidence bounced back after crash, board finds in consumer-attitude survey
Canadian consumers seem to have shrugged off any worries they might have had about the prospects for the Canadian economy after the October stock market crash, the Conference Board of Canada says. The board says in a report on its latest survey of consumer attitudes that confidence bounced back in the first quarter of 1988 after a decline in the second half of 1987 that was largely caused by the crash. The board's Index of Consumer Confidence climbed to 123.5 in the first quarter of this year, up from 119.8 in the last quarter of 1987. Mr. Rheaume said that the Consumer Confidence Index may dip in the second quarter of 1988 because of higher interest rates and slower growth in employment. He expects confidence to pick up in the third quarter of this year, however, as gains in disposable income from the new tax reform measures start to flow through the system. Measured by the board's index, consumer confidence peaked at 135 in the second quarter of 1987. During the second half of 1987, the index registered modest declines. Despite the recent decline in the index, consumer confidence is still considered to be at historically high levels.

Globe and Mail (June 3, 1988)

Prime boosted after huge rise in bank rate
The inflation fighting stance of the Bank of Canada has caused a huge jump in interest rates this week, prompting chartered banks to pump up the prime lending rate to its highest point in more than two years. Borrowers' costs for the banks' most credit-worthy customers moved half a percentage point higher to 10.75 per cent, the highest level since early May, 1986. Lending costs to consumers and businesses are expected to rise–imminently. The tide of higher rates is geared to putting on the brakes and slowing down the momentum of inflation. Growth in gross domestic product in Canada was surprisingly strong in March, steeling the determination of the central bank to cool off the economy. But heavy debt loads carried by consumers and some businesses raise worries about the effect of the increase. Because short-term mortgage rates are closely linked to the prime rate, the cost of these loans is likely to climb again soon. The last increase of one-quarter of a percentage point began last week.

Globe and Mail (June 3, 1988)

EXHIBIT 8

Statistical Trends

MARKET ECONOMY	Period	Latest	% Change from Prev.	Yr Ago
Gross domestic product/ seasonally adj., annual rate, 1981 $ bln	Mar.	390.6	+0.9	+4.4
Merch. exports/ seasonally adj., bal. of payments basis, $bln	Mar.	11.6	+3.7	+10.1
Merch. imports/ seasonally adj., bal. of payments basis, $bln	Mar.	11.0	+10.2	+17.2
Retail trade/ seasonally adjusted, $bln	Feb.	13.3	-0.9	+8.4

	Period	Latest	Prev.	Yr Ago
Merch. trade balance/ seasonally adj., bal. of payments basis, $ mln	Mar.	+578	+1193	+1137
New car sales/ seasonally adjusted, units, 000s	Mar.	89.0	85.9	89.6
Housing starts/ seasonally adjusted, annual rate, 000s	Apr.	217	217	248
Unemployment rate/ seasonally adjusted, %	Apr.	7.7	7.8	9.2
Service employment/ seasonally adjusted, mln	Apr.	8.7	8.7	8.4
Goods-producing employment/ seasonally adjusted, mln	Apr.	3.6	3.6	3.4

FINANCIAL ECONOMY	Period	Latest	Prev.	Yr Ago
Dollar/ weekly average, Toronto noon, U.S. cents	Last wk	80.59	74.49	80.87
Gold/ weekly average, London afternoon fix, $U.S.	Last wk	451.30	450.50	456.50
Money supply, narrow/ M-1, $bln	Last wk	36.2	35.7	35.0
Money supply, broad/ M-3, $bln	Last wk	240.9	239.6	226.8
Business credit/ seasonally adjusted, $bln	Apr.	320.4	317.5	291.9

Exhibit 8 cont'd

Exhibit 8 cont'd

Household credit/ seasonally adjusted, $bln	Mar.	195.2	193.0	165.2
Bank of Canada rate/ %	Last wk	9.49	9.17	8.50
Treasury bill yield/ 91-day, %	Last wk	9.24	8.92	8.25
Chartered bank prime rate/ %	Last wk	10.25	10.25	9.50
Canada bond yield/ weighted long-term average, %	Last wk	10.18	10.45	9.82
Corporate bond yield/ weighted long-term average, %	Last wk	10.88	11.05	10.46

PRICES	Period	Latest	% Change from	
			Prev.	Yr Ago
Consumer price index/ 1981 = 100	Apr.	142.5	+0.4	+4.0
Industrial production price index/ 1981 = 100	Mar.	126.3	+0.2	+4.2
Raw materials price index/ 1981 = 100	Apr.	97.9	-0.4	-1.2

U.S. ECONOMY	Period	Latest	% Change from	
			Prev.	Yr Ago
GNP/ seasonally adjusted, annual rate, 1982 $ bln (prelim.)	1Q	3918	+0.96	+3.86
Merch. exports/ not seasonally adj., c.i.f. basis, $bln	Mar.	29.0	+22.8	+33.0
Merch. imports/ not seasonally adj., c.i.f. basis, $bln	Mar.	38.7	+3.6	+11.6
Consumer price index/ 1982-84 = 100	Apr.	117.2	+0.4	+3.9

	Period	Latest	Prev.	Yr Ago
Merch. trade balance/ not seasonally adj., c.i.f. basis, $ bln	Mar.	+9.7	-13.8	-12.9
Unemployment rate/ not seasonally adj., %	Apr.	5.4	5.6	6.3
Federal reserve discount rate/ %	Last wk	6	6	5.5
Bank prime rate/ %	Last wk	9.0	9.0	8.25

EXHIBIT 9

Selected Interest Rates and Mortgage Rates–June 6, 1988

INTEREST RATES	30 Days	60	90	120	180	270	1 Yr	2 Yr	3 Yr	5 Yr
Banks										
Bank of Montreal	6.25	6.25	6.25	6.25	6.50	6.50	9.25	9.50	9.75	10.25
Bank of Nova Scotia	6.25	6.25	6.25	6.25	6.50	6.50	9.25	9.50	9.75	10.25
CIBC	6.25	6.25	6.25	6.25	6.50	6.50	9.25	9.50	9.75	10.25
Citibank	7.00	7.25	7.50	7.50	8.00	8.50	9.25	9.25	9.50	9.75
Hong Kong Bank	6.50	6.50	6.50	6.50	6.75	6.75	9.00	9.25	9.50	10.00
National Bank	6.25	6.25	6.25	6.25	6.50	6.50	9.25	9.50	9.75	10.25
Royal Bank of Canada	7.25	7.25	7.50	7.50	7.75	8.00	8.00	9.25	9.75	10.25
Trust Companies										
Canada Trust	7.00	7.25	7.50	7.50	7.75	8.25	9.25	9.50	9.75	10.25
Montreal Trust	7.25	7.25	7.50	7.50	7.75	8.00	9.25	9.50	10.00	10.25
Royal Trust	7.00	7.25	7.25	7.50	7.75	8.00	9.25	9.50	9.75	10.25
Other Financial Institutions										
Great West Life	—	—	—	—	—	—	9.00	9.25	9.50	10.00
Metropolitan Life	—	—	—	—	—	—	9.13	9.38	9.63	10.25

MORTGAGE RATES	Variable	6 Mo Open	6 Mo Closed	1 Yr Open	1 Yr Closed	2 Yr Closed	3 Yr Closed	4 Yr Closed	5 Yr Closed
Banks									
Bank of Montreal Mtg Corp	—	10.00	—	10.75	10.25	10.50	10.75	11.00	11.25
Bank of Nova Scotia Mtg Corp	10.25	10.25	—	11.00	10.50	10.75	11.00	11.25	11.50
CIBC Mort Corp	10.25	10.25	—	11.00	10.50	10.75	11.00	11.25	11.50
Citibank Canada	—	—	10.00	—	10.25	10.50	10.75	11.00	11.25
Hong Kong Bank	—	10.00	9.50	10.75	10.25	10.50	10.75	11.00	11.25
National Bank	—	10.50	—	10.75	10.25	10.50	10.75	11.00	11.25
Royal Bank Canada	10.25	10.50	—	11.25	10.75	11.00	11.25	11.50	11.75
T-D Mortgage	10.25	—	10.25	11.00	10.50	10.75	11.00	11.25	11.50
Trust Companies									
Canada Trust	10.25	10.25	—	—	10.50	10.75	11.00	11.25	11.50
Montreal Trust	10.25	10.25	—	11.00	10.50	10.75	11.00	11.25	11.50
Royal Trust	—	10.25	10.00	—	10.50	10.75	11.00	11.25	11.50

EXHIBIT 10

Client Financial Profile

Emotional Characteristics

You classify yourself as:

- Aggressive - willing to risk safety of principal for superior yield
- Prudent - prepared to accept reasonable risk to maintain or improve purchasing power
- Cautious - unwilling to risk principal

Your comfort zone:

Degrees of Concern

(0=none; 1=low; 2=slight; 3=moderate; 4=heightened
5=high)

Liquidity	0	1	2	3	④	5
Safety of Principal	0	1	2	3	4	⑤
Capital Appreciation	0	1	2	3	4	⑤
Current Income	0	1	2	③	4	5
Inflation Protection	0	1	②	3	4	5
Future Income	0	1	②	3	4	5
Tax Reduction or Deferral	0	1	2	3	④	5

Economic Characteristics in Determining Risk Preference

Categories	Low	Moderate	High
Age	+55	(45-55)	-45
Years to Retirement	0-5	(5-10)	+10
Annual Discretionary	$10,000	($10-15,000)	$15,000

Exhibit 10 cont'd

Exhibit 10 cont'd

Categories	Low	Moderate	High
Income			
Dependents	+ 3	1-3	(None)
Health	Poor	Fair	(Good)
Net Worth/ Annualized Expenses	1	(2-4)	+5

EXHIBIT 11

Mortgage Amortization Schedules

Scenario A

Amount borrowed, June 1988	$ 39,139.00
Annual interest rate, compounded semi-annually	11.25%
Monthly payments, blend of principal plus interest	$442.73
Number of monthly payments to amortize mortgage	180
Last payment date	May 2003
Total amount of interest paid over 180 months	$40,000.00

Scenario B

Amount borrowed June, 1988	$39,139.00
Annual interest rate, compounded semi-annually	11.25%
Weekly payments, blend of principal plus interest	$212.72
Number of weekly payments to amortize mortgage	235
Last payment date	December 1992
Total amount of interest paid over 235 weeks	$10,684.00

Drug Testing at Warner-Lambert

Wayne Britt, Vice-President of Human Resources at Warner-Lambert Canada Inc (W-L), contemplated the first draft of the company's April 1987 issue of the employee publication, *UpDater* (Exhibit 1).

W-L's parent company in the US had recently implemented a limited drug-testing program on a trial basis. Wayne was using this issue of the *UpDater* to inform the Canadian employees of what was happening within W-L in the US. Although his research and consultations with both management and staff groups had resulted in a favorable response to the idea of drug-testing, Britt still felt apprehensive about recommending a similar program in Canada. Wayne knew that following the distribution of the *UpDater* he would, sooner or later, have to take some position on the issue of drug testing in the Canadian company.

COMPANY BACKGROUND

Warner-Lambert Canada Inc, a wholly-owned subsidiary of Warner-Lambert Company of New Jersey, marketed and manufactured health care products through its Parke Davis division and confectionery products through its Adams Brands division. W-L employed 1,500 employees Canada-wide in manufacturing locations in Scarborough and Brockville, six regional distribution centres, and a research institute. It had sales of over $200 million and was considered one of the global company's most successful affiliates.

The Parke Davis division marketed and manufactured "ethical" pharmaceutical products such as Ponstan and LoEstrin which were retailed to doctors and distributed through drug wholesalers and pharmacists,

Case material of the Western School of Business Administration is prepared as a basis for classroom discussion. This case was prepared by Nadine Hayes under the supervision of Professor Jeffrey Gandz.

as well as "over the counter" products such as Sinutab and Listerine which were advertised to the general public and distributed through wholesalers and drug and food stores. The Adams Brands division marketed and manufactured brands such as Certs, Clorets, Chiclets and Trident through wholesalers and drug, food and variety stores. The two divisions were served by centralized corporate human resources, finance, research and development, and manufacturing groups but each had its own sales and marketing functions. An organization chart, showing the number of people in each department and division, is shown in Exhibit 2.

W-L Canada had earned a reputation as a fair and equitable employer. The corporate culture produced a "family type" atmosphere, and W-L had recently been recognized by the Financial Post as one of the 100 best companies to work for in Canada. Several key employee relations policies served to promulgate that atmosphere:

Affirmative Action

By 1975, International Women's Year, W-L had identified the increasing number of women entering the workforce as an opportunity for the company to ensure that they were an "equal opportunity employer." W-L voluntarily established an Affirmative Action program and five years after its implementation female representation in the Supervisory/Management ranks had risen from 18 percent to 25 percent in 1980 and 39 percent by 1986.

The Affirmative Action program was expanded in 1981 (International Year of Disabled Persons) to cover the disabled. W-L undertook a three-point program that would:

1) ensure wheelchair access to W-L facilities;

2) provide the most effective employment access to W-L for disabled persons by maintaining contacts with agencies dealing with disabled persons;

3) inform current W-L employees of the needs/capabilities of disabled people.

As one of the first 150 companies to participate in voluntary Affirmative Action programs, W-L was active in government discussions on the issue at both the federal and provincial levels, as well as serving as a model to other Ontario employers considering a similar program.

Communication

Communication at W-L had always been open, with regular staff meetings instituted in the early 1960s. These were expanded to all-employee orientation/information meetings that are held twice a year. Two key tools of communication were the in-house publications: a quarterly newspaper (*By-Line*) and a monthly newsletter (*UpDater*). These were in addition to regular memos keeping employees current on any changes, and articles of interest that were widely circulated. Opinion surveys were given annually to different employee groups with the results published in the *By-Line*.

Job Security

W-L management had made a commitment to all permanent employees that the company would make every reasonable and practical effort to ensure continuing, long-term employment. While this was not an absolute guarantee of employment, job security was a priority and a continuing management objective. This commitment was presented through the eight-point "Employment Security" Program:

Communications: disclosing potential and actual staffing plan changes and directly communicating with affected employees.

1st Choice - Qualified In-House Employees: posting vacancies; hiring from within; providing training and relocation counselling.

Service Recognition: recognizing seniority and pay-rate maintenance.

Career and Financial Counselling: providing in-house seminars.

Training and Development: subsidizing job-related courses; offering skill development and cross-training.

Separation: offering special leave, packages and counselling for separations.

Out-Placement: publicizing external assistance and developing alternative employment opportunities.

Study and Action Plans: experimenting with special programs, leave, educational options and contracts.

HELP Program

Since 1975, W-L had provided an assistance, support, information and counselling program for all employees and their families. Participation could be voluntary, suggested and/or mandatory depending on job performance. The HELP program (Helping Employees Liberate Problems) dealt with personal problems such as family-related problems, depression, alcohol, drugs, legal, work and financial difficulties, and was based on the philosophy that most of these problems were treatable and/or capable of being resolved by the employee concerned provided he or she was motivated at an early stage and had access to appropriate treatment resources. There was a clearly articulated corporate policy for the program that identified the types of referrals as well as the steps of the mandatory referral process (Exhibit 3). The administration was undertaken by a HELP Advisory Committee consisting of a team of workers, the Warner-Lambert Nurses, a representative from Mental Health/Metro, and a Family Services Association Counsellor who was assigned part-time to the Warner-Lambert HELP program. Voluntary assistance was guaranteed in strictest confidence with no written entries in the employees' records and no exchange of information with the Human Resources department without the consent of the employee concerned (unless required by law). Statistics for the HELP program are presented in Exhibit 4.

The Creed

In 1985, W-L Canada introduced a corporate creed to all employees throughout the country. The creed (Exhibit 5) was a series of statements expressing W-L's commitment to five specific "publics"—customers, employees, shareholders, suppliers and society. It was developed by W-L Company of New Jersey with the assistance of key people from the affiliates. The creed was designed to move W-L even closer to being an "excellent" company, and to provide a set of goals, values and principles of management against which performance could be measured.

Through mechanisms such as special "creed awareness sessions," all W-L Canada employees were exposed to the idea and expected to assist with the development of recommendations that would help W-L live up to standards set by the creed.

The creed is important to W-L, both in Canada and around the world, and continues to be frequently referenced in W-L Canada's annual employee attitude surveys, the monthly and quarterly in-house publications, and in performance appraisals.

Mandatory Retirement

Effective January 1, 1987, W-L Canada eliminated mandatory retirement at age 65. The results of a 1982 in-house survey had shown that while 69 percent of respondents felt the company should remove the "age 65 lid," 86 percent indicated they would probably leave by age 65. Based on those results and similar findings published by the Conference Board of Canada, W-L decided that by allowing employees a choice of their retirement date, the company would not be denying job opportunities to others. The decision was seen to be in the best interest of all concerned.

DRUG-TESTING AT WARNER-LAMBERT—THE IMPETUS

In December 1986, Wayne Britt was reading the monthly newsletter of Warner-Lambert, World, when he noticed a lead article outlining the new drug-testing program being implemented at W-L headquarters (Exhibit 6). The new Controlled Substance Abuse Practice was to be started on a trial basis in the Morris Plains, NJ, area and limited to job applicants and employees in high risk and executive positions. After evaluation and possible modification, the program was expected to be extended to other company operations in the US during the second half of 1987.

Joseph D. Williams, Chairman and Chief Executive Officer, explained the reasoning behind the new program:

> ...business bears an obligation to society. We are looked to for leadership in our communities in setting standards of personal behavior and participation in public affairs. Drug abuse is a national problem, and we must do what we can to help resolve it.

Britt was concerned. The program seemed to be one which would be invading personal privacy, and he wondered if the problem was large enough to justify the testing planned. As he read on he began to see what was driving the US management team to consider such a policy.

The Drug-Testing Issue

The proliferation of drug tests on American workers began in 1981 with the introduction of the first mass urine screening test for marijuana. A recent study by the Research Triangle Institute in the US set the cost of drug abuse at $25.8 billion a year, $16.6 billion of which was attributed to lost productivity from absenteeism, sick leave, drug-related deaths and imprisonment. The National Institute of Alcohol Abuse and Alcoholism had estimated the cost of alcohol abuse alone at $19.6 billion in lost production, and $12 billion in related medical bills.

Those kinds of statistics, as well as the highly publicized anti-drug stance of President and Mrs. Reagan, had served to see nearly 30 percent of the Fortune 500 corporations in 1986 take up routine urinalysis on employees and job applicants, up from 25 percent the previous year.

The Canadian Situation

Britt read the statistics outlined in the World newsletter with heightened interest. He wondered how Canada fared in the battle against drugs and also about the implications of informing employees of the US situation. He felt he needed information from several areas and began his data collection.

Wayne first contacted W-L legal counsel and requested the most recent information on drug testing in Canada. He then acquired a report from the Alcoholism and Drug Addiction Research Foundation (ADARF) in Toronto. In addition to accumulating media opinion on the issue, Britt contacted the US Human Resources people, as well as their Medical Director, to be sure he was fully informed on the current situation in Morris Plains, NJ. The various pieces of information convinced Britt that the issue warranted further study.

In Canada, the approach to drug testing had been more cautious than in the US. Although there was an estimated one million days of hospital care claimed each year as a result of alcohol and drug problems, the Addiction Research Foundation confirmed that no Canadian statistics were available on the extent of alcohol and drug abuse in the workplace.

The few companies in Canada that had implemented a drug-testing program tended to be in high-risk industries where a drug-induced error could result in serious harm to the public or fellow workers (eg off-shore drilling, airlines). American Motors of Canada had recently tested every short-listed candidate for the 3,000 jobs at its new Brampton, Ontario, plant. They saw it as protecting their $60 million training investment.

The major obstacle in the implementation of a drug-testing program seemed to be the invasion of privacy and/or unlawful search and seizure. However, there were also testing difficulties. Some tests were not accurate and had resulted in false positive results. The most reliable test involved a technique called gas chromatography/mass spectrometry. Performed correctly by laboratories, the results were as indisputable as fingerprints. But costs were high—from $25 to $100 per sample, compared with $10 to $25 for the simpler tests. This was the method recommended by the Addiction Research Foundation.

Although Canadian statistics were unavailable, the ARF report presented several observations with respect to employment-related drug screening:

- Initial studies indicated drug monitoring was having beneficial effects;

- Drug testing appeared to have lowered the incidence of job accidents in at least two US sectors (transportation and nuclear);

- Pre-employment testing as a term/condition of employment appeared to be legal;

- Reasonable cause was required for testing existing employees in other than high risk positions, to avoid an unlawful search and seizure allegation;

- General random testing was ill-advised;

- There was, as yet, no precedent on this issue.

The response from the lawyers suggested that the law had only begun to be developed in this area and several cases presently before the courts could mean new developments by the fall of 1987. Also, merely communicating to employees about the US program and the prospect of such a limited program at some future time in Canada presented no legal difficulties. Moreover, the *UpDater* information made clear that W-L Canada was only considering this approach in an effort to try to ensure a drug-free workplace for everyone.

DRUG TESTING AND W-L CANADA

Having decided that some action was necessary, Wayne Britt wanted to undertake some form of opinion polling. He presented the situation to the Executive Committee and received unanimous approval to proceed with further investigation on the issue. They were also in agreement that if any form of limited drug testing were to be implemented, senior management would voluntarily participate. Their only concern, raised by the Director of Scientific Affairs, was why the testing was limited to drugs only, and did not include alcohol.

Having received the go-ahead from senior management, Wayne took the issue to the three safety committees in the Scarborough locations, as well as senior management in the Brockville plant. He again received unanimous agreement that W-L should pursue some form of limited testing (ie those in high risk jobs, those applying for high risk jobs, or where there was reasonable medical cause to believe an individual was using drugs). The concerns raised by the safety committees centered on what would be considered high risk jobs, the criteria that would be used to classify them, and how many there were.

Wayne's final problem was to come up with a way of presenting the situation to the Canadian employees. He chose the *UpDater* as the vehicle, as it was used to feature special interest issues. He then considered the appropriate format. The W-L World edition had presented a second drug-testing article in a question and answer format with the Medical Director. Wayne felt this would be appropriate for Canada, as well.

WHAT NEXT?

As Wayne thumbed through the drug-testing edition of *UpDater,* he still had not decided what W-L Canada should do. On the one hand, a drug-free workplace was a goal no one would argue with. Malcolm Seath, President of Parke Davis, had summed the situation up quite simply: "After all, we are manufacturing ethical pharmaceuticals." However, Wayne still had several concerns:

- There was no Canadian evidence to suggest that the casual use of drugs and alcohol upset employees in the workplace.
- Was the current HELP program sufficient to handle the situation?
- If some form of drug-testing program was implemented, would it be an unreasonable invasion of an individual's privacy and therefore contradictory to the creed?

As Wayne prepared for the distribution of *UpDater,* he was comfortable with the flexibility he had retained for himself and the company. He felt that he would have no problem going back to his people and saying the issue required more thought. However, he also wondered whether he should be planning the next step.

EXHIBIT 1

Drug Testing at Warner-Lambert Updater

Warner-Lambert has launched a drug-testing program for all job applicants as well as employees in "high risk" positions in the Morris Plains, New Jersey area, effective January 3, 1987. After evaluation of the program and possible modifications, drug testing is expected to be extended to other company operations in the U.S. during the second half of 1987.

Ray Fino, Vice-President, Human Resources, says the company decided to establish the limited drug testing program to maintain a safe work environment for all employees and to avoid drug-related work performance problems by striving for a drug-free workplace.

Warner-Lambert will be joining an estimated 30 percent of "Fortune 500" companies which now require some form of employee drug testing.

Warner-Lambert's "Controlled Substance Abuse Practice" which has been explained personally to employees who will be affected will require testing of all job applicants and random testing of those in identified "high risk" positions. In addition, the 18 members of the company's Management Committee, which includes the Office of the Chairman, will be subject to random testing for drug abuse.

Joseph D. Williams, Chairman and Chief Executive Officer, explained that the Management Committee is being included in the testing program to send a clear message to employees that executive management fully supports and endorses the importance placed on maintaining a drug-free workplace.

Mr. Williams added that "business bears an obligation to society. We are looked to for leadership in our communities in setting standards of personal behavior and participation in public affairs. Drug abuse is a national problem, and we must do what we can to help resolve it."

Testing of employees in "high risk" positions will be done at least once a year on a random, unscheduled basis with no advance notice. All drug testing procedures and urinalysis will be under the supervision of the Employee Health Services Department.

The Controlled Substance Abuse Practice offers employees an opportunity to seek help with drug abuse problems. Employees must seek such help prior to being scheduled for random testing for abuse. Once an employee seeks help through Employee Health Services, a suitable

Exhibit 1 cont'd

Exhibit 1 cont'd

rehabilitation program and timetable will be developed for the individual.

For many years Warner-Lambert has offered drug rehabilitation to employees at most locations through the Employee Assistance Program (EAP) *[Project H.E.L.P. in Canada].*

Through, EAP, employees can receive confidential counseling and rehabilitation completely outside the routine framework of Employee Health Services.

In noting the growing problem of drug abuse in the U.S. workplace, Mr. Fino cited current national estimates of a $35 billion loss in productivity each year because of drug abuse. The figure rises to as high as $60 billion a year including medical costs, accidents, theft and other factors. Fino said that the U.S. Department of Health and Human Services recently estimated that in any one month, one in six workers smokes marijuana and one in 20 uses cocaine.

The company drug testing program is being instituted as a 'Practice,' meaning that it applies only to one location, in this case the Morris Plains area. Once the program is extended companywide it will be labeled as a 'Policy.' Fino explained that rollout of the program to other locations will be based on the experience of the pilot program in Morris Plains.

EXHIBIT 2

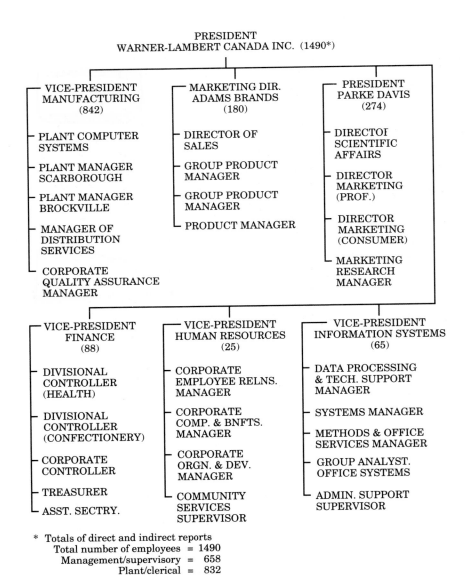

PRESIDENT
WARNER-LAMBERT CANADA INC. (1490*)

VICE-PRESIDENT
MANUFACTURING
(842)

- PLANT COMPUTER SYSTEMS
- PLANT MANAGER SCARBOROUGH
- PLANT MANAGER BROCKVILLE
- MANAGER OF DISTRIBUTION SERVICES
- CORPORATE QUALITY ASSURANCE MANAGER

MARKETING DIR.
ADAMS BRANDS
(180)

- DIRECTOR OF SALES
- GROUP PRODUCT MANAGER
- GROUP PRODUCT MANAGER
- PRODUCT MANAGER

PRESIDENT
PARKE DAVIS
(274)

- DIRECTOR SCIENTIFIC AFFAIRS
- DIRECTOR MARKETING (PROF.)
- DIRECTOR MARKETING (CONSUMER)
- MARKETING RESEARCH MANAGER

VICE-PRESIDENT
FINANCE
(88)

- DIVISIONAL CONTROLLER (HEALTH)
- DIVISIONAL CONTROLLER (CONFECTIONERY)
- CORPORATE CONTROLLER
- TREASURER
- ASST. SECTRY.

VICE-PRESIDENT
HUMAN RESOURCES
(25)

- CORPORATE EMPLOYEE RELNS. MANAGER
- CORPORATE COMP. & BNFTS. MANAGER
- CORPORATE ORGN. & DEV. MANAGER
- COMMUNITY SERVICES SUPERVISOR

VICE-PRESIDENT
INFORMATION SYSTEMS
(65)

- DATA PROCESSING & TECH. SUPPORT MANAGER
- SYSTEMS MANAGER
- METHODS & OFFICE SERVICES MANAGER
- GROUP ANALYST. OFFICE SYSTEMS
- ADMIN. SUPPORT SUPERVISOR

* Totals of direct and indirect reports
Total number of employees = 1490
Management/supervisory = 658
Plant/clerical = 832

EXHIBIT 3

Flow Diagram of Mandatory Referral Process

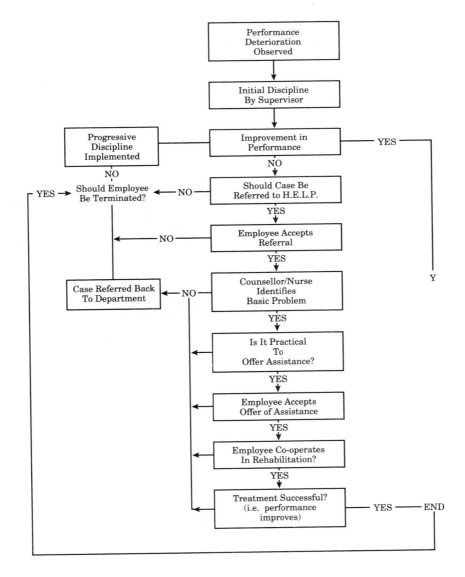

Exhibit 3 cont'd

<u>Exhibit 3 cont'd</u>

KINDS OF REFFERALS

Level of Referral	*Confidentiality*
1. Voluntary (includes kind of referral covered when employee requests help from supervisor)	Maximum (except by Law) (other exceptional case - eg. suicidal)
2. Suggested (discipline connotations) Early recognition as a result of job performance affected. Prevention operative here. Person suggesting anticipates a correction.	Maximum (general — not specific)
3. Mandatory Clear discipline required - other action has failed. Checks with supervisor as to which route. Proceed with discipline? Mandatory? Performance reviewed. Meeting with Counsellor condition of employment - put in writing	Less than maximum (with consent of employee) a) Was appointment kept? b) Willing to undertake counselling/ treatment — will employee benefit? c) Time frame (If consent not given this is communicated) If employee will not take treatment, this is communicated to Supervisor.

EMPLOYEE IS AT ALL TIMES RESPONSIBLE FOR HIS OR HER OWN BEHAVIOR

EXHIBIT 4

CONTRACT : WARNER-LAMBERT

FAMILY SERVICE ASSOCIATION OF METROPOLITAN TORONTO
EMPLOYEE ASSISTANCE DIVISION — SUMMARY OF ACTIVITIES

	01 Apr 86- 31 Mar 87	01 Apr 85- 31 Mar 86
Time Capture (hours)		
1. Counselling Services	446:40	740:15
2. Training and Public Information	19:00	13:00
3. All Other Activities	332:30	240:15
4. Total Time Reported	798:10	993:30
5. Total Time Allocated	800:00	800:00
6. % Over/Under Allocated	-.2%	24.2%
Service Activity (People)		
1. Carried over from Previous Period	41	31
2. Total Incoming Cases	139	101
a) Opened Cases	49	49
b) Brief Service Cases	90	52
3. Total Caseload Served (1+2)	180	132
4. Penetration Rate (865 employees)	16.1%	11.7%
5. Total Service Closed[1]	135	91
a) Interview Cases	37	35
b) Telephone Service Cases	8	4
c) Brief Service Cases	90	52
6. Carried Forward to Next Period	45	41
7. In-Person Interviews Given	317	575
a) On-Site	207	408
b) Off-Site	110	167

1 The Interview cases are in-depth discussions, usually set up in advance. The Brief
Service cases are for information only, such as requests for referrals.

Exhibit 4 cont'd

Exhibit 4 cont'd

CONTRACT WARNER-LAMBERT

CLIENT CHARACTERISTICS - CLOSED IN-PERSON INTERVIEW CASES

	01 Apr 86- 31 Mar 87	01 Apr 85- 31 Mar 86
WHO SEEN		
Employee	31	29
Family Member	2	1
Both	4	5
Total	37	35
GENERAL PROBLEM FOCUS		
Marital	9	6
Parent/Child	7	2
General Family	4	7
Individual	15	19
Environmental	2	1
Total	37	35
IDENTIFIED PROBLEMS		
Alcohol Abuse	4	7
Drug Abuse	0	3
Financial Management	3	6
Health and Care	7	2
Work	5	6
EVALUATION OF SERVICE		
Very Helpful	4	3
Helpful	18	24
Somewhat Helpful	13	8
Not Helpful	2	0
Total	37	35
REFERRAL TYPE		
Voluntary	33	27
Suggested	4	6
Mandatory	0	2
Total	37	35

Exhibit 4 cont'd

Exhibit 4 cont'd

CONTRACT WARNER-LAMBERT

CLIENT CHARACTERISTICS - CLOSED IN-PERSON INTERVIEW CASES

	01 Apr 86 - 31 Mar 87	01 Apr 85 - 31 Mar 86
YEARS OF SERVICE		
0-2 Years	4	8
2-5 Years	7	9
5-10 Years	11	7
10 Years Plus	14	9
Other	1	2
Total	37	35
TYPE OF WORK		
Supervisory/Management	11	4
Clerical	12	17
Hourly	13	12
Other	1	2
Total	37	35
LOCATION		
2200 Eglinton[2]	21	16
40 Bertrand	14	17
Research	0	0
Sales	1	0
Other	1	2
Total	37	35

2   The 2200 Eglinton and 40 Bertrand locations are both in Scarborough, Ontario.

EXHIBIT 5

Warner-Lambert Creed

OUR MISSION is to achieve leadership in advancing the health and well-being of people throughout the world. We believe this mission can best be accomplished by recognizing and meeting our fundamental responsibilities to our customers, employees, shareholders, suppliers and society.

To Our Customers WE ARE COMMITTED to providing high-quality health care and consumer products of real value that meet customer needs. We are committed to continued investment in the discovery of safe and effective products to enhance people's lives.

To Our Employees WE ARE COMMITTED to attracting and retaining capable people, providing them with challenging work in an open and participatory environment, marked by equal opportunity for personal growth. Performance will be evaluated on the basis of fair and objective standards. Creativity and innovation will be encouraged. Employees will be treated with dignity and respect. They will be actively encouraged to make suggestions for improving the effectiveness of the enterprise and the quality of work life.

To Our Shareholders WE ARE COMMITTED to providing a fair and attractive economic return to our shareholders, and we are prepared to take prudent risks to achieve a sustainable long-term corporate growth.

To Our Suppliers WE ARE COMMITTED to dealing with our suppliers and all our business partners in a fair and equitable manner, recognizing our mutual interests.

Exhibit 5 cont'd

Exhibit 5 cont'd

To Society

WE ARE COMMITTED to being good corporate citizens, actively initiating and supporting efforts concerned with the health of society, particularly the vitality of the worldwide communities in which we operate.

Warner-Lambert

ABOVE ALL, our dealings with these constituencies will be conducted with the utmost integrity, adhering to the highest standards of ethical and just conduct.

EXHIBIT 6

Drug Testing at Warner-Lambert

Warner-Lambert will launch a drug testing program for all job applicants as well as employees in "high risk" positions in the Morris Plains, New Jersey area on January 3. After evaluation of the program and possible modifications, drug testing is expected to be extended to other company operations in the U.S. during the second half of 1987.

Company has "added incentive"

Raymond M. Fino, vice-president, Human Resources says the company decided to establish the limited drug-testing program to maintain a safe work environment for all employees and to avoid drug-related work performance problems by striving for a drug-free workplace. "We have an added incentive to try and eliminate drug abuse within Warner-Lambert," says Fino, "because as a company, our mission is to improve health care around the world." Warner-Lambert will be joining an estimated 30 percent of "Fortune 500" companies which now require some form of employee drug testing. The number of companies testing, according to Newsweek magazine, is expected to experience "a quantum leap" by the end of 1986.

Among pharmaceutical companies already doing some form of drug testing are Merck, Johnson & Johnson, Pfizer, Hoffmann-LaRoche, Ciba-Geigy and American Cyanamid.

Warner-Lambert's "Controlled Substance Abuse Practice," which has been explained personally to employees who will be affected, will require testing of all job applicants and random testing of those in "high risk" positions. In addition, the 18 members of the company's Management Committee, which includes the Office of the Chairman, will be subject to random testing for drug abuse.

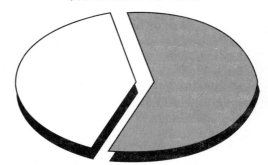

LOSSES TO INDUSTRY
DUE TO DRUG ABUSE
$60 BILLION PER YEAR

$25 billion in medical bills accidents theft, etc.

$35 billion losses in productivity

Joseph D. Williams, chairman and chief executive officer, explained to WORLD that the Management Committee is being included in the testing program to send a clear message to employees that

Exhibit 6 cont'd

hich test will be used?

Exhibit 6 cont'd

executive management fully supports and endorses the importance placed on maintaining a drug-free workplace.

Mr. Williams added that "business bears an obligation to society. We are looked to for leadership in our communities in setting standards of personal behavior and participation in public affairs. Drug abuse is a national problem, and we must do what we can to help resolve it."

Employees to be randomly tested because of their "high risk" positions include the following:

- Aircraft pilots and mechanics;
- Drivers of forklift equipment;
- Drivers assigned to company vehicles responsible for transporting other persons. (This includes employee drivers of company commuter vans and their back-up drivers.);
- Employees having access to the controlled substance cage and vault in manufacturing areas;
- Employee Health Services personnel, including the clerical support staff, and
- Employees of the Security Department.

In addition, drug rehabilitated employees will be included in the pre-employment physical examination. It is expected to serve as an up-front statement to potential applicants that Warner-Lambert does not tolerate drug use by employees.

Any applicant who refuses to be tested or whose test is confirmed as positive for drug use will not be hired.

Testing of employees in "high risk" positions will be done at least once a year on a random, unscheduled basis with no advance notice. All drug-testing procedures and urinalysis will be under the supervision of the Employee Health Services Department.

Signed consent form required

Prior to the drug screening, employees and job applicants will be required to complete and sign a consent/authorization form, including information on medication taken in the previous 96 hours which might affect the results of the drug test.

According to Dr. Timothy P. Lee, director-Corporate Employee Health Services, extensive study preceded the selection of test methods to be used and the laboratory to perform the diagnostic tests.

Initial screening will be by enzyme-multiplied immunoassay test, known as EMIT. Nine classes of drugs can be detected, even in extremely small amounts. Each drug will have its own cut-off limit for detection.

Drugs to be tested for are: amphetamines, barbiturates, benzodiazepine, cocaine, marijuana, methadone, methaqualone, PCP and the opiates, such as morphine and codeine.

Any positive EMIT test will be automatically subjected to a confirmation test by the extremely sophisticated gas chromatography/mass spectrometry method,

Exhibit 6 cont'd

Exhibit 6 cont'd

known as GC/Mass Spec. It is acknowledged to be the most sensitive, accurate and reliable method for confirming the presence of drugs of abuse in biological samples and is recognized as state-of-the-art by the courts.

Testing of samples will be performed by Compuchem Laboratories in Research Triangle Park, North Carolina. Extreme cautionary procedures have been established for what is known as "chain of custody," namely, confidential and documented tracking and handling of all urine samples through shipment and laboratory analysis. Delivery of samples will be by overnight courier.

The company drug-testing program clearly states that upon confirmation of drug use, an employee in a "high risk" position, or a member of the Management Committee, will be terminated.

However, the Controlled Substance Abuse Practice offers employees an opportunity to seek help with drug abuse problems. Employees must seek such help prior to being scheduled for random testing for abuse. Once an employee seeks help through Employee Health Services, a suitable rehabilitation program and timetable will be developed for the individual. If the initial rehabilitation effort proves unsuccessful, the employee will be terminated. If successfully rehabilitated, the employee will be given the opportunity to return to work, dependent upon such conditions as availability of suitable employment, qualifications and follow-up drug screening as deemed necessary. Employees in "high risk" positions will not be allowed to return to a job in any "high risk" classification.

Help is available through EAP

For many years Warner-Lambert has offered drug rehabilitation to employees at most locations through the Employee Assistance Program (EAP).

Through EAP, employees can receive confidential counselling and rehabilitation completely outside the routine framework of Employee Health Services.

In noting the growing problem of drug abuse in the workplace, Fino cited current national estimates of a $35 billion loss in productivity each year because of drug abuse. The figure rises as high as $60 billion a year including medical costs, accidents, theft and other factors. Fino said that the US Department of Health and Human Services recently estimated that in any one month, one in six workers smokes marijuana and one in 20 uses cocaine.

The company drug-testing program is being instituted as a "Practice," meaning that it applies only to one location, in this case the Morris Plains area. Once the program is extended companywide it will be labelled as a "Policy." Fino explained that rollout of the program to other locations will be based on the experience of the pilot program in Morris Plains.

4 The Ethical Investment Decision

It had been a good year for Jim Morrison. His firm, Travis & Hayes, had recorded the highest profits in its 80-year history. Jim's personal performance had also been outstanding, and he was gratified to share in the firm's success when he recently received a substantial bonus. He and Kathy decided that they would make a major purchase they had been postponing, and would invest the remainder of the bonus.

Both Kathy and Jim were socially conscious young professionals. Both were ardent environmentalists and had also been active in groups opposed to nuclear power and nuclear weapons. Kathy was contemplating joining the local chapter of Amnesty International as a result of recent contact with this group at her church.

In keeping with their values and beliefs they had become interested in so-called ethical, or socially responsible, mutual funds as a possible investment vehicle. As early as 1927, investments promoted as ethical or socially responsible were introduced in the United States. In later years, with the general public's greater awareness of, and interest in, the activities of corporations and governments around the world, such funds had become increasingly popular. The good financial performance of many of these funds also contributed to their popularity. By 1988, $6 billion were invested in socially conscious funds in the US.[1] Kathy and Jim felt that these funds were appropriate for them. They were professionally managed and offered a good financial return on the equity or debt of socially responsible corporations.

---

1. *United Mutual Fund Selector*, Babson-United Investment Advisors, Boston, Mass. Issue No. 491, June 17, 1988.

Jim had received a prospectus from each of the funds that he had identified. He also did a computer search of periodicals on the subject of ethical investing. After reading each prospectus Jim narrowed his choice to three funds that suited his and Kathy's objectives. One was the Managed Growth Portfolio of the Calvert Social Investment Fund. The Calvert Ariel Growth Fund was also a possibility. Both of these were US mutual funds. The third was a Canadian equity fund, the VanCity Ethical Growth Fund.

Jim's reading of the prospectuses led him to think that most of the funds used similar screening criteria on a similar set of issues. The common issues were:

- Employee relations. Companies should be progressive, meaning that they should have good health and safety records; bargain in good faith with employees; and not discriminate in hiring;

- Environment. Companies and/or their products were not harmful to the environment and were leaders in pollution control;

- Weapons. Companies did not manufacture weapons; were not engaged in military activities; and were not involved in war-related industries;

- South Africa. Companies were not operating in South Africa;

- Products. Companies produced quality, safe, pure products.

In addition, funds might consider other criteria like the existence of corporate codes of conduct and ethics, consumer protection, truthful advertising, and a record of philanthropy. At least one fund would not invest in companies in the liquor, tobacco or gambling industries. Finally, some of the funds emphasized one particular concern such as promoting alternative sources of energy, world peace, or industries that enhanced the quality of life (health, housing, education).

The funds exhibited a wide range of returns, portfolios (equity, money-market, bonds) and social criteria. The difficult decision would be which fund had the most appropriate social criteria. After reading the prospectuses, Jim felt that the Calvert funds and the VanCity fund addressed his and Kathy's particular concerns more completely than did the others.

THE TWO FUNDS: OBJECTIVES AND SOCIAL CRITERIA

Calvert Social Investment Fund[2]

The investment objective of the Calvert Social Investment Fund was "to provide opportunities for investors seeking growth of capital or current income through investment in enterprises that make a significant contribution to society through their products and services and through the way they do business."

The Fund's philosophy was that "long-term rewards to investors will come from those organizations whose products, services, and methods enhance the human condition and the traditional American values of individual initiative, equality of opportunity and cooperative effort.... The Fund invests in a producer or service provider which:

---

2 *Prospectus*, Calvert Social Investment Fund, January 1, 1988. Reprinted with permission.

1. Delivers safe products and services in ways which sustain our natural environment.
2. Is managed with participation throughout the organization in defining and achieving objectives.
3. Negotiates fairly with its workers, provides an environment supportive of their wellness, does not discriminate on the basis of race, religion, age, disability, or sexual orientation; does not consistently violate regulations of the Equal Employment Opportunity Commission; and provides opportunities for women, disadvantaged minorites, and others for whom equal opportunities have often been denied.
4. Fosters awareness of a commitment to human goals, such as creativity, productivity, self-respect and responsibility, within the organization and the world, and continually recreates a context within which these goals can be realized.

"The Fund will not invest in an issuer primarily engaged in:

1. The production of nuclear energy or the manufacture of equipment to produce nuclear energy.
2. Business activities in South Africa or other repressive regimes.
3. The manufacture of weapons systems.

"The Fund believes that social and technological change will continue to transform America and the world for the balance of this century. Those enterprises which exhibit a social awareness measured in terms of the above attributes and considerations should be better prepared to meet future societal needs for goods and services. By responding to social concerns, these enterprises should maintain flexibility and further social goals. In so doing they should not only avoid the liability that may be incurred when a product or service is determined to have a negative social impact or has outlived its usefulness, but will be better positioned to develop opportunities to make a profitable contribution to society."

Jim was interested in a portfolio within the Calvert Social Investment Fund. The Managed Growth Portfolio sought "to achieve a total return above the rate of inflation through an actively managed, diversified portfolio of common and preferred stocks, bonds and money market instruments which offer income and capital growth opportunity and which satisfy the social concern criteria established by the Fund."

The Calvert Social Investment Fund was organized in 1981 and the Managed Growth portfolio began sales in 1982. The *Boston Globe* called the Calvert Social Investment Fund "the fastest growing and most respected, comprehensively screened mutual fund around, the acknowledged flagship of the industry."[3]

The *United Mutual Fund Selector*[4] stated:
Restrictions in portfolio selection have not impeded profits. Reasonable gains were posted not only in tumultuous 1987, but in the prior three- and five-year periods as well. Calvert seeks growth of capi-

---

3 *The Boston Globe,* November 15, 1987, as reported in the Calvert Social Investment Fund Prospectus. Reprinted with permission—*The Boston Globe.*
4 op.cit.

tal or current income and is designed for long-term investment.

Although a member of the Calvert Group, the Ariel Growth Fund was not one of the Social Investment Fund's portfolios. The Ariel Growth Fund sought capital appreciation by investing in undervalued and relatively unknown stocks. The fund emphasized smaller companies with a recognized competence, quality products, and steady earnings-per-share growth.

The *United Mutual Fund Selector*[5] commented that "management believes its contrarian approach, avoiding the blue chips and sticking with the unknowns, will be rewarded in the long run."

The social criteria of the Ariel Fund were less comprehensive than those of the Managed Growth Fund. Ariel's criteria were:

1. the Fund will not invest in issuers which the Investment Manager ascertains are engaged in business in South Africa, that is, issuers with five or more employees or agents in South Africa, issuers with subsidiaries, affiliates or franchises in South Africa, or issuers with loans to companies in South Africa or to the South African Government; and

2. the Fund will not invest in issuers primarily engaged in the manufacture of weapons systems, the production of nuclear energy, or the manufacture of equipment to produce nuclear energy.

VanCity Ethical Growth Fund

Encouraged by the success of US funds,

the Vancouver City Savings Credit Union felt it was time for Canada to have its first socially responsible mutual fund. In February 1986, the VanCity Ethical Growth Fund was launched. The fund was initially restricted to British Columbia, mainly due to distribution complications. In British Columbia, units of the Ethical Growth Fund could be sold through VanCity Credit Union branches. This method of distribution was not available in the rest of Canada because regulations prohibited other Provincial credit unions from selling securities. Therefore, the fund was started in BC, while VanCity applied to other Provincial securities commissions to sell units nationally through various brokerage houses.

The investment objective and policies of the Fund were stated as follows:[6]

"The Fund will be prudently managed by the Fund Administrator primarily as a common share equity fund in order to maximize capital return on the funds invested, all within the framework of the investment policies. The assets of the Fund may from time to time, however, be placed in different classes of assets such as short-term investments, bonds, debentures and equities (common or preferred shares).

"In addition to the fundamental investment objective of the Fund, the Trust Declaration provides certain investment policies. The Fund will be socially responsible (meaning, the Fund will use specified ethical and moral stan-

---

5 op.cit.
6 *Prospectus*, Ethical Growth Fund, October 7, 1987. Reprinted with permission—VanCity Investment Services.

dards in making investments) and the monies of the Fund will only be invested in securities of a Canadian corporation which meets the criteria established from time to time by the board of directors of the Trustee. For these purposes the following criteria must be met on any investment in a Canadian corporation:

1. The corporation must have either its registered or head office located in Canada and its shares must be either traded or about to be traded on a stock exchange in Canada.

A Financial Comparison[7]

CALVERT GROUP

		%Change in Net Asset Values[8]		
	Size	Year 1986	Year 1987	5Mos. 1988
Ariel Growth	US $ 8.5M	N/A	11.4%	24.9%
Managed Growth*	US $ 162.3M	18.0%	4.0	6.2
Standard & Poor's 500		18.5	5.6	6.1

* Average annual overall return from inception (10/21/82-6/30/88) was 14.36%

VANCITY

		Year 1986	Year 1987	6Mos. 1988
	Size			
Ethical Growth	C $ 21.1M	N/A	7.8%	12.1%
Canadian Equity Funds (Avg.)	C $ 81.9M	10.3%	0.1	8.1
TSE Total Return Index		9.0	5.9	10.6

Performance the Week of the Market Crash October 1987

	Closing Oct. 16	Closing Oct.23	Percentage Change
Ariel	US $ 19.12	16.23	-15.6%
Managed Growth	US$25.30	23.79	-6.0
Ethical Growth	C $ 5.45	5.25	-3.7
Standard&Poor's 500	282.70	248.22	-12.2
Dow Jones Average	2246.74	1950.76	-13.3
TSE Composite	3598.58	3079.39	-14.4

7 These data were taken from the following sources: *United Mutual Fund Selector, The Financial Post Survey of Funds, The Globe and Mail* and *The Wall Street Journal.*
8 Including dividends and capital gains.

2. The corporation should encourage progressive industrial relations with all members of its staff or employees. Initially in order to determine the corporations within this criteria, a review of current publications relating to employment practices is conducted and a specific analysis is made of any corporations on any published "hot lists." From time to time thereafter published reports are followed (particularly at the time of any labor strife) to determine if there is any pattern of significant deterioration whereby a corporation would be considered for removal from the Fund's investment portfolio.

3. The corporation should regularly conduct business in, or with, a country or countries that provide racial equality within its or their political boundaries.

4. The normal business of the corporation should be the provision of products or services for civilians (non-military).

5. If the corporation is an energy corporation or utility, its major source of revenue should be from non-nuclear forms of energy."

A Critical Perspective

As Jim read the articles he had collected, he discovered that socially responsible investing was not without critics. Some people felt that the distinction between what is ethical and what is not was a personal matter. As one stockbroker stated, "What's ethical to me may not be ethical to the next guy."

The funds were also accused of making subtle and arguable distinctions between ethical and unethical investments. A *Forbes* magazine article highlighted this concern:[9]

> Distinguishing between ethical and unethical investments can be a problem. For example: Franklin Research and Development Corp lists Stride Rite Corp, the sneaker company, as a socially responsible investment, yet Stride Rite is moving production overseas and has a subsidiary in Haiti, which is run by a corrupt dictator; US Trust Co deems hard liquor, but not beer, an unsafe investment, while Anne Domini, author of *Ethical Investments*, endorses investments in firms that promote women, but not in Playboy Enterprises, which has a woman president.

Another article[10] stated that the Calvert Fund invested in "R.R. Donnelly, the world's largest non-union printer; Harcourt Brace Jovanovich, a publisher not famous for its concern for employees; and Peoples Express, an airline that hired low-wage temporaries to answer the telephones and then released them, refusing to train them for other jobs or consider them for permanent employment."

---

9 *Forbes*, Vol. 136 No. 3, July 29, 1985, pp. 42-43.
10 "Social Investment Funds: Fortune or Folly," Milton Moskowitz. *Business and Society Review*, Spring 1984, No. 49.

The VanCity Ethical Fund had also received criticism. One of its major critics was Dr Werner Cohn, a retired sociology professor from the University of British Columbia. An article[11] reporting on Dr Cohn's analysis and criticisms observed that although the Ethical Growth Fund avoided companies doing business in South Africa, "it gladly embraces those involved with 'some of the most repressive regimes in the world,' most notably Saudi Arabia and the Soviet Union. The former refuses employment to Jews and women, the latter prohibits trade unions and, of course, political dissent."

The article reported that Dr Cohn's analysis of the companies in the fund showed that all of them violated the fund's criteria in some way. Many of the companies engaged in business with communist and Arab countries "despite the fact that such states contradict every one of the professed ethical principles of VanCity."

One company stated that it did not mine gold in South Africa but it had a joint venture in China which "pays its laborers equally poorly." One of Northern Telecom's major US customers (for switchboards) was the Pentagon. Xerox's US parent dealt with the Soviet Union, and another company operated a factory in Saudi Arabia and had signed a letter of intent with the Canadian Armed Forces.

These articles were all dated, thought Jim, but none of the material he received had listed the companies whose stock the funds currently owned. He decided he would have to get the current investment lists.

However, the articles had started Jim wondering about what was ethical and what wasn't, and he felt he needed to resolve the question for himself. Although he felt he knew right from wrong, he had never really examined what distinguished ethical from unethical behavior. He felt pretty secure in his convictions about environmental insult, nuclear power, and South Africa. However, some of the criticisms regarding social issues in the other countries left him uneasy and unsure. He made a list of questions to discuss with Kathy:

1. What is the difference between ethical and unethical behavior, and who defines what is ethical?

2. Are Saudi Arabia and the Soviet Union repressive regimes? Why?

3. Is there any difference between doing business in South Africa, Saudi Arabia, or the Soviet Union? If a fund excludes South Africa, should it exclude the other countries also?

4. Is it fair to compare wage rates in China and South Africa with North America? Is it exploitive and/or unethical to pay people a low wage even if it is at the market rate?

5. Is it unethical to relocate a business from the US or Canada to a country with a corrupt dictator? If so, why?

6. Were the social criteria of the funds adequate? Was Dr Cohn right when he observed that for one fund to boast moral superiority over another was hypocritical?

---

11 "Exposing the holy high rollers," Fay Orr, *Western Report*, October 27, 1986. This article reported on Dr Cohn's 26-page study entitled "More Ethical Than Thou."

5 Ethics Management At Imperial Oil

As Ron Willoughby, communications manager at Esso Petroleum Canada, looked back on his years with Imperial Oil Limited, (IOL), he wondered what useful recommendations he could leave the company in view of his approaching retirement. Specifically, he was concerned about several incidents that had taken place that were in conflict with the company's code of ethics. He wondered what the company could do to minimize the occurrence of these incidents and whether IOL was doing something wrong, not doing enough, or doing all it could be expected to do in its ethical considerations of issues.

BACKGROUND

Imperial Oil Limited and its family of companies was one of Canada's largest energy companies, with 1985 earnings from operations at $684 million. It consisted of three major operating segments:

- Esso Resources Canada Limited, a wholly owned subsidiary involved in the production of crude oil, natural gas and coal, contributed $542 million to 1985 earnings from operations;
- Esso Petroleum Canada, a division of Imperial, with 1985 earnings from operations of $93 million, operated five refineries and marketed petroleum products;
- Esso Chemical Canada, another division, produced and marketed a wide variety of fertilizers and petrochemicals and had earnings from operations of $5 million in 1985.

In addition to these major operating segments, Imperial was involved in several other areas: Building Products of Canada Limited, a wholly-owned subsidiary, produced construction materials; Esso Minerals Canada, a division of Esso Resources, explored for profitable investment opportunities in minerals unrelated

This case was written by Nadine Hayes, under the supervision of Professor Jeffrey Gandz.

to energy; and a property development group provided a variety of real-estate services to the company.

Although Imperial was 69.6 percent owned by Exxon Corporation of the US, approximately a quarter of its outstanding shares were held by some 31,000 Canadians. Most of the directors were Canadians, and Imperial was well known for its pursuit of policies and practices that supported the Canadian economy, such as its "buy Canadian" policy.

CORPORATE CULTURE

Incorporated in 1880 by 16 London, Ontario, businessmen, IOL had a reputation as a socially conscious and responsible organization. Frederick Fitzgerald, the first president of IOL and described as "a man of unbending honor and incorruptible honesty," was the first in a long line of patriarchal figures who established a strong corporate culture oriented towards high ethical standards. Imperial earned the reputation for fair and ethical business practices through progressive policies in the areas of internal organizational effectiveness and human resource management. It was the first Canadian company to adopt a system of joint industrial councils in 1918; one of the first to permit four- and three-day compressed work weeks and flexible hours in 1932; one of the first Canadian business corporations to offer major support to Canadian culture with the purchase of the Canadian film classic *The Loon's Necklace*; the largest Canadian corporate contributor to the arts, amateur sports, education and community service; and one of the first to support employee health centres that offered company medicals, with the frequency of visits correlated to the age of employees. As part of this commitment, Imperial believed that it provided excellent pay levels closely linked to performance, and administered comprehensive benefit plans with items such as physical fitness refunds or the payment of higher education tuition costs for children of current employees and retirees.

The extent and strength of Imperial's ethical culture was difficult to describe. It was spoken of by employees as "a way of life." This way of life was sustained by both control mechanisms and "a tremendous amount of trust" between the company and its employees. In fact, Imperial's ethical standards were often emulated by other companies attempting to upgrade their own standards. One Royal Bank employee commented, "as we begin the job of reviewing and refining our code of ethics and how to apply it, Imperial's code and the way it implements it are invaluable models."

ETHICS POLICY

The ethics policy at IOL was not administered from one functional area, but had bases of responsibility in several departments. The range of tools used to ensure employee participation in ethical business practices was best described in the form of two action phases: the proactive phase and the reactive phase.

The proactive phase of Imperial's ethics policy sought, through communication tools, to raise employees' awareness of potentially difficult situations, and to educate them in IOL's definition of appropriate business practice. Richard

Michaelides, vice-president public affairs and general secretary, described IOL's communication process as a central element in the company's ethical culture because, as he stated, "there is no point in enforcing something people know nothing about." The tools considered to be proactive consisted of:

- a corporate ethics booklet;
- an annual sign-off procedure;
- the integration of ethics into training and orientation material;
- an annual review process conducted at the individual department/division level;
- the integration of ethics into company policies and procedures through the Framework of Management Control;
- the Business Practice workshops that presented material contained in the Framework of Management Control to IOL employees.

Corporate Ethics Booklet

The 20-page corporate ethics booklet, outlining IOL's expectations of behavior with respect to business dealings, was the core tool of the ethics policy. It was prepared, coordinated, and updated through the general secretary's department and was therefore focused at the corporate level. However, it was applied, implemented and tested within all IOL's operating arms, and subsidiaries. The content was general and understandable, and designed to prevent any impediment in its application to unique business units.

The booklet stressed the need for integrity in relationships (both within the company itself and in its external dealings) and referred to a series of stakeholders that should be given due consideration during the decision-making process: employees; shareholders, including Exxon; customers; sales associates; suppliers; and the communities within which IOL operated.

The booklet was firm in its requirement for employees to follow the letter of the law in areas such as combines and conflict of interest. However, it was also explicit in its requirement for them to follow the spirit of the law. The concern for both the letter and spirit of the law stemmed from a desire to be fair and open to public opinion. This was considered an "absolute must" due to IOL's size and level of foreign ownership and was well summarized in the booklet:

> It has always been the policy of Imperial Oil and the Esso family of companies to maintain the highest standard of ethics in its relations with whomever it does business or is associated with—its employees, shareholders, customers, sales associates, suppliers, governments, and the public. No director or employee, from the chief executive officer to the newest staff member, is ever expected to commit an illegal or unethical act. Not in the name of business efficiency. Not to get results. Not for any other reason.

> In addition to strict compliance with all laws applicable to company business, the highest standards of integrity must be observed throughout the organization. The company's reputation for ethical practices is one of its most valued assets. This reputation was achieved through the efforts of its

employees and their avoidance of any activity or interest that might reflect unfavorably upon their own or the company's integrity or good name.

Since its inception approximately 10 years ago, the corporate ethics booklet was given to each new employee, and distributed to all employees whenever it was updated, approximately every two years. Several specific addenda were included for individuals in especially sensitive areas (Exhibit 1). To ensure that the addenda were understood and followed, an annual sign-off process was in place.

Annual Sign-Off

Each year approximately half of all IOL's 14,000 employees were required to sign an assent document stating they had read or re-read the corporate ethics booklet, that it was understandable to them, and that they had been in compliance with it over the previous year. This sign-off procedure, administered by the general secretary's department, was designed for supervisors who had responsibility for sensitive areas, but it was not uncommon for those supervisors to require their staff to sign the document. As well as being a tool that communicated the company's ethical orientation, the actual signing-off was intended to induce personal commitment from those employees who actively put their name on that document.

Integration into Training and Orientation

The corporate human resources department took an active part in communicating Imperial's high ethical standards,

beginning with the recruitment stage, through orientation and into management development.

While recruiters for Imperial Oil did not explicitly search out individuals they felt were relatively more ethical, the interview process did incorporate an implicit ethical criterion. It tried to attract individuals with a mental set that would be compatible with IOL's high standards. The interviewer maintained an awareness for what people said was important to them and how they spoke about what they had done, and when a suitable individual was found, the prospective employee was made aware of IOL's expectations of behavior with respect to relations with both co-workers and business associates before an employment contract was confirmed.

New management-level hires at IOL would spend their first two years at Imperial becoming familiar with the culture, the accepted methods of business practice and the general atmosphere of such a large corporation. They would then be taken through a two- to three-day orientation session as part of IOL's planning and development training. The ethics component would be discussed in the context of where the concern for ethical activity originally stemmed from, and what it did for IOL rather than to it. The tools used in these sessions included simulated ethical situations on videotapes, as well as group discussion about actual cases. A similar format was used in the annual review process.

Annual Review Process

Each department or division was responsible for conducting an annual ethics review. These were not consistently applied throughout IOL or its family of companies in order to allow managers in those companies to mold the process to their specific departmental requirements. (This flexibility allowed managers to discuss specifics with their staff, as well as retaining the autonomy in decision-making that was very much a part of IOL's management philosophy.)

Examples from two departments illustrate both the diversity and the common threads that ran through the reviews. The general secretary's department, which handled confidential information and corporate security, used a <u>Business Ethics Compliance Checklist</u> for its annual review process (Exhibit 2). The list addressed sensitive activities or situations commonly encountered in that area. Once a year the 60-member department would be divided into groups of 20 or 30, which would then analyze the previous year's activities against the checklist. Each situation on the checklist was discussed to ensure that everyone completely understood its implications, and to determine if re-definition was necessary. In addition to the situations specified on the annual list, situations were presented that had not been covered. One of the items asked if the individuals had re-read the booklet, and if they had understood it. This process ensured that policies outlined at the corporate level were both understandable and applicable to the day-to-day jobs.

(Hilda Mackow, communications manager in the Retail Department of Esso Petroleum Canada, used a <u>less formal</u>, more specific annual review process.) As her department had responsibility for dealing with suppliers for printed communication needs and promotion ideas, she felt that her department was vulnerable to unethical temptations. For this reason she chose to run a workshop with her 15 managers where they discussed specific situations that had occurred, or that they felt could possibly be encountered. These were used, not to pass judgement on whether the decision taken had been the appropriate one, but to determine how similar situations could best be handled. This format allowed open discussion where individuals could speak candidly about experiences they had encountered, and areas they were particularly concerned with.

Framework of Management Control

(The internal control system at IOL consisted of numerous policies and procedures.) Permeating this system was an orientation towards ethics. The IOL comptroller's office developed a framework of management control that established principles for ethical and responsible business and administrative practices. It gave a clear indication of IOL's expectations of management behavior by explicitly stating objectives, and offering examples of the characteristics of appropriate business conduct. Managers then measured their performance against these examples. The alliance of controls and ethics is illustrated by contract clauses.

All contracts entered into by IOL and its family of companies contained three customary clauses that outlined IOL's standards of business practice: an ethics clause stating that no gifts would be accepted; a standard of conduct clause stating that no false billing would be consented to; and an audit clause stating that IOL retained authority to perform an audit on contractors and suppliers with contracts and major purchase orders.

Another form of integration of ethics and the management control system was shown in the communications department. Mackow felt that contraventions of ethical codes tended to occur as the result of a misinterpretation or misperception. To prevent this from occurring she was careful to ensure that her employees were knowledgeable about what could be misinterpreted, and was able to rely on IOL's internal control measures to present guidelines for verifiable situations such as those involved in bidding procedures, idea gathering for promotions, and supplier presentations.

These procedures delineated information flows, documentation and reporting requirements, and were used as the base for the monitoring process. Mackow stated that although the systems and procedures sounded bureaucratic, their consistency gave the perception of fairness in the marketplace. Bill Beacom, vice-president and comptroller, saw the controls as minimal, due to the strength of the company culture, and he was explicit in stating that "the strong ethical orientation allows for less controls because people are very aware of expectations of business practices."

The controls not only established methods to monitor work flows and communication flows, they were also set up as guidelines for ethical business practices and measured with both actual compliance and the spirit of compliance in mind. On a periodic basis, internal company auditors entered the business units and analyzed these control procedures in business practices, ethics and controls audit.

Business Practice Workshops

At Esso Petroleum Canada, the framework of management control was reinforced through business practice workshops. The half-day sessions were attended by all management personnel, as well as the administrative and clerical employees with high customer involvement, and focused on four major areas: contracting, sales, moral dilemmas, and gifts and entertainment. The participants were placed in groups, where each group prepared an analysis of a case study. The results of the group work were then presented and discussed. Since the workshops had been implemented approximately two and a half years earlier, Jim Dunlap, business control manager at EPC was pleased. He frequently received calls from former participants regarding a decision they were in the process of making, and saw that as a sign of the program's success. Higher awareness was leading employees to consider their actions beforehand, rather than having to correct careless decisions.

Monitoring and Appeal Processes

All business practices, ethics and controls were subject to review by an internal audit group. Consisting of approximately 45 auditors reporting at the corporate level, the audit group looked at the internal controls, efficiency, and business practices of each business unit in IOL and its family of companies. The audits occurred every two to four years, and had a mandate to assess the overall state of control. They were followed up with auditors' reports offering an overall opinion (good, satisfactory, not satisfactory, unacceptable) and outlining some possible recommendations for improvement. The internal auditors also met on a quarterly basis with the presidents of the three operating companies in audit committee meetings to discuss ethics and control issues. They checked for compliance with corporate ethics as well as the other, more traditional, performance measures and operating procedures.

Also occurring quarterly were stewardship meetings where the presidents of the three major operating segments would speak with their respective internal management groups concerning line management accountability issues. The presidents would then speak with IOL management in the upward-reporting stewardship format.

These reporting mechanisms culminated in an annual representation letter from each company president to the IOL comptroller confirming their company's compliance with business practices, ethics and conduct. The letter explained any deviations, the recommendations developed to deal with them, and any action that had been taken.

The corporation emphasized the responsibility of every employee to engage in a continual monitoring process in all areas they were in contact with. Although it was not inconceivable for concerns to be received and actioned from the office of the CEO, there were four well-communicated channels for reporting ethical concerns: the comptrollers of IOL and its operating companies; internal auditors; the general secretary; and the legal department. While each incident was handled according to its type and seriousness, the investigative process followed a fairly predictable pattern upon receipt of a concern:

- the concern was passed to the internal auditors;
- an attempt was made to clarify and verify the information;
- an investigation would begin;

- the auditors would determine the type of contravention:
- if the individuals involved were acting in their own interest, the incident was treated as fraud under the criminal code and the appropriate authorities were contacted;
- if the individuals involved were acting in the interest of the company, the incident was considered to be a conflict of ethics, and dealt with internally;
- the auditors would report in writing to the president of IOL on the incident and its consequences.

The final steps were situation-specific depending on the nature and severity of the incident—some were considered grounds for dismissal, others were infractions of the law and subject to judicial consequences, while others were discussed and set aside.

FURTHER ACTIONS?

As Ron Willoughby analyzed IOL's process of disseminating its code of ethics, he wondered what else could be done. Having recently seen two incidents arise—one a conflict of ethics, the other a conflict of interest—he wondered how they could have happened and how they might have been prevented. Was there a hole in the process? Was the communication lacking directness? Or was the process thorough and the cause on the part of the individual? He wanted to answer these questions and make some recommendations to his successor.

EXHIBIT 1

Addendum 2 - Gifts and Entertainment

STATEMENT OF BASIC PRINCIPLES

It is company policy to discourage the receiving of gifts or entertainment by employees from persons outside the company, and to discourage the giving of gifts or entertainment by employees on behalf of the company to persons outside the company. Such practices are permissible only where they involve moderate values and conform to the following basic principles:

- they are infrequent
- they legitimately serve a definite business purpose
- they are appropriate to the business responsibilities of the individuals
- they are within the limits of reciprocation as a normal business expense

GIFTS

Employees should neither give nor receive cash gifts or commissions, loans, shares in profit, securities or the equivalent of any of these things.

Employees should neither give nor receive gifts with more than a nominal value without the knowledge and consent of their department head, or functional vice-president, or where appropriate, an executive vice-president of the company. The current level deemed to be of nominal value is $25 or less.

ENTERTAINMENT AND BUSINESS MEETINGS

The company discourages giving or receiving entertainment (dining or an amusement, sporting or recreational event); however, it is recognized that entertainment within the basic principles in the policy may be appropriate from time to time .

FULL STATEMENT OF POLICY

A full statement of the company's policy on gifts and entertainment is available from division or department management.

EXHIBIT 2

	EHB 030-003
EMPLOYEE HANDBOOK	SECTION: Corporate Ethics/Conflict of Interest
	SUBJECT: Business Ethics Checklist

September 4, 1986

PUBLIC AFFAIRS AND SECRETARY'S DEPARTMENT EMPLOYEES

BUSINESS ETHICS COMPLIANCE CHECKLIST

The business ethics checklist has been reviewed at secretary's division meetings to ensure everyone understands the requirements and that possible areas of concern are identified.

Changes to the checklist this year are minor, but you should note section (I) that requires each of us to be knowledgeable and adhere to the department's microcomputer security and control guidelines. (Copies of the guidelines and instructions are available thorugh business services)

If at any time you have any questions on any of the items on the checklist, or if you are aware of anything we are doing which is contrary to them, please talk to me or any one of our senior managers.

RJMichaelides/cac

DATE:
September 1986

Exhibit 2 cont'd

Exhibit 2 cont'd

	EHB 030-003
SECTION: Corporate Ethics/Conflict of Interest	SUBJECT: Business Ethics Checklist

PUBLIC AFFAIRS AND SECRETARY'S DEPARTMENT

The following list supports the company's policies and guidelines given in "Our Corporate Ethics" providing a checklist of items of particular significance to public affairs and secretary's department.

A) ETHICS

Corporate ethics booklet:
- employees aware of the standards set down in the booklet. Copies are given to new employees.

Conflicts of interest policy and combines law statement:
- all appropriate employees read and sign the form contained in this booklet, including new employees to the department. Employees sign-off for compliance on annual basis.

B) INFORMATION HANDLING AND REPORTING

Safeguarding company information:
- all public affairs and secretary's personnel recognize the responsibility to maintain the confidentiality of sensitive information. This would include items such as board and management committee matters, shareholder ownership records, earnings and other financial data, employee records, etc. Personnel must be concerned about verbal communication, security of paper documents, and security of documents in the electronic media, e.g. word processing.

Disclosure guidelines - investor relations:
- awareness of and understanding of up-to-date guidelines for discretionary disclosure; press releases, speeches and informal remarks to be checked against guidelines; questionable items to be cleared with law department and/or investor relations manager.

DATE:
September 1986

Exhibit 2 cont'd

Exhibit 2 cont'd

	EHB 030-003
SECTION: Corporate Ethics/Conflict of Interest	SUBJECT: Business Ethics Checklist

Reporting to government:

- copies of regulations on reporting are up-to-date and employees are familiar with the reporting requirements, e.g. corporate business acts filings, insider trading reporting.
- all accidents requiring the attention of a physician outside 111 St. Clair are *immediately* reported to Workers' Compensation by the supervisor through the business services manager. Employees report any first aid incidents or injury concerns to their supervisor. Supervisors maintain a record of these incidents or suspected injuries.

Applications to government departments and agencies for permits, etc:

- proper channels, using prescribed forms; no undue pressure or unusual communications, e.g.: changes to articles, Access to Information Act, etc.

C) CONTRIBUTION TO OUTSIDE ORGANIZATIONS

Contributions to political organizations:

- no direct or indirect donations permitted; employees attending events where part of the ticket price is considered a donation must buy the tickets personally; no reimbursement by company.

Employees requested by supervisors to become involved in outside organizations, professional bodies, charities, and to do personal work:

- differentiate between attendance as employee or in personal capacity; safeguard confidentiality or proprietary information and procedures; speeches and presentations to be cleared with supervisors; sensitivity to combines requirements re competition.
- review for instances where undue influence is exerted by the supervisor on employees to participate in outside activities not essential to carrying out their jobs.
- check to ensure that it is totally voluntary on part of individual and degree to which activity is to Imperial's benefit.

DATE:
September 1986

Exhibit 2 cont'd

Exhibit 2 cont'd

	EHB 030-003
SECTION: Corporate Ethics/Conflict of Interest	SUBJECT: Business Ethics Checklist

Use of company in-house facilities and services for personal purposes:
- clearly defined limits; clearance with supervisor.

D) ENTERTAINMENT AND GIFTS

Contact with and entertainment of government officials and other outsiders:
- legitimate business purposes; reasonable value; in line with industry norms; reciprocal relationships.

Entertainment of company associates and subordinates:
- legitimate expense if guest from another geographic area; generally no reimbursement if same area, unless special purpose (eg. sensitive or confidential topic best handled in an outside setting, anniversaries, terminations, or transfers.)

Granting and receiving transportation:
- proper permission to invite outsiders to use company planes; legitimate reason to accept ticket or transportation from outsiders; travel by spouse only when attendance required by custom; proper approval.

Acceptance of unsolicited goods or services:
- determine whether gift or sample; if over nominal value, return/decline it or pay for it.

Acceptance of gifts or entertainment from outside businesses:
- nominal value only ($25); anything above to be cleared by a manager; above $100 to be cleared by a senior vice-president.

E) TRAVEL

Choice of hotels and carriers:
- employees are required to use approved hotels and carriers through air transport and reservation, or accomodation at similar cost.

DATE:
September 1986

Exhibit 2 cont'd

Exhibit 2 cont'd

	EHB 030-003
SECTION: Corporate Ethics/Conflict of Interest	**SUBJECT:** Business Ethics Checklist

F) CONTRACTORS AND CONSULTANTS

Use of company-engaged contractors, company employees, caterers, etc, for personal use:

- avoid appearance of the unethical; proper documentation of legitimate use; clearance with supervisor if necessary; no acceptance without full payment.

Contracts with consultants and "independent contractors":

- terms are to be fair and ethical and outlined in a letter of agreement or contract.

Ethical obligation of consultants and independent contractors:

- assurance that they subscribe to the same standards as the corporation; managers to decide whether to formalize.

G) PURCHASING

Use of tenders and competitive purchasing:

- all purchasing will be handled by materials and services department who will ensure adherence to the necessary guidelines.

Use of Canadian suppliers:

- purchase decisions to be tested against the company's "buy Canadian" policy.

H) ACCOUNTING PROCEDURES

Accounting and coding procedures for purchases of goods and services:

- observance of established procedures; care taken not to hide or misrepresent an item.

DATE:
September 1986

Exhibit 2 cont'd

Exhibit 2 cont'd

	EHB 030-003
SECTION: Corporate Ethics/Conflict of Interest	SUBJECT: Business Ethics Checklist

- payment of expenses for staff social external functions should be by the senior person at the the function, eg. department manager or division manager. A subordinate should not pay the bill in order that the expense can be approved within the division. All such expenses are to be recorded on a travelling expense statement form, not reimbursed through a cheque requisition, and approved by the department manager or executive manager, as appropriate.

Documentation of cash transactions to individuals:

- full documentation, including names; while not in themselves illegal, cash transactions should be fully documented for our protection.

Unusual payment procedures:

- payments to third parties, discount arrangements to be used only if standard to the industry and ethical; to be fully documented.

I) COMPUTER SOFTWARE

Microcomputer software:

- the microcomputer security and control guidelines are to be adhered to (copy is available from Business Services). No software program is to be copied without written permission from the Business Services Manager.

J) RIGHTS OF AN EMPLOYEE

Human rights statement:

- if employees are aware of any violations of the company's human rights policy as identified in the corporate ethics booklet, they should report the violation as provided for in the policy.

DATE:
September 1986

Exhibit 2 cont'd

Exhibit 2 cont'd

	EHB 030-003
SECTION: Corporate Ethics/Conflict of Interest	**SUBJECT:** Business Ethics Checklist

Harassment guidelines:

- a copy of the corporate harassment guidelines, dealing with harassment in the workplace, has been circulated to employees and is available from business services. (It will be circulated for all details business ethics reviews.)

DATE:
September 1986

6 Fardo Industries

Ron Bellamy, senior tax partner for a large public accounting firm, was preparing for a meeting with John Gardner, president and chief executive officer of Fardo Industries. Fardo was about to conclude an acquisition of Shorter Software, a small company specializing in developing custom software for several large organizations. The only minor problem was not directly related to the acquisition at all but, rather, how Fardo should amortize the $1.5 million goodwill payment included in the purchase price.

FARDO INDUSTRIES INC

Fardo Industries was a privately held company with an estimated market value of $20 million and 1,000,000 shares outstanding. John Gardner, the founder, held 31 percent of the shares; two other corporate officers held 20 per-

cent between them; the remaining shares were held by 30 outside investors, none of whom held more than 5 percent.

Since its inception 10 years previously, Fardo had specialized in acquiring small firms in the information systems field. It had raised the equity capital for this from small investors, mainly professionals such as doctors and lawyers, and also had substantial lines of credit at two banks.

SHORTER SOFTWARE

Founded by two brothers, Ben and John Shorter, former systems analysts and programmers with large computer firms, Shorter Software had developed a specialized niche in the software market, developing customized software to tie together a number of frequently utilized and commercially available applications packages.

Copyright © 1988. The University of Western Ontario.

This case was prepared by Professor Jeffrey Gandz. All names and certain facts have been disguised. Funding for this case was provided by a grant from Imperial Oil Limited.

THE ACQUISITION

Ron Bellamy had helped the Shorters set up their business six years ago and had acted as their accountant since its start. He had been surprised when, some three months previously, Ben had indicated that they would like to try to sell the business. "It really needs more capital to expand and, quite frankly, John and I are not very good business people...we're much happier doing the technical stuff. Maybe if we could sell the business to someone, remain associated with it for a number of years, and then retire, we could see a much better business develop and have our own retirement nest eggs."

Ron Bellamy had mentioned this conversation to John Gardner since he thought that Fardo Industries might be interested. They were. Bellamy immediately suggested to Ben Shorter that they get some independent financial advice since he could not really act for both the buyer and the seller in this kind of acquisition. Shorter retained George Miller, an old friend who was an accountant with a small firm.

Negotiations proceeded very smoothly and a deal was soon struck. The Shorters were to get 10 Fardo shares for each of their shares, with Fardo issuing 100,000 new shares for the acquisition. Furthermore, after five years the Shorter's would have to tender their shares to Fardo for an amount equivalent to 10 times the earnings per share in the best of the five years following the acquisition. Ben Shorter called Ron Bellamy after the deal was agreed to. "We're real happy, Ron. This Gardner guy seems pretty good to us and we think the deal's a fair one. Thanks for your help in this."

RON BELLAMY'S CONCERN

Ron Bellamy did not feel quite as excited as Ben Shorter about this deal. Of the acquisition price of $2 million, $1.5 million was for goodwill, representing the relationships built up between Shorter and their customers over the years. Such goodwill was not deductible for Fardo, however. Furthermore, the conventional accounting practices allowed a very wide range of alternative methods and amounts for writing off such goodwill. It could be written off quickly, over five years, or much more slowly, up to 40 years! (See Exhibit 3 for guidelines.)

Clearly, writing this off over five years—as John Gardner wanted to do—would depress the earnings per share of Fardo Industries significantly in those five years. This would affect the amount that the Shorter's would actually get for their shares at the end of the five-year period. Beyond that, however, it would also affect the earnings per share and, presumably, the share price for all investors, including the small minority shareholders, several of whom were either clients of Bellamy's firms or personal acquaintances.

Ron Bellamy had to give Gardner some clear advice about what to do in this situation, but he was uncomfortable about the impact on the Shorters and other minority shareholders. Before meeting with Gardner he decided to discuss the matter with George Clarke, a senior auditing partner with his firm, who was known throughout the accounting profession as an expert in accounting ethics. He wondered what Clarke was likely to say to him and, indeed, what the case was for either a quick or slow write-off.

EXHIBIT 1

Condensed Balance Sheet
as at Dec.31 (000's)

	BEFORE ACQUISITION	AFTER ACQUISITION
Current Assets	$ 5,000	$ 5,500
Fixed Assets	25,000	25,000
Goodwill	0	1,500
Total Assets	$ 30,000	$ 32,000
Current Liabilities	$ 2,500	$ 2,500
Long Term Debt	17,500	17,500
Total Liabilities	$ 20,000	$ 20,000
Shareholders Equity	10,000	12,000
Total Liabilities and Shareholders Equity	$ 30,000	$ 32,000

EXHIBIT 2

Projected Income Statement for 6 Years Subsequent to Acquisition of Shorter Software

	YEAR 1	YEAR 2	YEAR 3	YEAR 4	YEAR 5	YEAR 6
Revenue	$30,000,000	$31,500,000	$33,075,000	$34,728,750	$36,465,188	$38,288,447
Operating Expenses	$25,500,000	$26,775,000	$28,113,750	$29,519,438	$30,995,409	$32,545,180
Amortization Goodwill	$300,000	$300,000	$300,000	$300,000	$300,000	
Net Income	$4,200,000	$4,425,000	$4,661,250	$4,909,313	$5,169,778	$5,743,267
Tax (2)	$2,025,000	$2,126,250	$2,232,563	$2,344,191	$2,461,400	$2,584,570
Earnings After Tax	$2,175,000	$2,298,750	$2,428,688	$2,565,122	$2,708,378	$3,158,797
Shares Oustanding	1,100,000	1,100,000	1,100,000	1,100,000	1,100,000	1,100,000
E.P.S.	1.98	2.09	2.21	2.33	2.46	2.87
Shorter Tender at 10 x Earnings	$1,977,273	$2,089,773	$2,207,929	$2,311,929	$2,462,162	$2,871,634

NOTES: 1. Revenue increasing 5 percent per year.
2. Amortization of goodwill is not deductible in determining taxable income.

EXHIBIT 3

CICA Guidelines

Goodwill

Goodwill is commonly considered to be a composite of all the factors which cannot be individually identified and valued and which contribute to or accompany earnings capacity of a company. In a business combination, goodwill is represented by the difference between cost and the acquiring company's interest in the identifiable net assets. .54

There are various possible approaches that may be considered in accounting for goodwill including the following: .55

(a) retain as an asset indefinitely unless a reduction in its value becomes evident;

(b) retain as an asset but permit amortization as an operating expense over an arbitrary period;

(c) retain as an asset but require amortization as an operating expense over its estimated limited life or over an arbitrary but specified maximum or minimum period;

(d) write off complete amount at time of acquisition;

(e) reflect as a deduction from shareholders' equity unless a reduction in its value becomes evident.

The accounting treatments which do not involve the amortization of goodwill are based on the contention that the value of goodwill is not consumed or used to produce earnings in the same manner as various other assets and therefore net income should not be reduced by mandatory amortization of goodwill. Furthermore, it is contended that net income should not be reduced by both amortization of goodwill and the current expenditures that are incurred to enhance or maintain the value of acquired intangible assets. Amortization of goodwill is also criticized as being arbitrary, since it is contended that the life of goodwill is indefinite and an estimated period of existence is not measurable. .56

Exhibit 3 cont'd

<u>Exhibit 3 cont'd</u>

In the opinion of the Committee, however, goodwill does not have a lim-   .57
itless life, and therefore, amortization of goodwill should have the same
theoretical recognition as is presently afforded depreciation of tangible
assets. Goodwill existing at the acquisition gradually disappears and
may, or may not, be replaced by new goodwill. Furthermore, goodwill is
a cost which is incurred in anticipation of future earnings, and should
be amortized by systematic charges to income over the periods of those
future earnings in order to produce a proper matching of costs against
revenue. The straight-line method of amortization should be applied.
An analysis of all pertinent factors should normally enable the company
to assess a reasonable estimated life of such goodwill. However, the
period of amortization should not exceed forty years.

The amount reflected as goodwill at the date of acquisition should be   .58
amortized to income by the straight-line method over the estimated life of
such goodwill; however, such period should not exceed forty years. The
period of amortization should be disclosed.   [APRIL 1, 1974*]

Because Recommendations are not normally given retroactive effect,   .59
the Recommendation in paragraph 1580.58 is not intended to apply to
goodwill arising from business combinations where the date of acquisitions (see paragraph 1580.39) is prior to the effective date of these
Recommendations.

Since goodwill is an asset (see paragraph 1580.42), it would be account-   .60
ed for as such both at the date of acquisition and in subsequent periods
to the extent that it has not been amortized. It would not be written off
in a lump sum at the date of acquisition or shown as a deduction from
shareholders' equity. A subsequent permanent impairment in value
would result in a write-down of goodwill which would be treated either
as a charge against income before extraordinary items, or as an extraordinary item, depending on the circumstances.

The amount attributed to goodwill should be shown separately on the   .61
balance sheet as an intangible asset, to the extent that it has not been
amortized or written down. It should not be shown as a deduction from
shareholders' equity.   [APRIL 1, 1974*

Where there has been a permanent impairment in value of the unamor-   .62
tized portion of goodwill, it should be written down. The write-down
should be treated as a charge against income. The charge against
income will be shown either in income before extraordinary items or as
an extraordinary item, depending on the circumstances which give rise
to the impairment in value. (See EXTRAORDINARY ITEMS, Section
3480)
[APRIL 1, 1974*]

7 Geocan Systems Inc

"I wonder how often I've had this kind of talk" thought Grant Sparkes, president of Geocan Systems' international division. "They send me some hot shot business school graduate who's never worked outside of North America, and I've got to explain to him what international business is all about. Still, I suppose that someone has got to do it."

The "hot shot business school graduate" was Martin Skorinski, an engineer who had worked in Geocan's domestic software development group before going back to school for an MBA. Newly graduated, he had been re-hired by Geocan and assigned to the international division. Fluent in four languages and brought up by missionary parents in several Latin American countries, Skorinski had completed a three-month study of the division's operations. He had written a memo to Sparkes indicating that he had some concerns about the way that Geocan used sales agents in many countries, particularly in the Middle East and Africa, and wanted to speak with him about them.

GEOCAN SYSTEMS INC

A wholly owned subsidiary of a crown corporation, Geocan Systems Inc (GSI) was a large engineering consulting company, specializing in complex control of systems in the telecommunications industry. It sold services: design, engineering, installation and supporting consulting following installation. Its international revenues were $70 million, reflecting an annual compounded growth of 15 percent per year over the last five years. Recent projects had included a control system for a hydroelectric project in Peru, a data security system for a bank in Brunei, and a communications network for a pipeline installation in the Philippines.

GSI had specialized in small to medium sized projects, preferring not to compete with AT&T, Bell, British Telecom, NEC, Siemens, or other multinational firms on major projects. It tended to get business based on word-of-mouth reputation for good, innovative systems and its preparedness to transfer technology to

This case was prepared by Professor Jeffrey Gandz and was funded by a grant from Imperial Oil Limited. All names have been disguised.

developing countries, unlike major US and Japanese companies which tried to retain control of the technology.

The opportunity to work on international projects came to GSI in one of two ways. Either there was a request for a proposal sent directly to GSI in Canada or to one of its area offices in Singapore, Cairo, London, or Nairobi. Or, one of its current or former agents in a country might learn of a potential project, advise GSI, and work on a consulting basis in developing a proposal or bid.

The GSI staff, numbering about 250 in total, would investigate the lead, decide on the information required to prepare a bid, analyze the information, and cost and price the bid. The proposal would then be presented to the customer either through the GSI area manager or the agent who worked on GSI's behalf.

AGENTS

It was the issue of agents which occupied Martin Skorinski's mind as he opened up his discussion with Grant Sparkes.

"Grant, I've been looking over our agreement with agents, and I'm a little confused. It looks as if they get quite a lot from us in the way of consulting fees and expenses...anywhere between 5 and 25 percent of the value of a contract. Why do we use agents instead of our own people? And how do we decide who to use? How much to pay them? What do they do with the money? What responsibility do we have for how they use it?"

Sparkes thought for a few moments before he responded to

Skorinski. "You must recognize that agents are fundamental to doing business in various parts of the world. We use them for three reasons. First, they have connections. They know who makes decisions—about everything from technical specifications to providing foreign exchange for projects. These agents can line up the right people to see, organize visas for our people, and so on. Second, a good agent can clue us in on the social and business customs in a country. When to bring up business matters and when not; whether to bring small gifts or not; what kind and level of entertainment is appropriate ...those kinds of things. Third, you have to recognize that in some countries you can only do business through local agents—the bureaucrats and managers in local companies will only work through agents."

Skorinski listened carefully to Sparkes but then posed another question. "Why is that, Grant? What's their objection to working directly with us?"

"Look, Martin, the reality is that they depend on the money they get from agents to supplement their own salaries," Sparkes replied.

"You mean, they accept bribes for giving us business?" Skorinski asked.

"Bribe is the wrong word to use," replied Sparkes, with a slight hint of impatience in his voice. "What's a bribe in our culture is simply a normal business practice in theirs. I know presidents of large companies and ministers of state who make less than $20,000 a year. No one expects them to live on their salaries. It's accepted practice for them to receive money from agents. Also, remember that everyone does this—so no one really gets an unfair advantage—it's the way business is done. If you want to do business in those countries, that's how you do it. The agent keeps about 25 percent of what we pay him and he spreads the rest around his contacts, distributing the wealth.

"I see the look of disapproval on your face...but why? Here in Canada corporations make political contributions. They also retain lobbyists to get close to government, senior bureaucrats and politicians. How is that so different from what we do in Africa or the Middle East?"

Skorinski had been quiet while Sparkes had given this explanation but he pursued the questioning. "But there is the Foreign Corrupt Practices Act in the United States. Isn't there an equivalent in Canada?"

"Not that I'm aware of," replied Sparkes. "The FCPA really creates problems for US companies operating abroad. The fact that the US hobbles their international companies by insisting on projecting their standards onto different societies simply makes it better for the French, the Japanese...and us!"

"How do we find these agents? Who are they?" Skorinski asked.

Sparkes considered this for a moment. "Finding the right

agent is difficult. You have to visit the area. You get names from various sources. Our own embassies will have names of agents and you can sometimes get contacts from banks, international management consulting firms, the Export Development Corporation, CIDA, External Affairs, and so on. Often our clients will suggest an agent ...that's really the best source. When several contacts in a potential customer suggest an agent, he's probably got the connections.

"Most of these agents are great bullshitters—oh yes, they know everyone, at least they have you believe they do. You have to meet them...several times. It can take several visits to get a feel of what they'll be like, what they can do for you."

"What do our auditors think of this practice of using agents?" asked Skorinski.

"It doesn't bother them at all," Sparkes replied. "We have a written agreement with every agent we use. We base it on a standard agreement with additional clauses which specify exactly what will be paid for what services, and to which account and in which country and currency we should pay it. We get invoices for everything— we pay by cheque; there is no slush fund of cash or anything like that. It's above board. We pay agents for services rendered...that's it! We never pay an agent until we've been paid ourselves. And, by the way, any agent who decides to pass on some of his fee to others does it in his own name, not ours. Our contract clearly spells out what we are responsible for and what the agent does in his own name.

"All of our people—the area managers and sales people in the field have received a copy of our code of ethics. We know that this code, plus our practice of having detailed contracts, is the best safeguard we can have."

SKORINSKI'S CONCERNS

As he reflected on his conversation with Grant Sparkes, Martin Skorinski was a little confused. He knew that corruption of government officials was rampant in many of the countries he knew and had lived in as a child. He had often heard his father blame the inefficiencies in those countries on such corruption. The people were poor and the bureaucrats were getting kick-backs paid into Swiss bank accounts! So Grant Sparkes' down-to-earth comments should not have been surprising. Nevertheless, it felt strange to be working for a company which was actually involved in such practices! Did Sparkes' explanations satisfy him? Was it sufficient to accept the activities of agents as just a normal business practice? Was it the same as paying a lobbyist? What, if anything, should he do about it?

EXHIBIT 1

Code of Conduct and Ethics Regarding the Hiring of Agents or Representatives

In our marketing endeavors where we require the services of an agent or representative the relationship between the two parties must be clearly defined and meet high ethical standards.

All arrangements and agreements between Geocan Systems and its agents or representatives must be covered by written contracts. These contracts are to be guided by the following:

1. Contracts appointing Agents or Representatives are to be officially documented in the Company's records.

2. Compensation other than retainers in the form of fees to Agents or Representatives shall be paid only upon the successful award of contracts.

3. The level of compensation must be in accordance with local legal requirements and local ethical standards and must conform to international business practices.

4. All contracts with Agents and Representatives must receive prior approval by the President.

EXHIBIT 2

Extracts from Standard Representative's Agreement

ARTICLE II - Appointment of Representative

2.01   Geocan Systems Inc hereby appoints the Representative as its representative for the purpose of determining potential opportunities, negotiation, awarding and performance of the Contract, subject to the following limited authority:

1. To research and make inquiries as to potential opportunities for Geocan Systems Inc to obtain the Contracts and which will be incorporated in this agreement and noted in Appendix I by mutual agreement.

2. To assist Geocan Systems Inc in the preparation and submission of proposals and bids for the awarding of the Contract.

3. To participate in negotiations in the Country in respect of the Contract to the extent requested by Geocan Systems Inc.

4. To otherwise assist, as requested by Geocan Systems Inc in the performance of its Contract obligations in the Country.

2.02   Except as otherwise expressly and specifically agreed upon by Geocan Systems Inc, the Representative shall have no authority to act for or make any commitments on behalf of Geocan Systems Inc and in particular, Geocan Systems Inc shall be advised, in advance, by the Representative as to the extent Geocan Systems Inc's name and reputation will be used and relied upon in the Country and in this regard Geocan Systems Inc shall have the right to place such restrictions on the use of Geocan Systems Inc's name as it may deem appropriate.

2.03   In supplying and performing the Services described herein, the Representative agrees it will assign Mr_____to fulfill the obligations of the Representative.

Exhibit 2 cont'd

<u>Exhibit 2 cont'd</u>

ARTICLE IV - Scope of Services

4.01   The Representative shall, upon request of and as directed by Geocan Systems Inc, provide to Geocan Systems Inc, its officers, employees, and agents the Services which are more particularly described in Appendix II.

4.02   In providing the Services, the Representatives shall at all times comply with the Country's laws and customs and shall use qualified personnel, appropriate office premises and other resources and shall generally use its best effort to further Geocan Systems Inc's interest in performing the Contract in the Country.

4.03   The Representative agrees to faithfully supply Services to Geocan Systems Inc and undertakes not to furnish its services to any competitor to Geocan Systems Inc in the Country to the detriment of Geocan Systems Inc's obligation under the Contract during the term of this Agreement and the performance of the contracts signed between Geocan Systems Inc and agencies or organizations within the Country except with the prior written approval of Geocan Systems Inc.

ARTICLE V - Renumeration

5.01   Geocan Systems Inc agrees to pay to the Representative a commission in accordance with the schedule specified in Paragraph 5.02 below. The amount of the commission shall be agreed upon by both parties on a contract by contract basis in advance of Geocan Systems Inc submitting a formal offer, bid or proposal on a contract.

ARTICLE IX - Confidentiality

9.01   All agreements and arrangements between the parties and any information received by the Representative with respect to Geocan Systems Inc and the Product shall be and remain confidential during and five (5) years following the term of this Agreement.

ARTICLE X - Notices

10.01   Any notice or request required or permitted to be given or made

<u>Exhibit 2 cont'd</u>

Exhibit 2 cont'd

under this Agreement shall be made in writing in the English language.

10.02   Notices or requests made by personal service shall be deemed to have been given once so served and if by cable, telegram or telex shall be deemed to be received one working day after the sending thereof.

ARTICLE XI - Laws

11.01   This Agreement and the obligations of the parties hereunder shall be interpreted, construed and enforced in accordance with the laws of the Province of _____ and the parties hereby attorn to the jurisdiction of the Province of _____.

11.02   The Representative undertakes to provide the Services, in strict compliance with the laws and regulations of the Country of Canada.

APPENDIX II - Services

The Services to be supplied by the Representative shall consist of the following:

1.   Assist with the negotiation, award and performance of the Contract within the Country;

2.   Maintain a constant contact and provide a continuous liaison with agencies and organizations within the Country having jurisdiction over all matters related to services which can be supplied by Geocan Systems Inc in respect of the Contract;

3.   Inform Geocan Systems Inc and give its opinion on the Country's administration practices, procedures, regulations and related matters as well as the risks and contingencies affecting the negotiation, award, sale and performance of the Contract;

4.   Prepare and present all applications for total or partial exemption of imposts, taxes, duties and other assessments which may be imposed by the Country's authorities, to the extent permitted by law;

5.   Participate as requested with the representative or representatives of Geocan Systems Inc in the negotiations of the various contracts with agencies and organizations within the Country and in all further negotiations or discussion with such parties, as well as with the Country's

Exhibit 2 cont'd

Exhibit 2 cont'd
_____

authorities concerning problems which may arise with respect to the Contract;

6. Do what is necessary to obtain all permits, licenses, and other documents required to enable Geocan Systems Inc's personnel to perform the Contract in the Country;

7. Do what is necessary to obtain work permits, visas for services, tax releases and other approvals required prior to the repatriation of Geocan Systems Inc's personnel and their families;

8. Participate in the preparation, negotiation, drafting and executions of contracts in the Country with agencies and organizations and suppliers of local goods and services to Geocan Systems Inc in respect of the Contract;

9. Advise on local conditions which may affect the performance of the Contract such as the laws, amendments thereof, obligations pursuant to the labor conditions, customs, procedures, and others;

10. Do what is necessary on behalf of Geocan Systems Inc to select and obtain other facilities, translation services, travel and hotel reservations in relation to the Contract;

11. Deliver to Geocan Systems Inc a monthly written report of services supplied in accordance with the foregoing.

8 Johnson & Burgess Limited

On November 4, 1985, Peter Johnson, President of Johnson & Burgess Ltd (J & B), one of Canada's fastest-growing advertising agencies, faced a complex and potentially explosive situation. Jack Kelly, CEO of the Regal Tobacco Company, a large Canadian cigarette manufacturer, had contacted Johnson to request that J & B make a speculative bid for a $5 million piece of Regal's $12 million account.

Since Kelly was a long-time friend, Johnson had been able to probe the reasons for moving the account from the incumbent agency. He concluded that it had gone stale creatively and was experiencing internal problems arising from weak leadership and excessive turn-over of account executives.

Over lunch and in a confirming letter, Kelly had stated that his top marketing people were very much sold on J & B because they were aware of the agency's outstanding work and reputa-tion. He had strongly implied that the switch to J & B would be simply a for-mality if they really wanted the business and if the presentation for the Regal marketing management group went as expected. Kelly asked for an answer in three days.

Johnson could not help but be con-scious of the irony of his situation. Two weeks previous, he had received an application for employment from an MBA graduate, who had asked in her covering letter if J & B handled a cigarette account. He remembered dic-tating in his reply that J & B did not. Now he was coming to grips with a deci-sion that might change that.

His decision was not as straightfor-ward as it once might have been but was complicated by other recent experiences. In September, while undergoing a rou-tine medical checkup, he and his doctor happened to discuss smoking. In the con-versation, his doctor had pointedly men-

This case was prepared by Professor Donald H. Thain with the assistance of Joseph C. Shlesinger, as a basis for classroom discussion rather than to illustrate the effective or ineffective handling of an adminis-trative situation. Revised 1986.

tioned cigarette advertising: "The sooner the government stops these companies from advertising, the better off we'll all be." Because the doctor was a personal friend and a smoker as well, the statement stuck with him for several days. Another circumstance disturbed Johnson even more. In mid October, he learned that a close friend, who had been a heavy smoker, was dying of lung cancer.

In many ways, he was surprising himself with his quandary. "Last year," he thought, "I would have jumped at the chance to take this business. I'd better put these second thoughts out of my mind and get on with it. I'm running an ad agency, not a charitable society." Moreover, he could easily predict what his older partner, Tony Burgess, would say: "Cigarette smoking is legal. It brings people pleasure. Nobody's forcing them to smoke. Therefore, I don't give a damn what effect smoking has on health. If we can make a buck advertising cigarettes, let's go for it!"

He knew that there were mixed feelings about smoking within the agency. It was converted to a non-smoking office[1] just six months after a bitter struggle during which two key creative people threatened to quit. He knew that some of his staff would not really care about the issue, but many, if not most, would. And he also knew that it was his job to think of the agency's future and balance the rights of all his employees to have their personal values respected in such an important decision.

THE ADVERTISING AGENCY BUSINESS IN CANADA

The Canadian advertising scene was characterized by corporate, customer, and geographic concentration. There were about 400 agencies in Canada in 1985. The vast majority were located in Toronto, although Montreal and, more recently, Vancouver were also major centres. Of those 400 agencies, 20 accounted for 48 percent of total industry billings of $2 billion. Moreover, the top 10 advertisers (see Table 8.1) accounted for nearly one-fifth of industry revenues.

The business was changing. There was a growing tendency for multi-national companies to advertise with multi-national agencies based in the US. Independent Canadian agencies were in jeopardy of losing US subsidiary accounts. Moreover, competition was stiff in the advertising agency business. Aggressive new business solicitation was a basic activity in all well-run agencies. New account selling began with finding potential prospects who could be encouraged to switch agencies. The process developed through building relationships, communicating the competence and value added by the agency, and convincing the marketing people of the potential new client that they should replace the incumbent agency. When this process reached the point of a formal review and appraisal by the client, efforts often reached a fever pitch culminating in a formal presentation selling

---

1 Smoking was prohibited in public areas as a result of a decision voted by employees, encouraged by a Federal Government Department of Health and Welfare sponsored anti-smoking program.

TABLE 8.1 **Top 10 National Advertisers, 1984**

Rank	Company (head office)	Advertising Spending ($ millions)
1	Government of Canada (Ottawa)	$ 95.8
2	Procter and Gamble (Toronto)	46.3
3	John Labatt Ltd. (London)	37.6
4	The Molson Companies (Montreal)	35.3
5	Kraft Ltd. (Montreal)	32.5
6	Government of Ontario (Toronto)	32.1
7	Rothmans of Pall Mall Canada (Toronto)	31.0
8	General Motors of Canada (Oshawa)	30.0
9	Nabisco Brands Ltd. (Toronto)	24.5
10	General Foods Inc. (Toronto)	22.9
	Total	$388

Source: *Marketing*, May 13, 1985, Page 1.

the agency, its client service team, marketing expertise, advertising ideas and creativity. While elaborate and costly speculative presentations were frowned upon by the advertising agency association, the final pitch for a major account was usually an elaborate affair with suggested marketing plans, sample advertisements, and whatever else was necessary to convince the potential client.

Eroding margins presented another problem. As competition increased, pressures mounted to provide for clients at lower costs more comprehensive services, including marketing planning, marketing and advertising research, sales promotion and public relations. Although most agencies made a conscious effort to keep salaries below 56 percent of total revenue (see Table 8.2), agency cost structures generally showed wages at 59 percent of revenue.

Although agencies aimed for a 20 percent pre-tax profit, most were closer to 15 percent. Those that got close to 20 percent were generally the smaller agencies. Larger agencies typically had larger clients who were more sophisticated, more bureaucratic and more demanding.

SMOKING IN CANADA

In 1985, 33 percent of Canadians regularly smoked cigarettes, down from 50 percent in 1965. The smoking rate was highest among teenage girls. Industry research indicated that cigarette smoking rates were relatively higher among the following market segments: marital status—separated or divorced; income—low; occupation—blue collar; sex—female; and age—younger and older. One result of the declining market was that manufacturers were, for the first

TABLE 8.2 **Agency Cost Structure Target**

Revenue (15% Commission and fees)			100%
Expenses-			
Payroll			
Management	9		
Client contact	16		
Creative	10		
Other services	20		
Travel and entertainment		55.0	
Office facilities		10.0	
General office expenses		10.0	
Total expenses			80.0
Net profit before tax			20.0
			100%

Source: Casewriter's estimate

time, initiating and pursuing aggressive price competition. The 8 percent sales decline in 1985 led to major promotional campaigns with producers sometimes selling products at or below cost. Another outcome was that tobacco growers were being hit hard by falling sales and prices. In 1985, the Canadian Federal Government allocated $90 million for financial help for tobacco growers to inventory their crop until prices rebounded.

Tobacco industry sales were around $3 billion in 1984 and it was estimated that nearly $6 billion was spent on smoking-related health care. Cigarettes were blamed for 30,000 deaths a year in Canada. In fact, more Canadians died from smoking every 18 months than died in World War II.[2]

Criticism of smoking by the medical profession began in earnest with the 1964 report of the US Surgeon General's Advisory Committee on smoking and health which argued that smoking was a major cause of lung cancer and several other diseases. The *New York Journal of Medicine* (July 1985) published a 200-page report stating that the tremendous marketing efforts by cigarette manufacturers to create a strong, favorable image (by sponsoring sporting events and art shows) dwarfed attempts made to combat smoking. It included a report showing that the industry was attracting females by advertising in women's magazines and sponsoring women's tennis tournaments at which samples were often distributed.

2 *The London Free Press,* "Encounter", May 6, 1985 p.6.

The Canadian Council on Smoking and Health and the Non-Smokers Rights Association had lobbied against tobacco for several years. However, the closest the Federal Government had come to regulating tobacco was in 1969 when a parliamentary committee recommended the elimination of all cigarette advertising. In response to this threat, tobacco manufacturers voluntarily withdrew all television and radio ads.

The only restriction on tobacco marketing was a voluntary code (see Exhibit 1) administered by the Canadian Tobacco Manufacturers Council. Except for political pressure through the Minister of Health and Welfare, the public had no say in the development, enforcement or interpretation of the code.

Only two Canadian newspapers—the Kingston *Whig-Standard* and the Brockville *Intelligencer* had banned cigarette advertising. In May 1985, the *London Free Press* had been pressured by the Non-Smokers Rights Association to drop it but refused to do so. Addressing the issues, Bob Turnbull, the paper's president and associate publisher, wrote: "The problem here is a medical problem. It has nothing to do with our integrity or anything else.... All of these (pressure) tactics are directed, I think, the wrong way. They should be directed at the smoking problem. I just can't be convinced that tobacco advertising in daily newspapers would have a significant impact on the medical problem. It is not our role to make these rules."[3]

To the best of Johnson's knowledge there were only two Canadian advertising agencies that had an explicit policy of no tobacco advertising. In the case of one, he suspected that it was a matter of "sour grapes" because they had lost a major cigarette account.

A group called Physicians for a Smoke-Free Canada were demanding a ban on all tobacco advertising within two years. Some experts predicted that all forms of cigarette advertising would be banned by the year 2000. The most threatening trend in the industry, many experts said, was the increasing frequency of cigarette advertising aimed at the youth market. RJR MacDonald Inc, a large Canadian cigarette producer, brought this issue to the forefront with its "Tempo" campaign (see Exhibit 2). Its focus on youth was accused of being purposely controversial. In response, the Federal Ministry of Health and Welfare—itself a no-smoking office—began a $1.5 million campaign aimed at the young to counter such advertising.

A small sample of the kind of media reports currently being read by many J & B employees is presented in Appendix A.

JOHNSON & BURGESS LTD

J & B was one of the largest Canadian-owned agencies, with commissionable billings of $60 million in 1984. The agency was known for its talented people and had recently won several creative awards. It was considered by many creative people in the industry to be a rising star. J & B had 160 employees of whom 145 worked in the firm's offices in Toronto and Montreal, both of which were designated non-smoking.

---

3 *The London Free Press*, May 29, 1985 p. A3.

Over the past 10 years J & B had grown rapidly. According to Peter Johnson, their strategy had been to "overspend on people so that our creative product and client service are second to none." With strong political connections, a first class marketing research group and some widely publicized work in public opinion polling, they had also attracted significant public relations business from three large companies with extensive public affairs activities. Several staff members had worked hard for the PC party in the last federal election. Consequently, they had picked up over $3 million in Federal Government advertising.

The agency was earning a profit and was in good shape financially (see Exhibit 3). However, there was significant slack in the organization as a result of learning-curve improvements, particularly on two large accounts the agency had taken over two years previously, after fierce competition with several other agencies. Management was concerned about the need to either add more business or reduce salaries and wages.

Management also intended at some future point to make a public offering of equity shares to build a financial base for diversification into communication ventures. Management shareholdings are outlined in Exhibit 4.

THE KEY PLAYERS

A chart of the J & B organization indicating the main areas of the business and the top managers responsible is presented in Exhibit 5. The six key managers in the agency were described as follows:

Tony Burgess, Chairman

Tony was a good advertising agency man but his greatest asset had always been his friendly, outgoing personality. He had many friends and an amazing network of contacts. For retirement income he was counting heavily on cashing in his J & B stock which was currently worth about $2,250,000. He was very much aware that the agency's average five-year earnings-per-share figure could improve rapidly because earnings had been low in 1980 and 1981. Johnson knew that Burgess very much wanted to buy an attractive home in Florida and would not be able to finance it unless the agency did very well in Burgess's remaining two years. A former college rugger player, Burgess had a strong constitution and had smoked since he was a teenager.

Peter Johnson, President

Several industry observers attributed the success of J & B primarily to Johnson's unfailingly pragmatic, open, and positive leadership, his education, training and experience, his ability to attract and hold good people, and his sincerity and honesty in dealing with clients and staff alike.

A reformed smoker, he stayed in good shape by jogging year round and playing in an old-timers hockey league in the winter. While he was idealistic and socially responsible, he could also rationalize a wide variety of questionable behavior if a contract was at stake.

Bill Nugent, Vice-President Administration

Bill was an unflappable but disorganized

workaholic. Of medium height and noticeably overweight, he was a heavy smoker who drank more than his share. Bill was everyone's friend and the confidant of many. His grown children were all married and his wife, the daughter of a once prominent politician, was involved in many charitable and social activities. Bill worked many evenings and after working hours his door was always open. Anyone from Tony Burgess to a junior copywriter might be found in his office chatting about personal or business affairs.

Wally Bick, Vice-President Creative

With an excess of brilliant creative talent, Wally was the key idea man and a driving force of the agency. He was well known as an active member of a large downtown church. A health food devotee, he neither smoked nor drank. On the request of a bishop of his church, he had given many hours of professional help to a group of parents organizing a political action group to fight drunk driving. The creative work for beer and liquor accounts was his general responsibility, but he showed little interest in them beyond seeing that they were handled by top-rated people. Client services personnel, particularly on the beer account, occasionally complained privately to Jack Spitzer that they did not have Bick's full commitment. Johnson hoped that in spite of Bick's condemnation of smoking, he would still see that the creative work on a cigarette account was handled professionally. Johnson worried, however, about what he would tell Kelly if he specifically asked for Bick to be heavily involved on the Regal account. He expected that while Bick would

oppose taking a cigarette account, he would stop short of outright action to block the freedom of colleagues to work on what they wished. Bick had in the past mentioned informally that there was no way he would accept any direct or indirect benefits from a cigarette account.

Jack Spitzer, Vice-President Client Services

Pleasant, capable, and efficient, Jack knew and stayed in close touch with client top management personnel and made sure they got what they wanted. Sometimes accused of being too political and pragmatic in giving in to client pressures, he nevertheless was widely respected. Jack had been the hard-driving leader of the agency's new business campaign and took great personal pride in its growth record. Johnson knew that Jack would be a vociferous opponent of anyone who raised barriers to new business.

Lou Destino, Vice-President Marketing and Public Relations

A business school graduate with good training and experience, Lou was the able leader of marketing and public relations. Lou did much of the market targeting and planning which guided Jack Spitzer's new business push. Foresighted and strategic in his thinking, he doubted that cigarette business was good for the long term because of falling sales, growing government reaction against tobacco products, medical opposition, and mounting product liability legal claims (none successful) which he was afraid might eventually involve the ad agencies that did cigarette advertising.

However, he had no real personal hangups about working on a cigarette account. While he occasionally smoked cigars and a pipe, he was opposed to cigarette smoking and had told several friends about how happy he had been when his wife, who was a heavy smoker, quit smoking because of the pressure their young children had exerted on her.

THE MEETING

Since Johnson had to make up his mind immediately regarding his reply to Kelly, he called a special meeting of the management committee for the next Saturday morning. Casually dressed, they assembled around the boardroom table. The meeting had been called for 10:00 am and Johnson thought it might take an hour and a half at most. As usual, Nugent and Spitzer smoked throughout. After Johnson started off by describing Kelly's request and his subsequent meeting, telephone discussions, and letter, he asked for their input to his decision. Excerpts representing the various points of view follow.

Bick: There is no way we can get around the fact that smoking is bad for everybody and lethal for many. We all know the terrible numbers—10,000 die from lung cancer alone and that's only one of the many possible side effects. And, we all know that's just the beginning—bronchitis, emphysema, cancer of the larynx, bladder, esophagus, mouth, lip and reproductive systems—you name them, they're all attributable to smoking. There's no way we should take this account. We should all be worried about ourselves for

even giving it serious consideration.

Spitzer: Come on Wally, that's a lot of anti-smoking medical propaganda. The scientists working for the tobacco industry deny that those statistics have ever been proved. For the big majority—must be over 90 percent—of smokers there's no problem at all. If all that medical crap is really true, how come so many doctors smoke?

Burgess: Regardless of the medical arguments, it's legal and fits in with today's lifestyle. Advertising simply informs people about what they obviously want. We can't make anyone smoke who doesn't want to! And we have no right or responsibility to act as judges of what's good for society. That's the job of government. As long as the government raises taxes from cigarettes and openly supports tobacco farmers, how can we be so self-righteous as to make moral judgements against the business?

Spitzer: If we're going to get on a soap box and make public moral statements, what about some of our other business...our beer and liquor business is almost $6 million this year. Our automotive business includes a sports car with such incredible performance that four out of five buyers—especially teenagers —are a danger everytime they get behind the wheel. Incidentally, yesterday, when I was out at _____, they told me they've got over $200 million worth of consumer liability legal actions going in North America. We all know that you just can't waste time thinking about this kind of stuff. And why should we? There's no business in the world that's perfect...

Nugent: I don't see what harm cigarette advertising does anyway. The tobacco industry says that it's all brand advertising to defend market share and not to promote primary demand. We all know that cigarette sales are falling in spite of all the advertising that's being done.

Burgess: I think we've got to look at the positive side of this opportunity. It would be the biggest piece of new business we've ever picked up. We'll get some great publication and trade exposure because it will be the biggest account to move this year. That means momentum, reputation, and success. And there's a good chance for a lot more of Kelly's business if we do an excellent job. I'd be less than frank if I didn't admit that it would be a tremendous benefit to me and my wife. I've given my total commitment for 27 years to this team and to making our operation the best. The boost this would give to the price of my stock in a couple of years when I cash out would have to be one of the bigger breaks in my career. Not to speak of what it means in profit sharing for all of us!

Destino: I'm not sure this would be good for us in the long term. Sure, it's morally objectionable and it's going to cause internal conflict. But the real problem is the opportunity cost. There is better business out there. If we take this account we'll have no capacity for another big account for quite a while. I wouldn't want to take this at the cost of having to pass on some better business a month or two from now.

Spitzer: Do you have anything specific in mind?

Destino: Not right now.

Spitzer: Well then, let's take what we can get right now and worry about our next new account when the time comes.

Destino: Yeah, but if we land this account, we might lose some government advertising because of it.

Spitzer: So what if we do? Government can deal with some other agency. They've got too big a bureaucracy anyway—you need client approval at five levels, and it's taking a lot more time than we planned for in our budgets.

Johnson: Okay, but what about the internal consequences? What team will we put on the account?

Spitzer: For an account this size, we'll need eight people: an account supervisor, an account executive, two assistant account executives, two artists and two copywriters. They would all work for Regal pretty well full time. I'd like to make sure we'd put our best people on this account, since it's so important.

Bick: But some of our best people, like Jim, Marie and Jan [three of J & B's best copywriters and artists] say they'd have nothing to do with cigarette advertising. In fact, I wouldn't be surprised to find that Jim would quit before we took this account.

Burgess: Look, I can't tell you what to do, but if we don't take this account, someone else will. Then what has our "statement" meant? Only a big loss for us in terms of dollars and exposure. Think about it. Look at what it would mean to our profit-sharing plan. We owe it to all our staff, now and in the future, to go after this account as hard as we can.

Johnson: Maybe we do. But you're making our short-term advances more important than long-term stability. What if we do lose some of our best talent, and don't actually get the account? What effect will that have on our future? Some of these idealistic young people will think we're prostituting the whole agency for a few more bucks. Who'd want to come work for us thinking we cared only about the bottom line? If Kelly's people weren't known to be such a professional and classy organization, it'd be easier to make this decision.

Nugent: Let's put the staff problem in a little perspective. Out of our total of 160 people I'd say only four or five at the very most would ever quit over this. Another 15 or 20 would be strongly against it and drag their feet or not give their top effort. Another 25 or 30 would be against it but forget about the problem in a week or so. At the other end of the spectrum we would have our 35 to 40 smokers and quite a few non-smokers who would think we were crazy for even thinking about passing up such a great piece of business. Many of them would think they are being shafted by a bunch of do-gooders.

Finally, after three hours, the meeting broke up when Lou Destino and Bill Nugent had to leave. Destino's parting comment to Peter Johnson was, "You and Tony better take the rest of the afternoon and decide what we should do. I gotta leave. See you tomorrow."

Johnson knew he had to make up his mind quickly. However, after a long talk with Tony Burgess he was even more confused about what he should do. As he reviewed the file of notes he had accumulated on the problem, he assessed the pros and cons of his options. The organization was strong and cohesive but he worried that the agency job market was good for experienced, high performers. The tangible costs and benefits were fairly clear but the intangibles were difficult to assess. The longer he pondered his dilemma the more he realized there were going to be serious consequences no matter what he decided.

EXHIBIT 1

Cigarette and Cigarette Tobacco Advertising and Promotion Code
of the Canadian Tobacco Manufacturers' Council

RULE 1

There will be no cigarette or cigarette tobacco advertising on radio or television, nor will such media be used for the promotion of sponsorships of sports or other popular events whether through the use of brand or corporate name or logo.

RULE 2

The Industry will limit total cigarette and cigarette tobacco advertising, promotion and sponsorship expenditures for any year to 1971 levels. The limits will be revised annually to compensate for cost increases or declines.

RULE 3

Advertising of sponsored events associated with a brand or corporate name or logo will be limited to non-broadcast media and such advertising together with promotional material will not include package identification, product selling line or slogan, or the words "cigarette" or "tobacco."

RULE 4

No cigarette or cigarette tobacco brand shall be promoted by incentive programs offering to the consumer cash or other prizes. Coupons redeemable for gifts and related gift catalogues will not be advertised.

RULE 5

Direct mail advertising will not be used as a medium to promote the sale of cigarettes or cigarette tobacco.

RULE 6

All advertising will be in conformity with the Canadian Code of Advertising standards as issued in 1967 by the Canadian Advertising Advisory Board.

RULE 7

Cigarette or cigarette tobacco advertising will be addressed to adults 18 years of age or over and will be directed solely to the increase of cigarette brand shares.

Exhibit 1 cont'd

Exhibit 1 cont'd

RULE 8

No advertising will state or imply that smoking the brand advertised promotes physical health or that smoking a particular brand is better for health than smoking any other brand of cigarettes, or is essential to romance, prominence, success or personal advancement.

RULE 9

No advertising will use, as endorsers, athletes or celebrities in the entertainment world.

RULE 10

All models used in cigarette and cigarette tobacco advertising will be at least 25 years of age.

RULE 11

No cigarette or cigarette tobacco product will be advertised on posters or bulletin boards located in the immediate vicinity of primary or secondary schools.

RULE 12

All cigarette packages, cigarette tobacco packages and containers will bear, clearly and prominently displayed on one side thereof, the following words:
"WARNING: Health and Welfare Canada advises that danger to health increases with amount smoked — avoid inhaling.
AVIS: Santé et Bien-être social Canada considère que le danger pour la santé croît avec l'usage — éviter d'inhaler."

RULE 13

The foregoing words will also be used in cigarette and cigarette tobacco print advertising (see Appendix I for size and location). Furthermore, it will be prominently displayed on all transit advertising (interior and exterior), airport signs, subway advertising and market place advertising (interior and exterior) and point-of-sale material over 144 square inches in size but only in the language of the advertising message.

RULE 14

Average tar and nicotine content of cigarette smoke from any brand of cigarettes will not exceed, within normal tolerances, 22 milligrams of tar, moisture free weight, and 1.6 milligrams of nicotine per cigarette.

RULE 15

The average tar and nicotine content of smoke per cigarette will be shown on all cigarette packages and in print media advertising.

Exhibit 1 cont'd

<u>Exhibit 1 cont'd</u>

RULE 16

Labels carrying the warning noted in Rule 12 are available through the Council to operators of cigarette vending machines. No cigarette brand advertising or Corporate symbol except for package facsimiles will appear on cigarette vending machines.

RULE 17

Consumer sampling of cigarettes or cigarette tobacco free of charge will be limited to new products or existing products in which significant technological changes have been made. Such free sampling will be limited to a period not exceeding twelve months from the date of introduction of the said product in any given area, and the function of sampling limited to those areas in which cigarettes are normally purchased and only to persons who may legally purchase the product and are perceived as in the act of making a purchase. Furthermore, the sampling function will be carried out only by regular employees of the Manufacturer. These restrictions will not preclude free distribution of cigarettes by manufacturers to their employees for their personal use, or to consumers in answer to complaints.

RULE 18

No cigarette or cigarette tobacco brand names will be used on future cigar or pipe tobacco products nor will cigar or pipe tobacco brand names be used on future cigarette or cigarette tobacco products.

RULE 19

The parties to this Code agree that adherence to the Code's provision will be subject to review by a Board of Arbitration and that the Board will have power to impose sanctions on an offending party or parties.

EXHIBIT 2

Cigaret Firms Try New Marketing Approach

By Adam Corelli

In what may be the beginning of a cigaret packaging revolution similar in scope to changes that have affected the brewing industry, two leading cigaret manufacturers have adopted more aggressive marketing techniques.

RJR-Macdonald Inc. has introduced Tempo brand, a mid-strength cigaret in a trendy package, and Rothmans Inc. has begun selling its Number 7 brand in packages containing 30 cigarets for the price of a 25-pack.

Spokesmen for both Toronto-based companies said the changes are designed to capture market share from the competition and not to increase the over-all size of the smoking market.

Jeffrey Goodman, vice-president of corporate affairs at RJR-Macdonald, said Tempo "breaks the mold" for cigaret packaging because of its very contemporary nature.

"We are going after smokers of competitive brands but we're not reacting to declining markets," he said. He said Tempo's marketing strategy, developed by J. Walter Thompson Co. Ltd. of Toronto, is not aimed at young people, as anti-smoking lobbyists have charged, but at mid-strength cigaret smokers, who make up about half the market.

The Tempo advertisements, currently in Toronto only but planned for all of Canada eventually, use bright colors in the background and young-looking people in the foreground who are perhaps best described as appearing to be "hip."

Mr. Goodman said his company has no plans as yet to follow Rothmans' lead in offering different package sizes. He said his company suspected some time ago that Rothmans was going to introduce Number 7s in the 30-pack.

RJR-Macdonald has been expanding its current lines, and will probably digest such changes before introducing more changes, he said.

The company currently holds about 18 per cent of the Canadian market, Mr. Goodman said, with annual sales of about $400-million. RJR-Macdonald produces more than a dozen different cigaret brands as well as cigars and cigaret sundries.

The 30-pack introduced by Rothmans is likely to have even more impact than changes at RJR-Macdonald if smokers jump at what amounts to a price cut. "Obviously the competition won't stand by and watch us make a success of it," Peter Bone, a spokesman at Rothmans, said.

Mr. Bone said there are so many different varieties of cigaret packages on the market already he is not entirely sure what will happen next. He said an Ontario provincial "stick tax" limits what manufacturers can do economically.

Exhibit 2 cont'd

Exhibit 2 cont'd
_____

He pointed out that Rothmans once sold cigarets in a variety of package sizes and even gave away packages of five cigarets for promotional purposes. He said no plans exist for repeating such schemes beyond the 30-pack. "But someone may do something."

Rothmans sold more than $550-million worth of tobacco products last year, but profit was just over $17.4-million, down about $2-million from the previous year. The company paid almost $300-million in sales and excise taxes.

Mr. Bone said that many years ago, the Canadian cigaret industry agreed to adopt its fairly staid packaging format because such items as five-packs were uneconomical. The changes made by RJR-Macdonald and Rothmans effectively end that agreement.

The same kind of agreement existed in the beer industry until a couple of years ago, when the traditional stubby bottle gave way to a torrent of different shapes and sizes, all designed to increase lagging sales.

Mr. Bone said it "is awfully hard to tell" at this stage whether cigaret marketing will undergo a similar revolution, but Rothmans said recently, after major management changes, that it planned a major market offensive to increase market share.

The _Globe and Mail,_ Wednesday, October 2, 1985
Reprinted with permission of Adam Corelli.

EXHIBIT 3

Profit and Loss Statement 1984

REVENUES	($000s)	%
Gross commissionable billings	60,000	
Commission	9,000	
Services and other fees	8,000	
Gross Revenue	17,000	100
EXPENSES		
Client contact	3,400	20
Management	1,700	10
Creative	1,700	10
TV and radio	1,020	6
Public relations	680	4
Marketing	510	3
Research	340	2
Other	1,530	9
Total	10,880	64
OFFICE FACILITIES		
Rent	969	5.7
Amortization/leasehold facilities	51	.3
Depreciation/furniture, fixtures and equipment	136	.8
Heat, light, water	34	.2
Maintenance and repairs	102	.6
Municipal taxes	68	.4
Other	170	1.0
Total	1,530	9.0
GENERAL OFFICE EXPENSES		
Postage and courier	68	.4
Supplies and stationery	255	1.5
Telephone and telegraph	289	1.7

Exhibit 3 cont'd

Exhibit 3 cont'd

GENERAL OFFICE EXPENSES cont'd	($000s)	%
Donations	136	.8
Doubtful accounts	34	.2
Company contribution to pension plan	153	.9
Group insurance	102	.6
Enemployment insurance and other benefits	34	.2
Miscellaneous	289	1.7
Total	1,360	8.0
TRAVEL AND ENTERTAINMENT	850	5.0
Total Expenses	14,620	86.0
Net profit before tax	2,380	14.0
Income tax	1,190	7.0
Net profit	1,190	7.0
EPS (100,000 shares)	11.9	

Johnson & Burgess' profit sharing plan called for 40% of earnings to be distributed to 52 plan participants on a basis proportional to salaries.

Another 40% of earnings was customarily paid out in dividends.

EXHIBIT 4

Shareholders

	Number of shares	Percent
Tony Burgess	25,000	25
Peter Johnson	20,000	20
Bill Nugent	12,000	12
Jack Spitzer	10,000	10
Wally Bick	5,000	5
Lou Destino	5,000	5
21 others	23,000	28
	100,000	100

Shares were valued at 6 times average earnings per share for last 5 years plus $33.00 per share to cover per share portion of earned surplus and deemed good will.

Earnings per share for the past 5 years had been as follows:

1980	$6.80
1981	7.10
1982	10.25
1983	11.20
1984	11.90

Past 5 year average - $9.45
1985 EPS forecast - $15.25

EXHIBIT 5

Organizational Chart
(Age)

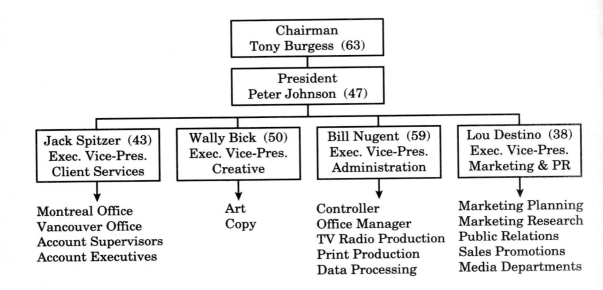

APPENDIX A

MDs Call for Two-Year Deadline in Tobacco Ad Ban

The federal Government should step up its campaign against smoking and ban all forms of tobacco advertising within two years, a group called Physicians for a Smoke-Free Canada says.

Dr. Andrew Pipe said yesterday that because federal politicians backed away from a proposed advertising ban 16 years ago, one more generation of young people has been exposed to an epidemic of smoking-related diseases.

"Where have our political masters been for the last 16 years?" he asked at a news conference. "I really wish some of our politicians would come into the back rooms of our hospitals and see the people who are dying of emphysema and lung cancer."

Physicians for a Smoke-Free Canada is a newly incorporated group with a core membership of 30 or 40 doctors in the Ottawa area and perhaps 50 more in other parts of the country.

Dr. Jim Walker, a member of the Canadian rowing team at the 1972 Olympics, said if cigarets were new products, health officials would never let them on the market because they are so dangerous.

"In short, we are facing Government-supported and Government-certified drug trafficking and allowing our children to be victimized," he said.

The Canadian Tobacco Manufacturers' Council has a voluntary code that says there shall be no cigaret ads on television and radio. The code also says that print ads will be aimed exclusively at adults and that all models used in them will be at least 25 years old.

Dr. Pipe called the code self-serving and ineffective and said tobacco manufacturers should be regarded as "pushers in pin stripes" rather than good corporate citizens.

The latest complaints against the code arose from print ads used to introduce Tempo cigarets. The advertisements feature young-looking people dressed in the latest fashions for youth.

"You just cannot tell me that this is not targeted at Canada's young people," Dr. Pipe said as he displayed two of the ads.

The doctors' group wants an immediate end to billboard and poster advertising, an end to promotional activities within one year and a total advertising ban that would cover all printed ads within two years.

Smoking studies done for the federal Health Department show that the percentage of regular smokers in Canada has been falling more or less steadily during the past two decades.

The latest study showed that roughly one of every three Canadians 15 years old or older was a regular cigaret smoker.

However, a Gallup poll done for the department earlier this year showed that nearly half the people in the 20 to

Appendix A cont'd

29 age group are smokers. The figure for men has gone up and down, but the figure for women has risen sharply in the past three years.

Dr. Pipe said he suspects young women are a special target of tobacco advertising. And they may be especially susceptible if they believe smoking will help them control their weight.

The doctors said they think Health Minister Jake Epp is sympathetic to their views, but they also believe that he has not yet been able to carry the day in Cabinet against colleagues with opposing views—Agriculture Minister John Wise for one.

"Obviously, there is a conflict of interest within the federal Cabinet that they have not sorted out yet," Dr. Walker said.

Source: *The Globe and Mail*, Friday, November 15, 1985. Reprinted with permission—CP Press News Limited.

Smoking Victims Sue Tobacco Firms Over Illness

Santa Barbara, Calif.—John Mark Galbraith, crippled by heart disease, lung cancer and emphysema, lived his final years on bottled oxygen.

Yet his widow and children contend he was so addicted after almost one-half century of smoking, he yanked back the oxygen mask to sneak a puff of Camel, Salem or Winston cigarettes.

This week, Galbraith's life and death will be spotlighted in his survivors' $1-million liability suit in the Santa Barbara County superior court against R. J. Reynolds Tobacco Co. and two stores.

Jury selection began Monday in the suit, the first among about 35 new liability suits against Reynolds to go to trial.

Meanwhile, in Austin, Tex., an elderly couple filed a $58-million lawsuit against three tobacco companies, including R. J. Reynolds, claiming their disabling illnesses were caused by years of cigarette smoking.

The suit claims cigarette manufacturers should be responsible for a percentage of damages even though the Bastrop, Texas, couple—Weldon Carlisle and his wife, Hazel — chose to smoke.

In the Santa Barbara suit, tobacco industry spokesmen and some financial analysts said a win for Galbraith's family could lead to a flood of similar claims against tobacco companies and open the door for liability suits against a wide range of goods, from liquor to fatty foods.

The wrongful death suit filed in 1983 against Reynolds and two stores that sold Galbraith cigarettes claims his 1982 death at age 69 was due to injuries that

Appendix A cont'd

Appendix A cont'd

resulted from cigarette smoking. It claims the cigarettes Galbraith smoked for about 50 years were "defective and unsafe for their intended purpose in that they contained contaminated, adulterated, impure, harmful, lethal and carcinogenic ingredients."

"The heart of the lawsuit is to have an American jury, having heard the medical and scientific evidence presented by both sides, find cigarettes cause human illness and especially, Mr. Galbraith's death," said Paul Monzione, associate to lawyer Melvin Belli, who is handling the case for Galbraith's widow, Elayne, of Stanton, and son and daughter.

Similar suits have been brought before but Reynolds spokesmen say the tobacco industry has never been found liable for damages resulting in death or disease stemming from cigarette smoking.

However, Belli, one of the leading personal injury lawyers in the United States, believes he can win. Belli has brought similar cases against Reynolds and lost them all, the first 25 years ago.

Belli sought out the Galbraith family—a practice prohibited by California law unless the lawyer pledges any proceeds to the public good. Belli says he will donate any income he receives from the case to cancer research.

Unlike previous cases, Belli said this trial will focus on smokers' addiction and on new scientific evidence linking smoking with diseases.

Belli said he will seek out smokers for the jury, since they will better understand his claim of addiction.

Testimony is expected from a University of California professor who contends cigarettes are more addictive than alcohol or heroin.

In the Austin case, Carlisle, 71, said he smoked a pack or two of cigarettes a day since he was 14. He developed throat cancer, forcing doctors to remove his larynx. He speaks through a mechanical voice device that he presses against a hole in his throat.

Mrs. Carlisle, 61, is dying of emphysema, has had a stroke and is confined to a wheelchair. The Carlisles were joined in the suit, filed in state district court in Austin last month, by the family of Hazel Boatright, a heavy smoker who died of lung cancer and emphysema last March.

Tobacco companies named as defendants in the lawsuit include Philip Morris Inc. and Liggett & Myers Tobacco. The Tobacco Institute, a tobacco industry lobby group, and Ponca Wholesale Mercantile, an Amarillo, Texas, cigarette distributor, were also named as defendants.

Don Davis, a lawyer representing the Carlisles, said the suit is based on a Texas supreme court ruling involving the crash of a small airplane in which the court ruled pilot error contributed to the accident but that a design flaw in the airplane was partially responsible. The ruling allowed a jury to assign percentages of culpability to the manufacturer.

Davis said if the same doctrine is applied to the Carlisles' case, the tobacco manufacturers could be responsible for 10 percent of the couple's damages.

"This is the first case where people are going in and saying 'we are at fault

Appendix A cont'd

Appendix A cont'd

but so is the tobacco industry,'" Davis said. The suit seeks $33 million in compensatory damages and $25 million in punitive damages. It charges that tobacco company advertisements suggest cigarette smoking is not only safe but "pleasurable, sophisticated, associated with success and glamour, sports, love and the wholesome outdoors."

Carlisle said he wished he had known the damage cigarette smoking can cause.

"I never would have started," he said.

Source: *The London Free Press*, Tuesday, November 19, 1985.

London Life - Investments Department (A)

Tom Allan, Senior Vice-President of Investments at London Life Insurance in London, Ontario, was faced with a decision. The president, Earl Orser, had recently requested that he introduce a document to be signed by all employees of the Investment department certifying that there was no conflict of interest between the employees' professional and personal investments. However, the meeting he had held with the department staff following the distribution of a draft of the document had identified numerous concerns about its contents. Allan wondered what he should do now.

LONDON LIFE

Founded in London in 1874, London Life had grown to a national operation with 168 offices throughout Canada. Ninety-eight percent of its stock was owned by Lonvest Corporation, which was in turn part of the Trilon Financial Corporation Group. With more than 2 million policies, assets of $7.6 billion and over 2,700 sales agents, London Life was one of the largest insurance companies in Canada. It had just received one of four Employment Equity awards from the Province of Ontario to reward fair hiring and promotion practices. In addition, the company was featured in "The 100 Best Companies to Work for in Canada," published the preceding year.

London Life's revenues came from three major sources—premiums, segregated funds (the administration of pension funds held on behalf of other companies) and investments. Investment income was $669 million (an increase of 12.1 percent from the previous year), which represented about one-third of the company's total income of $1.9 billion. Following the corporate strategy of asset diversification, more investment was being directed toward assets without a fixed term, such as equities and real estate. This type of investment represented 15.2 percent of London Life's total investment portfolio, up from 4.9 percent six years earlier.

This case was prepared by Beth Baker under the supervision of Professor Jeffrey Gandz, and was funded by a grant from Imperial Oil Limited.

The Investments department comprised 30 employees in nine functional areas (Exhibit 1). The atmosphere here was one of openness; several employees mentioned the department's team approach that came from employees working and discussing business together. Meetings were held daily with representatives from the department's bond, equity and private placement divisions, and weekly meetings involved the whole department. Most decisions resulted from discussions and consultations between the managers in the departments rather than from top-down edicts.

INDUSTRY SCANDALS

A series of events had recently scandalized Wall Street and was making businesses more aware of ethics. Dennis Levine, an investment banker at New York's Drexel Burnham Lambert investment firm, had recently been arrested for insider trading. The allegation was that he had made a great deal of money by selling tips to others, who then shared their profits with him. This way it was much more difficult to prove Levine's guilt. In fact, he netted over $2.6 million in profits before finally being caught, and was discovered only because of his boasting. Levine named many of his accomplices, which led to the arrest of risk arbitrageur Ivan Boesky. To lighten his own sentence, Boesky implicated Drexel's Martin Siegel for insider trading while at Kidder Peabody. Levine was sentenced to two years in prison and handed a $362,000 fine, while Siegel pleaded guilty to selling tips in exchange for briefcases full of cash. Siegel's own confessions led to the arrests of Kidder arbitrageurs Richard Wigton and Timothy Tabor, as well as Robert Freeman, Goldman Sach's chief of arbitrage. In all, investor complaints to the SEC regarding illegal practices had increased 55 percent over a five-year period, to a total of 25,000.

In Canada, insider trading had a lower profile since there had been fewer convictions, but Canadian business was no less conscious of it. A lower level of trading and a smaller financial community made illegal trading more difficult, but by no means prevented it. When Imasco Ltd was about to take over Genstar in March 1986, the latter's stock increased 25 percent (from $44 to $55 per share) in the two trading sessions prior to the takeover offer being announced. As a result, Imasco paid significantly more for the company than they should have. Several years earlier, one of the vice-presidents of Toronto's Scottish and York Holdings Ltd illegally sold some of his stock prior to the release of a financial statement. He was found guilty of insider trading, and fined $3,900, the largest penalty assessed in the decade to that date. Penalties were minuscule in comparison to potential gains, and convictions were rare. In addition, while a person selling inside information could be prosecuted, the individual receiving the tip had nothing to fear.

POSSIBILITIES FOR UNETHICAL ACTIONS

At London Life, employees who traded in equities had the greatest opportunity, at least in theory, to benefit from insider trading since their high volume trades could have influenced the market. (Daily trades averaged $2-3 million for stocks and $50 million for bonds, while total portfolio sizes were $600 million and $1.5 billion respectively.) However, all department employees openly discussed trades they carried out, so other investment employees could theoretically have benefited from that information.

Both a broker and trader had the potential to profit from entering into an illegal transaction. London Life's total brokerage commissions for the past year were estimated to have been approximately $6 million, equally divided between stocks and bonds. The company's stock transactions were split among 20 to 30 brokers with no one broker earning more than 10 percent of the commissions, while the maximum proportion of bond commissions earned by any one brokerage firm was 25 percent. (While commissions were not explicitly paid on bonds, they were built into their price.) Brokers earned commissions from both buy and sell ends of a transaction, so to gain even an additional 3 to 4 percent of London Life's business would have been lucrative. In the highly competitive investment business, one senior manager at London Life believed that a broker would "fight and scratch" to get an increase of that magnitude.

LONDON LIFE'S REACTION TO INDUSTRY SCANDALS

London Life's audit committee, consisting of one inside and six outside directors, was concerned that the company should take all possible steps to guard against real or perceived unethical or illegal trading practices. The company had recently updated its Code of Business Conduct (Exhibit 2), which provided general guidelines for employee behaviour. However, there was concern that it might be so general that people might either ignore it or not see its relevance to their activities. The audit committee questioned whether this statement was sufficient in the current context of investments management.

Orser contacted Allan and Bill Nursey, General Counsel and Secretary, to discuss how they should respond to the audit committee's request. The Investments department was a small and tightly knit one, and Allan knew his employees well. He was aware of most of their personal investment activities and absolutely believed that none of his employees would exploit their company affiliations for personal gain. Indeed, in the past he had advised people to minimize their exposure to personal loss on investments to ensure that they were not exposed to possible conflicts of interest. However, he understood the committee's concerns, and realized that a solid reputation was essential for an insurance company. He also wanted to avoid putting his employees in what he called "an awkward position," by having ambiguous or unstated expectations and policies. Following discussion between Orser, Allan, and Nursey, Allan drafted a document, "Policy Regarding Personal Investments by Investment Department Employees" (Exhibit 3). This policy called for the employees to submit a monthly statement of their personal investments to verify that there were no conflicts of interest. They would also sign a statement of compliance annually, promising to comply with the document for the next year.

EMPLOYEE RESPONSE TO THE POLICY

The document was handed out to department employees in April. They were surprised, since they hadn't been given advance notice that they would receive this draft. No schedule of those receiving the document was attached, so an employee did not know who else, if anyone, had received it. However, as employees began talking to each other, they realized that everyone in the department had received a copy, and it became the central topic of conversation. Some people thought it was a good idea and accepted it, but many others were opposed. Although they could understand why such a document was desirable, this did not alleviate displeasure and concern.

In response to the intense reaction generated by the document, Allan scheduled a departmental meeting to discuss the employees' concerns. While he answered most of their questions, not everyone was totally satisfied with the outcome of the meeting. It raised several issues that Allan had anticipated, and even more that had not occurred to him.

First, some of the employees considered the reporting requirements an invasion of privacy. Investment statements would be passed on to the employee's immediate supervisor, which meant that activities might be evaluated differently by different supervisors. This also raised the concern that it might somehow be used against the employee, for example, in a performance review. In addition, one employee mentioned that he tended to be somewhat speculative in personal investments, and might find it inhibiting that a supervisor would see his transactions. He

reasoned that the quality of his personal portfolio might suffer in the future, as a result of being conscious that someone else would see his investments.

Clause 7 explained that investment brokers, dealers and agents that employees dealt with would be informed of the document and be requested to inform Allan of any discrepancies. Employees were concerned that representatives with a grudge could incriminate them, and they would be unable to defend themselves.

Some argued that Clause 8 was too powerful. What designated "reasonable cause"? It was never even defined anywhere exactly what constituted an investment. Would employees have to report art purchases? Mortgages? And what about a spouse's investment activities?

One senior department manager objected to having to change his broker. Often the best broker for professional purposes was also considered best for personal purposes; Clause 2 prohibited that. Employees would be forced to deal with brokers that they considered second-best or worse, thus possibly decreasing their personal wealth. Although they understood this in principle, they balked at such a restriction.

Objections were raised to Clause 4, which stated that the size and degree of risk of an employee's investment should be proportional to his or her income and net worth. Employees argued that if they wished to borrow to invest in a risky venture, it was their own business; denying them the opportunity was paternalistic at best, and an invasion of privacy at worst.

Finally, the draft was seen as a one-way document. While the employee signed it to guarantee compliance, there was no return guarantee of either confidentiality or of the protection of rights.

NEXT STEPS

Allan realized that the meeting had not answered all of the employees' questions. He knew that several employees were very unhappy with the document, and he wondered if some might even consider leaving the company. The department had a team-like camaraderie, and he did not want to jeopardize that. He wondered how the document might affect their professional relationships with brokerage firms. In fact, the attitudes of the entire financial community, including their competitors, would have an impact on how the document was perceived. Allan was willing to make some changes in the document to appease employees, but did not want to water it down. The next move was up to him and, to prevent employees' concerns from escalating, he knew he must act quickly.

EXHIBIT 1
Investment Department Structure

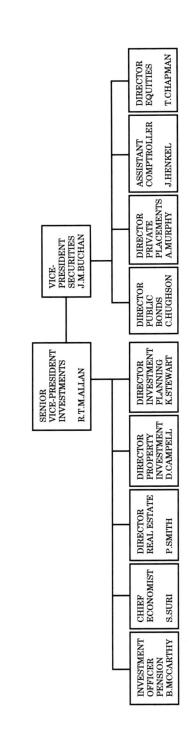

EXHIBIT 2

Excerpts from London Life's Code of Business Conduct

A) Introduction

London Life has always been committed to conduct its business in accord with the highest ethical and legal standards. Through our consistent pursuit of this goal, we have established a tradition of integrity in dealing with our customers while achieving the leadership position in the Canadian life insurance industry.

B) Purpose of Code

This code outlines the high standards by which we, as employees, must conduct ourselves with respect to our customers, shareholders, fellow workers, suppliers, governments and the public we serve. It applies without exception to every salaried London Life employee who acts in any capacity on behalf of the company.

Please read this Code of Business Conduct carefully. You must comply with its provisions as a condition of continued employment. Any breach of this code which causes serious embarrassment, harm or loss to the company or to an individual will result in disciplinary action or dismissal.

You will be expected to act appropriately and promptly to correct the situation whenever improper conduct is identified. Even the appearance of impropriety can damage either the company's good name or yours, or both.

(2) Company/Employee relationships

In the normal course of fulfilling employment responsibilities, an employee may gain information which has not been made known to the general public about the company's affairs and, consequently, is confidential. Examples are company plans, financial results, programs and product information. In fact, the disclosure of certain investment information is prohibited by securities legislation.

Employees may not buy or sell securities of London Life, Lonvest, other Trilon member companies, or any organization with which it does business, except in compliance with those securities laws that regulate insider trading, use of non-public information and trading of securities generally.

All patents, inventions, discoveries, computer programs and designs, and rights of authorship arising during employment with the company remain the exclusive property of the company. For instance, computer software is a trade secret, to be respected. Abuse of copyright or disclosure of or access to such information to anyone other than those who have a legitimate need for it, may cause serious injury to London Life or to

Exhibit 2 cont'd

Exhibit 2 cont'd

the owner of such information. The company may therefore seek compensation for damages, and obtain an injunction to stop such a breach or threatened breach of confidentiality, whether one is still employed with London Life or not.

An employee shall not use any such confidential information for personal gain or benefit, for the benefit of another party, or to the detriment of any customer.

(7) Conflict of Interest Relationships

The proper conduct of the affairs of London Life with its policy owners and with individuals in business outside the company, is a matter of vital importance. The best interests of the company must be a major consideration. Each employee occupies a position of trust in dealing with others outside the company. Whatever the area of activity or degree of responsibility, the company expects each employee to act in a manner which will enhance the company's reputation for the faithful performance of all its obligations.

(i) Policy Statement regarding Conflict

Interests of employees cannot play a part in any decision pertaining to the choice of individuals or businesses with whom London Life may have a business relationship. It is the duty of employees not to promote their own interests in a manner detrimental to or in competition with the company.

(ii) Standards of Conduct

Employees must avoid all situations in which their personal interests conflict or might appear to conflict with their duties to the company. A conflict of interest in a business context arises where:

(a) An employee has been or is likely to be put in a position to have the opportunity to use the authority, knowledge or influence derived from his or her employment in a way which benefits the employee or another person rather than the interest of the company;

(b) An employee acts in a way which benefits someone other than the customer to the disadvantage of the company.

Exhibit 2 cont'd

Exhibit 2 cont'd

(Example)
LONDON LIFE INSURANCE COMPANY
STATEMENT OF COMPLIANCE

I have reviewed and am familiar with London Life's Code of Business Conduct for employees.

I will comply with the Code, including its provisions for non-disclosure both during and after employment.

To the best of my knowledge, I am not involved in any situation that conflicts or might appear to conflict with the Code.

I also agree to notify my management, or for confidentiality either the Manager, Employee Relations or the Vice-President and Secretary of the company, immediately of any change that might adversely affect my compliance with the Code.

Name—————————————————————————
(please print)

Position———————————————————————

Department/Office—————————————————

Date————————————————————————

Signature——————————————————————
Please complete this page and return it to your management. It will be filed in your personnel folder.

Thank you.

EXHIBIT 3

LONDON LIFE INSURANCE COMPANY
Policy Regarding Personal Investments by Investment Department Employees

1. This policy shall be supplemental to the conflict of interest guidelines applicable to London Life employees generally and apply to those persons set out on the attached Schedule, as well as to the Senior Vice-President, Investments, and anyone else designated by him from time to time.

2. No person referred to or designated under paragraph 1 (a "designated employee") shall trade directly or indirectly, with respect to the investment activity (i.e. any one of Securities, Real Estate or Property Investments) with which he or she is associated by employment as listed on the attached Schedule, for his or her personal account with any representative of any broker, dealer or agent with whom London Life transacts business or with any specific office with which London Life transacts such business. The foregoing prohibition shall not apply to the London offices of securities brokers or dealers with whom London Life transacts business solely with respect to pre-confirmed purchases of new issue Government of Canada Bonds.

3. Each designated person shall report, on a monthly basis, the details of his or her investment activity. Such reports shall be made in writing to the Vice-President, Securities, in the case of all those designated on the attached Schedule under the heading "Securities", to the Director, Real Estate, in the case of all those thereon designated under the heading "Real Estate", and to the Director, Property Investments, in the case of all those thereon designated under the heading "Property Investments". The report of each of the Vice-President, Securities, the Director, Real Estate, and the Director, Property Investments, shall be made to the Senior Vice-President, Investments, and his report shall be made to the President.

4. The size and type of personal investments of a designated employee, and the degree of investment risk (including the amount of margin utilized) incurred in connection therewith, must be reasonable in the circumstances having regard to his or her income and net worth.

5. No designated employee shall enter into any financial arrangements such as loans or bets or other wagering or gaming transactions with a representative of any bro-

Exhibit 3 cont'd

Exhibit 3 cont'd

ker or dealer acting on his or her behalf, except where such arrangements are solely of a personal and friendly nature and which involve no more than nominal amounts of money or risk.

6. All personal investment activities of designated employees shall be subordinate to corporate activities and any conduct by any such person that places a priority upon personal investment activities to the detriment or prejudice of London Life and its activities shall be considered a serious conflict of interest.

7. Investment brokers, dealers, agents and representatives with whom London Life deals shall be formally advised of the existence of this Policy and the expectation of London Life that its employees comply with it to the fullest extent and without exception. All such third parties shall be made aware that London Life expects that information involving suspicious circumstances relating to the conduct of any London Life employee which comes to their attention, be reported to the Senior Vice-President, Investments, forthwith.

8. Upon reasonable notice to a designated employee, London Life or its nominee shall have the right to:

    (a) examine the personal and financial records of the designated employee, and

    (b) communicate with and obtain information and documents from third parties,

    for the purpose of ascertaining whether or not there has been a breach of this Policy. Such examination shall not occur unless there is reasonable cause to suspect a breach.

9. Any provision of this Policy may be waived or varied by the Senior Vice-President, Investments (or in his absence, by the Vice-President, Securities), with respect to any designated employee other than himself, but any such waiver or variation shall be on a case-by case basis only and only after review of all information then available and considered by him to be relevant to any particular request for waiver or variation.

W.C.N.
7 January 1987

10 Mansfield Minerals Inc.

Jim Mason, President of Mansfield Minerals Inc, put down the telephone slowly. Talk about a kick in the stomach! He had just heard from an old friend from business school who had some disturbing information. Apparently, his recently appointed Vice-President of Exploration, John Andrews, had been fired from one of his previous employers about six years ago for a serious drug-abuse problem. There had been no mention of this by Andrews, reference checks had not revealed the event, and the termination was not evident on Andrews' original application form.

JOHN ANDREWS

Age 35, married with three children, John Andrews had a degree in geophysics and had completed graduate work in geophysical engineering. Following graduate school, he had been employed for three years with one of the major mining companies but left them to join Eastern Minerals, a junior company involved in geophysical research. He was highly valued and well paid by Eastern and, so he had indicated when interviewed by the executives at Mansfield, had been very satisfied with the way that he had been treated.

After four years with Eastern, Andrews had decided to return to business school to complete an MBA, a long-time ambition. He had been an excellent student, graduating in the top quartile of his class and making the dean's list in both years of his program. While at the business school he was noticed by one of the professors who also did some consulting work for Mansfield. Indeed, it was this professor who had suggested to Jim Mason that Andrews was "a young man whose career was well worth watching." Mason contacted Andrews in the middle of the second year of his program and suggested that they meet and discuss his career interests.

Copyright © 1988. The University of Western Ontario.

This case was written by Professor Jeffrey Gandz, and was funded by a grant from Imperial Oil Limited. All names and certain identifying facts have been disguised.

Andrews met with Mason and three other members of the Mansfield management team. They were all impressed. He was obviously competent and, while somewhat reticent and a little withdrawn, he had a pleasant manner. He had explained his decision to leave the mining company and join Eastern as a move from a bureaucratic to an entrepreneurial environment, one where he could make a greater personal contribution and be rewarded accordingly. This explanation fitted perfectly with what Mason and the other Mansfield executives were looking for. Andrews' analytical skills were excellent and they thought he would blend in well with the Mansfield operation. Mason made him an offer to join Mansfield as Manager of Exploration, subject to the usual medical examination and reference checks. The Vice-President of Human Resources checked out Andrews' references from the business school and also checked with his previous employer, Eastern Exploration. The Vice-President of Exploration at Eastern described Andrews as "a first-rate person, one they would like to have back."

In his three years with Mansfield, Andrews' performance exceeded all their expectations. He was an excellent manager, had the intuitive judgement essential to the exploration business, helped to build a good staff of young geologists and geophysicists, and maintained excellent control of his operations. Four highly satisfactory performance appraisals had been completed. When "Doc" Jewell, Vice-President of Exploration at Mansfield for fifteen years, had decided to retire, there was no hesitation in promoting Andrews to the position.

THE TELEPHONE CALL

It was the day after Andrews' picture had appeared in the business press, with the announcement of his appointment, that Mason had received the telephone call from his friend, now the president of the mining company that Andrews had started his career with and also a client of Mansfield's. "I didn't know that you had hired John Andrews. He's really come up in the world since he used to work for me."

Mason replied, "Well, you guys never could hold onto the good ones! Life's too boring for anyone with some get up and go...you train 'em and we reward 'em!"

The well-intentioned ribbing went on for a few minutes before Mason's friend got to the point. "Look, Jim, this may come as a bit of a shock to you but Andrews didn't exactly 'get up and go.' We had to give him a push to help him on his way."

"What do you mean? What for?"

"Well, we were concerned about a few things. His performance on the job wasn't bad ... in fact he was a good guy technically. But he seemed to be tired a lot and, well, kind of moody and morose. We did some checking around, asked a few people ... you know the kind of thing. Several people told us that he was into drugs in a pretty serious way. I guess it wasn't that uncommon in those days. Hash, pot, I think even a little coke. I spoke with him about it—he was pretty evasive at first but after a while he didn't deny it. We had no option then ... we let him go immediately. Nowadays, maybe, we would have handled it differently—given him a leave of absence to attend a rehab program of some kind, perhaps. But back then if you had any problem with booze or drugs it was out immediately."

"Why didn't this surface when Eastern hired him?"

"I'm not sure, Jim. You know, I'm not even sure that Eastern checked out Andrews with us ... sometimes these small companies are pretty sloppy about those kinds of things. After we fired him, I think Andrews went to Europe for several months ... maybe he spun some kind of yarn to them about the gap in his resume."

"Well, I'm not sure whether I should thank you for this information or not. I don't know what I'm going to do about it. Do me a favor, keep this between us. I'd hate for rumors to start flying around."

NEXT STEPS

Jim Mason was disturbed about the telephone call, for a number of reasons. The more he thought about Andrews, the more he seemed to focus on his reticence and lack of openness about himself. Come to think of it, unlike the other executives and senior managers in the firm, Andrews did not mix much socially ... in fact Mason did not really know Andrews and his family well at all. Did he still have a problem? And what would happen if he was confronted about this issue?

What galled Mason most was that Andrews had hidden the facts from him—had, in fact, deceived them about his reasons for leaving the mining company and joining Eastern. But after all, thought Mason, would he himself have really done anything different? What chance would he have had of landing a job with Eastern or with us if he had come totally clean about his past? But how did this mesh with Mansfield's excellent corporate reputation for integrity? Could Mansfield have a senior officer with this kind of past? Above all else, what should Mason do now?

11 Matt Moreau's Dilemma

Matt Moreau, newly appointed Manager, Customer Services, for Bantings department stores picked up the telephone:

"We think we have the perfect person for you, Matt. She's a manager in one of the medium-sized suburban stores—been with the company for about 15 years, ambitious, smart, on-the-ball and, what's more, I think she'd jump at the chance of moving to head office."

CUSTOMER SERVICE DEPARTMENT

The voice on the other end of the phone was that of Steven Judson, Corporate Personnel Manager. Moreau had asked him to help in the staffing of his newly created department. It had been set up to improve the quality of customer service, developing new programs which would have organization-wide impact on how stores were designed and laid out, how staff were trained, and how customer satisfaction could be measured and factored into the company's merchandising and marketing programs.

The task that lay ahead for Moreau was a difficult and demanding one. The stores were managed through a strong line operations department which reported to the president of the corporation. His department would be "staff"—hopefully well respected and influential, but with very little real power or authority. It was critical for him to get good people, preferably those with some line management experience who had developed credibility with the operations types.

SALLY ARMITAGE

Moreau asked Judson to tell him a little more about his find.

"Well I've just been through her personnel records—by the way, her name is Sally Armitage. She's been with the company a

Copyright © 1988, The University of Western Ontario

This case was prepared by Professor Jeffrey Gandz and was funded by a grant from Imperial Oil Limited. All names have been disguised.

number of years, always had good performance appraisals. She started fresh out of high school as a clerk but, after a couple of years, started asking her manager to be put onto the management development program. As you know, we usually just put university and college grads on that program but in this case we made an exception. I think that her manager really went to bat for her on this one.

"Worked out great! She completed the program and then went into the Thunder Bay store as assistant manager in the white goods department. Rotated through a number of departments, then ... let me see ... Oh yes, she moved to the Toronto region as assistant manager of the Eastland Mall store—one of the biggest and, at that time, the worst performers. Well, she and Tony Abbott turned the thing around and I have a note attached to a performance appraisal from Tony which gives her much of the credit.

"Two years ago we gave her the Chute Hill store—it's small but she's doing a good job of enlarging it and also increasing profitability. As you know, Tony Abbott is the regional manager out there and I know he thinks the world of her. In fact he'd be hopping mad if he even knew I was talking to you about her."

"Why are you talking to me, Steve? What makes you think that she's in the least bit interested in moving into a head office job?"

"Well I was just looking over the results of her last performance appraisal and see that she indicated that she'd like to get some head office experience. And when Chuck Mackness [the president of Bantings] was on his last field visit, he called on her store and she mentioned to him that she saw her career at Bantings benefiting from some head office experience. He mentioned it to me and so I got out her file. So there it is, I think she's well worth looking at."

"What's the next step, Steve?"

"You should contact Tony Abbott and get a firsthand impression from him. He'll not be pleased but he's always been a booster of Armitage. Try not to tell him you heard of her through me."

DISCUSSION WITH TONY ABBOTT

The following day Matt Moreau called Tony Abbott and told him that he was interested in talking with him about any personnel in his region who might be candidates for a position in the newly formed customer service group. He arranged to meet with Tony early the following week at the regional office.

"I bet that it's Sally you're interested in," were the first words that greeted Moreau after he sat down in Abbott's office. "The ungrateful, ambitious, disloyal ... highly competent superachiever," he added with a grin. "How I'd hate to lose her."

Abbott and Moreau talked for about 30 minutes about Sally Armitage and during the conversation Moreau outlined some of the challenges that lay ahead for his group.

"As you know Tony, we have our work cut out for us. The public is getting pretty annoyed with the kind of service they've been getting at all department stores and ours is no better than most of the others. We have to improve. The president has detached me from my normal function to get this thing done and he wants to see results by Christmas. We can do it, but it's going to take maximum effort. Late nights, lots of tension, tough decisions, meetings, travel—a lot of old-fashioned blood, sweat and tears."

As he went through this, Moreau noticed some worry on Abbott's face.

"How much do you know about Sally's background?" he asked. "Do you know much about her personal circumstances?"

"No—at least no more than appears in her personnel file. Apart from some fairly extensive absences about three years ago— for medical reasons I think—it seems to point to a first class person."

"Let me give you some additional background. Sally's absences a few years ago were serious—she had cancer, I think it was cancer of the lymph glands. She was off work for several weeks and then went for chemotherapy for over two years. I don't know how she managed it ... for a couple of days after the treatments she looked like the walking dead. But she seemed to bounce back okay. She still goes in once every three months or so for regular check-ups.

"In her current position I think she can cope with the situation. She lives with her teenage daughter—she was divorced about six years ago—just about 10 minutes away from the Chute Hill store. She's got a good staff and on days when she's not feeling 100 percent she can coast a little bit.

"The job that you could offer her would change all that. First, she'd have a long commute into the city to work—maybe an hour each way unless she moved much closer to downtown and I doubt you guys would pay her that much extra to make that affordable. Second, it looks as if the job is very stressful and will require all sorts of extra work. I'm not sure Sally is up to that, that it wouldn't cause her condition to deteriorate. Oh, you'd never know it. Sally is just one of those people who always look cheerful, never let on that anything is wrong.

"By the way, I'm sure that if you offered her the job—even if you explained the situation to her, really pointed out all the problems and difficulties—she'd take it. One of the ways she has coped with her illness is to push even harder, show herself that she can do anything. This would be another challenge for her.

"But I wonder if it's the right thing to offer it to her. What if she took it and it did cause her situation to deteriorate? What good would that have done her? Or you, for that matter. Could you afford to have someone with a health problem on your staff, especially now? It's not like you're running a store where you can get someone else to fill in when a manager or employee is off ill. You know what it's like with cancer—it can recur any time."

THE DILEMMA

As he rode back to head office, Moreau mulled over this conversation. What options did he have? Should he even pursue the possibility with Armitage? Should she be given the option, knowing how tough things would be? Should he take the risk of an employee who, despite high performance and apparent good health, had such a medical history? How would he explain his decision to Tony Abbott? To Steve Judson? To Chuck Mackness?

12 NORFIN's Marketing Database

As Sandra Jasper, Executive Vice-President of Northern Trust Inc (NTI) studied the results of the marketing database project, she was struck by the tremendous potential for the company. Based on the project report's findings, there were significant opportunities to increase market share through the establishment of a shared marketing database which pooled information from NTI and other NORFIN affiliates and subsidiaries. She had to make a recommendation, within the next few weeks, on whether the database concept should be developed and implemented on a corporate basis.

COMPANY BACKGROUND

Northern Financial Services Inc (NORFIN) was a holding company that controlled several leading financial services companies and had interests in life and health insurance, merchant banking, real estate, and property and casualty insurance. Each of these related companies had quite separate identities and many customers of each would be unlikely to know that they were related through common ownership.

Although NORFIN was a holding company, it took an active role in guiding the strategy decisions of its operating companies and encouraged them to develop a strong marketing orientation. NORFIN coordinated with members of its affiliates through an active committee structure that assisted with the development of individual strategies designed to support the overall NORFIN mission. Permanent committees, chaired by senior executives from each of the member companies, reviewed joint projects in marketing, investments, administration and technology.

One of the first coordinated efforts between all of the NORFIN companies was a strategy paper compiled in the early 1980s known as the NORFIN Mission document.

Copyright © 1989, The University of Western Ontario.

This case was written by Nadine Hayes, under the supervision of Professor Jeffrey Gandz, and funded by a grant from Imperial Oil Limited.

This document asserted that competing effectively in the increasingly global financial services industry was the superordinate goal. The document outlined an explicit strategy for NORFIN, through to 1991, with a strong emphasis on increased market share, improved productivity, and incremental revenue to be gained by encouraging networking between the various NORFIN companies. Each affiliated company was urged to develop its own financial goals for the incremental business to be developed through this type of networking.

NORTHERN TRUST

Founded in 1926, Northern Trust was one of Canada's largest trust companies. With both a domestic and international presence, it provided a wide range of products and services, including personal and corporate banking services, international investment advice, and management and administration of financial assets for private and corporate clients. Northern Trust was purchased in 1982 by NORFIN.

Northern Trust stressed the importance of a flexible, non-bureaucratic organizational structure, innovative products, and coordinated work groups designed to meet client needs. In striving to meet those goals, it earned itself a reputation as a dynamic and forward-looking firm.

The decade of the 1980s saw many changes in the financial services industry, mostly through deregulation. To ensure Canada was a world player in international capital markets, ownership restrictions were lifted on securities firms, and banks and trust companies were allowed to take ownership positions. Those changes were scheduled to come into effect in late 1987, while the regulations that restricted banks from owning trust companies were expected to be lifted in early 1989. A third important change allowed foreign banks to develop branch systems, rather than be restricted to only one branch and a head office.

The changes allowed banks to compete in traditional trust company territory. That meant that the trust companies would compete for market share against the banks' branch systems—the banks had over 6,600 branches, whereas the trust companies had less than 900 branches. In addition, the foreign banks were expected to develop branch networks. That situation added support to the trust companies' focus on their current customer base as a primary target market, and to the concept of cross-selling other products and services as a competitive tool to increase market share in the industry. For example, a customer who had guaranteed investment certificates could also be a customer for mutual funds.

Extending this even further, a customer who had a mortgage with one of NORFIN's companies might also be a good candidate for property insurance, offered by another NORFIN company. The opportunity existed for cross-selling between related companies as well as cross-selling of products to one company's customers. Indeed, one vision talked about in the financial services industry was the concept of one-stop shopping at financial supermarkets, where customers could satisfy all their needs for financial services.

In addition to shifting competitive forces, changing demographics were an issue. Increased consumer sophistication forced the players in the financial services field to innovate and experiment with expanded product lines and more comprehensive services. And both the deregulation and the demand for new and better products paved the way for larger and broader conglomerates.

Such changes also induced consumer fears although these had not surfaced in an organized way. Concerns centred on the use of financial information by the conglomerates, as well as the safety and security of deposits. The security fears were based on the failure of several financial institutions in the early part of the decade, amidst allegations of self-dealing and misrepresentation, that resulted in considerable loss of investor savings. And those concerns led to calls for re-regulation and tighter controls of financial services companies.

STRATEGY

After the Mission document was developed, the NORFIN Marketing Committee, composed of senior executives from each of the affiliated companies, identified several methods of networking—a process that they termed "collectively focused business planning." Such issues as economies of scale in supply ordering, and promoting the non-duplication of products and administrative functions were obvious, while the concept of shared information was identified as useful for reducing redundancies, determining the appropriate markets for joint locations, and following up on direct mail and related purchases. Of particular interest to the committee was the concept of sharing information among affiliate companies for cross-selling.

The cross-sell ratio was defined as the average number of products of one company, held by a client. Data gathered from Northern Trust's internal marketing research indicated that the firm's average client had a tendency to purchase modules of products, and that there were certain times when modules, rather than single products, would be purchased. The committee determined that identifying and contacting those clients and the particular components of the product bundles could be made more effective by the use of a central database.

THE DATABASE PROJECT

A thorough study into the concept of a database was identified as a major priority. The overall goal of the database was to analyze and exploit the existing potential for cross-sell marketing programs in two ways: by determining which existing product modules were more popular, and by using it as a point-of-sale tool, to determine a client's portfolio of NORFIN products. It was also considered essential for the reduction of inefficient inter-company dependencies, as well as supporting program tracking and business planning.

The committee established the NORFIN Marketing Database working group, under the direction of Northern Trust through Sandra Jasper, which was to design and implement a marketing database for use by all NORFIN companies. The database was to contain well-organized, accessible information about each affiliate's customers: demographics, products purchased, size of purchase, and the history of transactions. The working group was the first of its kind within NORFIN.

When developing guidelines for the working group, the Committee often discussed the ethical issues surrounding the question of a marketing database. Although the general concept was well received by all Committee members, the specifics of the project raised issues such as:

- How should the database be used in marketing?
- What type of information should it contain?
- Who should be allowed access to the information?
- Under what rules should access be granted?
- Should customers be advised that the information they provided to one NORFIN company may be shared with another?
- Should they be given the opportunity to refuse to permit such sharing of information?
- Where does consumer confidentiality fit in?
- Do consumers have the right to know about the current working group and the prospective database?

The questions were intensely debated, and no consensus was reached. In order to get the project off the ground, Jasper decided that it was necessary to separate the ethical issues from the mechanics of the design. Therefore, the working group was given a mandate to design a database, make recommendations on its use, and "proceed independently of decisions on ethical use, security, and control." The objectives for the working group are presented in Exhibit 1.

In November 1986, Sandra Jasper appointed Randy Gregg as project manager. Gregg's team consisted of employees from each of the affiliates. Based on the guidelines and a specific budget, the team established a clear action plan. Examples of the type of data that could theoretically be accumulated included everything from Northern Trust client credit information to the insurance company's client medical information. In the end, the project team narrowed it down to the items presented in Exhibit 2.

The basis of the proposed database was Northern Trust's computerized client information in use at the time. Since 1984, Northern Trust had contracted with a specialized data processing company (EDP) to create customized computer databases and generate market information reports. The client data that Northern Trust gave to EDP for report preparation included: name, address, primary account type, subaccount type, balance, date account opened, branch, account number. From these primary data, EDP was able to develop a number of reports including analyses of cross-sell ratios, reports describing the combinations of services that households had, who had what combinations of products within households, and so on. By augmenting this information with additional data based on postal codes and proprietary NORFIN market research data on lifestyles, the various NORFIN companies would be able to identify areas of potential for cross-selling. They would have the potential to select groups of customers living in certain areas with specific characteristics, net worths, outstanding balances, and then target their marketing efforts. While some of this information would be sourced from NORFIN companies, some would be added from public services such as telephone books, Statistics Canada, credit reporting agencies, and so on.

The project proceeded according to schedule, with each affiliate submitting the necessary client information that matched the categories of information held in the Northern Trust EDP reports. Although the ethical issues were to be debated in the future, the working group remained sensitized to them as it completed the project, and many of the group's discussions touched on ethical concerns.

Because the structure and focus of the project was new to NORFIN, there was no established approval process, and ad hoc appeal for legal opinion was the only "check" on the project. One of the committee's members felt that the concept fell under the jurisdiction of the NORFIN Business Practices Review Committee, a committee of the board of directors of Northern Trust that dealt with conflicts of interest and ethical issues. They presented the concept to this review committee and received its opinion that no laws were being violated by the creation and exploitation of this database.

In November of 1986, Gregg submitted the final report to Sandra Jasper, complete with refined objectives and several key decisions. In this report the working group distinguished between a marketing database (MDB) and a customer information file (CIF). The CIF was defined as an operational database with procedures for updating information. It could be used to generate regular reports, as well as lists of clients for specific marketing programs. The MDB was

a "snap-shot" at a particular point in time. Gregg's group identified a clear need for NORFIN to decide which of these should be developed.

Gregg's group recommended and secured trustee agreements between Northern Trust and NORFIN affiliates prior to the transfer of any client information between NORFIN companies. This was to guarantee that access to customer identities be limited to a small group of professionals assigned to develop the database and analyze the data.

The major finding of the report showed that given the regional representation and lifestyle of the average customer and the type of product bundles that were popular, the cross-sell ratio amongst the NORFIN affiliates was not as high as initially expected. Therefore, there was an opportunity for further and more effective networking—an opportunity made even more significant by the working group's implementation of a marketing database.

The working group recommended that any immediate use of the database be limited to small-scale, well-controlled programs. Requests for access to another company's client information consisted of a written request to Randy Gregg, who then contacted the owner of the information to request access by another company.

THE LEGAL ENVIRONMENT

Before dealing with the ethical issues, Jasper decided to summarize the legal environment. She knew a Legislative Review Project had been set up by the government in early 1986 to review Ontario's consumer legislation. Although the review had only begun, Jasper felt that several areas demanded close attention: there were federal and provincial privacy statutes dealing with government-held personal information, and she wondered if the review would recommend similar restrictions for the private sector.

While there was no specific reference, in any statute, to the sharing of information between institutions, the Ministry of Consumer and Corporate Affairs was currently reviewing trust company legislation, and it was possible that some restrictions could be imposed. The Consumer Reporting Act was most relevant to the database project, and would be included in the government's review, but as it currently stood, the only mention of transfer of information between companies was in regard to consumer credit reporting agencies, companies which gathered information on consumer credit and sold that information to subscribers. The basic principles, however, could not be ignored: "the consumers' right to expect responsible conduct from businesses who gather, store, use or disseminate credit and personal information; to know what is being reported about them and to whom it is reported; and to correct inaccurate information about themselves."

Although the specific Acts governing trust and insurance companies did not speak directly to sharing of information, the broader issues of affiliation were addressed in several ways. Insurance companies were prohibited from realizing "hidden profits," such as referral commissions from an affiliate, and associated financial institutions were not allowed to share premises so as to avoid "tied-selling." Also, under the insurance laws, only licensed sales agents were allowed to receive insurance sales commissions.

THE DECISION

There was no doubt that potential existed to use the pooled data from related companies to identify and exploit cross-sell opportunities. Obviously, certain information—such as medical data—should not be shared. But what were reasonable limits on what could be shared? Overall, was this a direction in which NORFIN should go?

EXHIBIT 1

NORFIN Marketing Database
Working Group Terms of Reference

ORIGINAL OBJECTIVES:

To design and implement a marketing database for potential use by all NORFIN companies in pursuit of the 1991 profit target.

ASSUMPTIONS:

The Northern Trust database is a logical nucleus for the NORFIN database: it is an inexpensive head start; and it has a proven record of usefulness.

The design of the database can proceed independently of decisions on ethical use, security, and control since these issues can be addressed once technical feasibility has been investigated.

REFINED OBJECTIVES:

Design and implement a research database, modelled on Northern Trust's Marketing Database, to consolidate existing customer information from most NORFIN companies.

Use the database to analyze the existing potential for cross-sell marketing programs.

Develop a go/no-go recommendation for upgrading to an operational database, which has procedures for updating information, and can be used to generate regular reports as well as lists of clients for specific marketing programs.

REFINED ASSUMPTION:

There will be trustee agreements signed between NORFIN Trust and other NORFIN companies, prior to any company providing customer data to the project. The trustee agreement will guarantee that access to customer identities be limited to a small group of professionals assigned to developing the database and analyzing the data.

EXHIBIT 2

NORFIN Marketing Data Base
Recommended Data Inputs

Captured Data (Pooled from all NORFIN companies)

Client name
Address
Postal Code
Branch
Region

Age
Language Preference
Willingness to receive mail
Social Insurance Number

Product Purchase Data (for each product)

Product
Account Type
Account Number
Balance

Initiation date
Maturation date
Account closing date
Transaction history

13 North American Car Inc

Grant McNair, national sales manager of North American Car Inc (NACI) was thinking about the proposed advertising campaign for the new SFX 50 model. The advertising agency had suggested a head-to-head comparison of the SFX 50 with EuroSport's 550 sports sedan. The two cars would be shown racing on a slalom course and would be compared on the basis of straight-line acceleration, cornering, braking distance, and top speed at the end of the quarter-mile course. The SFX 40, a domestic sports sedan with a sticker price of under $17,000, would be shown to outperform the $33,000 EuroSport 550 in these comparisons.

The marketing research on the SFX 50 suggested that this advertising strategy would be effective. The potential purchasers had identified the EuroSport as a high-performance, quality marque—one which they would like to own if they could afford it. This suggested that positioning the SFX 50 as "the affordable alternative to the premier European sports sedan" would have powerful appeal to potential purchasers.

There were two things that bothered McNair about this proposed advertising strategy. First, while the SFX 50 compared very favorably on these four dimensions of performance, there were many other areas in which direct comparison would favor the EuroSport 550, including interior room, noise levels, quality of finish, trunk space, and standard 550 features such as electric sun roof, electric windows, and others. However, McNair thought that potential SFX 50 purchasers would understand that, at less than one-half the price of the EuroSport, the two cars obviously differed in a number of respects. Consequently, he did not feel that he was deceiving or misleading customers by selecting the bases of comparison.

Second, McNair was aware that the EuroSport 550 had been specifically designed by its maker as a *non-*performance, economy (in terms of gas consumption) sedan specifically for the European market, in which gasoline prices were extremely high. It had been marketed in North America at the time of gas shortages and rapidly increasing prices. EuroSport's advertising of the 550 never stressed high performance, unlike its advertising of the other models in its range. McNair wondered if it was legitimate to make the direct comparison between the SFX 50—specifically designed for high performance—and the economy-oriented EuroSport 550.

14 Royal LePage (A)

Oswald Jurock, President of Residential Real Estate Services at Royal LePage, read the monthly results with a mixture of excitement and concern. It was March 3, 1987, and the figures in front of him indicated that the month of February had been the second-best month ever for his division. While that news was cause for excitement, the real estate environment was cause for concern. The booming market was receiving a lot of media attention and there were rumors of rampant speculation, particularly in the area of reselling properties before the initial closing date. Jurock was aware that such practices were extremely risky for vendors and totally out of character for Royal LePage sales agents. He had not received any complaints about his agents engaging in such practices, but he wondered what could be done to ensure that such behavior would not occur.

COMPANY BACKGROUND

Structure

Royal LePage, the largest diversified real estate services organization in Canada and the third-largest in the world, was established in December 1984 by an amalgamation of two established industry leaders: A E LePage and Royal Trust. The new company formed an integral part of Trilon Financial Corporation, which held approximately 51 percent share ownership in the firm.

The company's principal subsidiaries were Royal LePage Real Estate Services United States Inc and Royal LePage Real Estate Services Ltd. The latter, the Canadian subsidiary, was divided into four divisions: Residential Real Estate Services; Commercial Real Estate Services; Real Estate Management

Copyright © 1988, The University of Western Ontario.

This case was written by Nadine Hayes, under the supervision of Professor Jeffrey Gandz, and funded by a grant from Imperial Oil Limited.

Services; and Capital Management Services. Each division was headed by a president, and had its own corporate support services.

The residential division employed over 6,400 sales agents in 312 offices in Canada's major residential markets. The locations were organized into divisions: British Columbia; Alberta—including Saskatchewan and Manitoba; Ontario—three divisions; Quebec; the Atlantic provinces. Each division was headed by a general manager, two or three regional managers, usually one human resource person, and a financial officer. Most offices accommodated 24 sales agents, one branch manager and two administrative personnel (Exhibit 1).

In real estate, volume was key. In 1986, Royal LePage sold a house every six minutes. In the Toronto area alone, salespeople were involved in about 32,000 resale home transactions. Altogether, the deals were valued at $3.3 billion. Performance figures are presented in Exhibit 2.

Commission Structure

The commission structure was said to be the driving force behind the success or failure of a real estate firm. In any brokerage house, local board fees were taken directly off the top when a commission—usually 6 percent of the selling price—was earned on the sale of a property. The remainder of the commission was split between the ends of the sale, the lister and the seller. Up to that point, the commission structure was the same for all brokerage houses. The next step was the distinguishing step: at Royal LePage, 2 percent was then allocated to institutional advertising. Before

the bonus system took effect, the remainder was divided equally between the sales agent and Royal LePage.

The amount of the split depended on whether an agent had attained bonus. After a certain level of earned commissions, an agent was qualified to receive bonus, which meant that the commission split shifted: it was increased for the agent, and decreased for head office. Both bonus eligibility levels and the amount of the split varied according to the region of the country.

There was intense competition for good real estate agents, both from existing established firms, such as Royal LePage and Canada Trust, and newer organizations such as RE/MAX which tempted high performing agents with higher commission rates, less corporate control of their activities, and a perception of less bureaucracy. The average turnover for sales agents in the industry was 40 percent a year, and when good sales agents left they often took their clients with them. Branch managers spent most of their time looking for good sales agents to join their teams and worked very hard to prevent unnecessary turnover. Turnover from Royal Lepage was about average for the industry.

There was no preference for experienced agents over newcomers within Royal LePage's recruitment and selection process. All new agents, with or without previous experience, were required to participate in the company's new 50-Day Team Program. It was designed to integrate a training component at Royal LePage's training centre with a practical component in a branch office. The orientation began with four days at the centre where new agents were given an introduction to the company and its mission. That was followed by seven days in a branch with a manager. The final phase was at the centre to summarize and debrief.

Royal LePage agents were offered in-house marketing support through television, radio, and print advertising, in addition to many specialized programs, such as the First Time Buyers program, the Executive Home program, the Carriage Trade Homes program, and Condominium Success.

Culture

Royal LePage was known for its integrity and sense of fair-dealing. Although the merged companies, AE LePage and Royal Trust, each had well-defined mission statements and statements of purpose, Royal LePage implemented its own mission in late 1986 (Exhibit 3).

ENVIRONMENT

The mid 1980s were an explosive time for the Canadian real estate industry. Affordable interest rates, combined with low inflation, declining unemployment, relative job security, and pent-up housing demand caused the market, throughout most of Canada, to ignite. There were, however, regional disparities that saw most of the growth concentrated in and around Ontario and Quebec, as well as the urban centres in both the far and near West, and parts of the Atlantic provinces. The Prairie provinces continued to experience difficult times. Across the country, the climate was reflected in the predictions for 1987 resale values (Exhibit 4).

Ontario was seen as the major benefactor of the booming market. Through-

out 1986, the market was described as a "seller's paradise." The province's housing starts for 1987 were projected to rise by 16 percent while the rest of Canada expected a rise of 5.5 percent. Average residential prices rose by 14 percent, and had been known to move between 12 percent and 20 percent over a period of four to five months. In some areas of Toronto, prices were up 24 percent over only a few months; the average price for a home was $135,300 compared to $93,500 as a national average. Resale values there were expected to rise by ten percent in 1987. The country-wide boom was expected to continue into 1987. Royal LePage predicted 286,000 residential resales, up from 265,650 in 1986, which itself was 7 percent over 1985 levels (Exhibit 5).

ROYAL LEPAGE'S CONCERN

Throughout 1986, the residential housing market soared, but the sustained upswing caused Jurock to fear a quick downturn. Newspapers printed daily reports on the rise in real estate prices and many articles projected even greater growth. But inconsistencies began to surface. A report in the *Globe and Mail* in late December stated that the market was slowing down, and predicted that there would be a serious decline in prices in a great hurry. Jurock felt that the inconsistency of opinion, combined with the rumored speculation, could result in a dangerous situation if the speculators began to panic and collectively sold quickly.

His specific concern had to do with the relatively large amount of speculating that was occurring in agreements to purchase in and around Toronto. Agreements to purchase were contracts, signed by a vendor and a purchaser, which stipulated that the purchaser would buy the property in question from the vendor for a certain amount, with a specified closing date. What was happening in the inflationary market was that purchasers were reselling the contracts before the closing date of the original transaction. Jurock knew that if the market fell and buyers became wary, a speculator who bought an agreement to purchase, solely with the intention of reselling it in a very short period, was unlikely to have adequate resources to maintain the property, thereby initiating a dangerous spiral; the probable result would be a default on the sale of each speculator involved. The original vendor, who had quite likely purchased another property by that time, would be left with two properties.

An interesting side to the situation was the role played by the agent. When a vendor decided to list a property, he or she would contact a broker, who would then value the property. Since properties were being sold before original closing dates, the credibility of valuations had come into question. The Registrar at the Ministry of Consumer and Commercial Relations—the government department which regulated real estate transactions—had received a number of complaints alleging that agents were under-valuing properties in order to engage in quick flips. If the agent worked for both vendors, he or she would, of course, be eligible for two commissions in a very short period of time.

That problem was exacerbated by the mini-auctions which were occurring in the Toronto market. Vendors were receiving a number of offers on a property almost immediately after it was listed, and conducting auctions around coffee tables. This resulted in many sales being made at a hefty increase above the original asking price. This situation also brought into question the original valuation of the property; there was concern that agents could be tempted to under-value properties to induce excitement and an auction.

Traditionally, the key to preventing defaults and downward spirals was the "subject to sale" clause. It was inserted into the agreement to purchase, and stipulated that the purchaser would complete the transaction only on the condition that his or her own property was sold by a certain date. However, subject to sale clauses had become almost extinct due to the hot market. Purchasers did not want to jeopardize their chances of winning an auction by presenting a conditional offer: listings were moving so fast that offers with conditional clauses were being rejected.

Relevant Policies and Procedures

Royal LePage had explicit corporate disclosure policies for agents, managers, and salaried employees who were either directly or indirectly involved in a real estate transaction for their own account. The Real Estate and Business Brokers Act also dealt with disclosure, but not to the extent of Royal LePage. By industry standards, Royal LePage's policies were considered restrictive.

A related policy was known as "policy 14" (Exhibit 6). It prohibited a Royal LePage agent from listing or selling a property over the period of one year after a previous sale of the same property by a Royal LePage agent. The policy had been in place in the firm for many years, although only recently had the time limit been specified. It had previously been referred to as "a reasonable time period." The restriction was by-passed only in exceptional circumstances.

During 1986, Royal LePage also introduced an alternative to the subject to sale clauses. Jurock was an avid proponent of the clauses, but knew that requiring them would put clients at a disadvantage in the hot market. To circumvent that problem, Royal LePage directed all sales agents to encourage vendors to require a 10 percent cash deposit before signing agreements to purchase. If the closing period was in excess of three months, agents were to insist that the vendor take a deposit. Although the firm could not force vendors to follow the suggestion, Jurock felt it would offer some protection from speculators who, with only a low down-payment at risk, could back out of a deal at the first sign of a market downturn.

Other Concerned Parties

The activity of the market had many of the key players concerned. The Real Estate Boards were aware of a market for agreements to purchase in Toronto, but had no regulatory authority over sales agents. The registrar at the Ministry of Consumer and Commercial Relations was also concerned. His department had received numerous complaints from individuals regarding possible violations of the provincial law on real estate activities. Many of the complaints had to do with inadequate disclosure of properties purchased by sales

representatives, not disclosing the individuals involved in the deal, the alleged selling of agreements to purchase, and even deliberate undervaluing of properties. He vowed to "scrutinize" the industry, but to forgo immediate action until the legislation had been analyzed.

THE DECISION

Oswald Jurock was concerned enough about the volatility of the market to do some investigation. He knew that for 26 out of 30 years the Canadian real estate market had risen, and that in three of the four years it reversed, the drop was less than one percent. He was also aware that, from year end to year end, the Toronto market had reversed only twice in 35 years. And each time, the drop was less than 2 percent; the last reversal was in 1963.

But those figures were deceiving. Taken from year end to year end, they neglected to present the fluctuations that occurred during the year. For example, in 1980 the average year end price of a home was $75,000, and in 1981 it was $97,000, a comfortable appreciation for an individual who purchased in late 1980 and sold in late 1981. The difficulty occurred when someone purchased at the highpoint of the 1981 market, which was in April, when the average price of a home was $125,000. By the end of the year, that purchaser was down $30,000. Jurock felt that it was just such a situation that necessitated vendor protections.

Although he was aware that some agents would object to any restrictions, Jurock was also aware that the company had a long-standing tradition of prohibiting speculation, and felt that he should act consistently with that tradition. One possibility was to completely prohibit Royal LePage agents from accepting listings unless the vendor was actually the registered owner of the property. This would effectively take Royal LePage out of the speculative segment of the market. But Jurock was concerned that his agents might react negatively to this interference with their income potential. Maybe now was not the time to act since surely this overheated market would soon come to an end. Or perhaps some action which simply urged his agents to be very careful about the deals they got involved in, without actually prohibiting any of them, might be sufficient. What should he do?

EXHIBIT 1

Residential Real Estate Services Organizational Chart

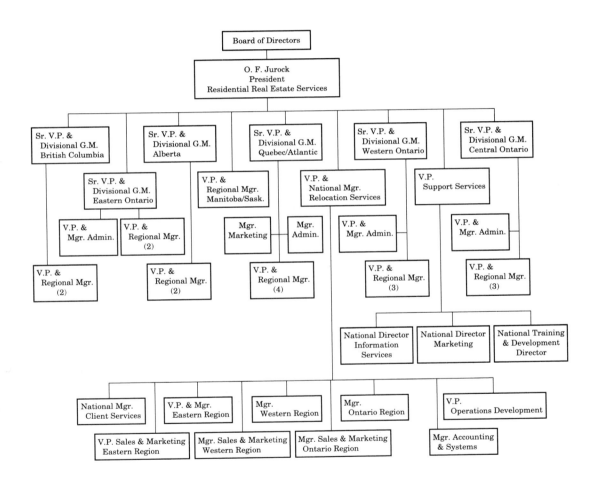

EXHIBIT 2

Operating Performance

Selected Financial Information
(thousands of dollars except per share amounts)

	1986	1985
Gross Commission and other revenue	$526,031	$460,269
Gross revenue	432,854	381,354
Net Income	14,188	4,684
Earnings per share	1.16	0.40
Total Assets	282,674	130,489
Return on average common equity	44.9%	20.6%

	Fees & Commissions		Sales Agents		Business Sources	
	$000	% Change	No.	% Change	Conventional/ Franchise %	Residential/ Comm.-Ind. %
1986	$432,900	14.0	6,877	0.5	100/0	77/23
1985	385,221	16.0	6,845	n.a.	100/0	78/22
1984	321,860	(0.5)	7,461	1.9	100/0	74/26

Source: *Canadian Business* performance rankings, 1985-87

EXHIBIT 3

Commitments

Our mission is to be Canada's finest, most professional real estate services organization.

In fulfilling our mission, we make these commitments:

To clients who are serviced by Royal LePage, we commit to delivering high quality, industry leading and innovative real estate products and services on a complete cost-efficient basis. Our business relationships will be characterized in the highest degree by honesty, credibility, and fair dealing. We are committed to setting the pace in service excellence.

To our fellow sales representatives, management and support staff at Royal LePage, we commit to providing a work environment, industry leading support and service systems, along with compensation and recognition programs that encourage the highest level of personal contribution and achievement, while maximizing opportunities for personal development and fulfillment.

To the common shareholders of Royal LePage, we commit to consistently increasing your total return as measured by earnings, asset values and share price.

To those who share the business community with Royal LePage, we commit to delivering a level of real estate professionalism that contributes to the overall well being of the community.

Setting the pace in service excellence.

EXHIBIT 4

Predictions for 1987 Resale Values

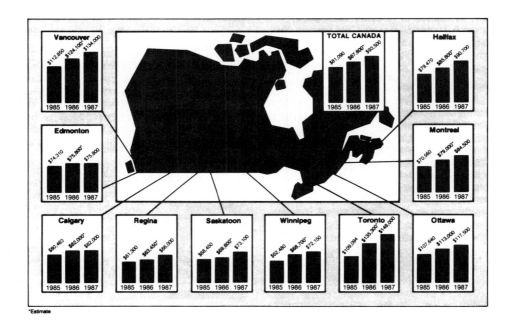

*Estimate

Source: *The Royal LePage Market Syrvey*

EXHIBIT 5

Predictions for 1987 Number of Resales

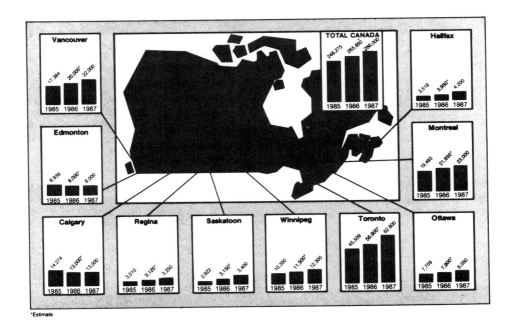

*Estimate

Source: *The Royal LePage Market Syrvey*

EXHIBIT 6

Policy 14

CORPORATE POLICY

POLICY NO.   14

TITLE   EMPLOYEE TRANSACTIONS DEALING IN REAL ESTATE
FOR THEIR OWN ACCOUNT

INTRODUCTION

People are Royal LePage's most important asset. Because they are also Royal LePage's direct contact with all its various publics, it follows that the manner in which employees conduct themselves has a tremendous impact on the perception, or image, that the public has of your Company. And, over the longer term, the most successful companies are those that are perceived to conduct their affairs with honesty and integrity.

In our business, one of the most sensitive areas which could call the integrity of the Company into question is an employee dealing in real estate for his/her own account. These transactions must be, and must appear to be, completely without prejudice to the public at large.

The steps that must be taken by all staff in these kinds of transactions in order to avoid negative reaction toward employees, the Company or any of its subsidiaries are outlined in the attached Corporate Policy.

All employees should read the following as being in their own best interests.

1. Part 1 of this Policy applies to all employees.

PURPOSE

To outline what an employee of the Corporation must do when entering into a real estate transaction for his/her own account either directly or indirectly.

The employee is required to follow the policy so as to prevent situations which may bring into question the integrity of the Corporation, its employees and subsidiaries.

Exhibit 6 cont'd

Exhibit 6 cont'd

DEFINITIONS

Employee: Every person, permanent or part-time, licensed or not, whether on salary or commission, who is working in any capacity in any part of the Corporation.

Corporation: Royal LePage Limited and its subsidiaries. Please see Appendix 'A' attached for list of subsidiaries.

Real Estate Transaction: Buying, exchanging, optioning, selling, developing and syndicating real estate, and leasing commercial or industrial real estate. In the case of a broker or sales representative, leasing or renting residential real estate is also included.

THE LAW OF AGENCY

The Law of Agency is that area of law which, apart from statute, governs the relationship of a real estate representative/broker to the public. While every employee is not a licensed real estate representative or broker, *it is the intention of this policy that the employee should govern himself/herself as if he/she were a representative/broker.*

A real estate sales representative or broker cannot personally become involved in a real estate transaction unless he/she delivers to the other parties a written statement to the effect that he/she is a sales representative/broker and herein he/she sets out all facts pertaining to the transaction. A full disclosure includes all material facts known by the sales representative/broker or facts which should have been known. A simple definition of material facts are those things which, if known, would likely influence the other parties' judgment. The onus lies on the sales representative/broker to show that he/she has made full disclosure.

POLICY STATEMENT

An employee entering into any real estate transaction in which he/she has a direct or indirect interest in his/her individual capacity, through a family member, partnership, syndication, corporation or any other business entity, must disclose all material facts with respect to the purpose for which the employee will be purchasing or selling the property, in writing, to the other parties to the transaction, *before entering into the transaction*, and his/her status as an employee of the Corporation and other pertinent facts as they relate to the real estate transaction which may affect the other parties' decision to enter into such transaction.

Exhibit 6 cont'd

Exhibit 6 cont'd

It is expected that an employee, when entering into real estate transactions, will do so, wherever possible, through the offices of the Corporation.

Employees may not speculate in real estate either directly or indirectly. An employee will be assumed to be speculating if any property is sold within one year from the date of its acquisition, unless the employee can show good reason, other than that of profit, for such a rapid turnover of property.

Prior approval, in writing, of the Board of Adjudication referred to in this Policy shall be required for transactions which may not comply with this Policy.

Where the Corporation becomes involved in a legal action as a result of an employee not complying with this Policy, the Corporation will hold the employee responsible for all damages and costs arising from the legal action.

It must be understood that any employee who does not comply with this Policy is liable to dismissal from employment.

PRE-EMPLOYMENT CONDITION

It is a condition of employment that each employee shall read this Policy and acknowledge, in writing on a duplicate of this Policy, his/her intention to comply with the Policy terms.

EXISTING EMPLOYEES

Any existing employee who has not done so must sign an acknowledgement that he/she has read and will comply with this Policy.

BOARD OF ADJUDICATION

The Board, from time to time, shall be comprised of any three persons appointed by the President and Chief Executive Officer from the following persons:

President of Commercial Real Estate Services
President of Residential Real Estate Services
President and Chief Executive Officer
General Counsel of the Corporation

An ad hoc member who shall be the senior manager of the department/area in which the employee works

EXAMPLES

The following are examples only of written disclosures which can be made to a prospective Vendor/Purchaser, etc., and are not meant to be an all-inclusive list:

Exhibit 6 cont'd

Exhibit 6 cont'd

House/Apartment Purchase
- I am an employee of Royal LePage and I wish to purchase your property for a principal residence.
- I am an employee of Royal LePage and I wish to purchase your property to rent to other parties.

House/Apartment Rental
- I am a sales representative with Royal LePage and I wish to rent your property for use as my residence.

Leasing a Commercial Property
- I am an employee of Royal LePage and I wish to lease your premises for a family owned business.

Selling a Home
- I am an employee of Royal LePage and I am selling my home to relocate to another city.
- I am an employee of Royal LePage and I am selling my home as I now need a larger/smaller residence.
- I am an employee of Royal LePage and I am selling my home as I now wish to live in an apartment.

Purchasing a Commercial Property
- I am an employee of Royal LePage and I wish to purchase your property for long term investment purpose.

In addition to the above disclosures, a real estate sales representative/broker must disclose, in writing, the points mentioned in the second paragraph of Page 2 of this Policy (The Law of Agency).

II. Part II of this Policy applies to officers, managers and salaried employees.

PURPOSE

The purpose of requiring officers and all other employees, with the exception of commission sales representatives, to report purchases of investment real estate is primarily to ensure that they do not become so involved with their activities outside the office that they devote time elsewhere which should be spent on the Corporation's business. Purchases of principal residences are not covered by the Policy.

MAJOR TRANSACTIONS

The purchase of investment real estate where the price paid, including debt assumed or taken out, exceeds $1,000,000 for any one transaction, is regarded as a major transaction. Before an employee commits himself/herself to a

Exhibit 6 cont'd

Exhibit 6 cont'd

major transaction, it must be referred to the Operating Committee or the Chief Executive Officer of the Corporation for approval. Employees should allow two weeks for this approval to take place. It is not necessary for sales of investment real estate to be approved.

Applications for approval shall be made to the Corporation's General Counsel who will have the responsibility of maintaining a record for each individual.

MINOR TRANSACTIONS

Any purchases by employees of investment real estate, not a major transaction, do not require any approval before being entered into but must, within Thirty (30) days of the signing of the offer, be recorded with the employee's manager or supervisor. The report must be in writing and contain particulars of the address, purchase price and financing and shall be recorded by the supervisor or manager in a record maintained separately for each employee. The manager or supervisor shall report the same particulars in each case to the General Counsel of the Corporation, who also shall maintain a record for each such employee. It will be the responsibility of the manager or supervisor to ensure that the employee does not assume a burden, either from the point of view of the time involved or financial obligations, which would interfere with the efficient performance of his or her duties.

15 Sears Canada Inc and Sunday Shopping (A)

Richard Sharpe, chairman and chief executive officer of Sears Canada Inc, considered his morning telephone conversation with the vice-president of corporate planning and public affairs. The media were anxious for the Sears position on Sunday retail openings. Only two days previous, on November 30, 1986, Hudson's Bay Co,—a major competitor whose holdings included the Bay, Simpsons, and Zellers—announced that it would open its stores on Sunday, December 7, 1986, in violation of Ontario's Retail Business Holidays Act. The following day, Sears' other competitors in general merchandise retailing also announced their openings. Eatons, Sears' most direct competitor, had not yet revealed its intent. Now Sharpe had to decide what Sears should do.

Two individuals whose attitudes and preferred business practices had great influence on Sears' corporate culture were Gordon Graham and Jack C. Barrow. Graham was president of Simpsons-Sears[1] from 1956 to 1962, chairman of the board from 1962 to 1966, and retired after 38 years of service. As the brother-in-law of Edgar Burton, who was at one time president of Simpsons and the first chief executive officer and president of Simpsons-Sears, Graham was a powerful figure in the company. Barrow, Graham's successor, was a long-time employee and also a well-respected leader. Both men were also steadfast opponents of Sunday shopping, an attitude that endured with subsequent Sears executives.

After Barrow retired in 1978, C. Richard Sharpe was appointed chairman of the board. He had spent his entire

---

1 Created in the early 1950s through a joint venture arrangement, which was terminated in 1978 when the Hudson's Bay Company acquired Simpsons.

Copyright © 1988, the University of Western Ontario.

This case was written by Nadine Hayes, under the supervision of Professor Jeffrey Gandz, and was funded by a grant from Imperial Oil Limited.

career with Simpsons, Simpsons-Sears, and Sears. Sharpe was also an anti-Sunday shopping advocate. His views were explicit: "We see no merit in opening on Sunday and will only do so if forced to by legitimate competition which elect to stay open."

Other aspects of the Sears culture included concern for customer value and product quality. The company also considered itself a responsible corporate citizen with a genuine concern for its employees. It organized an annual Employees' Charitable Fund drive, participated in the United Way Campaign and Variety Club Telethon, and offered university scholarships to employees' children. Sears maintained a National Employees' Suggestion Program with cash awards, as well as the Chairman's Challenge to honor those employees who had demonstrated outstanding performance in attaining planned goals. Indeed, the strategic mission and direction statement embraced by Sears described employees as "our greatest resource, recognizing that it is mainly through them that customer satisfaction and retention is achieved." (Exhibit 1).

THE HISTORY OF SUNDAY SHOPPING

The controversy over what should be considered acceptable Sunday activity had raged for centuries. Some of the key players changed and the breadth of the issue evolved; however, many of the problems, the arguments for and against, and even the actions of the government, recurred in similar form.

Federal Legislation

When Canada was still a collection of colonies, two British statutes, the Sunday Observance Acts of 1677 and 1780, prohibited "Sabbath Desecration." The colonies proceeded to pass their own Sabbath observance acts, the last one being the Upper Canada Act in 1845. That act prohibited everything except religious observances and works of necessity and charity, such as carrying travellers, the mail, or selling medicines.

As urbanization and industrialization occurred in Canada, there were additional opportunities for businesses to open on Sundays. As transportation became more readily available, the demand for entertainment on Sundays increased. The government of Ontario put the transportation issue of whether streetcars should run on Sundays to a plebiscite in 1897. Those in favor of loosening the restrictions on Sundays won out.

Enforcement was irregular, and interest groups for and against Sunday activity increased their pressure on government. It became apparent that the Upper Canada Act was unable to deal with the issue and a federal Lord's Day Act was proposed in 1907. The document made it illegal for any persons "to sell or offer for sale or purchase any goods, chattels, or other personal property, or any real estate, or to carry on or transact any business of his ordinary calling, or in connection with such calling, or for gain to do, or employ any other person to do, on that day, any work, business, or labour."

The debate surrounding the proposed legislation was intense. The business community was well represented and successfully negotiated exemptions into the Act. The exemptions were extensive, but concentrated on "work of necessity or mercy" such as: work in connection with divine mercy, work for the relief of sickness and suffering, and transportation requirements. Another exemption was the provincial clause which allowed provincial legislation to expand the list of federal exemptions.

Provincial Legislation in Ontario

When the provinces were formed, the Upper Canada Act in Ontario became An Act to Prohibit the Profanation of the Lord's Day, followed in 1922 with the One Day's Rest in Seven Act, which was in turn followed in 1950 with the Lord's Day Act, but was expanded to allow previously prohibited sporting and gaming events on Sundays. It was also amended several times to allow concerts and exhibitions, theatre performances and films and trade shows, fairs and exhibitions.

The increasing number of exemptions in the legislation attempted to address the increased number of retail openings and new challenges in retail marketing that occurred during the 1960s. Changing demographics saw more women entering the workforce who demanded more convenient shopping hours. For the overall population, working hours were shorter, and leisure was more popular. The retail marketplace was becoming less differentiated, with decreasing consumer loyalty to any one establishment, and different types of shopping environments, such as shopping malls, offered new enticements to consumers.

After a provincial commission to study the matter, the Retail Business Holidays Act (RBHA) became law on January 1, 1976. The intent of the legislation, according to the Solicitor General, was "to slow the growing commercialism and materialism about us" by regulating Sunday and holiday retail store openings. This piece of legislation added two new features to the preceding legislation. The first was an attempt to distinguish between corner stores and large grocery stores. The government saw the corner stores' only competitive advantage as being allowed to stay open for extended hours and on Sundays. Thus only those stores with less than 2400 square feet and three or fewer staff on duty could legally open on Sundays. The second addition was a new exemption for tourist areas. The Act allowed municipalities to pass by-laws exempting certain stores and/or areas "where it is essential for the maintenance or development of a tourist industry." These two exemptions laid the groundwork for twelve years of turmoil and confusion.

Other Provincial Legislation

In addition to the statutes outlined below, some provinces had Lord's Day acts or Sunday observance acts which were generally permissive in nature and provided exemptions to Sunday closing laws for activities of an educational or recreational nature. Beginning in 1980, British Columbia allowed Sunday shopping by municipal referendum in accordance with the province's Holiday Shopping Regulation Act. Following that decision, Sunday became the second most popular shopping day of the week after Saturday. Where there had been initial resistance to Sunday openings, it appeared to have eased. However, in other provinces in which the acts were challenged (Quebec, Nova Scotia, New Brunswick, Newfoundland), they were upheld by the courts. Prince Edward Island governed Sunday openings under the Days of Rest Act. It was not challenged through the courts, but retailers tried to circumvent it by sending invitations to potential customers to shop on Sundays. There were three successful prosecutions of store owners over those actions.

Federal Legislative Challenges

In 1984, three retailers from Alberta, before the Supreme Court of Canada, charged that the federal Lord's Day Act violated their right to religious freedom guaranteed in the Canadian Charter of Rights and Freedoms. On April 24, 1985, the Supreme Court struck down the federal Act on the basis that it was discriminatory to those of a faith other than Christianity. The decision stated that if the legislation had been secular, a piece of labor legislation rather than one which was premised on religious purposes, it would have been considered constitutional.

Provincial Legislative Challenge (Ontario)

Since the early 1980s, the Retail Business Holidays Act (RBHA) had not only been flouted several times but was even being challenged in the courts. The most notable and familiar of those challenging it was Paul Magder, a fur retailer located on Spadina Avenue in Toronto. Beginning in 1978, Magder opened his store each Sunday, on the basis that the RBHA was an infringe-

ment of his freedom. In 1983, Magder and two other retailers had their cases heard by the Ontario Court of Appeal. When that decision upheld the many charges against them, they proceeded to the Supreme Court of Canada. By the time the case reached the Supreme Court, the Charter of Rights and Freedoms was in place. The arguments focused on whether the possible infringement on freedom was justified for the greater public good. The court hearings were held in the spring months of 1986 and a decision was expected by the end of the year.

THE KEY EVENTS (ONTARIO)

1975-1984

For several years after the RBHA was passed there were few reported violations of the legislation. Although Paul Magder was accumulating charges and moving through the Ontario court system, he and his case received little media attention. However, the early 1980s saw a rash of openings, as well as the challenges in the courts.

1985

After the federal Lord's Day Act was found to be unconstitutional in April of 1985, independents and small grocery stores began to open on Sundays. They were still under the jurisdiction of the Ontario Retail Business Holidays Act (RBHA), which meant that the openings were illegal, but they apparently felt that because the federal legislation had been found unconstitutional, the provincial Act, which Magder was taking to the Supreme Court, could be as well. Enforcement continued to be the domain of the municipalities, resulting in variations in the conditions under which charges were laid and investigations conducted.

1986

The following year was quite different. Magder et al were heard in the Supreme Court during the month of March. Also bringing the issue to the forefront was a task force, struck by the opposition Conservative party, that was touring the province trying to determine the public's stance on the issue of Sunday shopping. Although the task force began under the assumption that the RBHA needed to be liberalized, it found the populace opposed to Sunday shopping, and therefore recommended tighter restrictions, with the exception of several Sundays before Christmas. The task force members unanimously agreed that there should be a common day of rest.

By September of 1986, the issue was again in the news. Large grocery stores were opening in an attempt to combat the drug stores, especially in Metro Toronto. Loblaws, Mr Grocer, Food City, A&P Food Stores and Miracle Foodmart stated that they were "responding to the competitive pressure," as well as following the US lead.

The incident that sparked the most controversy occurred on November 30, 1986, when Hudson's Bay Co announced that it would open its doors at eleven Toronto stores on Sunday, December 7, 1986. Two days later, Eatons announced that it would open in Nova Scotia, but was vacillating on opening Sundays in Ontario. That move was quickly followed by announcements from Towers, K-Mart and Woolco which each indicated that they would open in Ontario. Dylex Ltd, a pro-Sunday shopping retailer, decided to remain closed as long as the openings were sporadic. The mall operators took the position that they needed to accommodate their tenants, so they would turn on the lights but leave it up to the individual retailers to decide whether they wanted to be open. They did, however, anticipate increased sales and revenues.

Sharpe suspected that the reason behind the announcements was basically a show of impatience. He saw it as an attempt to accelerate the Supreme Court deliberations on Magder's case. Various provincial governments across the country were also awaiting the decision, and rather than attempt to enforce their provincial Sunday legislation, they made overtures to the federal government to try and hasten the Supreme Court decision. Some felt that the delay was contributing to the problem of illegal openings.

Following the announcements to open, the pressure from both sides on the Ontario government reached a feverish pitch. Ian Scott, the Attorney-General, saw the announcements as "offensive and shocking" and indicated that those retailers who violated the law would be charged. Some questioned whether there were enough police officers to enforce the law evenly and charge all offenders. The debate received considerable media attention. Joan Smith, the Solicitor-General, sent a message to police officials across the province stating that "it is imperative that even more rigorous law enforcement take place with respect to the RBHA."

Government, church and union groups were appalled at the retailers' intention to disregard the law in order to change it, and they vocally attacked such methods (Exhibit 2). The People for Sunday Association and the official opposition submitted the largest petition in Ontario's history (110,000 names) to Queen's Park.

Stories began to surface in the media about infringements on employees' rights. Employers were reportedly offering to cover employees' legal costs if they found themselves fined for working in a store that was illegally open on Sunday. Other employees were apparently told that their names would be taken off the payroll if they did not work Sundays. Still others were told to be silent on the issue if approached by the media. Many retail employees were caught in the dilemma of not wanting to break the law, but feeling forced to do so to protect their jobs. They wanted guaranteed job protection from the government.

Unions were concerned about the implications of illegal Sunday openings for their collective agreements, many of which stipulated that employees be paid double time for working on Sundays, which was unlikely to be upheld if the openings were illegal. There was also concern for the unrepresented part-time employees who would not be eligible for premium pay for working on Sundays. They too wanted protection for refusing to work on Sundays.

The media maintained interest in the issue and editorial opinions covered it thoroughly, if from opposing sides of the spectrum (Exhibit 3). The newspapers, however, reported similar opinions from retail employees: the majority were strongly opposed to Sunday shopping (Exhibit 4). Finally, the federal Attorney-General announced that a decision on the Magder case would be announced as early as December 18, 1986.

INTEREST GROUPS

The People for Sunday Association

People for Sunday, previously called the Lord's Day Alliance, was a recognized opponent of Sunday shopping. The Association was organized by Presbyterians in 1888 as a national organization with board members from several denominations. Politically, it was non-partisan with both Liberal and Conservative ties. Although the primary purpose of the organization was originally to preserve the purity of the Sabbath, the changing role of the church a century later brought social issues and worker rights into the forefront of their opposition. By the mid 1980s members of major corporations sat on both the board and the executive. The group was funded by individuals, church groups, and corporations. The support of labor organizations for People for Sunday was also growing.

The Sears Perspective

For Sears the issue was both a moral and a legal one. On moral grounds, Sears opposed Sunday openings for several reasons: there was a negative impact on family life; there was no appreciable job creation; it was unfair to retail workers; there was no real customer demand; and, it was bound to have a domino effect. Some retailers could virtually force it on the rest merely by opening their stores, which meant that those not in favor of opening would have to follow suit to maintain their share of the market.

On legal grounds, Sears found it distasteful for its competitors to attempt to change a law by breaking it. Sears was also uncomfortable with the idea that the retail industry would have to deal with a change in regulations, while other forms of business, such as liquor stores, beer stores, and government offices, could continue to operate as usual. Of equal concern was the quality of staff that would be drawn to the retail industry if Sunday shopping was allowed. Sears staff were loyal, dedicated employees who enjoyed spending time with their families. If there were Sunday openings, Sears felt that it might have difficulty attracting good employees and competent managerial talent. Sears was also concerned that their quality of service might decline.

Sears saw the RBHA as reasonable legislation which was inconsistently enforced. Its particular concern was the inequity of the law. What was outlined in the legislation as a drugstore was becoming more than a drugstore. It had grown to 50,000 to 100,000 sq. ft. of space, and its product lines were increasingly diversified. The legitimate general mechanisers, and particularly the grocery stores, were feeling pressured as they lost market share to pseudo-drug stores.

Although Sears had experience with Sunday openings in the West, in Sault Ste Marie, and through the US parent, the results had not been analyzed. There was no central collection or manipulation of data on Sunday results, but the executive group felt sure that Sunday openings were not economically advantageous.

Hudson's Bay Perspective

As the catalyst for the general merchandiser announcements, the firm contended that the stores which were opening on a regular basis, either legally or illegally, were eroding its market share and that it had to open in self-protection. Hudson's Bay Co stated that it weighed current market trends against the law, and found that the law was inequitable. The executive declared that the decision to challenge the law was made "with great reluctance and only because of the chaotic state of enforcement." The firm just wanted "equal application of the law." In fact, the firm saw the issue as not about Sunday shopping, but about a law that was not being obeyed.

Another concern was with the large drug stores and grocery stores that were selling an increasing amount of general merchandise, therefore eroding the firm's market share. Not only did Hudson's Bay feel a need to protect that share, it saw an opportunity to increase it. The firm contended that the experience of British Columbia and Alberta showed economic advantage to opening on Sundays, and cited statistics showing that Sunday had the second-highest daily sales in a given week and yielded the highest volume of sales per hour. Hudson's Bay Co also claimed that there would be 12 percent more "man-hours" to be gained by opening. The urge to open at that particular time was based on the firm's statistical projections that indicated one Sunday during Christmas was equal to an entire week in July or August.

Dylex Perspective

Wilfred Posluns, one of the co-founders, president, and CEO of Dylex, a major fashion retail conglomerate with stores such as Fairweather, Big Steel, Thrifty's, and Susie Shier, put a different perspective on the Sunday shopping situation. He pointed out that if the shopping malls were open Sundays, they would draw business from the stores that were not in the malls, because families would want to go to attractive shopping malls as a Sunday activity. He pointed out that Sunday was the second most popular shopping day in the US after Saturday. He believed that the marginal contribution of any incremental volumes made from Sunday opening was substantial, since all of the fixed costs of the business would be spread over more sales. He also predicted no difficulty finding people to work part-time on Sundays.

Mall Owners Perspective

Mall owners made their revenues on a percentage of their tenants' gross sales. They saw shopping on Sunday as a form of leisure and recreation to be enjoyed by families. They stated that such excursions could result in impulse buying, therefore increasing the total dollars to the retailers, rather than simply redistributing a fixed amount of consumer income. The owners also emphasized that they would not force retailers to open, although they pointed to the US and the Western provinces to illustrate that Sunday shopping was inevitable.

Sectarian Perspective

The reactions of religious groups to the announcements centred on two issues: the inappropriateness of retailers' conduct and the principle of a common day of rest. All denominations were unanimous in their denunciation of the retailers who announced their intentions to break the law. Dr Suzanne Scorsone, Director of the Office of Family Life of the Toronto Diocese, outlined the collective opinion: "I find it very disturbing that major retailers, who are supposed to be the pillars of society, are taking the position that they can break the law, and thus force the law to be changed. It is a very grave change in the way of approaching parliamentary democracy." In regard to the specifics of the Sunday shopping issue, Dr Scorsone stated that it was not a matter of a religious holiday, but the need for a common day of rest. The sectarian perspective was particularly concerned for single mothers, women in retail, and the potential for increased costs to consumers.

Union Perspective

The labor voice was relatively quiet on the issue of Sunday shopping. Unions and labor federations responded to questions on the issue, but did not mount an active campaign against it. Few of the retail workers in Ontario were unionized and therefore the collective voice was small. However, there was sufficient uncertainty over workers' rights to induce some union concern.

Other Perspectives

Those with the most to lose in a decision to allow unrestricted Sunday openings were the corner stores, such as the 7-Elevens and the Macs Milks. They were adamantly opposed to open Sunday shopping, stating that it would completely destroy their competitive advantage.

THE SEARS LOBBY

For many years Sears Canada Inc had actively opposed Sunday shopping. In the late 1960s when the issues of extended store hours and shopping on Sunday came to the forefront in Ontario, Sears lobbied the provincial government along with other interest groups. In the early 1970s Sears was a member of Provincial Uniform Store Hours (PUSH), an organization formed to lobby against extended store operating hours and Sunday shopping.

The firm also encouraged all levels of employees to become involved in the campaign to oppose Sunday shopping. The corporate stance was that night shopping on a province-wide basis should be kept to a three-night maximum, and that there be a ban on Sunday openings (excluding drug stores, jug milk stores, and other corner stores). Employees were informed of the stance, then encouraged to make their views known to the provincial committee. The corporate office sent letters to all employees suggesting that they, as private citizens, write to the Provincial Secretary for Justice or their member of parliament. Sears also offered some support to People for Sunday through financial contributions and the volunteer time of some of its personnel.

After the Retail Business Holidays Act was passed in 1975, Sears activity on the issue of Sunday shopping abated and did not resume until the mid 1980s, when the issue was again in the public eye. Throughout 1986, Sears observed the illegal openings by the grocery stores and kept an eye on the Magder trial, aware of the new dimension that had been added to the issue by the Canadian Charter of Rights and Freedoms. Although Sears knew that the RBHA was potentially discriminatory, the firm felt the law was defensible and expected it to be upheld. Both Richard Sharpe and the public affairs department also expected that retailers, such as Magder, would be forced to obey it.

THE DECISION

As Richard Sharpe considered the situation, he was aware of the complexities involved. It appeared to be a matter of principle versus protection against competition. He believed that if all of his direct competitors were to open, he would have no choice but to protect his share of the market even if opening would violate the law. He had to decide what position he wanted to take, and how he should present that position to both the media and his employees.

EXHIBIT 1

Mission Statement

STRATEGIC MISSION AND DIRECTION

Sears Canada Inc is a national merchandising corporation committed to satisfying customers by providing products and services of superior value. Fulfilment of this commitment requires integrity in everything we do, competent and motivated employees, healthy communities in which to operate and earnings that will not only satisfy the requirements of our shareholders but ensure the long-term real growth of the Corporation.

CORPORATE PHILOSOPHY

Sears believes in the need to excel in every facet of our business so that maximum earnings are achieved from our efforts. The corporation has basic philosophies in specific areas which are fundamental to the way it pursues its mission. They are:

CUSTOMERS

Sears believes that its very existence depends on treating its customers with integrity and providing them with the assurance that they will receive satisfaction or their money refunded on the products and services they purchase.

EMPLOYEES

We believe in treating our employees as our greatest resource, recognizing that it is mainly through them that customer satisfaction and retention is achieved.

MANAGEMENT

We believe in encouraging individual initiative and input in the achievement of Corporate goals and objectives and to stimulate the pride of accomplishment that is derived from a task well done.

SHAREHOLDERS

We believe we have a major responsibility to our shareholders to protect their investment and to provide them with an acceptable return on that investment.

Exhibit 1 cont'd

Exhibit 1 cont'd

COMMUNITIES

We believe we have a responsibility to help ensure the well-being of the communities we serve by being an ethical, responsible, caring, and successful Corporation. We believe in an ongoing interaction with all levels of government on issues that affect our Corporation, our employees, our customers, and our shareholders.

SUPPLIERS

Our suppliers of products and services are an important component of our business and they must be treated with integrity. We believe in mutually beneficial long-term associations with suppliers.

EXHIBIT 2

Spread of Sunday Shopping Denounced
(Media Coverage)

2 December 1986

By Rudy Platiel

Retailers were accused by a Roman Catholic church spokesman yesterday of resorting to "a kind of legal terror tactic" in an effort to break the Ontario Government's will to enforce the Sunday closing law.

A flood of announcements since the weekend by major retailers that they are moving to Sunday openings in Ontario—at least for December—has triggered concern from government, church and union groups that the trend will soon spread across the country.

Ontario Government officials have condemned the planned actions. Solicitor-General Kenneth Keys said yesterday that police across the province have been told to lay charges against any stores that violate the closing law. He said every force has been told through the Ontario Police Commission "to be sure they are extra diligent this weekend in laying charges against any stores whatsoever that are breaking the Retail Business Holidays Act."

Gordon Wilson, president of the Ontario Federation of Labor, said yesterday that the law should be enforced. And he urged consumers who shop on Sunday to consider the fact that they could also find themselves working on that day, too.

Suzanne Scorsone, director of the Office of Family Life of the Toronto Diocese, said the retailers' actions seem part of an increasing tendency in society generally for people to defy laws with which they disagree "and dare the Government" to move against them.

Archdeacon Harry Hilchey, general secretary of the Anglican General Synod of Canada, said it is "a dangerous precedent for major financial or business institutions to say, 'I don't care what the law says, if someone else does it, I'll do it.'"

Dr. Scorsone said the move by so many retailers amounts to an attempt to force the Government into changing the law by using "bludgeon tactics"—a mass defiance that places "so much pressure on the legal system" that it cannot function.

"I find it very disturbing that major retailers, who are supposed to be the pillars of society, are taking the position that they can break the law, and thus force the law to be changed," Dr. Scorsone said. "It is a very grave change in the way of approaching parliamentary democracy."

What's more, she said, it carries implications for other parts of the country.

Trilea Centres Inc. announced yesterday that it had decided to open its Yorkdale and its Scarborough Town Centre in Metropolitan Toronto and Shoppers World Mall in Brampton, Ont., on Sundays.

Exhibit 2 cont'd

Exhibit 2 cont'd

William Seli, vice-president of Trilea, said Yorkdale and the Scarborough centre have always been physically open for window-shopping on Sunday.

However, retailers, previously prohibited from opening for business, will now be allowed to do so if they choose during the four Sundays in December. No decision has been made on opening beyond the last Sunday in December, he said.

The latest round of declarations follows a weekend announcement by Simpsons — a division of Hudson's Bay Co. —that it is opening because of the threat to its market share by those who were doing so in defiance of the law.

The Bay, Woolco, K-mart, Zellers and Towers have since said they are also forced to open to protect their competitive position.

Cadillac Fairview Corp. Ltd. announced this week that its major malls, The Eaton Centre, Fairview Mall, Cedarbrae Mall and the Woodbine Centre, will now open.

In September, Loblaws supermarkets joined such other major food chains as Miracle Food Mart, Mr. Grocer, New Dominion, A&P Food Stores and Food City in opening on Sundays.

Under the Ontario Retail Business Holidays Act, store owners are required to close for 52 Sundays and eight additional holidays or face a $10,000 fine.

Dr. Scorsone said the fight in Ontario is more than a provincial one.

"When you are dealing with national corporations, then provincial borders mean very little.

"If they choose to mount a campaign for or against some kind of legislation, then it doesn't necessarily reflect feeling in those provinces, it reflects decisions in the boardroom."

Dr. Scorsone said the issue is not a religious holiday but the need for "a common day of rest." Sunday shopping is a threat to family life because Sunday is the one day that families and single parents can be assured that they and their friends and relatives can get together.

More than half of retail workers are women, she said, and if mothers of school-age children have to work on Sunday, "that is yet another day that the kids don't see her."

What's more, she said, if ultimately all stores are open on Sundays, it will only mean higher costs for consumers because the existing number of consumer spending dollars will have to be covered by the overhead and labor costs for seven days of operations instead of six.

However, Mr. Seli said that while at this point Trilea is simply responding to the opening by others, he believes Sunday shopping is inevitable.

He said the pattern in two company malls with Sunday shopping—one in Vancouver and one in Calgary—indicates that shopping for many families represents entertainment and "a family time together."

He said once families make that trip to the shopping mall "very often dollars not (previously) earmarked" for such items are spent and "represent money that wouldn't have necessarily been spent" in the malls.

Exhibit 2 cont'd

Exhibit 2 cont'd

"There is a certain transfer from expenditures that would not have been possible in a shopping centre environment into the shopping centre situation and let's face it...We're out there trying to fight for customers."

Mr. Seli said company research across the country indicates that a majority of customers want to be able to shop on Sunday because it is more convenient.

Mr. Seli said it is not company policy yet to go into Sunday shopping beyond December, but if that eventually arrives, it will probably not mean longer operating hours because other more unproductive hours during the week will be dropped, either by opening later or by closing earlier.

EXHIBIT 3

The Sunday Shopper
(Editorial Opinion)

2 December 1986

There is no joy in seeing retailers not only flout the civil law, but advertise their intention to do so. Several department stores have decided to open their doors this Sunday in contravention of Ontario's Retail Business Holidays Act, which requires most stores to remain closed on Sundays and eight other days during the year. In this, they follow the lead of independent stores and retail grocery chains which have opened on Sundays for some time, risking fines of up to $10,000 a day. The philosophy that the law's maximum fines are a practical and acceptable cost of doing business is deplorable.

That said, we repeat our long-held position that the law should be repealed. It may die in any case, if the Supreme Court of Canada overturns a 1984 ruling by the Ontario Court of Appeal and finds the law unconstitutional—a violation of freedom of religion under the Charter of Rights. But even if the Supreme Court were to agree with the lower court that "the inclusion of Sunday and other holidays is incidental to the main purpose"—giving Ontario residents a common day of rest—Ontario should dismantle the law on its own, as a flawed document whose continued existence is not in the public interest.

We side with those who find the Ontario bill a thinly-disguised sectarian document: it happens to choose Sunday as a common pause day, and happens to let people who want to pause on Saturday instead open their stores on Sunday. (It imposed certain restrictions on those people, until the court of Appeal ruled in 1984 that the restrictions violated freedom of religion.) The state, taking over the role once played by the church, orders Sunday to be special, whether people regard it as special or not.

Ontario cannot claim to have the shoppers' interests at heart; the public has flocked whole-heartedly to stores open on Sunday. The labor argument is weak as well. Certainly there are people who would rather not work Sundays, just as there are many who don't like working night shifts; but a great number of part-time workers would be glad of the new employment that Sunday openings create. To deny them that opportunity in the name of giving them a "pause day" is paternalism at its most perverse.

In any case, Ontario undercut its own arguments by lacing the law liberally with exemptions. You may legally sell antiques, handicrafts, "tobacco or articles required for the use of tobacco" or, if you're in a designated "tourist area," whatever you wish. From here we wade into the contradictions. You may open small food stores, but not big ones. A fruit market may open seven days a week from April to November, but must close on Sundays for the rest of the year. Magazine dealers may open on Sundays

Exhibit 3 cont'd

<u>Exhibit 3 cont'd</u>

and holidays; book stores may not. ("In Toronto, you can buy *Penthouse* or *Playboy* on Sunday," said lawyer John Brown, representing Edwards Books and Art before the Supreme Court, "but not Robertson Davies or Margaret Atwood.") Tourist areas that aren't officially designated as such must watch as neighboring merchants rake in the dollars.

If the Supreme Court of Canada were to uphold Ontario's law, and if Ontario were to maintain against the evidence that its act serves the public good, it could of course take harsh action against the scofflaws: it might strip the contradictions from the act, increase the penalties dramatically and enforce the law in so tough a manner that retail sales on Sunday would be but a distant memory. But the law isn't worth it; it lacks respect because it deserves none. If the court doesn't strike it down, Ontario should throw the act out.

Reprinted with permission—*The Globe and Mail.*

<u>Exhibit 3 cont'd</u>

Exhibit 3 cont'd

Ontario Ignores Reality on Sunday Shopping Law
(Editorial Opinion)

18 December 1986

By Timothy Danson

Mr. Danson is a Toronto lawyer who presented furrier Paul Magder's case against the Ontario Retail Business Holidays Act to the Supreme Court of Canada.

THE SUPREME COURT of Canada is scheduled to hand down its decision on Sunday shopping today. If it declares the Ontario Retail Business Holidays Act invalid, the issue will be dead until the province, or the federal Government, can draft new legislation that follows the criteria established by the court. But if the constitutional validity of the legislation is upheld, the debate will return to the political arena, where recent threats by large department stores to open on Sunday clearly have elevated its profile.

There is a significant difference between what is legally valid and what is politically expedient. The courts have no jurisdiction to pass judgment on the wisdom of the legislation outside its legal framework, despite public-opinion polls that have shown consistently that the public wants to shop on Sunday. The polls reflect some fundamental changes in society. The substantial influx of women into the work force and the growing number of single-parent families have made mid-week shopping unrealistic and impractical for many people. This leaves only Saturday to carry out the numerous commercial details of modern life.

Unfortunately, the Ontario law as it stands is prohibitive, making conduct that is acceptable six days of the week a crime on the seventh. This is neither realistic nor fair. Ontario Attorney-General Ian Scott expressed outrage when major department stores threatened a few weeks ago to defy the law. However, the province has no alternative but to express such anger. First, it is still illegal to open for business on Sunday (unless the store falls within the law's myriad exemptions); second, the Ontario Court of Appeal has already stated that the legislation is valid; third, Queen's Park has argued its case supporting the legislation before the Supreme Court of Canada, and it would be highly improper at this stage to take a contrary position. Clearly, the province's hands are tied.

On the other hand, instead of focusing so much attention on the fact that a law is being disobeyed, it might be time to consider that the law itself is bad. The Government's most recent and comprehensive public-opinion poll showed that 69 per cent of Ontarians want Sunday shopping, while 28 per cent are opposed and 3 per cent have no opinion. Other major polls have had similar findings. In staying open, retailers simply are

Exhibit 3 cont'd

<u>Exhibit 3 cont'd</u>

responding to an overwhelming public demand. It is high time that governments across the country recognized the new social economic realities of the day.

The fact that the Retail Business Holidays Act is a poorly drafted piece of legislation riddled with contradictions that result in highly discriminatory and unfair practices only aggravates the problem. Even opponents of Sunday shopping agree that it's inconsistent. As a result, the law commands little respect and the public has become cynical.

In addition, fears that Sunday shopping will cause family life to deteriorate have clearly been proved to be alarmist. The practice has not thrown family life in Alberta and British Columbia into disarray. In fact, taking the family shopping on a Sunday afternoon can be as much a form of recreation as going to a ball game.

As for economic impact, six months after Massachusetts allowed Sunday shopping, 4,000 new jobs had been created, adding an estimated $80-million to the state's economy in personal income and increasing sales-tax revenues by $12-million. This demonstrated that Sunday shopping does produce a bigger pie, not just the same pie cut into more pieces. It also showed that it is not difficult to enact legislation that protects retail workers' rights, just as there is legislation protecting workers in industries that run seven days a week. With the boon and social benefits Sunday shopping brought to the Massachusetts economy, it was no surprise that it was supported by both the Archdiocese of Boston and local trade unions. It is perplexing that their counterparts in Ontario—particularly the unions—take a contrary view.

Surely the key to a free society is that a person's liberty is absolute—unless, in exercising that liberty, others are harmed in some way. When it comes to Sunday shopping, some merchants complain that they are being harmed because they feel compelled to stay open to maintain their share of the market. That's a business decision they're free to make—not something injurious to the public at large.

EXHIBIT 4

Prospect of Having to Work Sundays Angers Some Clerks at Eaton Centre
(Employee Opinion)

2 December 1986

By Heather Bird

Some clerks at stores in Toronto's Eaton Centre who are faced with working Sunday shifts are not impressed with the idea of giving up their only weekend day off.

Jeff Edelist, the manager of the Town Shoes franchise, said he and his staff are dead-set against working Sundays.

"I don't want it. I think it stinks," Edelist said.

His head office is also against the idea of Sunday shopping, Edelist said.

"The only reason we would open is if all our competition opens. As of right now, there's no way we'll open."

The Christmas shopping hours are already extended enough to accommodate shoppers, he said.

At Christmas, the shops which are normally open from 10 a.m. to 6 p.m. are open from 9:30 a.m. to 9:30 p.m. On the Saturday before Christmas, Town Shoes will be open from 8 a.m. to 9:30 p.m.

"Everybody who is in retail already has a day off (during the week) to do their shopping and everybody who works Monday to Friday can shop on Saturdays," Edelist said.

He added that he didn't think it would mean an increase in business.

"Personally, all I think it's going to do is split your big Saturday into two days," he said.

Town employee Preet Nagra, 24, said she doesn't want to work on Sundays.

"I think we work enough hours as it is...that's the only day everybody is (her family) at home."

Colleague Gwen Duchesne, 27, agreed.

"It's supposed to be a day of rest anyway," she said.

Hildegarde Schmiedhammer, who works at Jewels by Koby, said all of the clerks she has spoken to in the mall are against working Sundays.

"Boy, do we hate it all. I think it's horrible. That's my opinion."

Schmiedhammer said she thinks her family life will be "destroyed."

Clerk Lori Hazuka, who works in Chadwicks, said the thought of working Sunday doesn't upset her.

"I'm from Alberta and I've always worked Sundays," she said.

16 Tremobin

For the third time on the morning of August 8, Dan Flanigan, quality control manager at Delta Industries, verified the test results. Neither Delta, nor its sister facility, was able to meet the recently increased quality control testing requirements for the drug Tremobin. And those standards were even lower than they might have been because of the successful campaigning of Mel Salari, director of quality control technology at head office. Only two years ago, Salari had convinced the pharmaceutical industry regulators that the standards for a particular test were too high, and they were immediately lowered. But now it was the new, lower standards that Flanigan's laboratory could not meet. Meanwhile, the annual batch of Tremobin was due to begin production, and Flanigan had to decide how to proceed.

COMPANY BACKGROUND

Delta Industries Inc (D-I) was the Canadian pharmaceutical affiliate of the CPW Company of Los Angeles, California. Delta operated in more than 100 countries around the world and marketed a wide range of both prescription and over-the-counter (OTC) drugs. The D-I manufacturing plant in Sudbury was only one part of CPW's Canadian operations which included administrative offices in Windsor, Ontario, and distribution centres in six cities across Canada.

Delta established an international reputation in the manufacture of prescription and over-the-counter pharmaceuticals. It came to be known as the cream of the drug industry, and was respected for the strict quality control standards it employed in the manufacture of its products. In 1967, CPW

This case was written by Nadine Hayes, under the supervision of Professor Jeffrey Gandz, and was funded by a grant from Imperial Oil Limited.

Company, a marketing-oriented firm in both the pharmaceutical and medical/surgical equipment industries, acquired Delta's assets. D-I continued to operate autonomously until 1979 when the CPW line of prescription pharmaceuticals was transferred to the Delta product line.

PHARMACEUTICAL MANUFACTURING AND REGULATION

The *Food and Drug Act* governed the manufacture and sale of pharmaceuticals in Canada through the Health Protection Branch (HPB) of Health and Welfare Canada. HPB was responsible for new product approvals, general administration and regulation of the industry, and annual site inspections of pharmaceutical manufacturers and importers under the jurisdiction of the Act. The HPB also published an interpretive booklet on the legislation. "Good Manufacturing Practices for Drug Manufacturers and Importers" outlined good manufacturing practices (GMPs) for plant conditions, employee hygiene, as well as general quality control. Excerpts, specifically related to quality control, are presented in Exhibit 1.

The Act designated the United States of America Pharmacopoeia (USP) as the primary regulatory manual for Canadian pharmaceutical products. The pharmacopoeia was a 1,700-page tome that established guidelines for quality assurance of raw materials and finished products, and was considered the authority on pharmaceuticals. It laid out specifications for the purity, potency, and safety of ethical pharmaceuticals.

The pharmacopoeia was published every five years by an independent body of academics, medical specialists, and industry experts. There was no Canadian pharmacopoeia, but there was a British edition and a European edition. If a particular product did not appear in the USP, the Canadian legislation stated that the British edition, then the European edition, were the order of authority. If a drug did not appear in any of the references, a similar composition was identified and the relevant specifications followed.

QUALITY CONTROL AT D-I

Quality control (QC) at the Sudbury plant fell within the broader realm of quality assurance (QA), and the managers of those departments reported to the Windsor offices. Their reporting relationship was unlike that for other managers in Sudbury; those managers reported to the Sudbury plant manager, who was directly responsible to the vice-president, manufacturing operations. A Q.A. organizational chart is presented in Exhibit 2.

The QC department dealt with the specifics of quality control, such as sampling/testing procedures, stability programs, documentation, and final product approval. Quality assurance dealt with the broader aspects of monitoring and designing the overall system, as well as ensuring that Delta met GMP standards.

Dan Flanigan was hired by Delta in 1974 as a supervisor in sterile manufacturing and moved through the ranks to his current position. By reporting directly to the corporate quality assurance manager in Windsor, Flanigan's department was relatively autonomous. Its budget was incorporated into the total QA budget, which was prepared each year by corporate finance in Windsor, based on the previous year's costs. A summary of quality assurance costs is presented in Exhibit 3. Any unexpected QC costs, such as extended testing or damaged product during testing, were assumed by the QC department.

Supplier quality control was an area of increasing concern to Delta. The firm had recently implemented a Vendor Qualification Program, as per GMP guidelines, and requested a "Certificate of Analysis" from all vendors to guarantee purity, potency, and safety of their delivered products. Most suppliers complied with the request; however, it was difficult to enforce, since many of the raw materials were imported by warehouses and large distributors which did not require such certificates.

Another initiative that addressed vendor quality was CPW's new corporate Business Principles (Exhibit 4). Implemented in late 1986, the Business Principles identified several stakeholder groups and attempted to influence CPW's business to make it compatible with the needs of each group.

TREMOBIN

Background on the Drug

Tremobin, which controlled neurological disorders, was comprised of an active agent, delonuprimide, that was used by some people with Parkinson's disease who could not be treated with a newer product, Trelobin, in the same family of pharmacologic agents. Because of the nature of the agent's action on the nervous system, the effect that a neurological drug would have was critically dependent on the lack of variability in the manufacturing process. The amount of active agent in the final dosage form was crucial: it had to be enough to control the critical disorder, but not so much as to confuse the nervous system. Abrupt withdrawal of the drug could reinstate the disorder with serious consequences for patients previously under control. Dosages had to be individualized according to response and tolerance, and determining the correct dosage for the patient was a long process of trial and error, with incremental changes carried out slowly and with careful evaluation of the patient's response.

Delta had produced Tremobin for close to 20 years, and was the only Canadian manufacturer of the drug. The CPW manufacturing operation in Toledo, Ohio, was responsible for US production for the US market. There was currently no Tremobin imported into North America. Tremobin accounted for $73,000 of total Delta sales of $56.2 million, and represented a fraction of one percent of total unit production.

Because of the size of the market—in 1985 there were only 200 Tremobin users in Canada—Delta manufactured one batch per year. The sophisticated Material Requirements Planning (MRP) system at the plant scheduled production for 18 months in advance, with the amount produced based on the number of prescriptions dispensed in the previous year. The batch was scheduled with approximately three to four weeks worth of inventory remaining in the warehouses, while the pharmacies held approximately two weeks worth of inventory. Tremobin had a shelf life of four years.

The Manufacturing Process

The manufacture of Tremobin was basically the blending of two powders, delonuprimide and starch, and occurred in three steps: mixing, filling, and polishing. Although the equipment used in the manufacture of Tremobin was only used by six to eight other products, the specific equipment and the entire surrounding area were thoroughly cleansed before manufacturing could proceed—a generally recognized GMP.

Tremobin was mixed in a 15-year-old, 20 cu. ft. blender, specifically designed for powders. The pre-measured quantities of starch and delonuprimide were poured into the vat, mixed for not less than one hour (+/- 10 minutes) before shipment to the filling operation. The filling operation generated a large amount of dust which required the capsules to be put through a polisher. From polishing, the Tremobin was sent to TBL Inc for packaging. The operation took approximately eight hours, and went from there to the warehouses where it awaited QC clearance after final testing.

Quality Control Checks

Quality control checks were employed at each stage of the manufacturing process. The first was on receipt of the bulk delonuprimide, where the usual incoming raw material QC checks were conducted: the purchase orders were checked for the correct labels, the correct number of containers, and the apparent overall acceptability of the product. The total shipment was then delivered to the sampling room where the QC sampler consulted delonuprimide's analytical data sheet which indicated the size of bulk sample to be sent for chemical testing. The laboratory tests verified the purity (the shipment did not contain any unrelated substances), potency (it was within the required specifications), and identity (it was the actual product ordered and required) of the bulk delonuprimide. At this point, the bulk delonuprimide was either approved or rejected. If it was rejected, notifications were sent to purchasing, production planning, and materials handling. Because of the MRP systems employed by the suppliers, and the small quantity of delonuprimide required for Delta's annual batch, replacement could take up to 18 months.

During the highly sanitary and critical dispensing operation, quantities and identities were checked and double-checked by different QC checkers. After the blending operation, the equipment operators documented the actual machine times and final product weights, and signed for the results, all of which were then verified by a QC checker. Sample product was retained in the event of future problems at either the filling stage or even for customer complaints. The sample was stored in the plant storage areas for approximately four years.

QC at the filling stage occurred at three different points in time: before the operation began, intermittently during the process, and after the filling was complete. Before the operation began in earnest, 100 capsules were filled and submitted to the chemistry laboratory for a dissolution test. Because of recent problems with the dissolution testing results, the entire filling process was put on hold until QC completed the pre-encapsulation tests.

During the filling process, the operator removed 10 capsules every 20 minutes and weighed the 10 capsules collectively. Every hour a QC checker also weighed 10 capsules, both in a group and individually. After the filling was complete, the operator weighed the total yield, and the results were verified by both a QC checker and a supervisor. Following the polishing, the capsules underwent a traditional Delta QC test, a visual inspection of each capsule. The capsules moved from the polisher onto a conveyer belt that was illuminated from below. One of three operators checked each capsule for physical defects, such as cracks, dents or empty capsules, and for the quality of the polishing. Total waste was calculated at approximately 2 to 3 percent. The inspection took approximately 10 hours. The capsules were then put into special containers to be weighed. The total yield, average capsule weight, number of capsules and total waste were calculated and compared against standards based on historical data.

More samples were taken at the bulk testing stage. Approximately 400-500 capsules were submitted to QC for weight testing (each capsule had to be +/- 10 percent of a pre-determined weight). Also, further dissolution testing was required, in an attempt to circumvent extensive testing after the product was packaged. During the final dissolution testing, the product inspection group examined all documentation related to the batch. The group checked sign-offs, testing results, and basically verified that the weights and lot numbers were consistent with specifications.

During the packaging stage at TBL Inc, label control was very strict: it was emphasized both in GMP guidelines and by regulatory bodies. There were extensive checks to ensure the accuracy of label identification, expiry dates, and lot numbers.

DISSOLUTION

During the 1970s, companies vying for new product approvals from FDA were required to conduct content uniformity tests on their products. The tests were to ensure that, on average, there was a specified amount of a specified agent per capsule; in other words, that there was content uniformity or a low variability from capsule to capsule. A related concern was to ensure that the specified amount of the specified agent in each capsule was *actually available* to the body, after ingestion, for the necessary action to take place (bioavailability). The only test for bioavailability, outside of clinical research, was dissolution.

Dissolution was controversial. The object of the test was to measure the bioavailability of a drug in a medium, usually water, and the purpose of the test was to simulate what happened in the human body upon ingestion of a drug. Dissolution measured the amount of active agent which dissolved in the medium after certain periods of time. The test was conducted by immersing a tablet or capsule in a basket in a container filled with a medium, then subjecting the medium to agitation by stirring. The medium was then tested to determine the amount of active agent it had absorbed.

Dissolution was a very sensitive test requiring tight controls. The difficulty with dissolution was the number of variables which could impact on the test results: the speed of the stirrer; external vibration; the room temperature; shape, size, and/or composition of either the container or the tablet; and even the air content in the water. Nevertheless, dissolution was a discriminating and valuable QC test to ensure uniformity of batches, even if it was less than reliable in regard to bioavailability.

TREMOBIN AND DISSOLUTION

By the late 1970s, dissolution was a recognized QC testing procedure. However, the FDA noted that there was extreme variability in both the equipment used for the tests, and the resultant measures of bioavailability. That observation prompted the FDA to set a QC dissolution testing standard for pharmaceuticals containing delonuprimide. The standard required 75 percent of the active ingredient to be dissolved in the medium after 45 minutes.

Dan Flanigan felt that the new standards were unattainable, and tested some retained samples of various lots of Tremobin. As expected, his results did not meet the new standards. Flanigan telephoned Los Angeles and spoke with Mel Salari, the director of quality control technology. Salari was highly respected, both in the pharmaceutical industry and in the field of QC testing, and Flanigan felt Salari could persuade the USP authorities to lower the new requirements.

Salari conducted some dissolution tests on Tremobin in his laboratory, using Toledo samples, all of which appeared to meet a standard of 75 percent dissolved in 120 minutes. Salari's reputation, combined with the fact that D-I and Toledo had been the only manufacturers of Tremobin for the last 20 years, convinced the regulators, and they agreed to modify the standard, which went into effect in November, 1983.

In the early stages of the dissolution testing for the 1984 batch of Tremobin, D-I found that it could not meet the 75 percent in 120 minutes standard. Flanigan contacted the QC group at Toledo, and confirmed that they were also unable to meet the new standard. However, when samples of both Sudbury and Toledo production were forwarded and tested in Salari's laboratory they were found to meet the dissolution requirements (75 percent in 120 minutes) and the issue was put on hold.

Flanigan considered the situation: neither D-I nor Toledo could meet USP standards; however, no part of the production process had changed, and only one batch per year was produced, as had been the case for almost 20 years. He had suspicions about the testing apparatus and procedures used by Salari, but was hesitant to pursue it. Therefore, Flanigan directed that the 1984 lot be released for sale, but that samples of the lot be placed in their routine stability program and be retested at scheduled intervals. A similar approach was taken by the Toledo facility. Stability testing was a study conducted over a period of time to demonstrate that a product would continue to meet its specifications up until its expiration date. For Tremobin, the results were to be monitored at intervals of 6, 12, 18, 24, 36 and 48 months.

The problem, in the short term at least, seemed to have been solved. However, in early 1985 Dan Flanigan read in a routine notice from corporate headquarters that Toledo was drastically reducing their expiry dating to 18 months from 60 months for Tremobin capsules. Flanigan was immediately concerned that this might indicate a problem with the active ingredient which both Toledo and Sudbury sourced from the same supplier. He contacted Toledo and found that non-conformance with the new USP standards for dissolution was at the heart of the matter: FDA inspectors had recently conducted a routine inspection of the Toledo facility and discovered a "stability problem" with Tremobin capsules. At time of manufacture in 1984, the lot had passing results—as measured in Salari's laboratory—but on stability the results were failing at the 18-month interval. These results were generated in Toledo's own laboratory and were consistent with all previous results on all lots of Tremobin. The FDA insisted that Toledo could no longer justify a dating of more than 18 months, hence the notice that Flanigan had read. The reduction in dating was unwelcome because it would increase the number of returns of outdated stock and would also likely lead to questions from regular dispensers of the product as to the reason for the change.

THE TREMOBIN DECISION

Flanigan again ordered dissolution testing on a sample of Tremobin held over from the 1984 batch, and, as before, test after test mirrored the results from Toledo. He was unable to match the Los Angeles results and therefore unable to meet USP standards.

As Dan Flanigan examined the most recent dissolution tests, he was certain that there was a problem with either the procedure or apparatus being used in Los Angeles. There was no other explanation for a result as high as they reported. And now Salari was retired, and the 1985 batch of Tremobin was scheduled to begin production. How to proceed?

EXHIBIT 1

Excerpts from "Good Manufacturing Practices For Drug Manufacturers and Importers"

C.02.013 (1) Every manufacturer and importer shall have on his premises a quality control department that is supervised by personnel described in section C.02.006.

     (2) The quality control department referred to in subsection (1) shall be a distinct organizational unit that functions and reports to management independently of any other functional unit, including the manufacturing, processing, packaging or sales unit.

RATIONALE

Although manufacturing and quality control personnel share a common goal of assuring that high quality drugs are produced, their interest may sometimes conflict in the short run as decisions are made that will affect a company's output. For this reason, an objective and accountable quality control process can be achieved most effectively by establishing an independent quality control department.

The rationale for the requirement that the quality control department be supervised by qualified personnel is outlined under Section C.02.006.

INTERPRETATION

1. A person responsible for making decisions concerning quality control requirements is on site at the manufacturer and importer.

2. The quality control department has true and effective access to equipment and facilities for inspecting and testing, having regard to the nature of the products produced.

C.02.014. (1) No lot or batch of drug shall be made available for sale unless the sale of that lot or batch is approved by the person in charge of the quality control department.

     (2) A drug that is returned to the manufacturer or importer thereof shall not be made available for further sale unless the sale of that drug is approved by the person in charge of the quality control department.

     (3) No lot or batch of raw material or of packaging material shall be used in the production of a drug, unless that material is approved for that use by the person in charge of the quality control department.

Exhibit 1 cont'd

Exhibit 1 cont'd

    (4) No lot or batch of a drug shall be reprocessed without the approval of the person in charge of the quality control department.

RATIONALE

The responsibility for the approval of all raw materials, packaging materials and finished products is vested in the quality control department. It is very important that adequate controls be exercised by this department in order to guarantee the quality of the end product.

To maintain this level of quality, it is also important to examine all returned drugs and to give special attention to reprocessed drugs.

INTERPRETATION

1. All decisions made by the quality control department pursuant to Regulation C.02.014 are attested to by the signature of the head of the quality control department or an authorized alternate and dated.

2. Raw materials, packaging materials, drugs in dosage form and returned drugs are effectively quarantined until released by the quality control department.

3. The reprocessing of any lot or batch of drug is approved by the quality control department. Attention is given to the stability of the reprocessed drug.

C.02.015. (1) All production and transportation methods and procedures that may affect the quality of a drug shall be examined and concurred with by the person in charge of the quality control department prior to their implementation.

    (2) The person in charge of the control department shall cause to be investigated every complaint on quality that is received and cause corrective action to be taken where necessary.

    (3) The person in charge of the quality control department shall cause all tests or examinations required pursuant to this Division to be performed by a competent laboratory.

RATIONALE

Production procedures should be examined independently by the quality control department. Matters such as dosage, chemical and physical compatibility should be assessed.

Suitable systems should be provided to investigate every complaint on quality that is received. Useful information can often be obtained from these investigations. Problems of physical, chemical or biological nature are often identified when complaints are evaluated by competent personnel.

Exhibit 1 cont'd

<u>Exhibit 1 cont'd</u>

This Regulation requires that for all raw materials, packaging materials and finished products, tests be carried out by a competent laboratory thus providing an assurance that test results are genuine and accurate.

INTERPRETATION

1. All decisions made by the quality control department pursuant to Regulation C.02.015 are attested to by the signature of the head of the quality control department or an authorized alternate and dated.

2. The tests are performed by a competent laboratory:
    i)   laboratory facilities are designed, equipped and maintained to suit the testing and approval (or rejection) of raw materials, packaging materials and drugs;
    ii) the individual in charge of the laboratory is an experienced university graduate holding a degree in a science related to the work being carried out and has some practical experience in his responsibility area or reports to a person having these qualifications (see Regulation C.02.006 INTERPRETATION 1);
    iii) laboratory staff are sufficient in number and are qualified to carry out the work they undertake;
    iv) equipment is serviced and calibrated (when appropriate) at suitable intervals and records are kept;
    v)   suitable arrangements are made for protecting sensitive apparatus (e.g. against humidity, temperature, vibration).

EXHIBIT 2

Organizational Chart

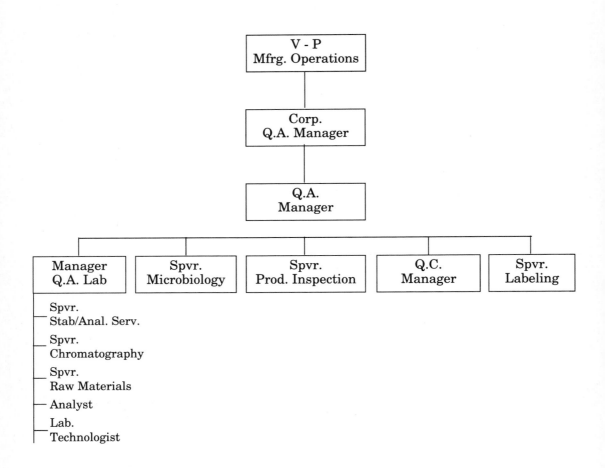

EXHIBIT 3

Quality Assurance Costs

	Amount	% of Total Quality Costs	% of Cost of Goods Made
	(000's)		
Prevention costs[1]			
Salaries	$ 770.0		
Expenses	8.0		
TOTAL	$ 778.0	22.9	1.8
Appraisal costs			
Salaries	$ 893.8		
Expenses	5.0		
Allocated Prd'n Q.C. (@ 40% excluding TBL)	834.1		
TOTAL	$1732.9	51.2	4.1
Failure costs			
Disc./Obsolete/Expired	$ 398.0		
Rework (Mfg (Pkg	11.3		
Q.A. Rejection	435.4		
Damaged or lost	30.7		
Product Recall	0		
TOTAL	$ 875.4	25.8	2.0
TOTAL QUALITY COSTS	$3386.3		7.9
COST OF GOODS MADE	$42710.8		

1 Quality control costs are contained within prevention costs.

EXHIBIT 4

Business Principles

CUSTOMERS
- Provide high quality products to our customers.
- Act ethically in all our business dealings.
- Identify and respond to customers' needs and market trends efficiently and effectively.

EMPLOYEES
- Recognize and reward employees for their achievement of objectives.
- Encourage creativity and prudent risk-taking to come up with new solutions.
- Provide training opportunities for employees to develop their skills and abilities.
- Encourage an open and participatory work environment.
- Provide high quality service to the internal client.
- Demonstrate respect for the contribution of all types of company employees, functions and units.
- Develop the future leaders of the company from within.

SHAREHOLDERS
- Improve the productivity of our physical assets, e.g. plants, equipment, material.
- Ensure that R&D provides new products to support our business strategies.
- Meet profit and sales growth objectives.
- Capitalize on synergies and shared know-how across company businesses and around the world.
- Provide an attractive rate of return to our shareholders.
- Market and sell our products aggressively.
- Develop and implement effective business plans.
- Create a lean organization through maximizing the utilization of our work force.

SUPPLIERS
- Foster fair and equitable relationships with our suppliers.

SOCIETY
- Initiate and support activities that improve the well-being of the communities in which we operate worldwide.

17 The Zeebrugge Car Ferry Disaster (A)

It is with profound sadness that I must introduce this report with the tragic loss of the *Herald of Free Enterprise* off the Belgian coast. The *Herald* is a Townsend Thoresen ship and, as you know, Townsend Thoresen became part of P&O in January. At the time of writing the precise cause of the disaster is unknown. We have instituted an immediate investigation and of course both the British and Belgian governments are conducting enquiries. Whatever the outcome of these you may be assured that the safety of our ships and those who man them and travel in them is our overriding priority.

So began the sombre letter by Chairman Jeffrey Sterling introducing the 1986 P&O Annual Report. The roll-on/roll-off passenger car ferry *Herald of Free Enterprise* capsized in the approaches to the Belgian port of Zeebrugge en route to Dover in England at 7.05 p.m. local time on the 6th March 1987. There was a light easterly breeze and the sea was calm. The ship had a crew of 80, and carried 459 passengers, 81 cars, 3 buses and 47 trucks. She capsized in about 90 seconds soon after leaving the harbour, ending up on her side half-submerged in shallow water. Only a fortuitous turn to starboard in her last moments prevented her from sinking completely in deeper water.

Following the capsize a heroic search and rescue operation was mounted. At least 150 passengers and 38 members of the crew lost their lives, most inside the ship from hypothermia in the frigid water. Many others were injured. It soon became apparent to the rescuers that the *Herald of Free Enterprise* had left the port of Zeebrugge with her bow doors open. The death toll was the worst for a British vessel in peacetime since the loss of the *Titanic* in 1912.

THE CROSS-CHANNEL TRANSPORT MARKET

The English Channel between England and the Continent of Europe is one of the most heavily travelled waterways in the world. In 1985 a total of 20,056,000 passengers and 3,387,200 cars, buses, trucks and unaccompanied trailers were ferried across the Channel. The most popular crossing is the shortest one, between Dover and Calais in France, a 22 mile trip that takes 90 minutes. Exhibit 1 shows selected data on sea and air travel to and from the United Kingdom.

Fares for cross-channel travel had historically been high in comparison to other intensive ferry routes in the world, and drew criticism from British consumer groups. In the 1980's, however, prices began to decline, as shown in Exhibit 2.

The mixture of demand for channel ferry services was changing. Passenger travel had remained stable since 1982, but freight traffic was increasing. Part of this increase was due to increased trade (particularly since Britain became a member of the European Economic Community), and part was due to the technological advance represented by the introduction of roll-on/roll-off (ro-ro) ships. These ships, essentially flat pontoons covered by a superstructure, have bow and stern doors which enable vehicles to be driven on and off via adjustable ramps at the dock. The speed of ferry loading and unloading is vastly improved for a ro-ro ship, which reduces the unproductive time a ship spends in port.

For the freight shipper, ro-ro ferries also improve productivity. A tractor-trailer (or just the trailer unit) can be driven straight on and off the ferry's deck as if it were part of the road to the freight's destination. Costly intermediate transfers of cargo are eliminated, and the quantity of inventory in the distribution pipeline is reduced by speedier transportation. Exhibits 3 and 4 show data on cross-channel ro-ro freight growth.

Competition on cross-channel ferry services was influenced by the British Government's July 1984 privatization of Sealink UK Ltd., previously a subsidiary of government-owned British Rail. At that time Sealink UK, its European state-owned counterparts, and Townsend Thoresen dominated the industry. Historically, channel ferry services had functioned mainly as the sea link between rail terminus points at channel ports.

Other recent developments in the industry had included the introduction of high capacity mixed freight and passenger "jumbo" ferries; reductions in crew levels, despite the strong opposition of the maritime unions; the modernization of dock-side facilities to help speed ferry turn-round time; the introduction of special freight-only ro-ro ferries; and the promotion of a wider range of fares, especially for day trippers and off-peak travel.

The Channel Tunnel poses an extreme threat to the ferry industry. After 100 years of aborted attempts to initiate a tunnel project, the French and British governments finally allowed the project to go ahead in 1986. This was bitterly opposed by the ferry operators. Eurotunnel, the Anglo-French company that will finance and manage the tunnel, plans to have the 30 mile long dual railway tunnels underneath the Channel in operation by 1993. Eurotunnel's finances of [£]1 billion in share capital and [£]5 billion in loan facilities compare with planned spending on the project of [£]4.9 billion.

TOWNSEND THORESEN

The following description is from the 1985 Annual Report:

> European Ferries Group plc[1] is a UK public company, with three separate classes of shares listed on the London Stock Exchange, giving a current market capitalization approaching £500 million.
>
> The origins of the Group can be traced back nearly 60 years to the time when Captain Stuart Townsend pioneered the first specialist car ferry service between Dover and Calais. Through a mixture of skilful management and acquisition the Group's Shipping Division, under the marketing name Townsend Thoresen, is now the major ferry operator in Europe, with services from Dover, Portsmouth, Felixstowe and Cairnryan to destinations in France, Belgium, Holland and Northern Ireland.
>
> In the 1970's the Group began diversifying, initially into Harbour Operations with the acquisition of Larne Harbour in Northern Ireland and the Felixstowe Dock & Railway Company, and then by the formation of a UK Property Division. The major asset within this UK Property Division is a 34.7% holding in Stockley plc, a listed property company operating in London and the south-east of England.
>
> The Group became involved in US property (real estate) in 1979, and this particular area has seen significant expansion in the intervening period, such that the Group now has an interest, both directly and through joint ventures, in substantial holdings of land in Denver, Atlanta and Houston. The 1980s have seen further property acquisitions at La Manga Club in Spain, and, in a smaller way, in Germany.
>
> Significant development projects have been in progress since the beginning of 1985 in our shipping and harbour divisions. Six vessels are being substantially extended ("jumboisation") and two new vessels have been ordered for delivery next year. We are also developing a major new terminal, the Trinity Container Terminal, at the Port of Felistowe which will be completed later this year.

Exhibit 5 lists the Directors of European Ferries Group plc, and the managers of Townsend Thoresen, as detailed in the 1985 Report. Background financial data is given in Exhibits 6 and 7.

In 1982 the Townsend Thoresen ferry *European Gateway* capsized with the loss of 6 lives after a collision with a

---

1 plc is an abbreviation of public limited company

Sealink ship in the approaches to the port of Harwich. The speed of the capsize drew speculation on the lack of stability of ro-ro ferries when water enters the main vehicle deck[2]. Like the *Herald* after her, the *European Gateway* came to rest on her side half-submerged in shallow water, narrowly avoiding a deep water sinking with heavy loss of life.

In January 1984 European Ferries purchased from The Peninsular and Oriental Steam Navigation Company (P&O) its loss-making Normandy Ferries subsidiary for £12.5m. In January 1986 P&O acquired a 50% interest in a firm that held shares equivalent to 16.1% of the voting share capital of European Ferries. Sir Jeffrey Sterling, the Chairman of P&O, was invited to join the Board on 21st January 1986.

On 4th December 1986 the Boards of European Ferries and P&O jointly announced a recommended £340 million takeover offer for the shares of European Ferries by P&O. Geoffrey Parker, Executive Chairman of European Ferries, gave reasons for his firm's recent poor performance in a letter to shareholders:

> In the early part of the year our property activities in Houston were affected by the severe fall in the price of oil, upon which the economy of Houston is critically dependent. In the late spring our shipping activities were seriously affected by strike action which was not resolved for 10 weeks. Your Board estimates that the strikes will be responsible for some £10m in lost profits in 1986....and that our US activities will now make a negative contribution compared with profits before taxation of £17m in 1985.

The majority of European Ferries shareholders accepted the P&O offer by the deadline of 3.00 p.m. January 16th 1987. Exhibit 8 outlines P&O's recent business history.

THE CAPSIZE OF *MV HERALD OF FREE ENTERPRISE*

The *mv Herald of Free Enterprise*[3], like her sister ships *Pride of Free Enterprise* and *Spirit of Free Enterprise*, was a modern ro-ro passenger/vehicle ferry designed for use on the high volume short Dover-Calais ferry route. She could accelerate rapidly to her service speed of 22 knots. She was certificated to carry a maximum total of 1400 persons.

At 433 feet long and 7,950 gross tons, the *Herald* was of record size at her launching in 1980 and was one of the prides of the 22 ship Townsend Thoresen fleet. She had two main vehicle decks, and at Dover and Calais double-deck ramps connected to the ferry, allowing simultaneous vehicle access to both

---

2 According to Lloyd's Register in London, over 30 accidents to ro-ro ferries had involved loss of life. The worst previous British accident was in 1953, when the *Princess Victoria* sank in the Irish Sea killing 134. The world's worst disaster was in 1981, when 431 died on an Indonesian ferry which caught fire and sank in the Java Sea. In roughly two-thirds of the cases, the capsize took less than 5 minutes.

3 *mv* is an abbreviation of motor vessel

decks. At Zeebrugge there was only a single level access ramp which did not allow simultaneous deck loading, and thus ferry turn-around time was longer at this port. Also, this ramp could not quite reach the upper vehicle deck, and water ballast was pumped into tanks in the bow of the *Herald* to facilitate loading.

When the *Herald* left Zeebrugge on 6th March 1987 not all the water had been pumped out of the bow ballast tanks, causing her to be some three feet down at the bow. Mr. Stanley, the assistant bosun, was responsible for closing the bow doors. He had opened the doors on arrival at Zeebrugge, and then supervised some maintenance and cleaning activities. He was released from this work by Mr. Ayling, the bosun[4], and went to his cabin. He fell asleep and was not awakened by the "harbour stations" public address call alerting crew to take their assigned positions for departure from the dock.

The bosun left the car deck at the "harbour stations" call to go to his assigned station. He later said, "it has never been part of my duties to close the doors or make sure that anyone is there to close the doors." The Chief Officer, Mr. Leslie Sabel, stated that he remained on the car deck until he saw— or thought he saw—Mr. Stanley threading his way through the parked cars towards the door control panel. He then went to the bridge, his assigned position.

The *Herald* backed out of the berth stern first. By the time the *Herald* had swung around the bow was in darkness and the open bow doors were not obvious to the ship's Master, Captain David Lewry. As the ship increased speed, a bow wave began to build up under her prow. At 15 knots, with the bow down 2-3 feet lower than normal, water began to break over the main car deck through the open doors at the rate of 200 tons per minute.

In common with other ro-ro vessels, the *Herald's* main vehicle deck had no subdividing bulkheads. If water entered the deck it could flow from end to end or from side to side with ease. The flood of water through the bow doors quickly caused the vessel to become unstable. The *Herald* listed 30° to port almost instantaneously. Large quantities of water continued to pour in and fill the port wing of the vehicle deck, eventually causing a capsize to port. The *Herald* settled on the sea bed at slightly more than 90°, with the starboard half of her hull above water.

Under the 1894 Merchant Shipping Act, a Court of Formal Investigation of the capsize of the *Herald of Free Enterprise* was held in London between 27th April and 12th June 1987 before the Wreck Commissioner, the Hon. Mr. Justice Sheen, a respected judge. The proceedings of the Court were subject to intense public scrutiny, with the tabloid press in particular concentrating on the more sensational aspects of the tragedy.

To encourage full disclosure at this Court of Investigation, the UK Department of Transport, which is responsible for enforcement of the various shipping acts, indicated that it did not intend to prosecute anyone responsible for the fact that the *Herald* went to sea with her

---

4 The bosun (a variant spelling of the word boatswain) is responsible for ship maintenance. The rank is equivalent to sergeant; assistant bosun is equivalent to corporal.

bow doors open. This was a common practice for such courts of enquiry. The Court had investigative powers, the power to suspend or remove a Merchant Officer's Certificate of Competency and the power to determine who should contribute to payment of the Investigation's costs. The Court had no other powers.

EXTRACTS FROM THE REPORT OF THE COURT OF FORMAL INVESTIGATION

mv Herald Free Enterprise

The remainder of this case study consists of verbatim extracts from the Report of the Court of Formal Investigation written by the Hon. Mr. Justice Sheen, and released on July 25th 1987. Statements of opinion and interpretation of facts are his, and not the case-writer's. [Any comments or elaborations by the case-writer are shown in square brackets.]

The Manning of the *Herald* on the Zeebrugge Route

On the Dover-Calais run these ships are manned by a complement of a Master, two Chief Officers and a Second Officer. The officers are required to work 12 hours on and not less than 24 hours off. In contrast, each crew was on board for 24 hours and then had 48 hours ashore. . . The sea passage to Zeebrugge takes 4.5 hours. . . .which gives the officers more time to relax. For this reason the Company employed a Master and two deck officers [instead of three] on this run. . . .

Captain Kirby was one of five masters who took it in turn to command the

Herald. He was the Senior Master. . .a co-ordinator between all the masters and officers in order to ensure uniformity in the practices operated by different crews. As three different crews served with five different sets of officers, it was essential that there should be uniformity of practice. Furthermore there were frequent changes among the officers. Captain Kirby drew attention to this in an internal memo dated 22nd November 1986 addressed to Mr. M. Ridley, Chief Superintendent.

The existing system of Deck Officer manning. . .is unsatisfactory. When *Herald* took up the Zeebrugge service our Deck Officers were reduced from 15 to 10. The surplus 5 were distributed around the fleet. On *Herald*'s return to the Calais service, instead of our officers returning, we were and are being manned by officers from whatever ship is at refit. Due to this system, together with Trainee Master moves, *Herald* will have had a total of 30 different deck officers on the books during the period 29th September 1986 to 5th January 1987. . .

Captain Kirby returned to this theme with a further memorandum dated 28th January 1987 which was also addressed to Mr. Ridley:

I wish to stress again that *Herald* badly needs a *permanent* complement of good deck officers. Our problem was outlined in my memo of 22nd November. Since then the throughput of officers has increased even further, partly because of sickness. During the period from 1st September to 28th January 1987 a total of 36 deck officers have been attached to the ship. We have also lost two masters and gained one. To make matters worse the vessel has had an unprecedented seven changes in sailing schedule. The result has been a serious loss of continuity. Shipboard maintenance, safety gear checks, crew training and the overall smooth running of the vessel have all suffered....

Pressure to Leave the Berth

Why could not the loading officer remain on deck until the doors were closed before going to his harbour station on the bridge? The operation could be completed in three minutes. But the officers always felt under pressure to leave after loading. . . .

The "Bridge and Navigation Procedures" guide which was issued by the Company included the following:-

Departure from Port

a) O.O.W./Master should be on the Bridge approximately 15 minutes before the ship's sailing time. . . .

That order does not make it clear whether it was the duty of the O.O.W.[5] or the Master to be on the bridge 15 minutes before sailing, or whether the officer was to remain on the bridge thereafter.) If the O.O.W. was the loading officer,

this order created a conflict in his duties. The conflict was brought to the attention of Mr. Develin[6] by a memorandum dated 21st August 1982 from Captain Hackett, Senior Master of *Free Enterprise VIII* in which he said:

It is impractical for the O.O.W. (either the chief or the Second Officer) to be on the Bridge 15 minutes before sailing time. Both are fully committed to loading the ship. At sailing time, the Chief Officer stands by the bow or the stern door to see the ramp out and assure papers are on board etc. The Second Officer proceeds to his after mooring station to assure that the propellers are clear and report to the bridge.

The order illustrates the lack of thought given by management to the organization of officers' duties.) [On the Zeebrugge run there was a reduced number of officers, and the loading officer's task was more complex because of the single-level loading ramp.]

The sense of urgency to sail at the earliest possible moment was exemplified by an internal memorandum dated 18th August 1986 sent to assistant managers by Mr. D. Shipley, who was the operations manager at Zeebrugge:

. . . put pressure on the first officer if you don't think he is moving fast enough. . . .Let's put the record straight, sailing late out of Zeebrugge isn't on. It's 15 minutes early for us.

---

5 [O.O.W. stand for Officer of the Watch, who is one of the deck officers and not the Master.]
6 [Mr. Develin joined the Company in May 1975. In 1978 he became the Chief Marine Superintendent, and in 1986 he became a Director of the Company.]

Mr. A.P. Young sought to explain away that memorandum on the basis that the language was used merely for the purpose of what he called "motivation." But it was entirely in keeping with his own thoughts at the time. . . .The Court was left in no doubt that deck officers felt that there was no time to be wasted. The Company sought to say that the disaster could have been avoided if the Chief Officer had waited on deck another 3 minutes. That is true. But the Company took no proper steps to ensure that the Chief Officer remained on deck until the bow doors were closed.

The Negative Reporting System

The Company has issued a set of standing orders which include the following:-

01.09 Ready for Sea
Heads of Departments are to report to the Master immediately they are aware of any deficiency which is likely to cause their departments to be unready for sea in any respect at the due sailing time. In the absence of any such report the Master will assume, at the due sailing time, that the vessel is ready for sea in all respects.

(That order was unsatisfactory in many respects. . . .Masters came to rely upon the absence of any report at the time of sailing as satisfying them that their ship was ready for sea in all respects.) That was, of course, a very dangerous assumption.

On the 6th March, Captain Lewry saw the Chief Officer come to the Bridge. Captain Lewry did not ask him if the ship was all secure and the Chief Officer did not make any report. Captain Lewry was entitled to assume that the assistant bosun and the Chief Officer were qualified to perform their respective duties, but he should not have assumed they had done so. He should have insisted on a report to that effect.

In mitigation of Captain Lewry's failure to ensure that his ship was in all respects ready for sea a number of points were made on his behalf, of which the three principal ones were as follows:

1. Captain Lewry merely followed a system which was operated by all the masters of the *Herald* and approved by the Senior Master, Captain Kirby.

2. The Court was reminded that the orders entitled "Ship's standing orders" issued by the Company make no reference, as they should have done, to opening and closing the bow and stern doors.

3. Before this disaster there had been no less than five occasions when one of the Company's ships had proceeded to sea with bow or stern doors open. Some of these incidents were known to management, who had not drawn them to the attention of other Masters. . . .

The system. . .was defective. The fact that other Masters operated the same defective system does not relieve Captain Lewry of his personal responsibility for taking his ship to sea in an unsafe condition. In so doing he was seriously negligent in the discharge of his duties. That negligence was one of the causes contributing to the disaster. The Court is aware of the mental and emotional burden resulting from this disaster which has been and will be borne by Captain Lewry, but the Court would be failing in its duty if it did not suspend his Certificate of Competency.

The Management of Townsend Thoresen

A full investigation into the circumstances of the disaster leads inexorably to the conclusion that the underlying or cardinal faults lay higher up in the Company. The Board of Directors did not appreciate their responsibility for the safe management of their ships. They did not apply their minds to the question: What orders should be given for the safety of our ships?

The directors did not have any proper comprehension of what their duties were. There appears to have been a lack of thought about the way in which the *Herald* ought to have been organized for the Dover-Zeebrugge run. All concerned in management, from the members of the Board of Directors down to the junior superintendents, were guilty of fault in that all must be regarded as sharing responsibility for the failure of management. From top to bottom the body corporate was infected with the disease of sloppiness. . . . .It is only necessary to quote one example of how the standard of management fell short. . . . .It reveals a staggering complacency.

On 18th March 1986 there was a meeting of Senior Masters with management, at which Mr. Develin was in the Chair. One of the topics raised for discussion concerned the recognition of the Chief Officer as Head of Department and the roles of the Maintenance Master and Chief Officer. Mr. Develin said, although he was still considering writing definitions of these different roles, he felt "it was more preferable not to define the roles but to allow them to evolve." That attitude was described by Mr. Owen[7], with justification, as an abject abdication of responsibility. It demonstrates an inability or unwillingness to give clear orders. *Clear instructions are the foundation of a safe system of operation* [original emphasis].

It was the failure to give clear instructions about the duties of the Officers on the Zeebrugge run which contributed so greatly to the cause of this disaster. Mr. Clarke, [counsel] on behalf of the Company, said that it was not the responsibility of Mr. Develin to see that Company orders were properly drafted. In answer to the question, "Who was responsible?" Mr. Clarke said "Well in truth, nobody, though there ought to have been." The Board of Directors must accept a heavy responsibility for their lamentable lack of directions. Individually and collectively they lacked a sense of responsibility. This left, what Mr. Owen so aptly described as, "a vacuum at the centre."

. . . Mr. Develin [Director and Chief Superintendent] was prepared to accept that he was responsible for the safe operation of the Company's ships. Another director, Mr. Ayers, told the Court that no director was solely responsible for safety. Mr. Develin thought that before he joined the Board, the safety of ships was a collective Board responsibility.

. . . as this Investigation progressed, it became clear that shore management took very little notice of what they were told by their Masters. The Masters met only intermittently. There was one period of two and half years during which

---

7 [Counsel for the National Union of Seamen, certain surviving crew, and the next-of-kin of deceased crew.]

there was no formal meeting between Management and Senior Masters. Latterly there was an improvement. But the real complaint, which appears to the Court to be fully justified, was that the "Marine Department" did not listen to the complaints or suggestions or wishes of their Masters.) The Court heard of four specific areas in which the voice of the Masters fell on deaf ears ashore [each detailed in separate sections below].

Carriage of Excess Numbers of Passengers

During the course of the evidence it became apparent from the documents that there were no less than seven different Masters, each of whom found that from time to time his ship was carrying substantially in excess of the permitted number [1400].

[The Report then details a series of memoranda between various Masters and Mr. A.P. Young, the Operations Manager, on the topic of excess passengers. These were exchanged in 1982, 1983 and 1984]....But the matter became really serious in 1986. The Court heard evidence from Captain de St. Croix, who was Master of the *Pride of Free Enterprise*. On the 1st August 1986 he sent a memorandum to Mr. Young....

Passenger Numbers on 15.00 D/C, 1.8.86

On the above sailing from Denver, the first passenger total given to the RO [radio operator] by the Purser was 1228. A call from the manifest office then informed the RO to add on another 214. The RO queried this as the total then had been

way over the top. After a short delay the manifest office came back with a figure of 1014 plus an add-on of 214 making a total of 1228.

As seeds of doubt had by then been sown in my mind I decided to have a head count as they went off at Calais. The following were revealed...[detail of count omitted]

Total passengers	1587
Crew	95
Total on board	1682

This total is way over the life saving capacity of the vessel. The fine on the Master for this offence is [£]50,000 and probably confiscation of certificate. May I please know what steps the company intend to take to protect my career from mistakes of this nature.

[The Report details 6 more memos sent to Mr. Young between August and October 1986 by various Masters complaining about overloading. In a memo sent on 31st October 1986, Mr. Develin attempted to arrange a meeting with Mr. Young to discuss the problem with a representative of the Senior Masters]. . . . Mr. Young did not invite Mr. Develin to meet him to discuss the subject. Mr. Young took the view that this was not a marine matter and deliberately excluded Mr. Develin from further investigation of the problem.

. . . . . *The Court reluctantly concluded that Mr. Young made no proper or sincere effort to solve the problem* [original emphasis]. The Court takes a most serious view of the fact that so many of the Company's ferries were carrying an excessive number of passengers on so many occasions. . . .

. . . .After it became apparent that this Court was greatly interested in the system for checking the number of passengers carried on each ship further thought was given to the matter by the Company. On 29th May 1987 Mr. Young produced a memorandum containing some ideas for improving the system of counting the number of passengers.

Door Status Warning Lights for the Bridge

On the 29th October 1983 the assistant bosun of the *Pride* neglected to close both the bow and the stern doors on sailing from No. 5 berth Dover. It appears he had fallen asleep. . . .On 28th June 1985 Captain Blowers of the *Pride* wrote a sensible memorandum to Mr. Develin:

> In the hope that there might be one or two ideas worthy of consideration I am forwarding some points that have been suggested on this ship and with reference to any future new-building programme. Many of the items are mentioned because of the excessive amounts of maintenance, time and money spent on them.
>
> 4. Mimic Panel - There is no indication on the bridge as to whether the most important watertight doors are closed or not. That is the bow and stern doors. With the very short distance between the berth and the open sea on both sides of the Channel this can be a problem if the operator

is delayed or having problems in closing the doors. Indicator lights on the very excellent mimic panel could enable the bridge team to monitor the situation in such circumstances.

Mr. Develin circulated that memorandum amongst managers for comment. It was a serious memorandum that merited serious thought and attention, and called for a serious reply. The answers which Mr. Develin received will be set out verbatim. From Mr. Alcindor, a deputy chief superintendent: "Do they need an indicator to tell them whether the deck store-keeper is awake and sober? My goodness!!" From Mr. Reynolds: "Nice but don't we already pay someone!" From Mr. Ellison: "Assume the guy who shuts the doors tells the bridge if there is a problem." From Mr. Hamilton: "Nice!" It is hardly necessary for the Court to comment that these replies display an absence of any proper sense of responsibility. Moreover the comment of Mr. Alcindor on the deck store-keeper was either ominously prescient or showed an awareness of this type of incident in the past.

If the sensible suggestion that indicator lights be installed had received, in 1985, the serious consideration which it deserved, it is at least possible that they would have been fitted in the early months of 1986 and this disaster might well have been prevented [original emphasis]. [The Report details further requests for indicator lights made by two Masters in 1986, and also records their written rejection by Mr. King:-]

> I cannot see the purpose or the need for the stern door to be monitored on the bridge, as the

seaman in charge of closing the doors is standing by the control panel watching them close.

[The Report notes]. . .that within a matter of days after the disaster indicator lights were installed in the remaining Spirit class ships and other ships of the fleet.

Ascertaining Draughts

[Following the loss of the passenger ferry *European Gateway* in 1982, Townsend Thoresen instituted an investigation into passenger safety]. . . . As a result of that investigation, on the 10th February 1983, Captain Martin sent a report to Mr. Develin. That report was seen by Mr. Ayers. It begins with the words:

The company and ships' Masters could be considered negligent on the following points, particularly when some are the result of "commercial interests":

(a) the ship's draught[8] is not read before sailing, and the draught entered into the Official Log Book is completely erroneous;

(b) It is not standard practice to inform the Master of his passenger figure before sailing;

(c) The tonnage of cargo is not declared to the Master before sailing;

(d) Full speed is maintained in dense fog.

. . . .For the moment we are only concerned with the draught reading. Later in the report under the heading "recommendations" there is the statement "company to investigate installing draught recorders[9] on new tonnage." Mr. Ayers was asked if he did investigate. His answer was "somewhere in this period the answer was yes." In the light of later answers given by Mr. Ayers, that answer is not accepted by the Court.

. . . .Mr. Ayers may be a competent Naval Architect, but the Court formed the view that he did not carry out his managerial duties, whatever they may have been. Mr. Ayers was asked whether each director of Townsend Car Ferries was given a specific area of responsibility. His [verbatim] answer was "No; there were not written guide lines for any director." When he was asked how each director knew what his responsibilities were his [verbatim] answer was "it was more a question of duplication as a result of not knowing than missing gaps. We were a team who had grown together." The amorphous phrasing of that answer is typical of much of the evidence of Mr. Ayers. He appeared to be incapable of expressing his thoughts with clarity.

[Mr. Ayers had previously not answered another Master's request for the installation of draught recorders. The draught of the *Herald* turned out to be a

8 [The depth of a loaded vessel in the water, taken from the level of the water-line to the lowest point of the hull. Section 68(2) of the Merchant Shipping Act 1970 makes it a legal requirement for a master to know the draught of his ship and to enter this in the official log book each time the ship puts out to sea.]

9 [Such recorders enable anyone on the Bridge to determine how low in the water the ship is. Without such devices the draught markings can only be read from outside the ship.]

critical question. Research undertaken for the Court revealed that the *Pride* and the *Spirit* each weighed about 300 tons more than previously thought. The origin of most of this excess weight was a mystery. The *Herald* was probably 300 tons overweight also. Further loading miscalculations arose from the estimates of the tonnage of freight vehicles on the ship. No weigh scales were used, as the tonnage was calculated by using drivers' declarations of vehicle weights. Experiments revealed that these were frequently false. An average ferry-load of trucks was found to weigh 13% more than the sum of drivers' declarations]

Captain Lewry told the Court quite frankly that no attempt had been made to read the draughts of his ship on a regular basis or indeed at all in regular service. Fictitious figures were entered in the Official Log which took no account of the trimming water ballast. . . .

The difficulties faced by the Masters are exemplified by the attitude of Mr. Develin to a memorandum dated 24th October 1983 and sent to him by Captain Martin:

> For good order I feel I should acquaint you with some problems associated with one of the Spirit class ships operating to Zeebrugge using the single deck berths. . . .
>
> 4. At full speed, or even reduced speed, the bow wave. . . comes three quarters of the way up the bow door. . . .
>
> 6. Ship does not respond so well when trimmed so much by the head [i.e. with water ballast in the bow], and problems have been found when manoeuvring. . .
>
> 8. As you probably appreciate we never know how much cargo we are carrying, so that a situation could arise where not only are we overloaded by 400 tons but also trimmed by the head by 4.5 feet. I have not been able to work out how that would affect our damage stability.

Mr. Develin was asked what he thought of that memorandum. His answer was: "Initially I was not happy. When I studied it further, I decided that it was an operational difficulty report and Captain Martin was acquainting me of it." Later he said: "I think if he had been unhappy with the problem he would have come in and banged my desk." When Mr. Develin was asked what he thought about the information concerning the effect of full speed he said: "I believe he was exaggerating." In subsequent answers he made it clear that he thought every complaint was an exaggeration. In reply to a further question Mr. Develin said: "If he was concerned he would not have sailed. I do not believe there is anything wrong sailing with the vessel trimmed by the head."

The Need for a High Capacity Ballast Pump

On 28th February 1984 Mr. R.C. Crone, who was a Chief Engineer, sent a memorandum to Mr. Develin. . . .

> Ballasting Spirit Class Ships on Zeebrugge Service
>
> Normal ballasting requirements are for Nos. 1 and 14 tanks. . . to be filled for arrival at Zeebrugge and emptied on completion of loading. . . .Using one

pump the time to fill or empty the two tanks is 1 hr. 55 mins. With two pumps the time can be reduced to 1 hr. 30 mins. . . . Problems associated with the operation. . . . .

(a) Pumping time amounts to approximately half the normal passage time.

(b) Ship well down by the head for prolonged periods causing bad steerage and high fuel consumption.

(c) Continuous pressurising of tanks to overflow/vent level.

(d) Time consuming for staff.

(e) Bow doors subjected to stress not normally to be expected, certainly having its effect on door locking gear equipment.

(f) Dangerous complete blind operation that should not be carried out as normal service practice, i.e. no knowledge of tank capacity during operation, the tanks are pumped up until the overflow is noticed from the bridge, thereafter emptied until the pump amperage/pressure is noted to drop!

Purely as a consideration realising the expense compared with possible future double ramp berths. . .[he recommends fitting a high capacity ballast pump]

Mr. Develin. . .said that he did not agree with some of the contents. He appeared to think that the chief engineer was grossly exaggerating the problem. . . .Mr. Develin said that Mr. Crone came to his department on several occasions to press for the implementation of his recommendations but that after discussion he must have been satisfied. . . In due course an estimate was obtained for the installation of a pump at a cost of £25,000[10]. This cost was regarded by the Company as prohibitive.

The Court's Conclusion

The Court. . .finds. . .that the capsizing of the *Herald of Free Enterprise* was partly caused or contributed to by serious negligence in the discharge of their duties by Captain David Lewry (Master), Mr. Leslie Sabel (Chief Officer) and Mr. Mark Victor Stanley (assistant bosun), and partly caused or contributed to by the fault of Townsend Car Ferries (the Owners). The Court suspends the certificate of the said Captain David Lewry for a period of one year. . .[and] suspends the certificate of the said Mr. Leslie Sabel for a period of two years. [The Court had no power to sanction the assistant bosun, who was not a certificated officer. The final section of the Report addresses the issue of payment of costs of the enquiry. The last paragraph deals with Townsend Thoresen:]

There being no other way in which this Court can mark its feelings about the conduct of Townsend Car Ferries Limited other than by an order that they should pay a substantial part of the costs of this investigation, I have ordered them to pay the sum of £350,000. That seems to me to meet the justice of the case.

---

10 [Equivalent to $45,000 at an exchange rate of US$1.80=£1.00]

EXHIBIT 1

Selected U.K Air and Sea Travel Data, 1975-85
(by country of embarkation or disembarkation, arrivals plus departures)

	1975	1976	1977	1978	1979	1980	1981	1982	1983	1984	1985
BY SEA:											thousands
Note: Some traffic through these 3 countries is in transit to or from adjacent European countries											
Belgium	3,641	3,975	4,391	4,428	4,421	5,192	4,714	4,678	4,415	4,608	4,411
France	7,739	7,861	8,602	9,805	11,112	12,621	14,734	15,747	16,140	15,353	15,645
Holland	1,496	1,841	1,977	2,056	2,044	1,940	1,958	1,968	2,210	2,191	2,207
Totals	12,876	13,677	14,970	16,289	17,577	19,753	21,406	22,393	22,765	22,152	22,263
BY AIR:											thousands
Belgium	788	850	854	874	867	809	757	748	824	942	988
France	2,740	2,901	2,904	3,026	3,102	3,070	3,105	3,193	3,275	3,537	3,746
Holland	1,634	1,835	1,934	1,994	1,959	1,903	1,813	1,843	1,808	2,014	2,227
Sub-totals	5,162	5,586	5,692	5,894	5,928	5,782	5,675	5,784	5,907	6,493	6,961
FR of Germany	2,277	2,470	2,619	2,882	3,081	3,136	2,948	2,998	3,006	3,384	3,644
Switzerland	1,093	1,181	1,289	1,372	1,413	1,444	1,469	1,576	1,711	1,875	2,016
Italy	1,860	1,941	2,037	2,279	2,550	2,692	2,335	2,378	2,494	2,582	2,583
Greece	691	882	884	1,162	1,562	1,839	2,095	2,123	2,006	2,301	2,875
Portugal	309	296	399	474	591	701	849	963	1,068	1,248	1,547
Spain	5,298	4,667	4,617	5,553	5,654	5,592	6,332	7,624	8,293	9,543	7,751
All air	16,690	17,023	17,537	19,616	20,779	21,186	21,703	23,446	24,485	27,426	27,377

Source: U.K. Department of Transport Statistics Digest 1975-85

EXHIBIT 2

Ferry Routes at 1985 Prices for Short Sea Routes Across the Channel
(4.5 metre car, Ford Cortina, 2 adults plus 2 children, one-way.
£1.00=US$1.80)

	1975	1980	1985
Peak (most expensive single fare)	£78.21	£72.72	£81.00
Standard (cheapest published no discount single fare)	£69.83	£55.61	£38.00

Source: Flexilink

EXHIBIT 3

Roll-on/Roll-off Road Goods Vehicles to Mainland Europe, by Country of Disembarkation, 1975-85
(departures from U.K. only)

	1975	1976	1977	1978	1979	1980	1981	1982	1983	1984	1985 thousands
Powered vehicles:											
Belgium	75.1	72.7	103.9	110.3	123.0	122.1	119.6	136.3	146.1	163.7	163.3
France	94.4	107.8	128.7	131.1	150.6	140.4	152.9	168.0	187.3	215.8	230.6
Holland	31.7	32.4	32.9	31.9	39.8	36.8	41.3	41.5	40.3	40.8	48.0
Totals	201.2	212.9	265.5	273.3	313.4	299.3	313.8	345.8	373.7	420.3	441.9
Unaccompanied trailers:											thousands
Belgium	33.6	37.1	45.8	44.6	57.5	48.2	63.5	99.1	104.4	103.6	129.9
France	25.3	28.8	35.8	43.0	56.4	53.7	63.1	58.2	61.5	59.9	65.8
Holland	72.2	81.7	69.8	94.0	103.3	97.6	110.4	128.1	140.8	146.7	145.0
Totals	131.1	147.6	151.4	181.6	217.2	199.5	237.0	285.4	306.7	310.2	340.7
Grand totals	332.3	360.5	416.9	454.9	530.6	498.8	550.8	631.2	680.4	730.5	782.6

Source: U.K. Department of Transport Statistics Digest 1975-85

EXHIBIT 4

Port of Dover Ferry Traffic 1981-85
(arrivals and departures)

	1981	1982	1983	1984	1985
Passengers (millions)	12.46	13.82	13.95	13.86	13.78
% change from prior year	+12.96	+10.94	+0.94	-0.67	-0.56
Passenger vehicles (millions)	1.65	1.78	1.74	1.73	1.72
% change from prior year	+11.41	+7.42	-1.99	-0.69	-0.06
Freight vehicles (millions)	0.51	0.61	0.69	0.74	0.80
% change from prior year	+5.88	+19.48	+13.36	+14.73	+7.96

Source: Port of Dover Authority

EXHIBIT 5

European Ferries Group plc.
Directors as listed in 1985 Annual Report

Kenneth Siddle	Chairman and Group Managing Director (*Succeeded by Geoffrey Parker in July 1986*)
W. James Ayers	Group Technical Director
Rodger G. Braidwood	Group Finance Director, Director of Stockley plc., Controller of Group Property interests.
John J. Briggs	Managing Director of Townsend Thoresen's Dover operations, Group Freight Director.
John W. Dick	Chairman of E F International Inc, Director of Stockley plc.
Geoffrey J. Parker	Chairman and Managing Director of Harbour Operations Division, Managing Director of Townsend Thoresen's Felixstowe and Larne Operations.
John R. Parsons	Deputy Managing Director of Townsend Thoresen's Dover operations.
William B. Pauls	Vice Chairman and Chief Executive Officer of E F International Inc

Non Executive Directors:-

Roald P. Aukner
David J. Bradford
Knut Dybwad
Colin H. Fenn
Sir Jeffrey Sterling (Alternate - Bruce D. MacPhail)

Townsend Thoresen Management
As listed in European Ferries Group plc 1985 Annual Report

Dover	J. J. Briggs	- Managing
	J. R. Parsons	- Deputy Managing
	A. P. Young	- Operations

Exhibit 5 cont'd

Exhibit 5 cont'd

Portsmouth	D. S. Donhue	- Managing
	R. N. Kirton	- Operations
Felixstowe & Larne	G. J. Parker	- Managing
	S. Livingstone	- Operations
Technical Services	W. J. Ayers	
Tourist Marketing	B. H. Thompson	

EXHIBIT 6

European Ferries Group plc Five Year Financial Record

	1985	1984	1983	1982	1981
(£1.00=100p=US$1.80)	£m	£m	£m	£m	£m
Sales Revenue	403.5	309.4	322.9	292.9	277.7
Profits before taxation	48.4	44.4	45.0	30.4	26.8
Earnings per share	13.7p	14.9p	12.3p	10.5p	9.4p
Net dividend per ordinary share	4.75p	4.3p	3.8p	3.35p	3.1p
Dividend cover	2.9x	3.5x	3.2x	3.1x	3.0x
Year-End Share Price	139.5p	128.0p	88.5p	57.0p	74.0p
Year-End FT Industrials Index	1130.0	945.2	775.7	593.6	528.8
	£m	£m	£m	£m	£m
Capital expenditure	82.6	45.3	16.2	14.4	18.2
Depreciation	17.7	15.0	13.3	12.3	12.0
Tangible fixed assets	267.7	206.9	176.6	183.1	180.5
Investment in associates	118.5	73.4	79.2	62.1	30.2
Stocks	163.3	302.7	121.1	110.3	75.3
Borrowings net of cash and deposits	159.7	164.6	113.4	121.0	88.6
Shareholders funds at 31st Dec.	327.1	302.4	254.9	225.2	207.8

Source: European Ferries Group 1985 Annual Report

EXHIBIT 7

European Ferries Group plc: Division Sales and Profitability

| | Sales Revenue | | | | | Profit before taxation | | | | |
	1985	1984	1983	1982	1981	1985	1984	1983	1982	1981
	£m	£m	£m	£m	£m	£m	£m	£m	£m	£m
Shipping	280.1	236.4	226.7	207.7	183.0	19.0	17.5	16.6	12.8	1.9
Harbour Operations	46.3	42.1	38.4	34.4	29.4	10.9	9.6	9.5	8.5	6.2
UK Property	14.6	14.0	13.7	33.9	33.3	2.0	3.0	2.3	2.4	9.2
US Property	48.8	13.9	43.0	16.5	31.4	17.4	14.6	12.7	(0.9)	7.7
Spain Property	13.7	3.0	1.1	–	–	(0.5)	(4.3)	(3.4)	–	–

Table ignores some interest charges, other income, and exceptional items and excludes the small Banking Division, disposed of in April 1984.

Source: European Ferries Group Annual Reports

EXHIBIT 8
The Peninsular and Oriental Steam Navigation Company (P&O)

P&O was incorporated in England on 31st December 1840 in order to establish a shipping service between the United Kingdom and the Far East and to take over shipping services, established in August 1837, to Spain, Portugal and Mediterranean Ports.

Shipping routes were established throughout the Near and Far East and to Australasia and the business expanded both organically and by acquisition over the ensuing century. However, in the 1960's radical changes began to affect P&O's cargo and passenger shipping activities as a result of the introduction of cargo containerisation and the growth of intercontinental passenger air transport.

In view of the high level of capital expenditure which containerisation required, P&O and three other United Kingdom shipping companies formed OCL (Overseas Containers Limited) to take over their cargo liner trades as they were converted to container shipping. By the early 1970's P&O had phased out its scheduled passenger liner services to the Far East and Australasia, while during the same period the concept of ocean cruising was being developed as a leisure market.

As a result of the economic recession and the rapidly changing environment for both cargo and passenger shipping, P&O began to diversify its activities in the 1970's. This led to the acquisition of the house building and property construction group Bovis, with its banking subsidiary TCB Limited, and to the continued development of P&O's integrated road and sea through transport freight haulage operators, Ferrymasters Limited and Pandoro Limited, as well as the growth of its integrated subsidiary, P&O Australia, largely in materials handling, off-shore supply services and cold storage and distribution.

Investments were also made by P&O in this period in oil and gas related activities mainly in the US and in the North Sea, in ferry services (to Orkney and Shetland, Northern Ireland, and the Republic of Ireland, Sweden, Holland, Belgium and France), and in liquefied petroleum gas ("LPG") carriers and other bulk ships. The oil and gas related activities were subsequently sold. In January 1985 P&O sold its cross channel ferry activity and in May 1985 P&O sold a 50% interest in its LPG carriers operation.

In February, 1985 P&O merged with SGT, thereby bringing into the P&O Group the ownership and management of a substantial portfolio of offices, shops and commercial properties located largely in the UK (owned by Town and Country Properties) and in the USA.

In the financial year ended 31st December 1985, profits before tax of the P&O Group were £125.6 million on sales of £1,629.3 million. At 31st December 1985, stock-

Exhibit 8 cont'd

Exhibit 8 cont'd

holders' funds amounted to £746.8 million. In May 1986, P&O acquired that proportion of OCL that it did not previously own, and in June 1986, P&O acquired Stock Conversion, a UK property company.

Reasons for the Offer

The directors of P&O believe that there is a clear commercial logic for the acquisition of European Ferries by P&O, which will undoubtedly result in improved profit potential for both companies. European Ferries will bring to P&O a range of businesses, including Townsend Thoresen, the principal European car ferry operator, and the Port of Felixstowe, the UK's leading container port. P&O's management is familiar with these businesses, which are allied to those in which P&O is already engaged both in the UK and overseas. The combination of the two groups will be a further logical step in P&O's strategy of developing its existing businesses and will increase the scope for maximising returns to stockholders.

European Ferries' ferry services and port interests complement P&O's shipping interests and will increase P&O's participation in the continuing growth of trade within Europe. European Ferries will benefit from the addition of P&O's skills and resources in property management and development and P&O's size and financial strength will enable the problems currently being experienced in European Ferries' US property portfolio to be dealt with effectively over an appropriate timescale.

Source: Various circulars sent to shareholders by P&O

18 Women in Management at London Life (A)

In September 1981, a management task force was established to discuss the managerial development and promotion of women at London Life. Specifically, the task force was responsible for reviewing policies, procedures, and attitudes affecting the development of women into supervisory and management positions. They had just one month to recommend to the senior management operating committee what action, if any, London Life should take to address the current under-representation of females in management positions.

LONDON LIFE INSURANCE COMPANY

London Life was founded as an insurance company in 1874 to serve a small number of London clients and, by 1981, had the fourth largest assets of all Canadian insurance companies and was one of the largest mortgage lenders in Canada. The company served Canadians at all levels with life insurance, health coverage, pension and other financial products through more than 100 regional offices. Operating statistics are summarized in Exhibit 1. The company had a sales force of 2,089 employees—The largest insurance sales force in the country—supported by an administrative staff of 2,535. Approximately 1,000 of these administrative personnel worked at the head office in London, Ontario.

In 1977, Brascan Ltd, a Canadian holding company, acquired a significant stake in London Life. Earl Orser was brought in from Brascan and appointed as chief operating officer and subsequently as president and chief executive officer. His evaluation of the organization led him to restructure management and focus the company strategy on marketing and investments. No layoffs occurred during the restructuring, but the previously highly paternalistic company atmosphere was transformed to a performance orientation in which employees were expected to make a pro-

Copyright © 1988, The University of Western Ontario.

This case was written by Gavin Hood and Professor Jeffrey Gandz and was funded by a grant from the Change Agents Program of the Ontario Women's Directorate.

ductive contribution to the company's operations.

The new management philosophy was based on improving service, increasing employee productivity and reducing costs. In addition to structural reorganization, head office renovations, employing state-of-the-art office planning and new computer technology aimed at making the company's operations more efficient, were begun in 1981. It was clear at that time that the future organization would be flatter, with fewer levels of management, and that there would be a gradual reduction in total number of staff as more computer technology was introduced. (Exhibit 2 outlines the projected number of management openings at head office and in the sales divisions.)

WOMEN IN MANAGEMENT AT LONDON LIFE

When Earl Orser joined London Life he raised the issue of the relatively few women in management at a strategic planning meeting. In 1981, females held 14 of 595 management and senior technical positions at London Life despite the fact that 73 percent of the head office staff were female (Exhibit 3). At the next level below this (supervisory and specialist) females represented 47 percent.

In 1981, the Ontario Provincial Government was strongly urging employers to create equal working opportunities for women. There were various initiatives taken, including the establishment of the Ontario Women's Directorate and the creation of a ministerial portfolio responsible for women's issues, and active consideration was being given to various legislative initia-

tives including employment equity and pay equity in the public and private sectors.

At the time, many insurance companies—which were very large employers of women, primarily in administrative and clerical roles—were addressing the concerns of women. Of the "Big Eight" life insurers which dominated the industry, Prudential, Metropolitan, ManuLife, Mutual Life, and Sun Life all had women board members. While London Life had no women on its board, its female distribution and management representation were about average for the industry.

Orser's view was that London Life could be missing an opportunity to improve its performance because it was not developing the managerial potential of female employees, many of whom had extensive experience in the insurance industry and had a high level of commitment to London Life. This view was apparently shared by some other managers and executives in the company although not many considered the issue to be a high priority. He encouraged the human resources department to hire an experienced consultant, Fran Kennedy, and develop a strategy and action plan to address this issue.

In response to Orser's expressed concerns, the human resources department held a series of three meetings, in which a total of 30 women, representing positions ranging from clerical to management, discussed women's opportunities, the attitudes in the company toward promoting women into managerial positions, and women's level of aspirations. Two of the generalizations drawn from these sessions were: (a) women were not aware of the opportunities that existed in their departments or, for that matter, in other departments, and (b) women did not receive the necessary support from their spouses to pursue managerial opportunities) Most married women reported that they assumed sole responsibility for household management and were in no position to take on the longer and more irregular hours, and travel, required of management personnel. In fact it was quite difficult to assess the attitudinal environment because most women had simply never considered the possibility of moving into management.

Following these sessions, the Director of Human Resources recommended a program to encourage more career-oriented women inside and outside of London Life to become aware of, to get interested in, and to prepare themselves through effective career planning for managerial and higher specialist career opportunities throughout London Life. Excerpts from the memo are outlined below:

By learning to assess their personal/career needs realistically and to acknowledge their strengths and limitations, more women should gradually qualify and be appointed to managerial and higher specialist positions over the next three years.

Developing the potential of employees is good business. This program would affirm better utilization and efficiency of our human resources and payroll dollars as more women progress to higher responsibilities. Such equal career opportunities could attract more qualified, career-oriented women to the company

legitimately outside the current restraints of our present job posting program, whenever necessary. Both the morale and quality of work life should be enhanced. Lastly, such action should lessen the potential attractiveness of third party pressures/intervention, whether they be from government (federal, provincial, municipal) or unions.

We have very few women in higher level positions. This is a current and historical fact. With a few encouraging exceptions, the past five years have seen minimal senior appointments of women for finance, marketing (home office), investments, actuarial, group and administration, while many men have been promoted internally and appointed from outside. There are 5 women compared to 138 men in positions at or above manager level at home office today.

There is a need to take "affirmative action" to correct past career inequities to make sure every employee has the chance to reach his or her full potential, based on performance and personal responsibilities for one's own career growth.

We would like to see more women qualify and be selected for such future opportunities. Both Premier Davis and Labor Minister Elgie are also encouraging voluntary affirmative action programs for 1981. As we know, this movement is not a fad, but a major social force with growing impact on business.

Subsequent to the submission of the memo, 12 managers holding the following positions, were appointed to a task force to study the situation, assisted by the external consultant, Fran Kennedy:

> Human Resources Consultant
> Program Coordinator, Employee Relations
> Vice-President, Investments
> Director, Human Resources
> Manager, Group Regional Office Services
> Manager, Individual Product Design, Marketing
> Vice-President, Group Insurance
> Operations Improvement Consultant
> Manager, Underwriting Operations
> Manager, Group Underwriting
> Manager, Administrative Services

Their mandate was to recommend to the operating committee the particular steps that should be in a development program and to suggest changes to company policies which discriminated against women. The task force scope for making recommendations was unlimited.

HUMAN RESOURCE POLICIES AT LONDON LIFE

London Life had many policies and procedures which the task force realized had some impact on the progression and status of women within the company.

Salaries

Salaries were determined by market wages, job complexity, and individual performance. Benchmark internal salaries were compared annually with those at other local companies and large national employers by a management committee and the senior job evaluation staff. Internal job comparisons based on know-how, problem solving, accountability and working conditions, determined relative salary ranges. Immediate supervisors reviewed employee achievements and development to determine their salary within the defined range. Employees transferred for development received salaries corresponding to their performance and the salary range for the new job.

Maternity Leave

Eighteen weeks of maternity leave were available to women at London Life. During this maternity leave unemployment insurance covered 60 percent of salary up to a maximum of approximately $20,000 over 15 weeks. A woman's position was not posted unless she resigned before going on leave, declared that she was not returning from the leave, or did not return to work at the end of the leave.

Flexible Hours

With management's consent, employees could select start and stop times for their job within ranges which were deemed acceptable to the function of the departments in which they worked. In practice, people could elect a working day which was somewhere between the hours of 7.30 a.m. and 6.00 p.m.

Promotion

Promotion to supervisory and managerial positions depended on training and technical knowledge, attendance, ability to work with others, and self-development. Progress was reviewed annually by an employee's immediate supervisor. Positions up to first line supervision were posted at London Life. Management, senior technical positions, and task force opportunities were not posted and were filled by candidates nominated by their senior managers. The job posting system is outlined in Exhibit 4.

Personal Development

London Life offered nine different life insurance courses and reimbursed 100 percent of tuition and 50 percent of text book costs for external self-improvement courses. Funding for external courses was subject to approval by the human resources department and the employee's manager. It was extremely rare for individuals in non-managerial positions to request or take such courses.

Women at London Life

Before the introduction of job posting and an extensive compensation review in the early 1970s, female high school graduates were essentially hired to be clerks. Because there was no maternity leave policy before 1970, pregnant women had to leave the company and reapply for their old jobs if they wanted to return.

Diane Haas, a member of the task force established to look at this issue and one of the very few women who had risen to the middle management level in the company, gave other members of the task force with less experience at London Life a brief history of what it was like for women in the company in the fifties and sixties:

When I started working here, women earned approximately half of what the men earned and women's raises were typically one-third of what the men's were. So there was definitely pay discrimination in those days.

Women tended to be longer-term employees. They trained most of the males who were hired, in anticipation that within two years those same men, better or worse, would become their bosses. I remember challenging my boss about this in the mid-1960s and basically what he said to me was, "Hey lady, you're a second salary. He has to support a family. Tough luck!"

In the early 1970s, there were some major corporate changes made with regard to measurable things, pay equity, and job evaluation based on the job, not the incumbent, In 1973, London Life completely changed its salary positioning. We used to be one of the worst payers in the city. Now we are good, around the median. The interesting thing is that I wasn't aware of the changes taking place. There was no announcement, the changes were evolutionary rather than revolutionary. What hasn't changed are the soft factors. Most men don't recognize that there are talented women around who want to get ahead.

I believe that a lot of long-term female employees have said to themselves,"Hey, getting ahead here is a lost cause. I'm not going to fight the system, I'm going to come in, work my 9-5 and then go home." It was really uncomfortable to be one of the scrappers. You were fighting an uphill battle against discrimination. Most women didn't even think about promotion. It was just too frustrating.

The task force coordinator, a member of the employee relations department, added her own views:

There is a lot of subtle discrimination at London Life. Most male managers don't realize that they are preventing women from being promoted.

As entry level employees, men tend to promote the fact that they are career oriented. When they ask to take self-improvement courses, they get management approval, because the courses develop their ability to meet future responsibilities.

Women, on the other hand, are limiting their horizons to becoming supervisors. That's perceived as their ceiling, and we don't have many examples to contradict the perception. If women don't tell their manager that they aspire to a higher position, their requests for the same courses will be turned down, because the development isn't necessary for their current job. Therefore, men get the posted jobs, because they are better qualified.

The human resources manager on the task force pointed out that the recent hiring history and practices of the company made it difficult but not impossible to address the issue of moving more women into management:

From the early seventies to the eighties, all of our recruiting has been at entry level positions. We are hiring at the clerical level, not university graduates, male or female.

I would also agree that we aren't encouraging women to excel. There is very little cross-fertilization and we aren't encouraging women to take extra courses, to take a chance. I think that opportunities exist and women aren't taking advantage of them, but I also think that because they aren't considering themselves as potential candidates they aren't coming forward.

Diane Haas, who had spent most of her career in operations as a clerk, a senior clerk, a section supervisor and then a division supervisor, related her experience of some men's attitudes to her progression into management:

Men in this company, with some exceptions, don't think they have to be concerned about women as competition. There is the odd woman like myself starting to progress, but as much as anything my progress has been based on tenure and experience. In most men's minds, I am a credible person, not necessarily a female. Men accept that there will always be the odd female who will bubble up, but there's certainly no concern on their part about having to be as good as the women.

The new director of human resources really rattled my own cage about three years ago. He told me to get moving and start to chase opportunities that were there.

Three or four months after I moved to human resources I was promoted to a manager. The immediate talk was, "She got the job because she was a woman." Subsequently, I got a position as a more senior manager in marketing. There were 22 applicants for that job. The manager who selected me told me that he thought I was the best candidate but an awful lot of the other 21 people indicated to him that they felt he had made the decision based on the fact that I was a woman.

A senior manager of Property and Investments talked about his views on the promotion of women:

There are issues associated with promoting women that have nothing to do with competence.

To start with, I don't think that society has accepted the concept of role reversal. If a woman is not a single career person, there is a whole set of associated problems. Not very many married women will uproot their spouse from his career. The concept still is that the male partner's career should be fostered. This is a real problem, because

one of the conditions of contest in my organization is that you have to be mobile. I believe very strongly that the qualitative judgement needed to become an investments manager is only going to be achieved by working in three or four different marketplaces. The dynamics that influence value in each area, in each region of our country are very different. Without experiencing all of them, you are not a fully seasoned mortgage lender.

It's also my observation, without a lot of experience, that women don't focus on their career in the same way as men do. There is not the expectation in most women that they will work for 40 years. The path they are setting out at the age of 23 or 24 is not a 40-year path. It's until they get married, until they have children, until a lot of things happen. That's not a universal statement, because if a man or a woman were to approach something with a single-minded purpose, I think either one is going to achieve it. Not many men approach their career in that manner, but I think fewer women do, because they have these other uncertainties as to which direction they are going.

So it's my recent experience—and I guess it's not unique to me—that women have a harder time progressing even though they understand the conditions of contest for getting ahead. They are less willing to give up friends and a social environment outside of work. It's also a very rare exception where, when there is overtime to be done, the woman will stay and the husbands are home at four o'clock to pick up the children.

Another reality is that most women have gaps in their career. Women do get pregnant, and if a woman is going to have two or three children, the gaps in her career are more than an irritant. From a philosophical point of view, it's fine, but if you have a key person who disappears for five months every two to three years, it's going to be difficult to build around. We have become a lean organization and we don't have three or four layers of competent people who can fill the gap. We plan and make sure that we have someone to pick up the pieces, but the person who has to fill in is already fully employed, so it stresses the whole organization when you do it.

The biggest danger, I caution, is that you can't force increased female representation in management faster than natural growth will allow it to happen. I wouldn't like to see a United States quota program. If it was mandated that I had to hire a female manager from the outside, presumably I could, but I don't do that with men, because I believe very strongly in training our own managers for reasons of consistency of ideas and focus. Quality control is very important in investments. Loan

losses can be significant if you don't know what you are doing and it's an area where there is a wide divergence of thought. I don't think equal representation objectives for management should ever transcend the fundamental objectives of the business.

Diane Haas expressed her own concerns about quotas which specified the percentage of various levels of management which had to be filled by women:

I don't agree with the classic affirmative action program that says you must have 20 percent of women in management, for two reasons: first, from a corporate perspective, it's quite conceivable that you will get people who are not qualified in those positions because you are striving to achieve quotas; second, I think it's grossly unfair to put people in positions that they have trouble coping with. There are still days when I scare the living daylights out of myself doing what I'm doing, thinking, is this for real or am I a fake? So I can imagine what someone who is not qualified would feel in the job.

I'll be darned if I want to see women in management who are not good, who are not qualified and who cannot handle it. I think if that happens, the reflection of non-performance is on all the women in management, not just the ones who are failing. Right now, we are like giraffes in the forest. We are a very visible small minority and we are being watched. Therefore it's crucial that we do well. I don't want to see someone, a non-performer, promoted simply because of her sex.

At the same time, we have to get commitment from a predominantly male management to start encouraging women to develop.

THE TASK

As the meeting ended, the task force coordinator summed up the task:

We have only three or four meetings left to complete our recommendations, so we have to start developing our plan. Where should we start? What do we need to do to tackle this issue?

EXHIBIT 1

Operating Summary
($ Millions)

	1977	1978	1979	1980	1981
Premium Income					
Individual	284	286	299	332	396
Group	159	172	152	299	260
Total	443	458	451	631	656
Total Assets	2926	3223	3513	3860	4318
R.O.A. %	8.23	8.56	8.92	9.16	9.57
Net Income					
Total	n/a	29	35	53	46
Shareholder	n/a	10	12	23	23
R.O.E. %	n/a	9.6	11.1	18.6	16.2
Employees					
Sales	2112	2154	2071	2084	2089
Admin.	2480	2490	2478	2421	2535

EXHIBIT 2

Projected Management Openings
Head Office

	1983	1984	1985	1986	1987
Projected employee growth	22	12	10	4	4
Projected retirements	0	2	6	4	5
Projected terminations	0	0	0	0	0
Projected openings	22	14	16	8	9
GENERAL SALES DIVISION					
Projected employee growth	6	5	6	7	7
Projected retirements	4	4	3	4	4
Projected terminations	2	2	2	2	2
Projected openings	12	11	11	13	13
DISTRICT SALES DIVISION					
Projected employee growth	8	7	8	7	8
Projected retirements	9	9	10	10	11
Projected terminations	19	24	25	29	28
Projected openings	36	40	43	46	47
GROUP SALES DIVISION					
Projected employee growth	5	4	4	5	0
Projected retirements	1	1	1	0	0
Projected openings	6	5	5	5	0
Corporate projected openings	76	70	75	72	69

EXHIBIT 3

Female Management Representation by Division

	Male	Female
Total Corporate Management	98% (595)	02% (14)
Head Office Management	95% (231)	05% (11)
Individual Sales Division Management	99%	01% (2)
Group Sales Division Management	98%	02% (1)

EXHIBIT 4

Excerpts from the Job Posting Guidelines

ELIGIBILITY

All employees except for those employed on a temporary basis may apply for any post-ed position. You should, however, assure yourself that you have at least the minimum qualifications required for the position in which you are interested. The selection pro-cess gives consideration to education and experience, length of service, job perfor-mance, attendance and supervisor's comment on your recent performance appraisals as indicators of potential for advancement. Other factors could also play a key role, depending of course on the type of opening, e.g. ability to communicate verbally and/or in writing, diplomacy, telephone courtesy, ability to work with minimum supervision, etc.

POSTING PROCEDURES

Vacancies from the S02 position level up to and including division supervisor will nor-mally be posted. Positions posted remain open for at least three days while qualified applicants are considered. Since new postings are made regularly, it's a good idea to read the job postings daily on the bulletin board in your department or the staff lounge. The information posted includes job title, department, division, position level, a brief description of the job and any special qualifications, as well as the number of vacancies that exist. If a job appeals to you, you should post for it immediately.

Jobs on which no selection is made are normally posted a second time. The word REPOSTED will be printed on the second posting description. Only applicants who did not apply on the first posting are eligible to apply for the reposted position.

A record of all past job posting descriptions for each department is maintained in Employment Services for your perusal.

If you are interested in the regional office positions, contact Employment Services for further information.

WHAT TO DO NEXT

If you see a position that appears particularly well suited to you, pick up an applica-tion either in your department, the lounge or Employment Services. Fill it out and send it to Employment Services. You should feel free to talk with your supervisor or section head about your interest in the position. However, should you wish your post-ing application to be kept confidential, this will be done.

Exhibit 4 cont'd

Exhibit 4 cont'd

Attach a resume if available. This will be kept on file by Employment Services and included on future applications until such time as you wish to revise it.

When you post for the first time, a member of the Employment Services staff will contact you as soon as possible to discuss your work experience, qualifications and interests and try to answer any questions you may have. An interview with the supervisor in the department where the vacancy exists will then be arranged in Employment Services. At that time, the requirements of the position will be explained and other points discussed including an appropriate flexible hours schedule.

Should you take sick after the posting or be away because of any illness or maternity leave at the time a posting of interest arises, it is your responsibility to get in touch with Employment Services. Arrangements can then be made, if feasible, for an appropriate interview by the area involved either personally or by telephone.

If you should post on a job and know that you will be absent shortly thereafter, please bring your posting application directly to Employment Services. This will ensure that the appropriate interviews are conducted before you leave.

NOTIFICATION

After all candidates have been interviewed, you will be notified of the result of your application.

If you are successful, your transfer date will be determined after consultation with your present and prospective departments. The transfer should normally take place within two weeks from the day you are selected. If your application was not selected, you are free to consult your present supervisor and/or Employment Services concerning your career plans.

ADMINISTRATIVE GUIDELINES

If you are successful in receiving a new job posting, you would normally not be expected to apply again for a new position for at least six months.

Exceptions to the job posting principle will occur whenever:

1. personnel become available for transfer as a result of reorganization, reduction in the work load or the introduction of a systems change. In situations of this kind, the normal job posting policy may not apply, as those employees made available for transfer should receive first priority.

2. the reduction of a unit's staff complement occurs as the result of a resignation, posting, etc. and it is desirable to fill that vacancy from within the unit without restoring the complement to it's original strength.

3. the employee is following an approved career progression within the unit and the staff complement is not to be increased, e.g., progressing from a grade 1 to a grade 2 clerk.

Exhibit 4 cont'd

<u>Exhibit 4 cont'd</u>

4. when a position is re-evaluated, the person occupying it assumes the new level without the need for a posting.

5. a new job is created in the unit that can be filled by means of present staff, without requiring an increase in that unit's staff complement.

6. the employee's job has been phased out due to reorganization, redundancy or systems change and therefore no replacement is required.

7. temporary jobs, positions of a project nature and unique back-up training situations occur. The Company reserves the right to transfer or hire personnel throughout its operation without using the job posting system.

8. jobs require specialized qualifications and/or experience not available within the Company.

9. jobs are normally held in reserve for employees returning from maternity leave or extended illness.

19 Noram Foods

On August 20, 1982, Leo Marsden, plant manager for Noram Foods of Toronto, Ontario, was considering the impact of changing Noram's policy on package weight. He knew this was a matter of overall corporate concern. Before raising the possibility of a change in policy with the company's executive committee, he wished to have a clearer picture of the options available and the implications of any change in policy. He was particularly concerned about the capability of the plant to hold tolerances on weights.

NORAM FOODS

Noram Foods was a major producer of a variety of consumer food products, including baby foods, cereals, and assorted canned products. Noram Canada was part of Noram International which had plants in 12 different countries, with the head office in New York. Head office control was primarily financial, as part of Noram's success was based on giving its international units a large amount of local autonomy. Moreover, food tended to be subject to specific and different governmental legislation in each country in which Noram produced its products. Even though management had frequently been pressured to do custom packaging or produce "no-name" products, it had steadfastly refused to get involved in either. Management believed that exclusive concentration on the production of high-quality branded products was in the corporation's best interest.

Noram Foods in Canada had an enviable record of sound financial performance, although the 1981-1982 period had seen declining profits as the Canadian economy as a whole was suffering. In July, 1982, the president had called for special vigilance by all managers to look for opportunities to increase revenues or reduce costs. Leo Marsden believed the weight control issue represented a major opportunity for re-evaluation and increased performance.

Copyright © 1982, School of Business Administration, The University of Western Ontario.

This case was prepared by Professor M.R. Leenders and John Walsh, based on research by Professors Forsyth and Wood.

NORAM FOOD'S POLICY ON WEIGHT CONTROL

Leo Marsden's concern was with the company's current policy on weight control which stated that "at least 95 percent of all packaged net weights shipped will be above the stated net weight."

Leo believed this policy could result in too high a proportion of overweight packages at substantial cost to Noram. He had therefore requested a meeting with Noram's packaging engineer, Joe Turner, who was the recognized expert in the company on statistical quality control and filling and weighing equipment. In discussing the current policy with Joe, Leo said:

> I know that Noram has had this policy for about 20 years now and that during this period Noram has never been cited for putting out underweight products. A lot of things have happened over the past 20 years, however. For example, today's weighing technology is a heck of a lot better than what it used to be. We've also gone metric in the meantime and I think we could save a bundle if we took a more realistic look at our policy. The last time I brought this issue up at an executive meeting was about 10 years ago. At that time, the vice-president of marketing was completely opposed to any changes. I can still remember how upset he was. He said:
>
> > "The consequences of underweight product reaching the public could be disastrous for this company. We have a fantastic reputation to protect and I don't want to run any risk that we will lose something that took decades to build and on which we have spent tens of millions of advertising and promotion dollars. If you're proposing that we start playing statistical games with the government and the consumer, I don't want any part of it."

Leo continued:

> Nevertheless, especially in today's economic climate, we would be remiss if we didn't at least look at any major opportunity at cost reduction. Before I propose anything to the executive committee, however, I want to be sure I'm on safe ground. I want to be absolutely sure, for example, that I do not propose anything we're not capable of doing in this plant.

Joe Turner replied:

> Leo, I think I know what you're saying but it is more than just a matter of statistics and technology in filling and weighing. From time to time, I've had discussions with our marketing guys about this whole area. They keep insisting that if we ever get caught with underweight packages, it will be seen by consumers as just as serious as a citation for unsanitary conditions. It is a topic where a lot of corporate psychology is involved. We see ourselves as real corporate winners in the food field. Our current policies on sanita-

tion, weight control, package design, and a host of other areas all reflect that winning attitude. In that kind of an environment, how much of a risk should this company take? Also, as you can well appreciate, our wide product diversity makes it difficult to apply the same weight policy to everything we do. Even now, on some products, we have substantially less than 5 percent of our packages underweight, just to make sure we run no chance of running below the government permitted tolerances.

Both Joe and Leo agreed that raising the issue of weight control without getting down to specifics was going to be meaningless. They therefore agreed to concentrate on a specific product line, pre-cooked baby cereals, to see what options might be available and what impact any change in policy might possibly have. Leo and Joe decided they would go and have a good look at the pre-cooked baby cereal package line.

FILLING OPERATIONS

Noram used a variety of filling equipment in its plant. Almost all of the larger-volume product lines were produced on sophisticated, modern, high-speed filling equipment of recent vintage. An interesting design trade-off on filling equipment involved speed of fill versus tolerance-holding ability on weight or volume. Obviously, a greater filling speed resulted in a higher capacity of the equipment and a lower labor cost per unit produced. On the other hand, a

lower filling speed afforded better weight and volume control, resulting in a package weight and volume closer to specifications. Overweight packages resulted in higher material costs for Noram; underweight packages might result in adverse consumer reactions or government citation.

For pre-cooked baby cereals, the filling operation was performed on a double line consisting of nine pieces of equipment (see Exhibit 1). The parallel lines were designed to optimize staffing, since one operator could attend to two pieces of equipment at the same time. The first unit in each line, a bottom maker, formed the pre-made carton and sealed the carton bottom. The sacker, second in line, formed the wax-paper liner and inserted it into the carton, completing the package. From the sacker, the carton was moved to the Wair filler, which measured out by weight the cereal content and inserted it into the waiting carton. From the filler, the carton was moved to the top sealer for final closure and then to the packer. The crew consisted of five operators.

THE WAIR FILLER OPERATION

The net weight filler consisted of four separately-operated filler heads fed from a food bin located on the floor above the filler room. The capacity of the Wair filler was about 100 cartons of 454 gram pre-cooked baby cereal per minute. This amounted to a filling speed of about 25 cartons per filling head per minute.

The Wair filler operator was primarily concerned with package weight control. This job consisted of taking full cartons from each head (four cartons from one of the four heads every 10 minutes), pouring their contents into a plastic container, and check-weighing the pre-cooked cereal to determine the actual net weight. The operator recorded the weight for each head on a control chart (X and R chart) and noted its position between the control limits. If the point fell outside of the specified limits, the operator adjusted the questionable filler head. If the filler head continued out of control after the adjustment, the operator summoned the operator in charge of the line who decided on further action. Typically, the machine was allowed to continue if the condition was one of overweight. However, an underweight situation was cause for the discontinuation of the operation.

Joe Turner and Leo Marsden observed the filling operation on August 20, 1982, and noted that everything was running smoothly and the line seemed to be meeting its daily production goal of about 38,000 cartons. The equipment in the baby cereal area was about three years old and had operated well since its original installation. When Leo Marsden asked Joe Turner what new technology was coming along on the horizon to replace it, Joe replied:

> I'm not aware of anything at the moment that would make it worthwhile for us to pull out this line now and substitute something better. It may well be that in another year or so, somebody may have some new equipment that's attractive enough for us to take a good look at. Frankly, compared to some of the older equipment in other parts of our plant, the perfor-

mance of these two lines and this particular filler is quite astounding. We really have no problem staying within a plus-or-minus-one-percent range on weight control in this department, which, considering the speeds we're running at, is outstanding performance.

Joe Turner moved to the Wair filler operator and asked her to show Leo her weight control charts. Leo noted that the equipment was consistently running within the control limits specified. (See Exhibit 2 for a typical Wair filler plot). Joe also selected at random one of the sheets summarizing the previous day's operation (see Exhibit 3). It summarized both the day's performance for one of the filling heads, as well as the month's to-date statistics for the same head. Leo asked Joe to make a copy of this and also to bring him the latest government regulations on weight control. Leo knew that with the introduction of the metric system, the government had issued new regulations on acceptable tolerances. He wanted to be absolutely sure that he had the latest information available on consumer packaged goods.

GOVERNMENT LEGISLATION

Joe Turner returned to Leo Marsden's office later that day. He brought a copy of the Wair filler chart that Leo had requested, as well as copies of the consumer packaging and labelling act and various amendments and information brochures provided by the Department of Consumer and Corporate Affairs of Canada.

Joe said:

> Leo, I've gone through all of this governmental material. As you can well appreciate, the primary reason for its existence is to protect the consumer from misrepresentation by the manufacturer of consumer packaged products. Therefore, there are all kinds of packaging and labelling regulations which we must conform to. For example, we are required to label everything in French and English. Where we state weights, we can only do so in the prescribed form and with the appropriate spacing. I have underlined here a few specific points which deal with the net weight issue you're trying to raise. For example, "where a declaration of net quantity shows the purported net quantity of the pre-packaged product to which it is applied, that declaration shall be deemed not to be a false or misleading representation if the net quantity of the pre-packaged product is, subject to the prescribed tolerance, not less than the declared net quantity of the pre-packaged product and the declaration otherwise meets the requirements of this Act and the regulations."

Joe Turner continued:

> As I understand it, in March 1975, a further amendment was made to the consumer packaging and labelling regulations. The following sections are of greatest pertinence for us:

Tolerances

39. (1) For the purposes of Schedule 1, "catch weight product" means a product that because of its nature cannot normally be portioned to a predetermined quantity and is, as a result, usually sold in packages of varying quantity.

(2) Subject to subsection (3), the amount set out in column II of an item of the appropriate Part of Schedule I is the tolerance prescribed for the purposes of subsection 7(3) of the Act for the net quantity set out in column 1 of that item.

(3) Where the net quantity of a prepackaged product referred to in Part I, II, III, IV, V, or VI of Schedule I is declared by weight or volume and that net quantity is not set out in column I of that Part, the tolerance prescribed for the purposes of subsection 7(3) of the Act for that net quantity is an amount based upon linear interpolation between the appropriate tolerances appearing in column II of that Part.

Inspection

40. (1) Where an inspector wishes to inspect any lot, shipment, proposed shipment or identifiable quantity of prepackaged products all purporting to contain the same net quantity or product (hereinafter referred to as a "lot") to determine whether the lot meets the requirement of the Act and these Regulations respecting the declaration of net quantity and where, in his opinion, it is impractical or undesir-

able to inspect all the separate prepackaged products in the lot, he may inspect the lot by selecting and examining a sample of the lot. [1]

Leo Marsden thanked Joe Turner for his work. He concluded:

Joe, why don't both of us think this whole situation out for a week or so and then get together on it again. I want to be thoroughly familiar with this whole situation before I look at any options or propose any changes. I like the idea of concentrating first on the pre-cooked cereal line, because it is a steady seller and it is an area we appear to have under reasonable control. I know we can't stop there, but it is a good place to start.

---

1 Excerpt from CONSUMER PACKAGING AND LABELLING ACT, Consumer Packaging and Labelling Regulations amendment, P.C. 1975-479 4 March, 1975, see Exhibit 4.

EXHIBIT 1

The Pre-Cooked Baby Cereal Line

Bottom
Makers (2)   Sackers (2)   Wair
Filler   Counter   Top
Sealers (2)   Packers (2)

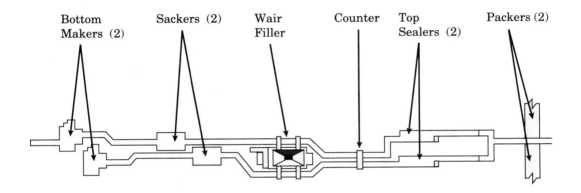

EXHIBIT 2

Wair Filler Plot, Head No. 3

A-2R	UCLR	LCLX	X	UCLX

\#   = Sample means
1,2,3,4 = Individual sample weights

EXHIBIT 3

Wair Filler Operating Results

Date	August 19th 1982
Product	Pre-Cooked Baby Food
Package Weight	454 g
Head	#3
Capability	1.65 g

	MONTH TO DATE	DAY
A-2R	2.281 g	2.829 g
Std. Dev.	1.517 g	1.882 g
Mean Range	3.124 g	3.876 g
UCL (Range)	7.123 g	8.837 g
LCL (Range)	0. g	0. g
5% Control	2.495 g	3.096 g
UCL (Mean)	4.778 g	5.925 g
LCL (Mean)	0.214 g	0.267 g
Sample Size (R)	630	45
Sample Size (A)	622	45
# Light	119	8
Total Lightweight	257.516 g	20.52 g
% Light	4.783 %	4.444 %
Total Overweight	6749.944 g	572.040 g
Mean Overweight	2.713 g	3.178 g
Mean % Overweight	0.598 %	0.700 %
Precentage Variability	8.061 %	-14.061 %

Exhibit 3 cont'd

Exhibit 3 cont'd

A Note on Control Chart and Control Chart Summary Calculations

DATE, PRODUCT, PACKAGE WEIGHT, HEAD : Each day summary tables of operations for the Wair Filler were prepared. On any given day there might be several summaries for each head as package weights or products changed. This summary refers to the previous day's run, Thursday August 19th 1982, of 454 gram Pre-Cooked Baby Cereal through #3 head.

CAPABILITY : This is the standard deviation determined by Noram management which under the filling conditions relevant to this product, speed, particle size, Wair manufacturer specifications etc., should be achieved in meeting the "95 percent of all packages shipped should be over stated net weight" policy.

A-2R : This is a factor calculated using Table C. For n=4, A-2 is .73 and R is the mean range of a number of samples. Thus, for the Month to Date figure,

$$\text{A-2R} = 0.73 \times 3.124 = 2.281$$

STD. DEV. : this is the sample standard deviation. Theoretically it is calculated as the square root of the sum of the squared deviations of n observations from the mean divided by n-1. The bigger the standard deviation the more "spread out" the distribution about the mean.

$$S = \sqrt{\frac{\Sigma \, (y_i - \overline{y})2}{n - 1}}$$

If MEAN RANGE is divided by D2 (a factor taken from Table B equal to 2.059 for n=4), we have a very close approximation of the population standard deviation. Thus, for the Month to Date figure,

$$\text{STD. DEV.} = 3.124 \, / \, 2.059 = 1.517$$

MEAN RANGE : This is the average of the ranges in the samples taken for the day.

UCL (RANGE) : This is the Upper Control Limit on the Range. It is calculated as D4 x MEAN RANGE where D4 is a factor equal to 2.28 for a sample of n = 4 (see Table C for D4 factors). Thus, for the Month to Date figure,

$$\text{UCL (RANGE)} = 2.28 \times 3.124 = 7.123$$

LCL (RANGE) : This is the Lower Control Limit on the Range. It is calculated as D3 x MEAN RANGE where D3 is a factor equal to Zero for a sample of n = 4. The Lower Control Limit on the Range is therefore Zero (see Table C for D3 factors).

Operators use the upper and lower control limits on the range to monitor the filling operation.

Exhibit 3 cont'd

Exhibit 3 cont'd

5% CONTROL : This is the mean setting to ensure that not more than 5% of the packages filled will be below 454 grams. At this setting 90% of observations will be between some upper and lower bound on a normal distribution, where the lower bound is 454 (there will be 5% observations in each tail).

We can calculate this 5% control level in the following way. Table A shows the percentage of observations which will be within a given number of standard deviations from the mean. If we want to find how many standard deviations on either side of the mean will contain 90% of observations (Noram policy), find .4500 in the body of Table A and read off 1.645. We can interpret this as 45% of observations will be between the mean and minus 1.645 standard deviations and 50% above the mean. Table A is a "one tail" table. Thus, for the Month to Date figure,

$$\text{5\% CONTROL} = 1.645 \times 1.517 = 2.497$$

UCL (MEAN) : This is the Upper Control Limit on the Mean. It is calculated as 5% CONTROL LEVEL + A-2R. Thus, for the Month to Date figure,

$$\text{UCL (MEAN)} = 2.497 + 2.281 = 4.778$$

LCL (MEAN) : This is the Lower Control Limit of the Mean. It is calculated as 5% CONTROL LEVEL - A - 2R. Thus, for the Month to Date Figure,

$$\text{LCL (MEAN)} = 2.497 - 2.281 = 0.214$$

SAMPLE SIZE (R) : This is the unadjusted sample size. Each sample consists of four packages. The 630 samples reported for the Month to Date represent 2520 individual packages.

SAMPLE SIZE (A) : This is the adjusted sample size. "Wild" samples are disregarded in calculations. The 622 samples reported for the Month to Date represent 2488 packages. In this regard we can think of two kinds of "causes" for package weight variation. There are statistical variations which we can regard as normal fluctuations around a mean and which arise from the acceptable operating characteristics of the equipment, and there are assignable variations where the variation from target is a result of some malfunction. If a blockage occurs, for example, and produces a half-filled package in a sample this would be termed "wild" by Noram and the whole sample discarded for computational purposes. The reasoning here is that Noram wishes to track statistical variation and not malfunctions. In the event of a "wild" sample being detected operators would take the appropriate action to ensure that affected packages were removed from production. A total of 8 such samples have been omitted for the Month to Date SAMPLE SIZE (A).

LIGHT : This is the number of packages in the samples under the net weight of 454 grams. For example if, in one of the samples of four packages, one of the packages was

Exhibit 3 cont'd

Exhibit 3 cont'd

less than 454 grams this would count as one light package. For the Month to Date figure 119 such packages have been recorded in the samples.

TOTAL LIGHT WEIGHT : This is the total amount in grams of underweight in the light packages. For example, if a light package has been detected in a sample, weighing in at say 451 grams, this would be recorded as 3 grams of light weight. The TOTAL LIGHT WEIGHT associated with the 119 # LIGHT for the Month to Date figure is 257.516.

% LIGHT : This is the percentage of packages in the adjusted sample under the net weight. It is calculated as # LIGHT divided by the number of packages in SAMPLE SIZE (A) and expressed as a percentage. Thus, for the Month to Date figure,

$$\% \text{ LIGHT} = 119 / 2488 = 4.783\%$$

TOTAL OVERWEIGHT : This is the total weight in grams in excess of the net weight requirements. Each package that weighed in excess of 454 grams would contribute to the TOTAL OVERWEIGHT.

MEAN OVERWEIGHT : This is the TOTAL OVERWEIGHT divided by the number of packages in SAMPLE SIZE (A). Noram does not deduct the number of light packages from SAMPLE SIZE (A) in computing MEAN OVERWEIGHT. Thus, for the Month to Date figure,

$$\text{MEAN OVERWEIGHT} = 6749.944 / 2488 = 2.713$$

MEAN % OVERWEIGHT: This is the MEAN OVERWEIGHT divided by the PACKAGE WEIGHT and expressed as a percentage. Thus, for the Month to Date figure,

$$\text{MEAN \% OVERWEIGHT} = 2.713 / 454 = 0.598\%$$

PERCENTAGE VARIABILITY : This can be interpreted as a measure of Wair Filler performance against "standard." It is calculated as CAPABILITY minus STD. DEV. and expressed as a percentage of CAPABILITY. A positive figure indicates performance better than standard, while a negative result suggests worse. Thus, for the Month to Date figure,

$$\text{PERCENTAGE VARIABILITY} = 1.650 - 1.517 / 1.650 = 8.061\%$$

Exhibit 3 cont'd

Exhibit 3 cont'd

TABLE A. **Areas under the Normal Curve**

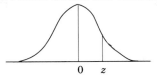

z	.00	.01	.02	.03	.04	.05	.06	.07	.08	.09
0.0	.0000	.0040	.0080	.0120	.0160	.0199	.0239	.0279	.0319	.0359
0.1	.0398	.0438	.0478	.0517	.0557	.0596	.0636	.0675	.0714	.0753
0.2	.0793	.0832	.0871	.0910	.0948	.0987	.1026	.1064	.1103	.1141
0.3	.1179	.1217	.1255	.1293	.1331	.1368	.1406	.1443	.1480	.1517
0.4	.1554	.1591	.1628	.1664	.1700	.1736	.1772	.1808	.1844	.1879
0.5	.1915	.1950	.1985	.2019	.2054	.2088	.2123	.2157	.2190	.2224
0.6	.2527	.2291	.2324	.2357	.2389	.2422	.2454	.2486	.2517	.2549
0.7	.2580	.2611	.2642	.2673	.2704	.2734	.2764	.2794	.2823	.2852
0.8	.2881	.2910	.2939	.2967	.2995	.3023	.3051	.3078	.3106	.3133
0.9	.3159	.3186	.3212	.3238	.3264	.3289	.3315	.3340	.3365	.3389
1.0	.3413	.3438	.3461	.3485	.3508	.3531	.3554	.3577	.3599	.3621
1.1	.3643	.3665	.3686	.3708	.3729	.3749	.3770	.3790	.3810	.3830
1.2	.3849	.3869	.3888	.3907	.3925	.3944	.3962	.3980	.3997	.4015
1.3	.4032	.4049	.4066	.4082	.4099	.4115	.4131	.4147	.4162	.4177
1.4	.4192	.4207	.4222	.4236	.4251	.4265	.4279	.4292	.4306	.4319
1.5	.4332	.4345	.4357	.4370	.4382	.4394	.4406	.4418	.4429	.4441
1.6	.4452	.4463	.4474	.4484	.4495	.4505	.4515	.4525	.4535	.4545
1.7	.4554	.4564	.4573	.4582	.4591	.4599	.4608	.4616	.4625	.4633
1.8	.4641	.4649	.4656	.4664	.4671	.4678	.4686	.4693	.4699	.4706
1.9	.4713	.4719	.4726	.4732	.4738	.4744	.4750	.4756	.4761	.4767
2.0	.4772	.4778	.4783	.4788	.4793	.4798	.4803	.4808	.4812	.4817
2.1	.4821	.4826	.4830	.4834	.4838	.4842	.4846	.4850	.4854	.4857
2.2	.4861	.4864	.4868	.4871	.4875	.4878	.4881	.4884	.4887	.4890
2.3	.4893	.4896	.4898	.4901	.4904	.4906	.4909	.4911	.4913	.4916
2.4	.4918	.4920	.4922	.4925	.4927	.4929	.4931	.4932	.4934	.4936
2.5	.4938	.4940	.4941	.4943	.4945	.4946	.4948	.4949	.4951	.4952
2.6	.4953	.4955	.4956	.4957	.4959	.4960	.4961	.4962	.4963	.4964
2.7	.4965	.4966	.4967	.4968	.4969	.4970	.4971	.4972	.4973	.4974
2.8	.4974	.4975	.4976	.4977	.4977	.4978	.4979	.4979	.4980	.4981
2.9	.4981	.4982	.4982	.4983	.4984	.4984	.4985	.4985	.4986	.4986
3.0	.4987	.4987	.4987	.4988	.4988	.4989	.4989	.4989	.4990	.4990

Source: W. Mendenhall and L. Ott, *Understanding Statistics* Duxbury Press, 3rd Edition, 1980.

Exhibit 3 cont'd

Exhibit 3 cont'd

TABLE B. **Factors for Estimating s from $\bar{R}$**

Number of observations in subgroup	Factor for estimate from $\bar{R}$ D2
2	1.128
3	1.693
4	2.059
5	2.326
6	2.534
7	2.704
8	2.847
9	2.970
10	3.078

TABLE C. **Factors for Determining from R the 3-Sigma Control**

	Limits For $\bar{X}$ and $\bar{R}$ Charts		
Number of observations in subgroup n	Factor for $\bar{X}$ chart A2	Factors for $\bar{R}$ chart	
		Lower control limit D3	Upper control limit D4
2	1.88	0	3.27
3	1.02	0	2.57
4	0.73	0	2.28
5	0.58	0	2.11
6	0.48	0	2.00
7	0.42	0.08	1.92
8	0.37	0.14	1.86
9	0.34	0.18	1.82
10	0.31	0.22	1.78

Source: Adapted from E.L. Grant and R.S. Leavenworth, *Statistical Quality Control*, 5th edition, McGraw-Hill, 1980.

EXHIBIT 4

Declaration of Net Quantity by Metric Units of Weight on Products Other Than Catch Weight Products[1]

Item	Column I Declared Weight	Column II Tolerances
1.	1 g*	0.16 g
2.	1.5 g	0.20 g
3.	2 g	0.25 g
4.	3 g	0.32 g
5.	4 g	0.38 g
6.	5 g	0.44 g
7.	6 g	0.50 g
8.	8 g	0.59 g
9.	10 g	0.68 g
10.	15 g	0.88 g
11.	20 g	1.05 g
12.	30 g	1.36 g
13.	40 g	1.63 g
14.	50 g	1.87 g
15.	60 g	2.1 g
16.	80 g	2.5 g
17.	100 g	2.9 g
18.	150 g	3.8 g
19.	200 g	4.5 g
20.	300 g	5.8 g
21.	400 g	7.0 g
22.	500 g	8.0 g
23.	600 g	9.0 g
24.	800 g	11.0 g
25.	1 kg**	12.5 g

---

1 Excerpt from CONSUMER PACKAGING AND LABELLING ACT,
   Consumer Packaging and labelling Regulations amendment, Schedule 1,
   Part III, P.C. 1975-479 4 March, 1975

Exhibit 4 cont'd

Exhibit 4 cont'd

Column I Item	Declared Weight	Column II Tolerances
26.	1.5 kg	16.0 g
27.	2 kg	19.4 g
28.	3 kg	25.0 g
29.	4 kg	30.0 g
30.	5 kg	34.0 g
31.	6 kg	39.0 g
32.	8 kg	46.0 g
33.	10 kg	53.0 g
34.	15 kg	68.0 g
35.	20 kg	80.0 g
36.	Over 20 kg	0.4 % of declared weight

* g = grams
** kg = kilograms

20 Metropolitan Bank

D. R. Johnston, a vice-president in the corporate finance department at the Metropolitan Bank, had just been speaking to officers of an organization that wanted Metropolitan to finance its takeover of another company. He would later consult with others in the bank, but first wanted to review the proposal, beginning with the standard criteria that Metropolitan deal-makers usually considered in such cases.

THE BANKING INDUSTRY

The banking industry in Canada was composed primarily of eleven large chartered banks. The "Big Five" banks, of which Metropolitan was one, in turn dominated this group. These five banks, with combined branch networks that overpowered those of all other Canadian financial institutions, had a virtual oligopoly in the industry. Together, their assets outnumbered those of the top 250 non-financial institutions in Canada. In some cases these banks acted as the lead or principal financier of mergers and acquisitions although such activity was normally done by specialized merchant banks. More frequently these chartered banks would be asked to provide some part of a financing package.

In the early 1980s, many of the large banks had either established their own investment arms (such as the Toronto-Dominion's Green Line Investor Service) or acquired established brokerage businesses (such as the acquisition of Dominion Securities by the Royal Bank.) This meant that the banks were even more involved in investment banking activities, although several of them went to considerable lengths to keep their investment and commercial banking businesses as distinct corporate and operating entities.

This case was written by Beth Baker, under the supervision of Professor Jeffrey Gandz, and was supported by a grant from Imperial Oil Limited.

DECIDING WHETHER TO FINANCE A TAKEOVER DEAL

When deciding whether it would be appropriate to finance a particular deal, Johnston and other officers of the bank first considered what the bank's primary responsibility was—to be profitable and efficient by making economically prudent decisions.

However, because the banks' reputations hinged on trust and acceptance within a society, bankers believed that public perception of their honesty and ethical behavior was as crucial as the reality of such behavior.

There were a number of questions that deal-makers such as Johnston had to ask about mergers and acquisitions in general and about any specific proposals.

Should the bank finance the acquisition of a company when the acquirer's objective depended on a reorganization with negative social consequences such as the elimination of divisions, slashing of overhead, or the forcing of pay cuts?

One argument often heard around banking circles was that if an organization wasn't "lean and mean," every job in the organization, not just the division, was threatened and the type of restructuring associated with mergers and acquisitions therefore served some useful social purpose, at least in the long term. Metropolitan would not usually avoid financing such a deal, although if the outcome looked particularly serious, deal-makers might reject it. A "serious" reorganization could involve the shutdown of a plant in a small, one-industry town, which could damage the bank's reputation. A less serious reorganization might involve the closure of one division of an organization in a large city, which would permit easier assimilation into new jobs by displaced employees.

Should the bank finance a deal which in the minds of some citizens involved an industry with an ethically troubling nature?

What constituted an "ethically troubling" deal changed with social attitudes: whereas 50 years ago such a deal might have involved a distilling company, today it might involve the nuclear industry, an organization with South African ties, or a tobacco company. Metropolitan officers felt that they should not cast themselves in the role of moral arbiters, and that the principal criterion should be whether the deal made good business sense. Nevertheless, if the loan transaction was one which could bring adverse publicity to the bank, it might elect to avoid any involvement.

Should the bank finance a hostile acquisition when management was opposed?

Metropolitan considered that shareholders' rights took precedence over management's. Different perspectives may have caused shareholders to support a deal which management considered to be unwelcome. Accordingly, Metropolitan would not necessarily refuse to finance a merger or acquisition just because the target's management team was opposed.

Should the bank finance a request from a raider who was an alleged greenmailer, that is, someone who was willing to be paid off as a result of merely threatening to take over an organization, as opposed to

someone who was interested in the business for the long term?

Shareholders were becoming increasingly incensed at greenmail situations, with the potential raider being paid off generously and management retaining its jobs, but shareholders being hurt because of the financial stress on the firm. In his attempted takeover of Walt Disney Productions Corp, noted corporate raider Saul Steinberg failed in his acquisition attempt, but was paid a consolation prize that included a profit of between $30 and $60 million, not including $28 million which covered out-of-pocket expenses. As a result, Disney shareholders brought the matter to court, and since then, shareholders of many companies have tried to press management to include anti-greenmail clauses. This type of situation might have troubled even some institutions that were willing to finance a hostile takeover. Metropolitan's attitude, which differed from that of some other banks, was to assess each case on its own merits.

Should the bank provide financing when the target had not been disclosed?

The acquirer may not wish to divulge its target in order to keep the deal as confidential as possible. Johnston believed that some banks would finance such a deal but most would reject it, and even those that would have accepted it usually reserved the right to refuse the deal once the target had been identified. When the target was unknown, Metropolitan rarely, if ever, provided financing.

Did the bank have a particular responsibility to those companies for which it was the principal banker? And should it react differently if the intended takeover target had only peripheral business with the bank?

An organization that dealt peripherally with the bank may have had only its payroll account there, for example. Loss of business and potential conflicts would have been greater in the first instance, but both were customers. Similarly, should the bank have a different response for a long-time customer as opposed to a more recent one? This question held for the potential acquirer as well as the target. While opinion on this issue was divided, some bankers argued that an institution that had always supported a customer should not suddenly discontinue this support, and that the length and extent of involvement in the banking relationship was indeed an important issue.

In general, the bank faced the question of whether it was inherently unethical for a financial institution to be a "common carrier," an institution willing to finance any deal that represented an economically viable transaction (assuming, of course, that it was legal). One such institution was Citibank, which had represented the hostile bidder in a takeover proposal of one of its major customers. One reported instance involved Revlon which, with Citibank's help, tried unsuccessfully to take over Gillette. As a result, Gillette took its business to another institution, after having been a Citibank customer for 22 years. Citibank argued that if it hadn't represented the hostile bidder, that party would merely have taken the deal elsewhere; it also believed that a final decision should be made by the shareholders of the company. While Metropolitan did not consider itself to be a common carrier, it did not find such a stance inherently inappropriate.

Finally, before the bank made a decision, it had to weigh the implications. If it refused to finance a takeover deal, not only would it lose that deal, but if the acquirer were a customer, the bank would likely lose that account too. Another bank that agreed to finance it would stipulate that the company must move its account to the second institution. If the bank did not finance an acquirer's bid for one of its customers, but the bid subsequently won the deal, that customer's account would likely go to the bank that had financed the hostile bid. These considerations were the price of doing business: the desire to retain a good customer (either the acquirer or the target) was a major factor when making the decision, but the quality of credit risk was still the major criterion.

ETHICS IN THE BANK

The bank's "sacred trust" was to protect the depositors' money above all else. Metropolitan's code of corporate conduct was very general (Exhibit 1), and since it could not cover all complex matters, individual employees were inevitably left to interpret and apply the code themselves. For example, one phrase read: "And in dealing with applications to finance mergers and acquisitions, the bank will endeavor to respect the relationship the customers enjoy with the bank and the customers' individual interests. Specific policy issues in this respect are numerous and therefore are established by a credit-policy committee made up of senior bank officers and

board members." Most corporate managers in a quality organization tried to do what was "right," but the result depended inevitably on each individual's subjective definition of right.

Conflicts of interest were a legitimate concern of the bank, and therefore the same process was followed every time a deal-maker was approached by a company wishing to make an acquisition. First the policy decision was made that it was the type of business that the bank was willing to accept. Only when it was accepted on that basis would the economic decision be made. Johnston would first assess the deal on his own, and if it appeared to involve a question of law, he would discuss it with the in-house lawyer. For example, if the bank had a relationship with the takeover target, its response may have been different depending on whether it was a significant relationship, which usually involved lending activity, or a peripheral one.

Likewise, the company's management may have had a close personal or professional relationship with top management of the bank, or it may have recently made an annual presentation to its senior officers, either of which would have complicated the decision. Whereas checking with a lawyer was left to the employee's judgement, running it by an ad hoc committee of senior officials was bank policy. The committee may have comprised one or several officers of the bank who approved or rejected the proposition. The higher the sensitivity of the deal, the more levels of authority had to review it. These officials would consider who might be offended by the deal and what business might be lost. Only once a deal had passed the above criteria would the economic viability be assessed. If and when the deal was approved, the acquirer was notified that the bank reserved the right to deal with other potential buyers, but at the same time they advised him of the "Chinese Walls" that existed to protect confidentiality.

PROTECTION OF CONFIDENTIALITY

Chinese Walls were any type of safeguard that segregated business between departments, and particularly between lending and investing activities. They were necessary because the Code of Ethics was too general to guide the individual in a specific situation, and they protected the confidentiality of both the acquirer and the target. A Chinese Wall protected confidentiality through control over both personnel and information.

Chinese Walls around personnel ensured that employees working on a particular account had no proprietary knowledge of other pertinent business, accounts, or deals. They were isolated from bank employees working on competing bids, and any employee working on a deal was forbidden to invest in any related securities at risk of losing his or her job. When making a presentation to credit committees, Johnston asked to make his presentation last if it was confidential, to keep the information from being known by more employees than was absolutely necessary. In spite of these safeguards, most employees in the bank didn't have to sign statements of compliance, although senior executives signed a document annually to verify that they had not acted contrary to bank policies.

The other type of Chinese Wall was erected around the information itself. Code names were often used for the projects and correspondence was kept confidential. Files from other divisions were never used to assess the merits of a bid, and department employees were prohibited from using any information already held by the bank that might give them an unfair advantage.

There was some doubt in the investment world regarding the effectiveness of Chinese Walls, largely due to the tremendous potential to benefit the customer, the employee, or the bank itself. One such example involved First Boston Corp, which was fined $264,000 for a violation of confidentiality. One of its customers notified the bank that it was about to undergo financial problems, and a portfolio manager who handled First Boston's own investments discovered this information and sold the bank's shares as a result, thus effectively using insider information.

There were at least three possible types of conflicts of interest that the bank tried to avoid for ethical reasons. These included: the misuse of confidential information to benefit someone personally, the misuse of confidential information to benefit the corporation, or the bank acting in such a way as to favor one applicant's deal over another's.

When assessing a deal, Johnston made the distinction between what was unethical and what was inappropriate. Ethical problems could have fallen into one of the above categories, whereas the question of appropriateness might have involved refusing to finance a deal for a non-financial reason, such as one of the six areas discussed above. As far as Johnston was concerned, all bankers faced these kinds of dilemmas in their day-to-day work and it required some experience and judgement to steer the right course.

EXHIBIT 1

Excerpts from the Metropolitan Bank's Code of Conduct

CODE OF CONDUCT

Metropolitan conducts its business in accordance with a straightforward credo: to operate in an ethical, socially responsible manner. The bank accepts its obligations to apply moral and ethical judgements in conducting its affairs.

GOALS AND OBJECTIVES

Banking is a commercial enterprise. As with any other business, its aim is to make a reasonable profit while avoiding undue risks.

Profits enable the bank to achieve its goals of maximizing the return on shareholders' capital and the bank's assets, as well as meeting its obligations to its employees, pensioners and the communities in which it does business. They also enable the bank to offer more and better services.

Above all, profits help the bank maintain the confidence of shareholders, depositors and prospective borrowers—for banks are creatures of confidence.

They are built on trust—trust in the security of depositors' money and in the soundness of their business practices.

The public's confidence in Metropolitan is attested by the more than four million families, farmers, professionals and independent businessmen and women who look to it for the banking products and services they require.

COMPLIANCE WITH THE LAW

Operating in more than 20 countries worldwide, the bank's first policy is to respect both the spirit and letter of all the laws and regulations that govern its business and to contribute actively and constructively in their formulation.

RELATIONS WITH CUSTOMERS

Our customers have taken the bank into their lives. The financial services we provide play an important part in the success of their personal and business objectives.

Trust and confidentiality are therefore at the heart of the bank's relationship with its clients.

Therefore, employees must be scrupulous in protecting the confidentiality of information obtained from bank customers.

Exhibit 1 cont'd

Exhibit 1 cont'd

When the bank is a party with a customer in a business venture, the business relationship is kept entirely separate from any financial services the bank may provide the customer.

And in dealing with applications to finance mergers and acquisitions, the bank will endeavor to respect the relationship the customers enjoy with the bank and the customers' individual interests. Specific policy issues in this respect are numerous and therefore are established by a credit-policy committee made up of senior bank officers and board members.

Alcan Canada Products Limited Kingston Works (A)

21

On September 19, 1984, Don Neil, Alcan Canada Products Ltd's Kingston Works Manager, announced Alcan's decision to discontinue the aluminum extrusion portion of its Kingston operation. As a result, 485 positions in Kingston—390 unionized and 95 staff positions—were to be eliminated over a period of up to 18 months.

In announcing the extrusion phasing-out, Mr. Neil emphasized that the company was committed to minimizing the impact of the workforce reduction on the employees, the community, and Alcan's Kingston aluminum rolling operations through the implementation of various employee support programs, including skills upgrading and retraining, job search assistance, early retirement, pre-retirement counselling, and a severance package.

THE ALUMINUM INDUSTRY— BACKGROUND

The North American aluminum industry experienced considerable growth in the 1960s and 1970s as the worldwide demand for the metal increased. The energy crisis of the 1970s resulted in a shift from steel to aluminum in many applications as North American industry (automobile, transportation, etc) focused on improving its cost and energy efficiency by taking advantage of aluminum's inherent high strength-to-weight property, and its excellent conduction, corrosion resistance, and reflective qualities.

The economic downturn in 1981 hit the aluminum industry hard, particularly in the construction, automotive, and transportation markets, resulting in large inventories and low price levels. With an emphasis on effective cost management to improve operating efficiency in the relatively mature industry, management re-evaluated the operations in light of the company's long-term strategic objectives. By the end of 1984, the major aluminum producers had adopted various strategies, such as production cutbacks (Alcan & Alcoa), plant closings of obsolete facilities (Reynolds), diversifi-

Case material of the Western School of Business Administration is prepared as a basis for classroom discussion. This case was prepared by Professor Jeffrey Gandz and Donald J. Polk.

cation into other more promising industries (Kaiser), and even leaving the aluminum industry completely (Martin Marietta, Arco).

ALCAN CANADA PRODUCTS

Alcan Canada Products (ACP), the Canadian fabricating and sales subsidiary of the Montreal-based multinational Alcan Aluminum Limited, had been extruding aluminum products at Kingston Works since 1940. (In 1985, Alcan Canada Products Limited ceased to exist when a corporate restructuring led to the realignment of operating groups. Kingston Works today is part of the newly formed Alcan Rolled Products Company.)

Kingston Works housed two of ACP's divisions: the Extrusion Division and Rolled Products Division. There was a Works-wide collective agreement with each of the three unions at the Works— the United Steelworkers of America (USWA) representing machine operators and laborers, the International Association of Machinists and Aerospace Workers (IAM) representing the skilled tradesmen and maintenance people, and the United Plant Guard Workers of America (UPGWA). In effect, members of the unions had Works-wide seniority rights, allowing them to "bump" more junior employees in jobs they were qualified for, even if this meant working in the other division which shared Kingston Works.

The equipment for making heavy extrusions was old and required extensive maintenance. ACP could not justify the multi-million dollar investment required to replace the old equipment, especially in light of the unstable and unpredictable market for heavy extrusions, which was subject to wide cyclical swings. Thus ACP decided to discontinue heavy extrusions fabrication in Canada while continuing to serve customers requiring them through Alcan-affiliated companies in Japan and the UK.

Market demand to provide rapid service and enable lower customer inventories resulted in a move towards regional fabrication facilities for medium and light extrusions. Consequently, Kingston Works' role in supplying light extrusions to the Canadian marketplace had been diminishing since Alcan began to acquire regional facilities in the 1960s and 1970s. Most of this business was being handled by Alcan plants in Laval, Que, Aurora, Ont, Winnipeg, Man, Calgary, Alta, and Richmond, BC.

ANNOUNCING THE DECISION

At various times in recent years, the Kingston rumor-mill had been anticipating a major corporate decision concerning the future of the extrusion operations. Decisions in 1983 and 1984 to close or relocate other smaller Kingston Works departments related to the extrusion production operation served to warn the employees of a change in direction for the Extrusion Division. Despite these moves, the announcement on September 19, 1984, of Alcan's decision to discontinue Kingston extrusions came as a complete surprise to many, the result of a rapidly-implemented, comprehensive management plan designed to preserve management's credibility among employees and the community, and minimize negative reaction.

Preparation for the Announcement

For ACP, its decision to discontinue Kingston extrusions resulted in the largest down-sizing effort it had ever attempted. Since the Alcan name had been synonymous with security and stability in the Kingston community for over 40 years, a primary corporate objective in implementing the decision was to do a first-rate job of handling the situation.

Because of the existence of both Extrusion Division and Rolled Products Division operations at Kingston Works and the Works-wide collective agreements that the company held with each bargaining unit, successful implementation of the decision was going to require effective coordination of the two operating divisions.

Since ACP management had no previous experience in carrying out a down-sizing effort of this scale, ACP first enlisted the services of a management consultant to educate key personnel on how best to carry out the downsizing. In an effort to guarantee security and to avoid starting rumors, these education sessions were held in Montreal—away from both head office and the operations.

ACP selected Wednesday, September 19, 1984, as the date it would announce its decision to allow the phasing-out of extrusions to be carried out over a period of up to 18 months. Given this 18 month phasing-out period, the management thought that the company would be able to maximize the benefit of the employee support programs to be implemented. Furthermore, September was felt to be appropriate as the busy summer-holiday season would be over, and the Christmas season was still a few months off. By announcing the decision on a Wednesday, management was hoping to avoid the problems of the "pink slip on Friday at 4:55" scenario by being available to respond to the many questions and concerns of both the affected and unaffected employees.

About 10 days in advance of the announcement, Toronto head office informed Kingston top management of its decision to discontinue Kingston extrusions. Given this short time frame, Kingston management was responsible for coordinating all aspects of the announcement without letting word of the decision slip out in advance.

During this period, Kingston management worked long hours and made several trips to head office in Toronto to prepare a workable scenario for making the announcement. Management was concerned with making sure that all parties were informed of the extrusion phase-out by the company at the same time, and that the company had a communications system in place to handle the anticipated flood of questions from employees. Above all, Alcan was concerned with maintaining its reputation as a responsible employer in the community by pledging its support to all those employees affected.

Towards this end, management coordinated a plan (outlined below) to inform the unions, all employees (both those on day shift and those on the back shifts), and the community of the decision. Management drew up the lists of employees eligible for early retirement under the corporate plan and those employees potentially affected by the phasing-out. Furthermore, Alcan put together a special edition of the plant newspaper (Exhibit 2) for distribution at the time of the announcement, informing all employees of the reasons for the decision, the impact of the decision, details of the corporate compensation packages (early retirement and severance), and places where employees could get their questions answered.

Making the Announcement

The following section outlines the key components of management's plan for announcing the Kingston downsizing.

September 17, 1984: Alcan contacted Flora MacDonald, MP for Kingston and the Islands and newly appointed federal Minister of Employment and Immigration, to inform her of its intentions. As one of the major employers in her constituency, Alcan wanted to allow her the opportunity to prepare for dealing with such a major announcement. Similarly, Alcan also contacted Keith Norton, MPP for Kingston and the Islands, and Kingston's mayor, John Gerretsen.

September 18, 1984: Alcan contacted the local print and electronic media, and prominent members of the Kingston-area business community, inviting them to a breakfast press conference hosted by Mr. Neil on September 19, 1984 at 8:00 am. The event was arranged on such short notice in order to minimize the rumors which would result from inviting people to such a rare event.

September 19, 1984:

6:00 am: Alcan contacted the local presidents of the USWA and the IAM, inviting each of the union executives to separate meetings to be held on-site at the 8:00 am shift change.

8:00 am: Mr. Neil announced the management decision to the community at the breakfast press conference.

Kingston management conducted simultaneous meetings with the USWA executive, the IAM executive, and Kingston Works foremen and staff. At these meetings, the various groups were informed of the decision and the impact that it would have.

Couriers were dispatched with notices of the decision to the homes of those employees currently working on the afternoon and night shifts. Alcan wanted to ensure that all employees were informed by the company of the decision rather than hearing of it by other means.

8:30 am: Senior Kingston management conducted meetings with the hourly employees on day shift. At these meetings, the employees were informed of the decision, and the impact that it would have. Management distributed a special edition of the plant newspaper (Exhibit 2) containing more details of the announcement to all employees. Employees were provided with a list of personnel who were able to provide information to any employee pertaining to any aspect of the extrusion phase-out.

9:00 am: Production resumed throughout Kingston Works and management continued to monitor
reaction to the announcement,
both on-site and in the community.

Reaction to the Announcement

The announcement of the layoffs was
broadcast across the country on both
radio and television, and was picked up
by the national wire services. In
Kingston, the announcement was front-
page news, with both the company and
union positions well documented.
Generally, Alcan management was
pleased with the coverage given the
announcement and felt that the company's image in the community was as
good as could be expected under the circumstances.

At Kingston Works, the employees
were taken aback by the announcement.
While some sort of announcement had
been anticipated, the magnitude of the
layoffs caught virtually everyone by surprise. Reaction throughout Kingston
Works ranged from shock to disbelief,
which resulted in a temporary reduction
in production efficiency. In addition, the
IAM circulated a petition throughout the
community urging management to
reconsider its decision.

In mid-December, Sanford M. Treat,
president of Alcan Canada Products Ltd,
visited Kingston to meet with senior
management and union-executive personnel, and the Kingston Area Economic
Development Commission. At these
meetings, Mr. Treat reiterated Alcan's
decision to discontinue the Kingston
extrusion operation, but emphasized
Alcan's commitment to operate world-

class sheet rolling and research facilities
in Kingston.

EMPLOYEE SUPPORT PROGRAMS

Early Retirement and Severance Packages

The details of the early retirement and
severance packages offered to affected
employees are outlined in Exhibit 2. The
details of each package were developed
by the national Alcan Pension Plan
group based on current standards, other
packages offered in the industry, and
acceptance rates of past offers. These
packages are the same as those offered
to employees when the tool and die shop
closed earlier in 1984.

Of the 390 hourly employees affected
by the phasing-out of the extrusion operation, 110 (85 USWA/25 IAM) were eligible for early retirement. While
retirement for those eligible was voluntary, management was hoping the combination of an attractive package and
peer pressure would result in high
acceptance.

In all, only three of 85 eligible
USWA members (96.5% acceptance) and
three of 25 eligible IAM members (88.0%
acceptance) refused the early retirement
offer. Consequently, the layoffs extended
to about 213 USWA and 73 IAM members. Abiding by the provisions for layoffs in the collective agreements, USWA
employees on the layoff list had up to 5
years seniority. In the IAM, those on the
layoff list had up to 25 years IAM seniority (due to departmental "bumping" on
the basis of seniority and skill). The

phase-out was planned to be completed by the end of 1985—layoffs were tentatively scheduled for April 26, 1985, August 1985, and the last quarter 1985, and early retirement for July 1985 and January 1986.

Employee Counselling

Since mid-1984, Alcan had sponsored an Employee Assistance Program (EAP) for its Kingston Works employees through the Family Counselling Service of Kingston. Through this free service, both staff and hourly employees had sought counselling on a range of concerns. The EAP was available to all employees, including those laid off or seeking pre-retirement counselling.

Retraining Program

For about 120 extrusion production employees transferring into Rolled Products operations, Alcan introduced a retraining program at a cost of over $1 million. The training staff was selected from the operating crews on the basis of experience, credibility, willingness, and ability to teach—each trainer having been given temporary staff status.

Under the program, groups of 20 employees (five on each of four shifts) were put through an eight-week training program in Rolled Products, consisting of both classroom sessions and on-the-job training. For those employees transferring to a lower paid job classification, their previous rate of pay would be maintained for 32 weeks; they then received the pay rate of their new job class.

As of March 1985, 68 production employees were being retrained in Rolled Products, with a further 22 transfers to occur in April 1985. The remaining transfers would occur as the extrusion department was closed out in late 1985.

Outplacement Services

In early October 1984, both management and the unions recognized their common goal of helping those employees to be laid off. Under the authority of the Ministry of Employment and Immigration (CEIC), two five-member, management-union Placement Assistance Committees (PACs) were formed (Alcan-USWA, Alcan-IAM), consisting of a neutral chairman and two representatives each from management and the union. The primary objectives of the PACs were as follows:

- Give people the opportunity to be placed in a career that they want by providing:
  - Career counselling
  - Skills upgrading
  - Information sessions
  - Resume development
  - Job search assistance
- Excellence in providing these employee support services;
- Make recommendations to Alcan concerning the nature and implementation of employee support services;
- Not act as a labor relations committee.

The Placement Assistance Committees' mandate was not to get jobs for displaced workers but to help them get one. Towards that end, the PACs rented office space in October and began setting up the Placement Centre. The location of the PAC Centre was chosen off the plant site—to minimize the effect on the ongoing operations and reflect the independent nature of the committees' activities—but close enough to the plant site to be convenient for all. All outplacement costs associated with the PACs were funded by the government (40%) and Alcan (60%).

OUTPLACEMENT ACTIVITY TO DATE

PAC News

In order to keep all employees facing layoff informed of the latest job opportunities, information sessions, and other tips, each placement committee began publishing its own *PAC News*. *PAC News* was published about every week and mailed to the home of those union members laid off or facing layoff. The USWA *PAC News* is attached as Appendix A.

Questionnaires

One of the PACs' first moves was to send a questionnaire to all employees facing layoff to get a better idea of the services desired/required by the employees. Using the questionnaire and a follow-up interview, the PACs hoped to be able to focus their efforts to help as many people as they could. Much of the PACs' early efforts focused on trying to get the questionnaires filled out and returned by employees.

Resume Development Program and Skills Training

The PACs arranged for two people from the CEIC to go on-site and conduct resume development workshops with small groups of workers facing layoff. After the workshops, the PACs had each employee's resume typed and copied, and kept copies on file to forward to prospective employers.

In addition to the resume development program, the PACs recommended that Alcan allow a number of affected employees the opportunity to learn saleable skills or to get their qualification papers where appropriate. A number of production (USWA) workers expressed an interest in learning how to drive a forklift truck, and Alcan provided them with the training on company time. Similarly, some of the affected IAM employees wanted some experience in computer numerical control (CNC) and hydraulics, so Alcan agreed to give them the suitable experience so that they were able to get their qualification papers and trade tickets.

UI-Assisted Worker Training

Interested Alcan production workers had the opportunity to participate in self-development programs in areas such as forklift driving, computer literacy, and first aid/CPR. These courses were approved by the provincial Ministry of Colleges and Universities and funded by UIC.

Extending this concept further, the PACs proposed that, in anticipation of some future hiring, the employer agree to train prospective employees in the plant provided that the training does not affect regular production. The PACs proposed that the training program (a combination of classroom and on-the-job) be approved by the Ministry of Colleges and Universities and be funded by UIC. Prior to the anticipated hiring date (and throughout the training program) the prospective employee would continue to receive UIC benefits, receiving a salary/wage only after being hired. Also, once hired, the employee would be fully trained—at virtually no cost to the employer. At this point, both the provincial and federal governments responded favorably to this idea. The PACs then worked on lining up an employer and setting up a prototype program.

Searching Out Prospective Job Opportunities

The PACs focused much of their efforts in helping employees identify where there might be potential jobs. Concentrating on the Belleville-Kingston-Brockville corridor, the PACs aggressively searched for opportunities, scanning newspapers and contacting various employers. Any opportunities identified were posted in the Placement Centre and passed along in the *PAC News*.

In one of their first experiences, the PACs contacted an Ontario steel company, and arranged for them to come to Kingston and interview a number of candidates on-site in connection with some prospective job opportunities. The steel company offered jobs to seven Alcan employees; however, since the steel company was not paying as much as Alcan and required relocation, each of the employees refused the offer. The PACs decided then to be more selective in pursuing job opportunities; they did not want to jeopardize their reputations among potential employers.

The PACs identified 10 job opportunities for people with a minimum Grade 12 education at an eastern Ontario cement factory. Despite publishing the information in the *PAC News* (*PAC News* Issue IX), the PACs received no response. Recognizing that their strategy of leaving the initiative to the laid-off employees was not generating satisfactory response, the PACs decided to assume the initiative. They began phoning qualified personnel on the layoff list, personally informing them of the opportunities at the cement plant. As a result, over 60 people applied for the jobs, 33 received interviews, 23 were given aptitude tests, and 9 received (and accepted) job offers.

RESULTS

Despite the initial period of frustration, the PACs were generally quite pleased with their results at the end of March 1985. Both management and the unions expressed satisfaction with the outplacement effort and felt confident that they would be able to deal effectively with the large number of laid-off employees to follow.

TABLE 21.1 **Placement Results as of 31 March 1985**

	USWA	IAM
Alcan employees laid off	27	0
Looking for work	15	0
Back to school (other)	6	0
Laid-off employees placed	6	0
Other employees placed (scheduled for future layoffs)	26	25
TOTAL EMPLOYEES PLACED	32	25

EXHIBIT 1

Corporate Organizational Structure

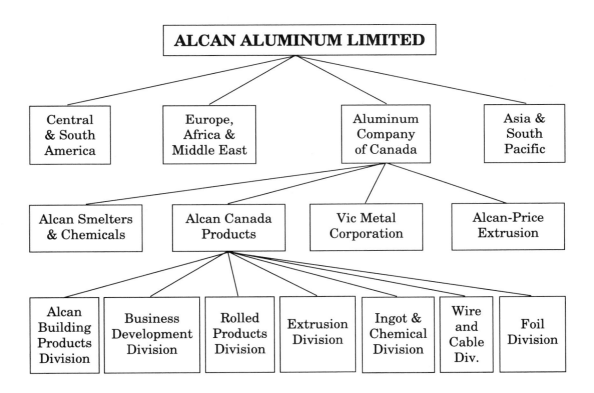

EXHIBIT 2[1]

the press

Alcan to Discontinue Kingston Extrusions

Sept. 19, 1984

The employee population at Kingston Works will be reduced by approximately 485 as a result of the company's decision to phase out its extrusion operation here.

Employees have been meeting with their supervisors since the day's first shift change to discuss how the move will affect them, and works manager Don Neil will inform media representatives of Alcan's decision at a press conference in Kingston this morning.

Neil emphasizes that the effects of the decision will not be immediate since plans call for a phasing-out of extrusion operations over a period of up to 18 months.

He says the company will do everything in its power to minimize the impact of the workforce reduction both on employees and on the community. (See accompanying report on support programs.)

Of the 485 positions to be eliminated, Neil noted that there are more than 100 unionized people who will be eligible for early retirement. An early retirement plan will also apply to some staff employees.

The phasing-out of extrusion operations at Kingston comes as part of a major program to restructure Alcan's extrusion division.

Kingston's heavy presses, now obsolete, were installed in 1939-40 to support the allied war effort, and have reached the end of their economic lifespan, Neil explains.

They are now at a point where they require extensive maintenance, and have been subject to increasingly lengthy and costly downtime. The company says it cannot justify the multi-million dollar investment it would require to replace the old equipment—especially in view of an unpredictable and unstable market for heavy extrusions, which is subject to boom-and-bust cycles.

Although this decision means that Alcan will discontinue the fabrication of heavy extrusions in Canada, it will continue to act as an agent for extrusions of this type, serving customers who require them through Alcan-affiliated companies in Japan and the U.K.

In the light end of the extrusion business, a move toward regional fabricating facilities has been under way for several years now, reflecting customer demands for rapid service and their need to keep their inventories to a minimum.

---

1 Source: *the press*, 19 September 1984, Alcan Canada Products Limited, Kingston, Ontario

Exhibit 2 cont'd

Exhibit 2 cont'd

Kingston Works' role in supplying light extrusions to the Canadian marketplace has been diminishing since Alcan began to acquire regional facilities in the 1960s and 70s. Today, most of this business is handled by Alcan plants in Laval, Quebec; Aurora, Ontario; Winnipeg, Manitoba; Calgary, Alberta; and Richmond, B.C.

Modernization in high gear

Neil says the same trend toward regionalization is developing in the medium extrusion business for the same reasons—the customer's desire for rapid service and low inventories. With the phasing-out of extrusion production here, this business will also shift to the regional plants.

Since Kingston's aging casting facility is primarily related to remelting extrusion scrap from sources that include the extrusion operation here, it no longer makes business sense to locate it in Kingston.

Without the scrap that is generated locally, the centre of gravity for extrusion scrap generation will shift to the Toronto area, where the company will build a new "state-of-the-art" casting centre at a cost of $10 million.

At the same time, the technical upgrading of Kingston's sheet rolling operation will continue, bringing the facility—already among the most advanced in North America—up to world-class standards.

"We expect that sheet for the production of aluminum cans will become Kingston's most important product," Neil explains.

In the U.S., cans account for 25% of the total market for aluminum. The can market is expected to develop the same way in Canada over the next few years, he says.

"Essentially what we're doing is discontinuing an operation that is no longer appropriate for Kingston, while concentrating on the secure rolled products business here.

"We're taking the decisions necessary to ensure the long-term health and profitability of the company," he adds. "The challenge for us locally is to do all we can to minimize the impact of this restructuring on the employees who will be affected by it."

Exhibit 2 cont'd

Exhibit 2 cont'd

Company Pledges Support

Skills upgrading, job search assistance, early retirement, pre-retirement counselling and a severance package are some of the support programs to which the company is committed in an effort to help offset the effects of the impending layoffs announced today.

In addition, a retraining program will be launched internally, at a cost of more than $1 million, to prepare employees transferring to the rolled products operation for their new assignments.

A total of 390 unionized employees will be affected by the phasing-out of Kingston's extrusion operation, of whom 110 will be eligible for early retirement. While retirement for these people is voluntary, the company is hoping they will take advantage of the option, says personnel manager Don Murray who has overall responsibility for the employee support programs.

If all who are eligible for early retirement accept it, Murray says that layoffs will extend to about 210 members of the United Steelworkers of America (USW), and about 70 members of the International Association of Machinists and Aerospace Workers (IAM).

Staff ranks are also expected to be reduced by 95 positions. "We are currently exploring options for the people in these positions," Murray explains, "including early retirements, transfers, deployments to other locations, and whatever else we can do to minimize the number of terminations.

"But as to how many people we can accommodate by these methods, and how many will be terminated, I'm just not able to be specific right now—bearing in mind that this is going to take place over a year or more, and there could be opportunities to place people at other Alcan locations."

To address the many concerns this morning's announcement will create among employees and the community of Kingston—and the huge challenge of finding new employment for the people affected—the company plans to form a task force whose responsibility will be to explore ways of making the situation easier for those involved.

The unions will be approached to sit on this task force, Murray says, as will community and government representatives, so that all avenues will be investigated in assessing ways of providing maximum assistance to people facing layoffs.

Once the company has identified those employees who will opt for early retirement, retraining will be the thrust to help the remainder affected by the phasing out of the extrusion operation.

Employees who transfer to rolled products will require new skills, and those to be laid off will find re-employment easier if they can acquire job-search skills in addition to upgrading their existing skills and/or acquiring new ones. The company is committed to providing whatever type of training is necessary, Murray says.

Del Mitchell, assistant to the works manager, is charged with helping employees who will be seeking new employment through a job placement program. He says that an office will be

Exhibit 2 cont'd

Exhibit 2 cont'd

set up in town to spearhead the re-employment effort.

Training major thrust

Mitchell foresees a training course for laid-off employees that would help them compose a resume, teach them how to prepare themselves for interviews and how to conduct themselves when they're talking to prospective employers, and raise their consciousness of their own abilities.

"We see ourselves contacting by mail large industries throughout Ontario. We'll be phoning other, smaller industries, explaining the situation," Mitchell says. "We'll scan newspapers. And we'll involve both federal and provincial governments in our job placement process. Alcan will supply the administrative infrastructure to support this effort.

"There may be people who, with very little effort, could be trained to acquire additional skills that would make them more employable.

"We'll have some time...it will be a number of months before some of our people will be laid off, and a lot of this can be done during those months.

"In addition, when we look nation-wide, I see us setting up some committees or task forces with Alcan people at other locations. They would be instructed to keep their eyes open in their own operations, as well as monitor developments in other industries where there may be job openings."

Another component of the support programs is the company's commitment to provide pre-retirement counselling for employees who opt for early retirement, and for their spouses.

This counselling will give participants information on finances, housing, recreation, health—"a whole gamut of issues that are important when a person is going from a working career into retirement," Murray says.

The personnel manager stresses that employees will receive all new information as soon as it is available, through meetings with their managers and through existing print channels.

"Presiding over the phasing out of our extrusion operation here is not a pleasant task for me," says Kingston Works manager Don Neil, "but I take comfort from the fact that the company is committed to a sensitive approach in helping those who are going to be affected.

"And there will be some after-the-fact satisfaction if we're successful in meeting the objectives of our support programs."

A Kingston resident since 1945, Neil understands the impact that Alcan's restructure and modernization program will have on the community.

"The name Alcan has, for so many years, been synonymous with security and stability here...and it will continue to be, once we've reorganized our extrusion business and positioned ourselves to be a leader in the aluminum can market.

"That's why it's so important for us to make sure the public understands that, in spite of the jobs affected now, we're going to continue to be a large presence in the Kingston area. Our sheet rolling facility will become a world-class

Exhibit 2 cont'd

Exhibit 2 cont'd

operation. And our total rolled products operation, in conjunction with our international research and development centre here, will continue to employ more than 1,200 people."

Alcan not immune

Reflecting on the circumstances that have led to the company's decision, Neil says: "Business conditions and opportunities in the 1980s have forced many corporations to make tough decisions; Alcan isn't immune to the realities of the international marketplace. I think what we're observing is our Kingston extrusion operation reaching the end of its life cycle.

"Every operation tends to have a life cycle, for one reason or another. It's management's job to recognize the symptoms of the dying phases of that cycle and to react responsibly and realistically—in spite of the fact that the consequences may be unpleasant and difficult to deal with. It's also part of management's challenge to deal with those consequences in a responsible way."

Neil admits that understanding the wisdom of the business decision in this case doesn't make it any easier to cope with the reality of people losing their jobs.

"We don't intend to leave a stone unturned in our efforts to assist our employees and the community through this difficult period of adjustment."

According to Neil, the changes announced this morning will be carried out over a period not longer than 18 months.

He cautions, though, that there is a certain amount of unpredictability in the time frame. "Depending on our business prospects over the next few months, we could find ourselves having to speed up the process."

As for the physical facilities of the plant, Neil says that presses number 1 and 6 will be decommissioned and probably scrapped; press number 7 will be decommissioned and mothballed until its future is determined; and press number 4 will probably be moved to Aurora. Press number 8 has already been transferred to Vancouver.

He adds that part of the remelt facilities will be retained to service the plate mill.

Team effort needed

The works manager emphasizes that the company hopes the unions will agree to be part of the team charged with exploring every possible means of helping displaced employees find re-employment.

"Our commitment is that we'll do the very best we can to make this situation easier for our people, and that goal will be much more attainable if we all work together toward it," he says.

During the coming days and weeks, all Kingston Works employees will have an opportunity for one-on-one discussion with a company representative who can answer their questions and respond to their concerns.

Now that the difficult decision to discontinue the extrusion operation here has been made and announced, the

Exhibit 2 cont'd

Exhibit 2 cont'd

work of implementing employee support programs can begin in earnest, Neil says.

Early retirement offer for P.T.S. employees

As reported elsewhere in this issue, one of the ways in which the company plans to reduce the number of employees who will face layoffs in the months ahead is by offering an attractive early retirement package.

According to personnel manager Don Murray, it is the same offer made to employees of the die shop when that facility was closed earlier this year. Murray says that the company has tried to make the offer beneficial enough to older employees that it will serve as an incentive for them to take advantage of the early retirement option.

The additional costs of this program will be paid entirely by the company, and will not come out of the pension fund.

YOU ARE ELIGIBLE IF:

- You will be 60 years old or older in 1985 and have accumulated at least 75 points (i.e., your age plus your number of years in the pension plan equal 75 or more). Depending on the time needed to train replacement personnel, retirement timing for those qualifying in 1985 is expected to be the third and fourth quarters of 1985.
- Similarly, if you reach age 60 in 1986 and have accumulated at least 75 points, you will be eligible.

Retirement timing for people falling into this category is expected to be the first and second quarters of 1986.

EARLY RETIREMENT PENSION WILL IMPROVE BY:

- The elimination of the early retirement discount: Normally, an employee's pension is first calculated as if he or she were 65, then reduced according to the actual age at retirement. (For example, at age 60 by 14%.) Under the special early retirement package, this calculation will be waived and your pension will be determined as if you were 65.
- The supplementary "bridge" pension normally payable between age 62 and age 65 will be paid at retirement below age 62, and will be improved from $125 per year x years in the pension plan to $180 per year x years in pension plan.
- Lump sum payment of $3000.

Severance package for P.T.S. employees

If you are an affected P.T.S. employee, you will have the option of accepting laid-off status, in which case you will be eligible for recall and may collect Supplementary Unemployment Benefits, as provided for in the collective agreements.

Alternatively, you may opt for termination at the time of layoff and receive the following benefits:

Exhibit 2 cont'd

Exhibit 2 cont'd

1 One week's salary for each year of service up to and including five years.
2 An additional 1.5 week's salary for each year of service in excess of five and up to and including 10 years.
3 Plus two weeks' salary for each year of service in excess of 10 years up to and including 20 years.
4 Plus three weeks' salary for each year of service in excess of 20 years.
5 Plus a cash payment consisting of one week's salary and an amount of $650 (which is equal to the amount you would have received in Supplemental Unemployment Benefits had you opted for layoff) for accepting termination instead of layoff.
6 Plus continued prescription drug plan and semi-private ward plan medical coverage for three months following termination or layoff.

If you initially opt for layoff but later decide to terminate, you will be entitled to all items in the severance package except the cash payment described in item 5.

If you have any questions about the severance package, please call one of the people on the contact list carried elsewhere in this issue.

Contact list

For information pertaining to any aspect of the phase-out of extrusion operations here, and the effect that this decision may have on you, please call any one of the people listed below. If they can't answer your questions immediately, they will either refer you to someone who can or will get back to you with the information you need.

> Gordon Marshall..........7420
> Don Murray...............7250
> Jim Richardson...........7252
> Jim Utley................7601
> Beth Young...............7509
> George Zakos.............7398

APPENDIX A

Issues of the USWA PAC News

ISSUE: I
PLACEMENT POSSIBILITIES U.S.W.A.

The new facility is now open for business and is located at

PLAZA 16
16 Bath Road
Kingston, Ontario
K7L 1H4

which is directly across from the Canadian Tire Pit Stop (upstairs)

Phone No. is 547-2365

VENTURE TRANS MILHAVEN

There were 66 U.S.W. people who submitted applications through us for the openings at Venture Trans. A small number of people have been interviewed and three have accepted positions there. Further information will be sent out next week.

DELORA STELLITE BELLEVILLE

There are openings for "Grinders" at Delora Stellite in Belleville. The rate is $9.89 per hour.
If you are interested please phone the Placement Assistance Office number as noted above.

OTHER ALCAN LOCATIONS

We are in the process of getting further information on the hiring situation at the other Alcan locations in Canada. This should be completed by next week.

THERE'LL BE MORE NEXT WEEK

Appendix A cont'd

Appendix A cont'd

ISSUE NO. II
PLACEMENT ASSISTANCE COMMITTEE U.S.W.A.

PLACEMENT OPPORTUNITIES

LOCAL AREA

If you are interested in one of the following areas please let us know.
Phone 547-2365 or drop in at 16 Bath Rd., Plaza 16
1) Belleville
2) Brockville
3) Gananoque

ALCAN LOCATIONS

Very quiet in all areas. Appears it will remain this way until at least well into 1985.

OTHER INFORMATION

Beginning Monday, November 5 Office hours are
7:A.M. - 6:00 P.M. and open Saturday 2:00 P.M. - 4:00 P.M.

QUESTIONNAIRES

Committee members will be having short discussions with each person who has returned their completed questionnaire. If you have returned your questionnaire you will be contacted. If you have not please do so immediately. Just address the envelope—"Placement Assistance Committee" and drop in Plant Mail.

RESUME TRAINING

Training of persons in the development of their own resume has begun. The employees who will be laid off early this month will be given the first opportunity to attend this course.
If you already have a resume that you are satisfied with, please send us a copy for your file.

> Placement Assistance Committee
> Doug Tousignant
> Reg Bauder
> Del Mitchell
> Don Murray

Appendix A cont'd

Appendix A cont'd

PAC NEWS ISSUE: III
PLACEMENT ASSISTANCE COMMITTEE
U.S.W.A.

JOB OPPORTUNITIES:

TRENTON: BATH ENGINEERING
Openings for Machinists and Welders
NC Machinist   Stainless Steel

THERE ARE A NUMBER OF MISCELLANEOUS JOBS IN THE OTTAWA, BELLEVILLE, BROCKVILLE AREAS. THESE ARE POSTED ON BULLETIN BOARDS AT THE P.A.C. CENTRE.

For additional information visit our office at Plaza 16, 16 Bath Rd., or phone 547-2365.

RESUME DEVELOPMENT & WRITING

The first session and follow-up was completed last week. The second session was held on Thursday 9 November with a follow-up on Friday 16 November, 1:30 P.M.

HOW TO START & RUN YOUR OWN BUSINESS

As a result of the interest shown, arrangements have been made to hold an introductory talk on this subject.

A Management Service Representative from the Federal Business Development Bank has been scheduled to speak on the 27th November from 7:30 P.M. to 9:00 P.M. The location to be announced later.

If you wish to attend phone 547-2365 before 16 November and leave your name.

PAC NEWS ISSUE: IV
PLACEMENT ASSISTANCE COMMITTEE
U.S.W.A.

JOB OPPORTUNITIES

Machinist Jobs in   PETERBOROUGH
ALGOODS IN TORONTO
BATTAWA TRENTON WELDERS
Equipment Operators in OTTAWA AREA

A number of you have been asking about the "Film Processing" company that is to be established in Kingston. The ultimate number of employees will be approximately

Appendix A cont'd

Appendix A cont'd

200. About 70 will be hired in the first year (1985). Further information will be issued as we receive it.

LAID-OFF EMPLOYEES

In depth interview held on 14 and 15 November had good turn outs. The objectives of these interviews were to
- A - Identify skills and needs of the individual as well as confirm information already on hand.
- B - Ensure understanding of committee's role and the role of the individual.
  e.g. The committee will assist in the development of a resume through to having it typed but the individual is responsible for mailing it to prospective employers.
- C - Outline an action plan for the employee to follow over the next week.

RESUME DEVELOPMENT WRITING COURSES

The fourth Resume Development and Writing Course begins on 19th November.

STARTING YOUR OWN BUSINESS

Sessions will be held 27th November 7:00 - 9:30 P.M. at Plaza 16, 16 Bath Road, Kingston.

REMINDER

Please send in completed questionnaires.

PAC NEWS ISSUE: V
PLACEMENT ASSISTANCE COMMITTEE
U.S.W.A.

JOB OPPORTUNITIES:

WELDERS AND FABRICATORS in Ottawa, Trenton and Belleville, Peterborough Areas.
TOOL AND DIE MAKERS in Oshawa Area
There are a number of miscellaneous jobs in the Ottawa—Toronto Areas. These are posted on the Bulletin Boards at the Placement Assistance Centre.

STARTING YOUR OWN BUSINESS

FOR THOSE WHO HAVE SUBMITTED THEIR NAMES FOR THE SESSION, IT WILL BE HELD AT THE PAC OFFICE, PLAZA 16, 16 BATH ROAD STARTING AT 7:00 P.M. ON THE 27TH NOVEMBER.

Appendix A cont'd

Appendix A cont'd

CAREER IN SALES

ANYONE WHO IS INTERESTED IN ATTENDING AN INFORMATIONAL SESSION ON "SELLING AS A CAREER" PLEASE PHONE PAC AT 547-2365 AND LEAVE YOUR NAME.

PLEASE RETURN QUESTIONNAIRES AND COMPLETED RESUMES FOR OUR FILES

PAC NEWS
U.S.W.A.
18 December 1984
ISSUE: VII

What are the objectives of the Committee and how does it plan to meet these objectives?

These two questions will be addressed in the next two or three issues of the PAC News.

One objective is to assist displaced employees in:

1. Finding suitable employment with other industries.
2. Identifying suitable programs to upgrade their skills and the support available for such programs.
3. Obtaining knowledge for individual needs such as "starting your own business."

However, it should be noted that the role of the Committee is to "assist." The primary role must be taken by the displaced employee.

How we plan to achieve this objective together will be discussed in the next two or three issues.

ADDITIONAL INFORMATION:

1. Questionnaire
   Only about 50% of the questionnaires have been returned to-date. In a final effort to get the required information from the other 50%, we have included a copy of the original questionnaire with this bulletin. If there is a copy with your bulletin, please complete and drop in the plant mail.
2. Resume Development Training
   To date, six courses of two sessions each have been scheduled. The last session was well attended but some of the other sessions have had a poor turnout. If you cannot attend when scheduled, please let us know beforehand—phone 547-2365.
3. Government Sponsored Programs By St. Lawrence College
   The Canada Employment people have arranged for a more convenient route to follow in obtaining information about these courses. Call Reg or Jasper about it at 547-2365.

Appendix A cont'd

Appendix A cont'd

4.   The P.A.C. office will close at 4:30 P.M. Friday, 21 December and reopen at 7:30 A.M., Wednesday, 2 January 1985.

MERRY CHRISTMAS - HAPPY NEW YEAR

P.A.C Office
Plaza 16
16 Bath Road
Kingston, Ontario
547-2365

PAC NEWS
U.S.W.A.
10 January 1985
ISSUE: VIII

In the next two or three issues we will be discussing possible ways to achieve our objective of finding suitable employment with other industries.

How can a person be as competitive as possible in placing their name, experience and abilities before a prospective employer?

There are a number of ways you can approach a possible employer, some of which are:

1)   Phone and tell him you are looking for a job.

2)   Drop in to his place of work and attempt to speak with him.

3)   Write him a note saying you are looking for work and would like to see him.

4)   Pick up an "application form" and send it in.

5)   Send him a resume.

Any one of these approaches may result in a job interview but experience shows that the most successful one is submitting a resume.

Because of this each person who may be facing layoff is being given the opportunity to obtain some training in how to develop a good resume.

To date 123 people have attended these sessions. A number of others have developed resumes previously and do not require further instruction. However, in order to be competitive in the "job search" game, those persons who do not yet have a resume should attend one of these training sessions.

Phone 547-2365 and discuss the situation.

Another opportunity to work together with the resume occurs when, in discussing future job openings with a possible employer, the Committee has sufficient detail to speak knowledgeably of candidates.

Appendix A cont'd

Appendix A cont'd

However, this type of co-operation can only develop if the committee has your resume on file.

To work together we need your resume.

MORE NEXT ISSUE

ADDITIONAL INFORMATION

1) General Motors—Oshawa—will shortly be accepting applications for assembly line workers.
   The process to be used in applying for these positions is to be strictly followed.
   Do not apply until you have discussed this with a member of the P.A.C.

"Start Your Own Business Courses" are progressing with second course sessions slated and another first session being set up for those who are interested. Please phone the P.A.C. office if you would like to attend.

P.A.C. Office
Plaza 16
16 Bath Road
Kingston, Ontario
547-2365

PAC NEWS
U.S.W.A.
17 January 1985
ISSUE: IX

LET'S LOOK AT ANOTHER PHASE in meeting our objective of finding suitable employment with another industry.

How can you identify which companies you should approach in order to find a job?

1) One question you must answer is, "What type of work am I looking for?"
2) Another question is "Where do I want to work?" e.g. Kingston? Belleville? Brockville? Toronto?

Once these basic questions are answered you can start looking. A number of routes can be followed in this search.

1) Check with the C.E.C. people.
2) Spread the word among relatives, friends and acquaintances.
3) Check newspaper ads.
4) When you talk with one employer, ask him for names of a couple more you should contact.
5) Keep in touch with the P.A.C. Office.

Appendix A cont'd

Appendix A cont'd

All of these routes should be used and when they are, they become a powerful vehicle in your search for "a prospective employer."

Hopefully, the P.A.C. route can play a greater role in this phase as time goes on. At the present time P.A.C. is:

1) Monitoring newspaper ads and having the appropriate ones displayed in the office.
2) Contacting a limited number of employers regarding possible job openings in the future.
3) Encouraging employers to contact the P.A.C. Office when they actually have openings.

FUTURE POSSIBILITIES ARE:

1) Much more contact with possible employers, both locally and other areas.
2) Further discussion with employer associations.
3) Advertisement in various newspapers.

Next week we will discuss how to find the answer to the question "What type of work should I look for?"

OTHER INFORMATION

1) GENERAL MOTORS OSHAWA
   will be accepting applications through the Oshawa C.E.C Office shortly.
   If you are interested, contact the P.A.C. Office within the next week.
2) CANADA CEMENT LAFARGE BATH
   is interested in looking at resumes from people with Grade 12 diplomas and higher. Contact P.A.C. Office immediately.

PHONE 547-2365
PLAZA 16
16 Bath Road
Kingston, Ontario
K7L 1H4

PAC NEWS
U.S.W.A.
25 January 1985
ISSUE: X

"WHAT TYPE OF WORK SHOULD I APPLY FOR?"

For some this question is easily answered. "I will look for the type of work I have been trained to do" (e.g. maintenance work or the type of work I have experience in, e.g. factory work).

Appendix A cont'd

<u>Appendix A cont'd</u>

For others the answer is more difficult because they feel that they would be more competitive in a job that is considerably different than their present one (e.g. a machine operator may feel he would be more competent and comfortable in some other type of work such as "sales").

For these people we can suggest some sources of assistance.

1) Canada Employment Centres Counselling Process which includes "Aptitude and Interest" tests.
    Contact the P.A.C. Office (547-2365) for information on this.

2) A short training program which would allow each participant to assess his vocational aptitudes and interests. This program is being developed by C.E.C., St. Lawrence College and P.A.C. and will be available as an evening course over a three- or four-week period. It is intended to give a person guidance in assessing his skills and interests before he is laid off. Contact the P.A.C. Office if you feel you may be interested in this type of approach.

ADDITIONAL INFORMATION

TRAINING PROGRAMS

A number of short programs to improve skills in various areas can be made available if the demand is there. These programs which are sponsored by the C.E.C. would be on a part-time basis. These would allow a person to take some upgrading before he is actually laid off by attending in the evening or on "Days Off."

More Next Week.

POSSIBLE JOB OPENINGS

1) G.M. OSHAWA
    The C.E.C. Office in Oshawa is accepting applications for jobs at the G.M. Plant, Oshawa. The period for accepting these is Jan 21 to Feb 7. Applications must be completed and given in person at the Canada Employment Office in Oshawa. More information regarding this is available at the P.A.C. Office.

PHONE 547-2365.

P.A.C. Office
Plaza 16
16 Bath Road
Kingston, Ontario
K7L 1H4

<u>Appendix A cont'd</u>

Appendix A cont'd

PAC NEWS
U.S.W.A.
29 January 1985
ISSUE: XI

JOB OPPORTUNITIES

GENERAL MOTORS OSHAWA

As mentioned in last week's "PAC News" the Canada Employment and Immigration Office in Oshawa is now accepting applications for production workers at General Motors, Oshawa.

The C.E.C. Office generally accepts G.M. applications for two three-week periods each year. If you don't get your application in during this three-week period you will have to wait some months before you have another opportunity.

1- The current period for accepting the applications will close at the end of next week.
2- Applications must be completed and handed in, in person, at the Canada Employment Office in Oshawa.
3- If you have a resume, take it with you and enclose in the application.
4- Some Tips:
   a) Read the entire form carefully.
   b) Answer each question only after reading it carefully once again.
   c) Before you sign, read your answers over.
      Do take time and be neat—it's your future.
5- Address: Bond Towers
              44 Bond St., West,
              Oshawa, Ontario.
6- Go prepared with addresses & dates relevant to previous employment.

ONE PART OF THE APPLICATION READS AS FOLLOWS:

"Previous Employment History"

"Starting with the most recent, list your previous places of employment including service with the armed forces. Approx. dates will be acceptable."

Date Started/Left	Employer & Supervisor	Employer Address	Job Description & Rate Pay	Reason for Leaving
1)				
2)				
3)				
4)				
5)				

<u>Appendix A cont'd</u>

Any further questions please phone 547-2365.

P.A.C. Office
16 Bath Rd.,
Kingston, Ontario
K7L 1H4

PAC NEWS
U.S.W.A.
20 February 1985
ISSUE: XII

UPDATE

1) The number of people applying at General Motors, Oshawa, was surprisingly low. (7)
2) Canada Cement Lafarge—search for suitable candidates among those who applied is going quite smoothly—
   23 of our people completed the aptitude testing portion of the selection process. We should be aware of further development within the next 10 days or so.
3) Congratulations and Good Luck to the five people who obtained work at Kingston Heading Service.

JOB OPPORTUNITIES

1) BLACK & DECKER, in Brockville are accepting applications for production workers. You submit your application through P.A.C. Phone 547-2365 for more information.
2) Six Sales People are required by a local office of Metropolitan Life. There is a two-week training program prior to writing for your licence. If you are interested phone 542-4955.

Any further questions please phone 547-2365

P.A.C. Office
16 Bath Rd.
Kingston, Ontario
K7L 1H4

<u>Appendix A cont'd</u>

Appendix A cont'd

P.A.C. NEWS
U.S.W.A.
11 March 1985
ISSUE: XIII

UPDATE

1. A large number of people have applied at Black & Decker, Brockville. We will update when they actually begin recruiting.
2. Congratulations to the nine people who have received job offers from Canada Cement, Bath. Good Luck in your new career.
3. It is hoped that we will have some more news next week regarding the Pre-employment Training Program for those of you who are currently unemployed.

ADDITIONAL OBSERVATIONS

The Resume Development Programs are virtually completed. However, there are a number of people who have not returned a copy of their resume to P.A.C. If we have a copy of your resume we can:

1) forward a copy very quickly to a company with which you would like to be employed.
2) identify suitable training programs which may benefit a person in obtaining a job.
3) give a critique and help fine tune your resume.
4) make additional copies as required.

Please bring in your resume and discuss it with a member of P.A.C.

Any further questions please phone 547-2365

P.A.C. Office
16 Bath Rd.
Kingston, Ontario
K7L 1H4

APPENDIX B

Alcan Products President Sees Bright Future for Company in Kingston

"Alcan faces a long and bright future in Kingston," says Sanford M. Treat, president of Alcan Canada Products Limited. His comments were made at a meeting with the Area Economic Development Commission held here in Kingston this morning. In addition, similar meetings are being held today with management employees and senior union executives.

"The combination of our sheet production facilities, plus our research centre, means that Kingston has the best we have to offer," says Treat.

Williamson Plant plays a key role in the aluminum fabrication industry in Canada. The Kingston plant is the only such facility operated by Alcan Canada Products Limited, and has a rated capacity almost three times greater than that of the country's only other cold rolling facility operated by Reynolds Aluminum Company of Canada Ltd. in Quebec.

"The two major growth markets in Canada are foundry alloys for the automotive industry and, most important, sheet for aluminum beverage cans. Growth for the latter will be phenomenal, from around 3,000 tonnes to nearly 45,000 tonnes in three years, with a potential market approaching 100,000 tonnes, not including export," said Mr. Treat.

"We have implemented programs, invested $8 million since 1981, and will invest more to ensure that the sheet rolling operation is at a world class level.

We are committed to participate fully and aggressively in the fast growing aluminum can sheet market," he said.

"Mayor Gerretsen, his Council, and others in the community have been very helpful over the past two years by their constant efforts to help us ensure that the Ontario Government moves to allow aluminum cans. As Ontario accounts for approximately one-half of all soft drink cans sold in Canada, it is extremely important to obtain a government decision on this issue which will provide additional and significant volume," he said.

A decision favourable to aluminum would be particularly well-received in Kingston as the can sheet market is a stable one, not greatly affected by swings in economic conditions, which results in relatively stable employment.

Mr. Treat went on to say as a matter of fundamental corporate policy, Alcan has re-emphasized the role of the Kingston research and development centre in the search for new products and end uses for aluminum in order to meet the challenges of the future.

He reiterated Alcan's position that the Extrusion division will close its operations here over the next 15 months as planned. "With a view to the eventual phase-out of the Extrusion operations in Kingston, we have formed Placement Assistance Committees which involve Company and Union representatives

Appendix B cont'd

Appendix B cont'd

with an independent chairman, under the authority of the Minister of Employment and Immigration. For employees who will eventually be laid off, the Committees will assist in the search for other employment," says Treat.

Turning to other aspects of Alcan's business, Mr. Treat said, "Our plate production facilities, and two of the four foil rolling mills, are very old and therefore the operation of that equipment will continue to require constant review and evaluation."

Addressing the question of vacated space at Kingston Works, Mr. Treat said,

"Fortunately, we have many months before this space becomes available. During that time we will examine possibilities for its use."

Finally, Mr. Treat emphasized that between Alcan Canada Products' operations and Alcan International's research and development centre, Alcan will continue to play an active and major role in Kingston. The Company's total employment in the City after the Extrusion phase-out is complete, will still be over 1,200.

Source: *the press*, 20 December 1984, Alcan Canada Products Limited, Kingston, Ontario.

Appendix B cont'd

Appendix B cont'd

Extrusion Phase-Out to be Completed by End of Year

The phase-out of Extrusion operations in Kingston will be completed by the end of this year, Works Manager Don Neil announced this week. A phase-out schedule has been determined that provides for the final closure of Kingston Extrusion in December 1985.

A series of lay-offs are planned to reduce Extrusion production manpower levels in stages over the intervening months with the first lay-off of 24 employees scheduled to take place 26 April. A further lay-off of approximately 50 production employees is expected to occur the end of August, and subsequent lay-offs will follow in the final months of the year.

Some time ago a tentative schedule was issued for the lay-off of IAM bargaining unit employees. In light of this week's announcement, the schedule for IAM lay-offs will be reviewed and re-issued by the end of February.

In addition, the majority of the first group of senior employees eligible for the special early retirement offer in 1985 will retire on 1 July. This is a change from the November 1984 announcement stating that retirements would likely be delayed until the fall of 1985. Retirements for the group of employees eligible for the special offer in 1986 will begin 1 January and continue through the early part of the year.

Another important component of the phase-out plans continues to be the retraining efforts for employees transferred from Extrusion to new areas within Rolled Products. Good progress has been made in this area and, to date, 48 Extrusion employees have been transferred into Williamson Plant and Coated Products for retraining. The schedule calls for 20 more transfers on 11 March 1985 to Williamson Plant, and a further 22 transfers into Coated Products, Foil Mill and Plate Mill in April 1985.

Transfers of Extrusion employees have already served to significantly reduce employment levels in that department. From a level of 12 press crews in September 1984, Extrusion has dropped to 9 press crews currently, and with further transfers and lay-offs, is scheduled for 6 press crews by the end of April and 3 press crews by the middle of the year.

Reduction of operations in the Casting Department will naturally mirror to a certain extent the gradual downsizing of Extrusion. As Casting, however, also serves other regional Extrusion facilities it will continue to meet the needs of the Extrusion Division until the new Casting facility in Pickering, Ontario comes on stream in the first quarter of 1986. Beyond that time, Casting operations will continue at a level necessary to support the Kingston Works Plate Mill.

Source: the press, 14 February 1985, Alcan Canada Products Limited, Kingston, Ontario.

Index